One Girl Who Barely
Lived to Tell . . .

Carol DaRonch, a pretty, seventeen-year-old brunette, immediately trusted the good-looking, dark-haired young man who introduced himself as a police officer. It seemed that there had been trouble with the Camaro she'd left in the shopping mall parking lot. She agreed to go to police headquarters with him.

In his car, it happened quickly. He grabbed Carol's arm and snapped a handcuff on her wrist. She recoiled, screaming, "What are you *doing?*"

"Shut up or I'll blow your head off," he snarled, reaching for her other wrist. Terror jolted Carol into a frenzy. Screaming, she struggled away from him. The other handcuff clicked onto the same left wrist, as Carol's right hand clawed for the door handle and found it. Then the door was opening, and she was falling, screaming, outward. He lunged toward her with a metal bar in his hand, raised to strike. She struggled against the blow, reaching up, gripping the steel. In a blur of terror, Carol wrestled free and went screaming, stumbling around the rear of his car and out into the wet, dark street, into the headlights of an approaching car. . . .

BUNDY
THE DELIBERATE STRANGER

RICHARD W. LARSEN

PUBLISHED BY POCKET BOOKS NEW YORK

Distributed in Canada by PaperJacks Ltd., a Licensee
of the trademarks of Simon & Schuster, Inc.

POCKET BOOKS, a division of Simon & Schuster, Inc.
1230 Avenue of the Americas, New York, N.Y. 10020
In Canada distributed by PaperJacks Ltd.,
330 Steelcase Road, Markham, Ontario

Published by arrangement with Prentice-Hall, Inc.
Library of Congress Catalog Card Number: 80-15795

ISBN: 0-671-63032-6

First Pocket Books printing May, 1986

10 9 8 7 6 5 4 3 2 1

POCKET and colophon are registered
trademarks of Simon & Schuster, Inc.

Printed in Canada

To Deanie.

And to my children, with apologies for hours and days we've not had together.

And to those families whose lives were touched by these and related events; many of you whom I do not know.

Contents

Acknowledgments

My special appreciation goes to James B. King, executive editor, Mason Sizemore, assistant managing editor, Lane Smith, city editor, Don Hannula, other editors, and the management of *The Seattle Times* who provided that ultimate support so cherished by a reporter—the encouragement and freedom to pursue the story, wherever it leads.

Scores of people provided hundreds of hours of their personal time in interviews with the author. For their assistance, their trust, their confidence, I am especially grateful. It is not possible to list all of you. Special thanks to Eleanore Rose and to James and Shirleen Aime; to Mr. and Mrs Lyle Manson; to the law-enforcement officers, Michael J. Fisher, Jerry Thompson, Ben Forbes, Paul Forbes, Ira Beal, Brent Bullock, Robert Keppel, Stephen Bodiford, Don Patchen, Bill Gunter, G. Larry Daughtery, Al Pickles, Bill Harris, Bob Campbell, and so many others; to the prosecuting attorneys, David Yocom, Milton K. Blakey, Bob Dekle, and Larry Simpson; to the admirable attorneys who serve the defense, Lynn Thompson, J. Victor Africano, Millard Farmer, John Henry Browne, and others. And special thanks to the helpful staff of the Leon County clerk's office, Tallahassee, Florida.

The author is grateful for special friendships which have resulted from this work.

Adele and Robert Monahan provided perfectly-timed support and assistance during preparation of the manuscript. Thank you.

Dick Larsen

AUTHOR'S NOTE: These events are true. In some rare instances a name has been changed to avoid possible embarrassment to the individual. Where conversations are portrayed, an effort was made to verify their accuracy through interviews with participants.

ONE | Ted

A heavy overcast pressed low on Puget Sound, so that the mountain ranges—the Olympics to the west, the Cascades to the east—were shrouded from view of the city by a thick, misty February veil. Up from the waterfront, a mottled gray seagull soared past upper windows of Seattle's hillside office buildings, on a silent flight above the hum of street traffic below and the sounds of the nearby harbor.

Abruptly, a brilliant white light bathed one seventh-floor room of the federal building, as television crews and newspaper and radio reporters readied themselves for a midmorning press conference in the office of the FBI.

"Ah, yes," said a TV technician, peering at his light meter, "Ted Bundy goes national."

Other hot lights were switched on. Reporters, opening notebooks, settled into their chairs as a silver-haired Federal Bureau of Investigation agent entered the room and took his place behind a cluster of microphones. John Reed, chief agent of the Seattle FBI office, began reading the official announcement being released across the nation at 10 A.M., local time.

"On this date, February 10, 1978," the agent began, "Theodore Robert Bundy has been added to the list of the Federal Bureau of Investigation's ten most wanted fugitives. . . . Bundy was a recent escapee from a jail in Colorado and is wanted for questioning in connection with thirty-six sexual slayings which began in California in 1969 and extended through the Pacific Northwest and into Utah and Colorado. . . ."

If Theodore Robert Bundy were to be convicted of all the killings in which he is a suspect, the FBI was explaining that day, he would be "the most prolific mass murderer in American history."

The most prolific mass murderer in American history.
Ted.

While the FBI man continued to read the prepared statement, my pen paused over the notepad in my lap, and I turned my attention to the newly issued "wanted flier"—the latest poster which would be thumbtacked on public bulletin boards across America, along with all the other "most wanted" felons.

"INTERSTATE FLIGHT—MURDER," said the headline. Beneath the ten swirl-pattern splotches, which were Ted Bundy's fingerprints, were the three photos of Ted's face, or, rather, three of Ted's faces: left profile—good browline, straight-sculptured nose, loose-knit cardigan on the shoulders, the earnest, scholarly face you'd associate with a college campus; then the full face—head cocked to the left and slightly downward, tousled hair, a stubble of beard, eyebrows arched roguishly over intense eyes (I recognized that one as the way he looked after his first escape and recapture); and the lower right photograph—full face, looking toward the right, dark turtleneck, long dark hair, a full beard, a flicker of mirth in the almost smoky eyes; a photo which could be that of a leading man in a Shakespeare festival playbill.

Below the photos, the text:

Wanted . . . Age 31, born November 24, 1946 . . .
HEIGHT: 5'11" to 6' . . . WEIGHT: 145 to 175

pounds . . . BUILD: Slender, athletic . . . CAUTION: Bundy, a college educated physical fitness enthusiast with a prior history of escape, is being sought as a prison escapee after being convicted of kidnapping and while awaiting trial involving brutal sex slaying of woman at ski resort. He should be considered armed, dangerous and an escape risk.

After the FBI man had completed the routine announcement, reporters asked their questions:

"Where do you think Bundy might have gone?"

With a shrug, Reed responded, "We're just looking for him all over the place." This very morning, he noted, there were news conferences like this one in Salt Lake City and Denver —cities in states where there had been many murdered and missing young women. Bundy, whose movements seemed to coincide with murders, had been major crime news in Washington, Utah, Colorado, and elsewhere in the West for months. Now, said the FBI spokesman, the "most wanted" flier on the man would go to police everywhere in the nation, to attain "maximum saturation."

Reed was asked: What about the thirty-six murders of which Bundy is suspected? Could the FBI detail them? Where and when—and how—did all those crimes occur?

He could only respond to that by saying that the FBI received that information from local police jurisdictions in the Western states. The FBI knew little about Bundy, other than that he had become an interstate fugitive when, forty-three days earlier, he had slipped out of jail in Glenwood Springs, Colorado, leaving behind a mound of law books and other items under a blanket on his jail-cell cot, and vanished in a snowstorm.

Local police in Colorado and elsewhere had pleaded with the FBI to put Bundy on the most-wanted list. That would assure a police alert across America, even though there would be no news-media interest in the man in such distant places as, for example, Florida.

As the news conference ended, TV crews dismantled lights, folded tripods, packed their gear, and headed back to studios to edit film and prepare it for the evening newscasts. Newspaper and radio reporters departed for telephones and news-room typewriters. It would be the day's lead story: TED BUNDY ON FBI'S MOST-WANTED LIST.

Hearing, reading that day's news would be scores of people who knew Ted Bundy in earlier years—as a friend, a college classmate, as a work associate, as that rather good-looking young man whom they had encountered somewhere, one day, by chance—people who would attempt to reconcile their own memory of him with the always darkening news reports which suggested that wherever Ted Bundy seemed to travel, young women vanished and were murdered.

For Mary Ellen McCaffree, a pleasant, middle-aged Seattle woman, an activist in Washington State politics and govern-ment, memories of Ted Bundy were vivid.

Often, when she had been at home, working in her yard, tending flowers or trimming the lawn, there'd be a honk from a passing Volkswagen, and Ted would wave and shout, "Hi, Mary Ellen."

"Ted, of course, was a very friendly person. And he lived right there in the neighborhood."

That was in North Seattle's University District, an attrac-tive area of tree-lined streets, where distinguished older houses, most containing student apartments, were inter-spersed with fraternity and sorority houses. To the south, across 45th Street, was the woodsy edge of the large campus of the University of Washington where, in 1972, Bundy had received his bachelor's degree in psychology. Even after graduation, he kept residence in a student apartment there in the "U District"; he seemed to enjoy the university atmos-phere.

It was the year of Bundy's graduation that Ken and Mary Ellen McCaffree came to know the young man well. Mrs. McCaffree, onetime member of the Washington State legisla-ture, became a key organizer in the '72 reelection campaign of Washington's Governor Dan Evans. Because Evans was a liberal Republican, a champion of environmental protection and other "citizen causes," legions of intensely loyal, bright young "Evans Republicans" turned out to help in his cam-paign.

Sometimes, after a session of work in campaign headquarters or of putting up yard signs, some of them would gather at the McCaffree home, to sit and talk and laugh in the comfortable living room. Often Ted Bundy was there.

The young man in turtleneck sweater, jeans, and tennis shoes confided that his dream was to go through law school. "But money's a real problem," he added. He talked excitedly of his new interest in the exhilarating world of politics—perhaps a career in politics.

"Well, Ted," she replied, "I always tell all the kids I know—the ones that get interested in politics early—that the most important thing is to get your education first. Ted, I really think you should get your law degree."

He nodded in agreement.

Jim Moore recalls first meeting Bundy during Moore's unsuccessful 1972 campaign for the nonpartisan office of Superintendent of Public Instruction. Mandatory school busing to attain racial desegregation had erupted early that year as a major issue in the Florida presidential-primary election and had spread as a hot issue into other campaigns across America.

That evening in October, Moore, a tall, mostly bald, bespectacled psychologist for the Seattle school system, delivered his antibusing speech to a candidate's forum at Lincoln High School. Afterward, some of the candidates mixed with the crowd in the auditorium, and a well-dressed young man approached Moore to talk about the issue.

"Watch it," Moore's campaign manager told him. "The guy's taping you." The young man held a partially hidden tape recorder. "It's okay," said Moore.

Moore's interviewer introduced himself as Ted Bundy, a campaign worker for Governor Dan Evans. He said he was researching issues. "He was a very sharp young chap," Moore would reflect later. "Nice-looking young man."

Moore had grown up in the distant small town of Lake City, Florida, where his closest boyhood friend, H. Morris Williams, also had gone into the field of education in their hometown. On that day, February 10, 1978, when Moore saw the news that Ted Bundy was on the list of the FBI's most-wanted fugitives, Moore's boyhood friend Williams, principal of the Lake City, Florida, junior high school, was fearful about a pretty dark-haired schoolgirl who had vanished mysteriously from his school the day before.

The coincidence of the date would dawn on Moore and Williams later.

In the predawn of that morning—a few hours before the FBI press conference in Seattle—Morris Williams had been roused out of bed at his Lake City home by a distraught mother and father. Mr. and Mrs. Thomas Leach were begging him to go with them to the junior high school and search for their daughter, Kimberly.

It was rather ironic, Cathy Swindler remembered with a chuckle, how Ted first seemed to her "sort of Kennedylike." There was a little personal-political irony in that.

During 1968, that year of turbulence and frustration for America, agonizing over the war in Vietnam and social upheaval at home, Cathy was an early, avid supporter of Senator Robert F. Kennedy in his campaign for the Presidency. Then came his shocking assassination in California, and Cathy was disconsolate. An acquaintance at Western Washington State College, where she was a student, persuaded Cathy to go to work for what her friend described as "the next best candidate available": Nelson Rockefeller of New York.

Although Rockefeller was a Republican, and Cathy was a loyal Democrat, she volunteered to work in the Draft Rockefeller headquarters in downtown Seattle. The office manager welcomed her with a cordial greeting: "Hi, I'm Ted Bundy. Welcome to the Rockefeller campaign." He was quite handsome, and Cathy, a pretty nineteen-year-old with long honeybrown hair, was impressed by her new supervisor.

"He was very well dressed and well mannered," Cathy recalled. "The kind of guy a girl my age would look at and just say *wow!* Sort of Kennedylike."

Day by day, as she performed her routine work—typing, sorting file cards, handling telephone calls and other campaign chores—Cathy also watched and admired the efficient, obviously confident young man. "Ted had control of what he was doing. He was really poised. He was friendly. He was always smiling." Ted had a way of letting volunteers know their work was appreciated. "He was terribly charismatic.

6

Obviously, he was someone who had a great deal of compassion in dealing with other people."

Then came that exciting moment when Ted approached Cathy's desk and asked, "Would you like to walk with me up to the public market for lunch?"

"I almost fell all over myself," she remembered. She accepted, of course, with as much composure as she could summon. That noontime, in the bright sunshine, the two of them—the suave, twenty-one-year-old man and the shining-faced younger woman—walked together, chatting happily, along the busy downtown street, northward to Seattle's Pike Place market, a quaint arcade of farm-fresh fruit and vegetable stands, fish markets, crafts shops, and tucked-away eating places.

"Why don't we have bagels and cream cheese?" Ted suggested.

"*What and what?*" Cathy laughed. Slightly embarrassed, she admitted she had never heard of bagels. Ted patiently explained that, while bagels and cream cheese might be unfamiliar to a native of Seattle, it was a common order, especially in the East. "Try it," he suggested.

Cathy and Ted took their bagels, wrapped in napkins, to a place behind the market, where they could sit and look down on Seattle's waterfront. The warm breeze ruffled their hair, and Cathy listened, fascinated, as Ted talked about his studies at the University of Washington, his interest in the law and politics and people. Cathy felt flattered that he treated her so equally, even though she felt very little-girllike in the presence of a young man of such urbanity.

"He was a champion of causes. He was concerned about the situation of the blacks, of all minorities. And the poor," she remembered. "He was unhappy with the injustices of society, and he wanted to do something about them."

After their first lunch together, there were other dates. Sometimes they went to a movie, sometimes they just had coffee and conversation.

Once Ted invited Cathy to his apartment in the University District to play chess. "I don't know how to play chess," she replied. "It's okay, I'll teach you," he offered. Ted's grin was encouraging and irresistible.

Cathy arrived at Ted's upstairs apartment a little early that afternoon and, because he wasn't home, she waited at the doorway until he appeared. Ted soon came bounding up the stairs, wearing his tennis garb—white shorts, white tennis shirt, socks, and shoes. He just looks healthier'n hell, Cathy thought.

"Hi, sorry to be late," Ted said, tucking his tennis racket under one arm and unlocking the apartment door. "Come on in."

Ted's small student bachelor apartment was tidy, with a neat arrangement of books and an orderly study desk. It was a warm summer day, and so the bed, in its folded-down position, was covered only by a white sheet. Ted opened the chessboard on the bed, and they sat down together, Ted arranging the chessmen and explaining the procedures of chess to her.

During the game, when Cathy began to move a pawn, Ted warned her softly, "*Look* at it, now. *Look* at it. *Think* about it." It was a gentle warning that the move she was about to make would put her in some trouble.

Cathy withdrew her fingers from the pawn and looked up at him in wonderment. He merely grinned back at her. "Think about it now," he encouraged. Ted made it clear she would have to think to contemplate each move until she understood what it might incur. Ted was an excellent chess coach.

Eventually their relationship progressed to the stage of an occasional embrace and kiss. If Ted's touching became too intimate, Cathy needed only to touch his hand, and the hand withdrew. "He was always just the perfect gentleman," she remembered.

Later that summer of '68, Ted went off to Florida to attend the Republican National Convention, to continue his work in the Rockefeller cause. That was a losing effort. Richard Nixon in 1968 swept to an easy nomination, en route to the Presidency. But Ted that year had discovered the world of politics and campaigning.

Years later, Cathy and her father thought back and tried to remember if, during the time she and Ted were dating, she ever introduced Ted to her dad. "I think I must have," Cathy said. Her father, Herb Swindler, confessed, "You know, I just can't remember for certain if I ever did meet him. But you know I'd sure like to be able to meet him and talk to him now."

Herb Swindler became chief of the homicide division of the Seattle Police Department in 1974, the year in which the series of murders of young women stunned the city.

Even after all the hundreds of news reports about Ted Bundy's possible connection with so many murders of young women across the nation, Cathy could only reflect on the Ted she had known:

> Ted Bundy was a figure that people met and loved. I mean, I thought I loved Ted Bundy. Not totally in a romantic way . . . but in terms of being moved by what he said and his feelings for other human beings . . . if you know him, you can't help but have a great deal of affection for him as a human being.

During the final weeks of the 1972 campaign for governor of Washington State, a tough political battle was being fought by Governor Evans, the Republican, and Democrat Albert D. Rosellini. Wherever Rosellini appeared, newsmen noticed the handsome, well-groomed young man who seemed always to be in the audience.

Eventually, when I asked him who he was, the young man introduced himself as Ted Bundy, a graduate student at the University of Washington. He said he was working on a political-science thesis.

One day, late in the campaign, both candidates were scheduled to address senior citizens at the Olympic Hotel in downtown Seattle—Rosellini at ten o'clock, Evans at eleven o'clock.

When I settled into my chair that morning, I noticed Bundy sitting a few rows in front of me. His tape recorder was beside him, and he took notes as Rosellini delivered his speech.

I stared at Bundy's back, feeling envy. His long brown hair fell in perfect waves over his ears. There was a special dapperness about him.

Shortly after 10:30, Rosellini wound up his speech and left the room. After a moment Bundy rose and started toward the ornate lobby of the old hotel. I followed. Within moments

Governor Evans and a small entourage came through the main doorway of the hotel and crossed to where Bundy stood.

The governor, a slender, dark-haired man, graying at the temples, greeted Bundy with a grin and leaned his head forward to listen. Bundy, referring to notes he'd taken during Rosellini's speech, quickly briefed Governor Evans: "And he used the usual line about an eight percent cut in employees, across the board, in all state agencies."

The governor listened, nodding, his eyes turned toward the mezzanine room where the audience awaited.

For Dan Evans, 1972 was an uncertain campaign year. President Richard Nixon was clearly on his way to a sweeping reelection victory over Democrat George McGovern. Evans, although a Republican like Nixon, couldn't count on much "coattailing" help from the President. On many issues, Evans had disassociated himself from Nixon. But the most troubling factor in Evans' reelection bid was the state economy, still ailing from the layoff in recent years of tens of thousands of Boeing Company aircraft employees.

Some Evans-Rosellini debates proved to be decisive near the end of the campaign. Rosellini fared poorly. In November '72 Evans won his third term. Bundy, who'd played a role and won some influential friendships in the campaign, got a postelection job as an aide to Ross Davis, chairman of the Washington State Republican Party.

Months after the election, United Press International carried a report from the state capitol at Olympia, quoting Bundy as admitting he had posed as a college student to travel with and secretly report on the Rosellini campaign. "Theodore Bundy, now special assistant to State Republican Chairman Ross Davis, said in an interview that his connection with the Evans campaign was kept secret while he traveled with Rosellini," said the report.

Gordon Schultz, state capital bureau chief for UPI, explained that he had noticed Bundy constantly shadowing Rosellini during the campaign, carrying his tape recorder, asking questions. When Schultz questioned Bundy about it at the time, Bundy explained, as he had to me, that he was a graduate student working on a political-science thesis. Later, when Bundy turned up as a paid staff employee of the state

Republican Party, Schultz got Bundy to confess that his campaign story about being a student was a ruse.

Republicans were furious at the report, calling it a distortion. Democrats charged that Evans' "spy" had been unethically seeking to dig up dirt on Rosellini.

I telephoned Bundy at the state GOP headquarters, and he happily agreed to come in to *The Seattle Times* newsroom for an interview. "Heck, yes," he said. "I want to talk about it. I'm not apologetic for anything we did in the campaign."

Ted arrived at the newsroom, again looking like the prosperous young executive-to-be, in a blue-gray jacket, slacks, shirt, and dark tie.

"Hi, Ted, nice to see you," I said as we shook hands. We moved past the reporters' desks and clacking typewriters to a partitioned interview room.

"Is it okay if I ask a photographer to come in and take some shots of you while we talk?"

"Certainly." Ted sat at a table in the small room. "Y'know," he explained, referring to the UPI article, "that really hurt. I'm not the least bit uncomfortable about what we did in that campaign. *You* know—you were there. You saw. We were just reporting everything Rosellini was saying and doing—the kind of things that a good campaign ought to do."

I nodded in agreement. A few years earlier, I told him, I was involved in a congressional campaign, and we tried to find out everything we could about what the opponent was saying.

A photographer arrived as we discussed the campaign and some of the new issues involving Governor Evans and the legislature. We talked derisively about some of the old-guard Democrats who were running the state senate. "What a sad bunch," Ted said with a grin. The photographer's strobe flashed a few times. His smiling face was recorded. A very good face, I thought. Although I knew little about him, I was intrigued, as a political reporter, by any new appealing face in the political crowd. Bundy seemed articulate and self-confident.

"Ted, have you ever had any thoughts of running for office yourself?"

"Well, I've given that some thought." (I sensed he was flattered by that question—always an ego-inflator—and was handling the response like a skillful pro.) "Maybe some day. Right now I'm planning to go into law school this fall. Down at the University of Puget Sound [in Tacoma]. And maybe, eventually—who knows? I really do enjoy politics, and I think a lot of things can be done through the political system."

I felt another twinge of envy. This twenty-five-year-old was obviously bright and had a promising future.

At interview's end, we shook hands. "Well, Ted, good luck in law school." I'd be writing an article which would dispute the "dirty tricks" allegation, I told him. (In fact, I eventually wrote that Ted Bundy was "a man who has become an accidental celebrity as, thanks to Watergate, the press and public discover with fascination some wholly proper kinds of activities which occur in political campaigns.")

Of course, Ted had fibbed a little—unnecessarily, really—saying he was a graduate student, when, in fact, he was being paid by the Evans' campaign. But fibs aren't rare in politics.

We agreed to stay in touch. Only casually, I watched Ted walk away through the busy, fluorescent-lit newsroom.

Later I'd try to remember that moment—his hair color, size, and height. My memory was that he was rather wiry and not very tall, perhaps 5 feet 9 or 5 feet 10, and had brown hair with golden or sandy highlights.

There would eventually be varying recollections, especially about the hair color and height, when witnesses later tried to describe the man who was thought to be the killer.

TWO | Voices Stilled

In the midwinter-shortened days of 1974, Seattle's morning rush-hour traffic began in the dark, usually in the rain. Out of the suburbs and neighborhoods, the headlights of the morning migration pointed inward toward the city. Over the sounds of traffic and the monotonous lapping of wiper blades on wet windshields, drivers turned up car radios to hear the latest on Watergate.

At the top of the news for commuters that morning was President Nixon's State of the Union message from the night before, January 31. His recorded voice was making a vow: "I have no intention whatever of ever walking away from the job that the people elected me to do."

Those dark days of the so-called Boeing recession—a painful memory for Seattle and the state—had passed. Seattle's economy was on the upturn. Boeing had many orders for new jets and was recruiting workers around the nation. The recovery and its new growth were not without problems. In an area where people held a possessive, protective affection for their uncrowded life-style and environment, there was resistance to sudden growth—especially the growth-at-any-price phenomenon which had arrived at, and, it seemed, despoiled other regions of the West.

One bumper sticker in the flow of traffic urged, "Don't Californicate Washington."

Among America's cities, Seattle, at the beginning of 1974, remained a rather fresh, cheerful adolescent. It had been spared the problem of chronic, violent crime which flourished in the streets of many larger cities. Surrounding the city, rural King County, with a population of about 400,000, had only six murders during the preceding year—twenty-two fewer than the FBI's national population and crime statistics indicated it could have expected. "Where'd we go wrong?" asked one King County homicide detective with a pleased grin.

The sparkling rivers of commuter headlights, reflecting on wet roadways, continued into the city on the north-south freeway and, from the east, over the two floating bridges which cross Lake Washington. Although the climate of Puget Sound can be wet and gloomy, most of its residents considered it worth enduring the drizzle to be able to live near so many shorelines, lakes, and mountains—places for boating, fishing, and camping. In an increasing number of homes, families kept a full set of ski equipment for Mom, Dad, and each of the kids. It was possible, after work that day, to drive the whole family to a nearby mountain for skiing.

The cheerful feminine voice on the radio was reminding commuters of that possibility:

> "Hi, skiers. This is Lynda with your Cascade Mountain ski report for Thursday. All areas are operating and all areas are reporting new snow. Snoqualmie Pass is reporting eight inches of new snow for a sixty-eight inch total. Crystal Mountain reports ten inches of new snow. . . ."

Beginning early in the morning, that clear, youthful voice with the latest ski news was being heard each day on several radio stations around the Pacific Northwest, a promotion broadcast for *Northwest Skier* magazine. For twenty-one-year-old Lynda Ann Healy, the girl with that melodic voice, her morning radio work was a handy part-time job. She was a psychology major at the University of Washington.

A tall, slender, pretty girl with long brown hair, Lynda had settled in with some other young women students in one of the many old two-story houses near the university campus. Lynda and another girl had adjoining basement rooms in the old house.

Her morning radio job meant rolling out of bed early. At her bedside, Lynda's clock radio was regularly set for 5:30. She had just enough time to dress, push her bike up a couple of concrete steps from the basement and out the side door to a sidewalk. Lynda enjoyed her solitary morning bike ride through the quiet residential neighborhood in the predawn, past the businesses of the U District, then over to the storefront office of *Northwest Skier* on Northeast 45th Street.

There she and other girls doing the ski reports had to work swiftly. Speed was important. The ski operators wanted to reach the radio listeners in the morning commuter traffic.

Lynda was reliable. So her absence was conspicuous that Friday morning, February 1. When Lynda hadn't appeared at her job by 6:30, Betty Bowen, her supervisor, thought she might have overslept. Betty telephoned Lynda's residence and heard, at the other end of the line, the drowsy voice of a housemate explain that Lynda must be on her way. Lynda's clock radio had gone off as usual.

But then Karen, the housemate, also noticed that Lynda's bicycle was still in the basement, in the place Lynda always kept it, outside her room. The bedcovers had been pulled up over Lynda's bed, too. That was unusual. In her morning rush to get to work, Lynda usually didn't bother to make her bed.

Through the day, after telephone calls between Lynda's mother, her supervisor at the job, and the other girls at the house, everyone began to feel uneasy. Lynda had invited her parents to the house for dinner that evening. To anyone who knew her, it made no sense that Lynda would have gone away somewhere without telling anyone. When police were summoned to the old house, Joanne Testa, another housemate, told them, "We think something's really wrong." She showed the officers Lynda's bed. When the covers had been pulled down, they discovered some blood on the pillow and more blood on the sheet. In Lynda's closet they found the short, cream-colored nightie Lynda had worn to bed. Around the seam of the garment, on the shoulder and back, there were more bloodstains.

One of the officers theorized that Lynda might have had a nosebleed or something in the middle of the night, then gotten out of bed and gone somewhere. Lynda's parents and other girls insisted that hadn't happened. "This is serious," said one of the girls. Seattle Police Sergeant Tom Burke

15

arrived at the house, looked over the scene, and made a detailed report. He tried to piece together Lynda's movements the night before.

During the early evening she had spent some time at Dante's tavern, one of several student beer-drinking hangouts. Around 9:30 she had walked home with two friends. After arriving there, Lynda had gone downstairs to her basement room, undressed, slipped into her nightie, and then returned upstairs to the living room. She lounged there in an easy chair for a while, watching television. The prime show that night was CBS's "The Autobiography of Miss Jane Pittman." Around midnight, after a conversation with Joanne about routine things, including her planned dinner with her parents and a psychology quiz next day, Lynda went downstairs to bed.

Karen arrived home a little later. She, too, remained upstairs for a while talking with Joanne. It might have been 1:30 when Karen went downstairs to her bed. As she crossed the open area of the concrete basement floor, approaching her own room, Karen noticed that, beyond the draped entryway, Lynda's room was dark. Apparently Lynda was asleep.

Only a thin partition separated Lynda's and Karen's basement rooms. They weren't exactly rooms, with construction walls—just areas divided by partitions of half-inch plywood. As Karen slept in her bed Lynda would have been sleeping only a few feet away, beyond that plywood. "I'm normally a light sleeper," Karen told the officer. "But I didn't hear a thing."

The top bed sheet was missing. Lynda's pink satin pillowcase, which the other girls said was always there, was now gone. Examining Lynda's wardrobe, her roommates decided that some items of her clothing also were gone: her bell-bottomed blue jeans, white blouse, hiking boots, and yellow ski cap. Her red knapsack with the gray stripes was also missing.

Girls frequently wander away impulsively, for any number of reasons, but the Seattle police concluded that Lynda wasn't the type for a flight of impulse. Something had happened to her. That seemed obvious. The investigators concluded that someone, standing outdoors in the darkness, in the narrow stretch of lawn on the south side of the house, could have peered down into Lynda's room as she undressed. Then it would have been possible for that someone to enter the door on the north side of the house—none of the other girls could be sure whether or not the door was locked or unlocked—and slip down the stairs into the basement, into Lynda's room. And then? Perhaps he used a knife to wound her, to frighten her into silence, forcing her to dress and accompany him somewhere. They could only guess. But why, they wondered, had Karen, sleeping just beyond the thin wall, heard nothing? Or had Lynda been taken out in that hour and a half or so, after midnight, before Karen came downstairs to her room?

Lynda's disappearance became news a few days later. A *Seattle Times* article, reporting the police puzzlement over the mystery, quoted a homicide detective: "We have interviewed seventy-two people and haven't learned what might have happened to her. We have talked with every guy she dated since age fifteen, and you'd be proud to have any of them as your son. It doesn't look good. It doesn't look good at all."

The article's headline, AFTER SHE PUT OUT THE LIGHT, WHAT EVIL CREPT IN? was to be the first of a series of troubling headlines.

That investigation led Seattle police back to another house a few blocks away in the University District. A vicious crime had occurred there twenty-seven nights before Lynda's disappearance. In an older house in the 4300 block on Eighth Avenue Northeast, Sharon Clarke also lived in a basement apartment. Sharon, a pretty young woman, had been upstairs watching television until quite late. Around two o'clock that morning she went downstairs to her bed in the basement.

Throughout the following day her housemates—all young men—noticed she hadn't been up and around. One of them late in the day approached Sharon's bed. Seeing the covers drawn over her head, he called her name. There was no reply. When he drew back the covers, he recoiled at the sight of all the blood. Her face was covered with dried blood, and her hair was a matted crimson. Blood had soaked into the pillow and sheets. With a faint moan, she coughed up more blood. She was still alive.

Sharon was rushed to a hospital. To the surprise of the

attending doctors, she lived. She had massive skull fractures and severe internal injuries. Other residents of the house told police they thought that a steel reinforcing rod, which had been outside the house, was missing.

An investigator stood in the narrow side yard of that house, and concluded it was almost identical to the setting where Lynda had disappeared. Someone could have stood there and looked down through a curtainless basement window as Sharon had prepared for bed. Then he could have slipped through a side door—a door trustingly left unlocked—and descended the few steps into the basement.

During her long, slow recovery, Sharon was questioned by police, but she could remember nothing of what had happened to her. She had suffered partial amnesia as a result of the beating. Police tried hypnosis on the girl, hoping that, through a heightening of her recall, she might be able to grasp some memory of the attack. It didn't work. Police concluded that Sharon's assailant must have knocked her unconscious while she slept, with the first crushing blow from that steel rod.

The Evergreen State College campus was located in a remote, meditative place, surrounded by a dense evergreen forest, a few miles east of the state capitol at Olympia. By that autumn 1974 quarter, its enrollment still hadn't reached 3,000. Not far away, in the legislature, Evergreen became a pet target of criticism for conservative legislators. They grumbled about Evergreen's cost, its "frills," its soaring per-student cost of operation, and the "hippie atmosphere" which seemed to prevail on the campus. One lawmaker delivered a speech of outrage, detailing what the kids' dogs were doing to the expensive carpeting in the library.

For many students, though, Evergreen's atmosphere was exhilarating. Many gifted instructors were drawn to it by the academic freedom and creativity it encouraged.

Blue-eyed, brown-haired Donna Gail Manson, a petite nineteen-year-old was naturally drawn to Evergreen. She had always insisted on and savored her personal independence. That trait in their daughter was accepted, though occasionally with some reservation, by her conservative parents. Lyle Manson was a music instructor in the Seattle school system;

Marie Manson was a part-time legal secretary and church choir director.

It was the evening of Tuesday, March 12, 1974. In her room at the student residence hall, Donna sat cross-legged on the floor, playing her flute for a while. Then she rose and began preparing to go out for the evening. She stood in front of her mirror, head tilted, brushing her long brown hair. Her roommate, Deanna Ray, recalled that Donna changed clothes, fussing with her appearance. Donna was going across campus to attend a concert in the student lounge. Some of the students and faculty members would be fooling around with jazz, improvising. Donna's father played jazz—his preference was Dixieland—and so she'd grown up with music.

Around seven o'clock, before she left, Donna stirred some vegetable beef soup in a pan on the stove and turned the burner knob down to "warm." She was wearing green pants and a bright striped shirt of red, orange, and green. Donna pulled on a long, warm fuzzy black coat and left the apartment.

Donna liked old-fashioned things. That fake-fur coat she was wearing had been her grandmother's. Wearing it, Donna, who was only about five feet tall, looked like a little bear cub, her friends told her. But that night the old coat was surely warm as Donna began her walk across the campus in the chilly, wet blackness.

From Donna's residence, the building where the concert was held would have been, perhaps, a five-minute stroll. Much of the route was in partial darkness. There were scattered lights along the campus pathways.

Donna never reached the jazz concert.

Several days later some local police officers in the small town of Auburn arrived at the front door of the Manson home to tell Lyle and Marie that their daughter had apparently run away from the Evergreen campus. The parents felt an instant uneasiness.

"She hasn't run away," said Donna's mother with certainty. "Something's happened to her."

Just the night before that concert, Marie Manson had had a long conversation on the phone with Donna. "Mom," Donna had said, "when we get to spring break at school, I'd really like to take a trip out to the ocean with you." Donna loved

19

the ocean beach, where she could walk the vast expanse of wet sand, watch the crashing waves, search for seashells, and watch for the treasures of smoothed, sculptured driftwood tossed in by the waves.

Her mother had told Donna on the telephone that the trip to the ocean sounded like a good idea. Marie thought she could get away from home for a few days. "Dad and Jimmy can batch it for a week," she'd told Donna. There was a gas shortage, and the drive to the ocean would be a long one, but Marie had told her daughter, "We'll find a way."

After he got the news from the police, Lyle Manson drove quickly to the Evergreen campus to find out what had happened. Donna's roommate had delayed reporting the disappearance for a few days. Even though the pot of soup had been left on the stove, the other girl assumed Donna had just impetuously decided to go away for a while. At the college, Thurston County Sheriff's Detective Paul Barclift tried to give some assurance to the worried father. "Maybe," reasoned Barclift, "she just went off somewhere with some boyfriend. That's the way these things usually turn out around here."

Lyle Manson's stern Scotsman's face showed cold disagreement. No, he said—Donna had no need to run away. "We've always given her freedom." Lyle and the detective walked to the residence hall, to Donna's room. She had left behind all her money, her toilet articles, the other things which she would have taken with her had she gone off somewhere voluntarily. The detective shuffled through some of Donna's papers and her address book, looking for something that could be a helpful lead. Swallowing hard, Lyle Manson picked up his daughter's flute and held it—gently. He knew Donna was gone and something serious had happened to her.

Eastward out of Seattle, Interstate 90 ascends through foothills densely covered by rain-loving cedar, Douglas fir and pine, to cross the Cascade Mountains at Snoqualmie Pass. From there, beyond the mountains eastward, the terrain becomes more open and arid—a rolling country of pine-topped ridges, bare buttes, and flatlands. In April 1974, spring again was retouching the winter-dulled landscape around the small town of Ellensburg. Cottonwoods along the

Yakima River had a new sprouting of foliage, the hay crop in farm fields was greening, and newborn colts were making their wobbly-legged debut on the ranches. Ellensburg is mostly a ranch town, a trucker town, a rodeo town, comfortable in denims and boots. Its biggest and steadiest industry is the college—Central Washington University. That spring its enrollment was nearly 7,000 students.

At a ranch five miles out of town, the campus police chief, Al Pickles, was settling into the saddle of a horse in the paddock of a riding stable when he noticed one of the white campus police cars braking to a stop near the fence. Whatever it was, Pickles thought, something important must have happened. The man climbing out of the car, waving at him, was Robert Miller, the dean of students.

"Hey, Al, Al," the dean shouted. "C'mon over."

Pickles jogged the horse over to the fence, swung out of the saddle, and tied the reins to a fence rail.

"What's up?" he asked.

"Al," said the dean, "we've got a girl missing."

"A girl missing?"

"One girl student just told me about it. Her roommate left the residence hall for a meeting last night and never came back."

"I'll be right in," said the chief.

After he reached his office, Pickles interviewed the roommate, Diana Pitt. She was in tears. The night before, said Diana—Wednesday, April 17—her roommate, Susan Rancourt, had gone out to attend a meeting across campus, at Munson Hall. On her way to that meeting, Susan had put some clothes in one of the washing machines in the basement of the dorm. She hadn't returned. The clothes had been left in the washer.

"All her things, her bike, her wallet—all her ID—are still in the room," said Diana. "It isn't like Susan at all. Just to go off."

Pickles jotted down a description of the missing girl:

Susan Rancourt, 18, 5'2", 118 pounds, blonde hair to shoulders, straight and parted in the middle, blue eyes, light complexion . . . Additionally described by roommate as busty . . . Last seen wearing yellow, short-

21

sleeved sweater, gray cord pants, brown Hushpuppies, yellow coat. Personality described as shy, quiet, withdrawn (lately trying to meet new people . . .).

The chief studied a photo of Susan. Against a campus background, strolling along a walkway, Susan was looking back, smiling, over her shoulder. Bright smile, beautiful girl, Pickles thought. Susan had been a high-school cheerleader, and Pickles vaguely remembered her as one of those students who'd been in that early-morning jogging class he attended.

When Susan's parents arrived from Anchorage, the mother examined Susan's medicine cabinet. Susan's dental floss was there. That, concluded Mrs. Rancourt, was the proof that something serious had happened. Susan would never go anywhere without her dental floss. Dental care was important to Susan. She'd had extensive dental work—ceramic crowns and bridgework.

"She lived for each day and was a happy girl," said Susan's father. "She would get up in the morning and just be very vibrant and knew exactly what she wanted to do and went ahead and did it. And this . . . this . . . is just completely out of character for her."

Time and again, in daylight and darkness, the campus chief walked pathways across the campus, following the route he thought Susan might have taken after she left her meeting at Munson Hall. One night, with another campus officer, Cheryl Schmeitzer, the chief again walked the most likely route— from Munson Hall, past the front steps of the library, then north and east in front of Black Hall, onto Chestnut Street, and from there northward.

Where Chestnut Street emerged from its underpass beneath the railroad tracks, Pickles observed, "It's darker'n hell right over there." He pointed to a place just north of the tracks, where the roadway turned to parallel the rail line. "You could park a car in there and nobody'd ever see it."

Schmeitzer nodded. The spot was in deep darkness, just beyond the campus lights. They searched the ground there, but found nothing.

Among the Central students who had read and talked about Susan's disappearance were two young women who had paid scant attention to separate nighttime encounters they had had with a young man on the campus around that time. In each instance, the coed had encountered a man outside the library. He appeared to have an injury to one arm and was fumbling with some books. Each girl had offered to help the man by carrying his books for him. Each girl had been led from the steps of the library to that darkened area just beyond the railroad underpass where his Volkswagen was parked. Each girl had felt uneasy about the man and had fled quickly. Nothing had really happened. Neither girl had bothered to make a report to anyone.

It's probably not related, I guess," said Bill Harris. "We're so far south of you. But we've got a missing girl down here. . . ."

Harris, campus security chief at Oregon State University, was having a telephone conversation with a detective to the north, in Washington State.

Harris' small office was in an obscure place, tucked away at the mezzanine level of Gill Coliseum, OSU's basketball arena. From his desk, through a window, Harris looked down onto a campus bathed in brilliant mid-May sunshine.

"She was walking across the campus last night, and that was the last time she was seen."

At the other end of Harris' long-distance call was Paul Barclift, a detective in Olympia, about 200 miles to the north. "Left all her things behind in the room," Harris went on. "Even left her study lamp turned on."

That sounded familiar to Barclift. He was investigating the disappearance of Donna Manson at Evergreen—Donna had left a pan of soup to warm on the stove in her room the night she disappeared.

Harris described the missing OSU coed: Roberta Kathleen Parks, always known as Kathy; pretty, slim, long, blonde hair, parted in the middle. A sensitive young woman, Kathy had been upset the night she disappeared, Harris explained. Kathy's father, in Lafayette, California, had suffered a heart attack. Kathy had been concerned, restless. She had decided to take a walk that evening—May 12—across the campus. It was quite warm. While she was walking near the student union building, she had encountered a girlfriend. They talked for a few minutes. The other girl invited Kathy to her room.

"No, thanks," Kathy had replied. "I just want to walk for a little while." She continued onward, across a rather well-lighted part of the pretty tree-lined campus. Walking the route she was on, Kathy would have reached the business district of Corvallis within a few more minutes. But no one had seen her there. Or anywhere since she talked with that other girl.

Barclift and Harris agreed there were eerie similarities between Kathy's disappearance and Donna's. Barclift mentioned the disappearance of the girl in Seattle and the missing coed across the mountains at the campus in Ellensburg. But the officers agreed it would be far-fetched to assume some connection between a missing girl at Oregon State and the Washington State coeds. Seattle was about 250 miles north of Corvallis. Then Ellensburg would be another 140 miles to the east.

It might seem far-fetched as hell, Barclift reflected afterward. Nevertheless, he gathered identifications of the missing girls from each campus and, on the authority of Sheriff Don Jennings, issued a regional police teletype. Directed to northern California, Oregon, Washington, Idaho, and Montana police, it summarized a possible pattern of disappearances:

ALL FOUR FEMALES . . . AGES 18-21, ARE CONSIDERED ATTRACTIVE. THEY ALL WERE ATTENDING COLLEGES OR UNIVERSITIES LOCATED ON OR NEAR AN INTERSTATE HIGHWAY. ALL DISAPPEARED, TELLING NO ONE THAT THEY WERE LEAVING AND THEY TOOK NO PERSONAL BELONGINGS WITH THEM. REQUEST OTHER AGENCIES WITH SIMILAR DISAPPEARANCES TO CONTACT DETECTIVE BARCLIFT, TELE 206-753-8122 OR WRITE TO THURSTON COUNTY SHERIFF'S OFFICE. . . .

In early June 1974, with a summer vacation approaching, there was no widespread feeling of fear on the college campuses—yet.

It was a warm night in Seattle. Occasional sounds of laughter and stereo music came from the fraternity and sorority houses of "Greek Row," just north of the University of Washington campus.

It remained rather noisy along the Row until past midnight. The date was June 11. At one of the houses in the block north of 47th Street there had been a "welcome summer" beer party. Together Georgann Hawkins and Jennifer Roberts, her sorority sister, were returning from that party, walking south on 17th Avenue, when Georgann paused in front of the Beta Theta Pi fraternity house. She told Jennifer she was going to drop into the Beta house to say good night to her boyfriend. Jennifer continued her stroll along the sidewalk to their sorority house at the far end of the block.

Georgann, a radiant, eighteen-year-old from the Tacoma area, had, understandably, been one of the community Daffodil Festival princesses during her high-school years; a pretty, brown-haired, brown-eyed girl, an outstanding student. She entered the Beta house and talked for a while with Marvin, her boyfriend, as he wearily finished his homework.

Later Georgann left the fraternity house through a rear exit, stepping into a brightly-illuminated alleyway, a familiar block-long tunnel of light and human presence leading "home"—southward a block to the rear entry of her sorority house.

When she stepped into the alleyway she heard her name being called: "Hi, George!" Georgann tilted her face upward where she saw, leaning from a window of the fraternity house, Duane Covey, a friend. "Hi, Duane," she replied. She stood there for a few moments talking with Duane. She looked especially glowing, even in the artificial light of the alleyway. Georgann had picked up a healthy suntan in the first sunny days of spring. It was getting late, she told Duane—after one o'clock. "I've got a Spanish test tomorrow," she told him. With a wave and an "Adios," she turned to her right and resumed her stroll down the alleyway toward her sorority house.

From that window, Duane could watch Georgann, in her red, white, and blue blouse, navy-blue pants, and white canvas shoes, as she walked—in the lights of that alleyway. Her sorority house door was perhaps 200 feet distant. Given the angle of his vision, Duane could see her until she was within perhaps a few seconds of her doorway.

In those seconds, Georgann disappeared.

* * *

Next day Georgann's roommate, Laura Heffron, worriedly told the house mother that Georgann hadn't returned to their room. At first the house mother's report to the Seattle Police Department stirred no response. But Laura's father, Norm Heffron, a news executive at KING-TV, made certain that a report on Georgann's disappearance was on the station's evening newscast. Another co-ed had vanished. Then came a heavy police response.

Detectives swarmed into Greek Row, questioning anyone who might have been in the vicinity. During the afternoon, standing in the alley, Captain Herb Swindler, new chief of the homicide and robbery detail of SPD, studied the scene. Beside him, Sergeant Ivan Beeson pointed to the spot where Georgann had stood, talking with Duane, beneath the window of the Beta house. "She was right here, and then she started walking down the alley there," the sergeant explained. Not far from where she had stood, two people sat in a parked car. "They could see her walking almost all the way, too," Beeson added.

The two officers walked the route Georgann had walked. On their left were the rear walls of the fraternity and sorority houses—a mixture of frame and brick with numerous doors and windows. On the opposite side of the alley, to the officers' right, buildings were scattered. There were some open parking areas.

Swindler puzzled over it. "All kinds of activity in here. Kids up late. Windows open. But nobody saw or heard a damned thing."

The sergeant nodded.

"Whoever took her," Swindler mused, "she must have gone willingly for some reason." Perhaps, he thought, it was someone she knew. Or perhaps someone pretending to be a policeman. "Well," concluded the captain, "I'll bet anything it's tied in with those others. I know damned well it is. And we've got another loser. No body. Nothing."

The captain had a personal thought about the special vulnerability of the cheerful, outgoing young women of a college campus. "Y'know," said Swindler, "I've got a girl here now. My own daughter's a student here."

* * *

After a few changing directions in her life, Cathy Swindler had decided she wanted to be a journalist. So, that spring of '74, she had become a communications major at the University of Washington. Earlier, Cathy had taken a few months away from college to live and work in New York City. Now she was happy to be back in her hometown, applying herself in a field which interested her.

Emerging from the Communications Building, carrying her books, Cathy stepped into the sunshine of that spring day, leisurely descended a few brick steps to the flow of students criss-crossing the campus between classes. Suddenly, among the passing young faces, she noticed that especially familiar one, the face of the young man to whom she'd been so attracted six years earlier—Ted Bundy.

He was riding his bicycle along the street, moving slowly through the traffic of bikes and pedestrians.

They saw each other. Cathy wanted to grin and wave and shout, "Hi, Ted!"

But somehow she didn't. "It was a noncontact, really," she reflected later. "We both looked at each other. And we saw each other. But we didn't say anything to each other. I often wondered why I didn't say anything."

Ted looked great, she remembered. Impeccable. On his ten-speed he appeared to be on his way to a tennis match, probably from his apartment near the edge of the campus. His tennis racket was tucked into a backpack. Ted was dressed almost exactly the way Cathy remembered him that day, in his apartment years before, when he taught her to play chess. He was wearing a white T-shirt, tennis shorts, socks, and shoes—his tennis whites.

THREE | Sunday in the Park

In each place where a girl had vanished, the officers interviewed the girlfriends, boyfriends, families, acquaintances. They sought known criminals who might have been in the area. They sorted through names of offenders who might have followed a similar mode of operation. They pursued tips by the hundreds. And hunches.

Obviously some mortal force was responsible. Someone had come there in the night when each young woman vanished. Yet, when they walked the ground where the girl had walked, nothing was found.

It was as though they were chasing yesterday's wind.

"I get the feelin' that some predatory bastard is sittin' out there, lickin' his chops, reading all those stories about the missin' girls and grinnin' at us." The frustrated thought of a Seattle detective was probably shared by investigators in each of the cases.

Nothing plus nothing plus nothing equals zero. That, said Herb Swindler, captain of the Seattle Police Department's homicide division, was the cumulative total of all the clues in all the disappearances during the early months of 1974. Swindler also played with another math problem:

"That first girl, damned near killed in her bed, is the 4th of January. . . . Lynda Healy disappears from her bedroom January 31. . . . March 12 is when the little Manson girl goes out of the Evergreen campus. . . . Susan Rancourt at Central, over at Ellensburg, is April 17. . . . Very, very remote chance that the Oregon disappearance is related, but Kathy Parks, there, was May 6. . . . Then there was the other missing person, Brenda Ball. Not a college girl, but about the same age and look. She disappears May 31 outside a tavern southwest of Seattle, around two o'clock in the morning. . . . And then Georgann Hawkins, June 11.''

If they were all related, that would be nearly one disappearance a month. Swindler counted the days between the incidents—almost a recurring pattern of time intervals—and he thought of the possibility that some astrological design was being followed in the apparent abductions.

Or, if there were some nut walking around in the night, with an alarm clock of madness in his head, ticking, ready to go off at certain intervals, it could happen again around the end of June or early July—*about now,* Swindler thought.

Most residents of the Puget Sound area have developed a sense of humor about their monotonously rainy climate. In fact the drippy weather is used by some of them in wry messages to discourage population growth. One T-shirt message: "In Seattle we don't suntan. We rust." Sometimes they dredge up the mossy story about the visitor to Seattle who, after days of constant drizzle, has a question for one of the natives:

"What do you do around here in the summer?"

"If it falls on Sunday, we have a picnic."

Sunday, July 14, 1974, dawned unmistakably as a vintage summer day, beginning the instant the sun signaled its rise with a red flare behind the Cascades before dawn. Then it climbed into the cloudless sky, turning orange, then white hot. Responding to the beckoning of the day, the people moved early in sports cars, vans, station wagons, and pickup trucks, many trailering boats toward seashores, lakes, and mountains. One direction of the flow was along Interstate 90, eastward out of Seattle, toward Lake Sammamish State Park. The arrivals began filling the parking lot early in the morning. From the cars a mixed crowd, mostly young, carried beach towels, lunches, portable radios, barbecues, and playpens into the park grounds—a stretch of sand beach at the edge of the lake, surrounded by the tree-shaded grasslands of the picnic areas.

Riding her yellow ten-speed bike, Janice Ott pedaled through the crowd to find a sunny place on the sand. A slim blonde with pretty, trim legs, Janice had enjoyed her easy morning bike ride to the park. It was only twenty minutes or so from her little basement apartment in the nearby town of Issaquah.

One of Seattle's rock radio stations had been promoting the day at Lake Sammamish—a picnic sponsored by the Rainier Brewing Company. Coincidentally, a couple of company picnics were also scheduled for the same day at the park. Before the day would end, an estimated 40,000 people would be there, filling the park's swimming waters, beaches, and picnic areas throughout the day.

In the crowd, a good-looking young man, wearing all white—T-shirt, tennis shorts, socks, and tennis shoes— engaged a pretty, petite brunette woman, a stranger, in conversation. He asked her if she'd go to the parking lot to help him unload a sailboat from his car. She could see he might need help—his left arm was in a sling. He explained with a smile that he couldn't manage the boat with just one arm.

"Okay," she agreed. He courteously assured her he appreciated her help. As they strolled together toward the parking lot, he introduced himself as Ted. She told him her name was Jennifer Rutledge. "How'd you hurt your arm?" she asked.

He explained he'd injured it playing racketball. "Ted," Jennifer thought, was a rather debonair man. There seemed to be a trace of a British accent in his speech. In the crowded parking lot, they came to his car, a brownish colored Volkswagen. Jennifer had expected a little fiberglass sailboat hull to be perched atop his car. She noticed only an empty bicycle rack.

"Where's the sailboat?" she asked.

"Oh," replied Ted, "it's up at my parents' house." He gestured toward the hillside a few miles away, toward the east. "Over at Issaquah." He explained it would be necessary to drive there together to pick up the boat.

Jennifer replied she couldn't take the time to drive there with him; she had to meet her husband and some other people back in the park.

"Okay, I understand," Ted said pleasantly. He apologized for inconveniencing her. Jennifer returned to the park.

Not long afterward, Jennifer, reclining in the sun, again noticed her friend, Ted. Hmmm, she thought, he's really hustling. Now Ted, the man in white with his arm in the sling, had begun a cheerful conversation with a slender, pretty blonde in a black bikini. He knelt beside her where the girl sat on a beach towel. Jennifer overheard him asking the blonde to help him with his sailboat. Nearby, in the crowd, a young man also watched and listened. He had earlier cast an appraising eye on the blonde in the bikini. A very foxy lady, he'd concluded. The good-looking guy in the whites had taste.

Those onlookers idly noticed it when, with a smile of agreement, the girl in the bikini arose. She slipped on a white knit overshirt, squirmed into her denim cutoffs, and stepped into her deck shoes. Then, pushing her yellow bike, she walked away with the handsome young man, through the crowd in the sunshine toward the parking lot.

Watching them go, Jennifer smiled to herself. "Ted," she mused, had apparently found his sailboat helper. And this time he must have improved his technique. Jennifer had heard him explain to the girl in the bathing suit that they would have to drive his car over to Issaquah to pick up the sailboat. The girl had told him, "Oh, I live in Issaquah." When the girl had wondered about her yellow bike, "Ted" had told her it would fit on his car rack.

When "Ted" and the pretty blonde disappeared into the crowd in the direction of the parking lot, Jennifer thought the time was around 12:30 or so.

The day grew hotter. The crowd increased. The park became a place of effervescing sound and activity. Overhead there was the drone of circling airplanes. From the lake came the steady growling sounds of motorboats, towing water-skiers. Under the eyes of lifeguards, young people splashed and shouted in the water. In the tree-shaded picnic area, amateur chefs fumbled in the blue smoke around barbecues, forking hamburger patties and hotdogs onto paper plates. A camera crew from a Seattle television station moved around the park, filming—gathering some fill-in footage for the Sunday evening news. Sunday was a slow news day.

After drowsing for a while in the sun beside her boyfriend Kenny, Denise Naslund arose from her towel and said. "I'm going to the bathroom. Be right back." Kenny acknowledged with an "uh-huh."

Denise, a striking nineteen-year-old with olive skin and

dramatically dark hair and eyes, walked away in the crowd toward a distant cement-block public rest room. She was wearing denim shorts, a blue halter, and sandals.

That was perhaps shortly before 4:30 in the afternoon, Kenny remembered.

After an hour had elapsed, Kenny began walking around the park looking for Denise, but she didn't seem to be anywhere. When he went to the parking lot, he found her 1964 Chevrolet where it had been parked. Denise had driven all of them—Kenny, Bob, and Nancy—out to the park from their homes in Seattle.

As it grew later, Kenny grew more puzzled. Nancy checked all the women's restrooms and couldn't find Denise. Kenny asked about her at the first-aid station and talked to a lifeguard. Nothing had happened to anyone in the water that day. By evening, there was no sign of Denise, either in the emptying picnic grounds or in other wooded places around the park.

The sun was lowering, reddening in the haze over the lake when Kenny and the others gave up searching.

It sure wasn't easy for Kenny to have to drive Denise's car to her mother's home that evening. And to try to explain to her mother that Denise had disappeared in that crowd at the park. Denise's mother, Eleanore Rose, was a frail, dark-complexioned little woman, who, it seemed to Kenny, was pretty nervous all the time anyway. Eleanore and Denise's father had been divorced. Then her second marriage hadn't worked out very well, either. When Denise decided to leave home and live in a little house on Graham Street, Eleanore Rose hadn't liked it at all. She didn't think Kenny was treating Denise very well, and Denise, in her mother's words, was always "my beautiful little girl, my shining star." Eleanore was of Lebanese extraction. From her mother, obviously, Denise had inherited her dramatic dark looks—and her vitality and passion for life.

As soon as Kenny slowed the car on Thirteenth Avenue Southwest, in Seattle's White Center neighborhood, nosing the Chevy into a parking place in front of the little home, Mrs. Rose came outdoors. Her mouth opened to speak. Her large, dark eyes grew round with wonderment at the sight of

Kenny—just Kenny—in Denise's car. *Where's Denise?* was written all over her face.

Kenny explained, in a faltering way, that Denise seemed to have disappeared at the state park over at Lake Sammamish. He began to explain how he'd looked all over. . . . That he'd tried, but the police wouldn't take a report from him, because . . .

"Oh, God, *no!* Dear God, *no!*" she shouted. There was no gradual dawning of the realization within the tiny woman. Eleanore recoiled, as though she had been struck in the chest—physically—by the blast of fear. "Not *Denise!* Not *Denise!*"

Eleanore's hands welded together in a fist of anguish, and her dark face turned upward in the summer night. She shrieked, turned, and ran into the house, to fumble for the telephone receiver. With stabs of her frantically shaking finger, she dialed the police emergency number. She sobbed out the information to an officer who told her that the police really couldn't do anything officially until twenty-four hours had elapsed. That was the police rule on missing-persons reports. "But Denise is my whole life," Eleanore sobbed.

All her life, Eleanore had yearned to have a daughter. Her first child had been her Denise. Later a son, Brock, was born, but Mother and daughter had always had a special, loving, hugging, vital relationship with each other. That's the way it had been in the Lebanese home where Eleanore had grown up.

"She's my whole life," sobbed Eleanore. She was slumped at the kitchen table, gripping the telephone. "Someone has to do *something!*" In desperation she dialed a local television station, KING-TV. A reporter agreed to have someone come out to the house.

Weeping, trembling, Eleanore stumbled from the telephone, from the kitchen, through the tiny living room, where the floor seemed to sway beneath her feet, outdoors to the curb where Kenny had parked Denise's car.

There, for an instant, the fantasy replaced her fear.

Abruptly, it's daylight. And cold. The tan Chevy Impala is there with a blue ribbon perched on the nose of its hood, where Eleanore had placed it. Denise is aglow with happiness. She and her mother hug. "Thanks, Mom, I love you," Denise tells her. "See," Eleanore replies, squeezing her girl, "I promised." Eleanore always had promised Denise that, when she became eighteen, Mom would get her a car. Eleanore had always worried about Denise's safety—fearful that, riding on a bus, or worse, hitchhiking, she would be vulnerable to strangers. If she had her own car, Eleanore thought, Denise would be safer. When Denise was just a toddler, Eleanore had begun saving fifty cents here, a dollar there. Gradually, it had added up so that, when Denise's birthday came around this October, Eleanore had the $400 to buy the '64 Chevy. Denise pats the hood. Then happily, she bounces around to the driver's door, opens it, and wriggles her cute little fanny onto the driver's seat. Sitting there, behind the steering wheel, Denise grins at her Mom and gives Denise's familiar little-girl wave: arm straight up, there is just the happy movement of fingers together—fluttering like a bird's wing.

In the glow of the amber porch light, Eleanore noticed numbly that the Chevy's surface was dull and dusty. It probably got that way, Eleanore thought, sitting out in the parking lot all day at Lake Sammamish.

When she and Denise had talked with each other on the telephone that Sunday morning, Eleanore had thought, Denise sounded as though she really didn't want to go on that picnic with Kenny and the others. Looking at the car in the darkness of that warm summer night, Eleanore decided she'd get the little Chevy all washed and polished, so it would look nice and shiny for Denise, when her little shining star came home to her. There probably would never be a day of her life, from that moment onward, when Eleanore Rose could deal with the contradicting certainties which had taken residence together in her mind at that moment: Denise was coming home. Denise was dead. Denise was coming home. Denise was dead.

Listening to a reporter at the other end of the phone line, Bob Monahan, working at the city desk of *The Seattle Times*, muttered the words again: "Bizarre. Absolutely bizarre

. . . Just a minute," he told the caller. "I'll getcha someone for dictation." The assistant city editor looked around the newsroom, across the desks where reporters sat typing, then transferred the call to an available typist.

Other editors and some reporters had gathered around Monahan's desk to learn the latest in the strange, developing page 1 story. Monahan gazed up at them, with a look of astonishment on his round face. "Apparently, some guy kidnapped one girl out of a crowd of forty thousand people over at Lake Sammamish sometime around noon Sunday. And then he comes back in the afternoon and, around four-thirty or so, takes out another girl."

"My God," murmured a reporter. "Were the girls together?"

"No."

"What's the deal? Have the cops got the guy?"

"No, not yet."

"Christ, what a weirdo."

"One girl in the morning. Another in the afternoon. He must have some kind of appetite."

It was Tuesday and, though details were still sketchily falling together, it was certain two more girls were gone. Monahan was handling information coming in from reporters who were tracking developments in the peculiar story— talking to detectives, trying to piece together what had happened, covering the search. Scores of volunteers were moving through the wooded areas and fields around Lake Sammamish. Skindivers had begun searching the waters of the lake. A helicopter was making an air search. Men in jeeps and on horseback were combing the nearby foothills.

Denise Naslund, eighteen, 5 feet 4, 110 pounds, dark hair and eyes, had been reported missing immediately. It had taken longer to discover that Janice Ott, twenty-three, had also vanished. Janice had failed to show up Monday morning for her seven o'clock tennis game with Betty Jo Stover. Then Janice failed to appear for work at the King County Juvenile Court in downtown Seattle, where she was a caseworker and counselor.

When Betty Jo had telephoned Janice's apartment in Issaquah, there was no answer. Growing concerned, Betty Jo notified police, then drove to Janice's residence—a tiny white frame house screened away from the businesses of Issaquah's Front Street by high shrubbery and overhanging tree branches. Betty Jo met a police officer there. On the front door they found a characteristically cheerful note which had been written by Janice and obviously left for her roommate: "I am at Lake Sammamish sunnin' myself." The note had been hanging there, apparently, for more than twenty-four hours. The roommate, for whom the note was written, had been gone all weekend.

Inside, in Janice's basement apartment, they found everything in order. The only things missing were Janice's black bikini, her denim shorts, and a sweatshirt. And her yellow ten-speed bike.

Two girls vanished, one after the other, in bright sunshine, from among a crowd of tens of thousands of people. The news shocked the Pacific Northwest.

The latest disappearances had occurred in the rural county area, so the investigation fell to the King County police. The county's chief of detectives, J. N. (Nick) Mackie, appealed for information. There was a heavy response. Hundreds of people who had been in the Sunday crowd at the park began telephoning.

Jennifer Rutledge reported her encounter with the charming young man named "Ted"—the man with his arm in a beige sling. She told how he had asked for her assistance with his sailboat. She recounted the other details—their walk together to the parking lot, the Volkswagen (she thought it was a metallic brown), his accent, his explanation that he'd hurt his arm playing racketball.

She identified Janice Ott as the bikini girl who, pushing her bike, had eventually walked away with "Ted."

Seattle's first "Ted" headlines began: POLICE SEEK "TED" IN MISSING-WOMEN CASE.

Beyond the mountains, at Ellensburg, the shocking news of the Lake Sammamish disappearances jogged the memory of a woman student at Central Washington University. She went to Al Pickles, the campus police chief.

"That man wearing his arm in a sling over at Seattle

reminded me of something I heard about here last spring," she told him. "Some girl—and I can't remember who she was—mentioned that the same kind of thing had happened to her. Over by the library here on campus."

"When was this?" asked the chief.

"It seemed to me it was right around the time that Susan Rancourt disappeared here. As I remember it, some guy had his arm in a sling, and he got her to carry his books for her. It was at night. And she got kind of scared of him."

"Thanks very much," said Pickles. "We'll see if we can't find her somehow."

Pickles issued an appeal through the campus newspaper:

> Campus police would like to talk to a female student who helped a young man carry some books from Bouillion Library to his car.
>
> They say it's possible that she could provide them with some important information in the investigation of several missing persons, including Susan Rancourt, missing from this campus since April 17. . . . The young man was wearing a cast on one arm. Because of the cast, he seemed to be having difficulty handling the books he carried. . . .
>
> Campus Police Chief Al Pickles . . . said he thinks it is possible there is a connection between that incident, the Rancourt disappearance and the Lake Sammamish disappearance(s). . . . Police feel the cast could be an excellent ruse for an abductor to use in gaining the confidence of young women who are normally cautious of strangers. . . .

Two young women students, who had been on the Central campus that spring, suddenly remembered events which they had previously dismissed—events which had happened at night, the previous April.

One girl, Janet Carstensen, wrote a report for the campus police:

> About 9 P.M. I walked out of the library to go back to my apartment. Right outside of the main entrance a

man carrying a large stack of books was having difficulty. . . . A castlike bandage was on his arm. He dropped the books and was making a noise [pain] as though his arm was hurting him. I went over to offer some assistance. I picked up the books and handed them back to him. But then I said, "Would you like me to help you carry them?" He said, "Yes." . . . We walked past Black Hall and walked under the railroad crossing. . . . I asked him how he hurt his arm. He told me it was a skiing accident. He [said he had] hit a tree. . . . He was grubbily dressed, with a dark wool hat on, and dark, long hair. . . . When he looked at me, it sort of bugged me—two big eyes staring at me weirdly.

As they walked on Chestnut Street, beyond the railroad underpass, she continued, they came to a darkened place where his car was parked. It was a Volkswagen. She thought the VW was yellow, but the light was poor.

But I remember the passenger's seat wasn't in the car. . . . It was gone. When we were standing next to the car, he started complaining about his arm: "Oh, my arm hurts." He opened the door and told me to start the car. I stood there and said, "No." He then said, "Get in." I said "No." I dropped the books, turned around, and ran back to my apartment.

She remembered that the cast or bandage on the man's left arm looked amateurish—"something he could do himself."

The second Central coed reported an almost identical happening about that same time in April. She, too, encountered such a man. His arm was in a sling. He persuaded her to help carry his books from the library to the same darkened place near the railroad tracks. At the side of his Volkswagen, he dropped his keys. He told that girl to bend down and pick up the keys for him. She placed his books on the Volkswagen and fled in the darkness toward her residence hall.

Pickles relayed his new information to the King County police in Seattle, and for the first time, police had a reason to believe that the disappearances could be connected. Descriptions of the suspect varied, but his age—middle or late twenties—was always the same. And his MO was the same—pretending to have an injury, soliciting the help of his intended victim, luring her to his Volkswagen.

Dr. Donald E. Blackburn and his wife, Janice Ott's parents, had traveled to Seattle to help, if they could, in the search for their daughter around Lake Sammamish. Blackburn was a former staff man for the Washington State Board of Prison Terms and Paroles. Inspired by her father's work in the field of corrections, Janice had become a caseworker for the courts. Her father, who had later become an administrator in the Spokane school system, spoke of his daughter and the way she had apparently been lured from the park: "All her life she wanted to please us and others. She had a burning desire to help. . . . It doesn't surprise me a bit that she would agree to help someone in need."

King County police interviewed hundreds of persons who had been in the state park that Sunday. They examined film taken of crowds in the park by amateurs and by the television crews who had been there, in the hopes of finding, in the background, an accidental picture of a young man with his arm in a sling. But July ended and August passed, and police had no solid lead pointing toward the "Ted" in the park, the man with a Volkswagen.

Just east of Lake Sammamish, near Issaquah, Interstate 90 spears between two steep foothills as it begins its rise toward the higher mountains. On one of those foothills, on a Saturday morning in early September, two grouse hunters made the discovery.

Lying in tall grass on the steep hillside above the highway was a human skull, attached to a spinal column and a rib cage. Some long dark hair was still attached to the skull.

Their telephone call to police caused an explosion of activity. Several police agencies dispatched cars and men to the scene, and officers swarmed to surround the hillside, to establish a security line to keep news reporters, photographers, and curiosity seekers out of the area.

When Eleanore Rose heard the news on the radio, she

went to the scene as quickly as possible. At the bottom of the hill, an officer restrained her. "But I'm Denise's mother," she cried. "I have to know if it's Denise up there."

"Sorry, ma'am," said the officer. "You'll have to wait here."

Eleanore slipped around the restraining line and began climbing the small mountain, through the tall grass and underbrush. Higher on the hillside, another officer stopped her. A skull had been found, he said, but he assured her, "It looked to be about the age of a fourteen-year-old. It can't be your daughter."

Still worried, Eleanore retreated to the bottom of the hill to await word. In the confusion of rumors, she received more encouraging news. The skull with the long dark hair had no dental work in the upper teeth. That meant it couldn't have been Denise.

With tears streaming down her cheeks, Eleanore's face was radiant as she spoke to news reporters. "I'm so very glad. So relieved," she said.

Atop the foothill, King County Detectives Bob Keppel, Roger Dunn, and other officers organized a controlled ground search for any human remains. It was a tangled area of tall grass, scrubby trees, and nettles. The isolated spot could have been reached by a vehicle climbing a steep, faint roadway from the highway below.

The skull, spine, rib cage, and two leg bones—all remains of one human—were found September 7. Next day the second skull was found. At first the searchers reasoned that the remains could not have been those of Denise and Janice, the girls from Lake Sammamish—the remains were too badly deteriorated.

Gradually, though, the detectives realized that coyotes, wild dogs, other predators, had been at work on the bodies. They had quickly become skeletons.

Gently, the detectives asked Eleanore Rose for Denise's dental records. She provided them. The officers, too, wanted to know if Eleanore could provide a sample of Denise's hair for comparison. Sensing the worst, the mother retrieved a few strands from Denise's curling rollers.

Within hours, the positive identification was made. The remains were those of Denise Naslund and Janice Ott, the girls from the state park. When the bones were taken to Dr. Daris R. Swindler, a University of Washington anthropologist, he concluded that there had undoubtedly been a third victim on the hillside, too. One small section of an articulated column had been found, which included some lumbar vertebrae—an extra skeletal part. There was also a leg bone which didn't belong with the two skeletons. But no skull or jawbone remained to help identify the third victim.

At one place in the tall, weedy grass, the searchers found telltale "grease spots"—places where the soil had been impregnated with oils, as though three bodies had once lain there, within a few feet of each other.

An inch-by-inch search of the hillside went on for days. A few more bones were found—mostly animal—plus scraps of rotting fabric and some items of clothing. But the latter all appeared to have been there for a long time. No garment of any of the girls was discovered. There wasn't enough left of the victims to determine how they died, but there were jaw and skull fractures.

The detectives could speculate, though. How "Ted," with his Volkswagen, could have driven his victim from the park onto the freeway, turned left toward Issaquah, and after about a ten-minute drive left the highway via a side road, to a tree-shrouded turnout at the base of the foothill. From there the Volkswagen could have ascended the hill on a faint, overgrown almost-forgotten roadway.

Then it would have been another ten-minute drive back to the park.

Denise's remains, the detectives explained to her mother, would have to be kept in an evidence locker. As tenderly as they knew how, they led Eleanore to an understanding that it had to be that way. There was a need to preserve the evidence in the event the killer was caught. The tiny woman, emaciated by her grief, seemed to understand.

Eleanore Rose stood there in her cold reality, looking at Denise's empty bed, and repeated: "I always wanted a daughter real bad, 'way back, years ago. I was afraid I might never have a little girl. But I had Denise. Long before Denise was born, I had a closet just full of little girl's clothing. I, really, you know, wanted a daughter so bad."

The priest told Eleanore that she should now reconcile herself to the fact that her daughter was gone, that she should take comfort in the knowledge that Denise was at peace and was happy now and there was no more pain.

"Well, I understand that," said Eleanore, groping for her thoughts and words. She was a good Catholic and all, and she knew what the priest was saying. "But Denise was peaceful and happy when she was here. She was happy *here*. She was planning her life." Her voice trailed upward, as though she were asking a question.

The closet remained filled with Denise's clothing. It would be untouched. Outside, on the street in front of the little house where Eleanore lived alone, Denise's car was left parked at the curb. Now and then someone came to the door and knocked, asking if the brown '64 Chevy were for sale. Eleanore always told them, "No, I'm just going to keep it for Denise."

FOUR | Wasatch Autumn

A bright September sun glints off the golden statue of the angel Moroni, trumpet raised, standing high among the slender spires of the great Mormon Temple, above the office buildings and traffic of downtown Salt Lake City.

By this autumn of 1974, the dominance of the church over the social, economic, and political life of Utah and its cities and towns was undiluted, even as more newcomers moved into the state.

A few blocks east of the Temple grounds, in the church's University Ward, Utah newcomer Ted Bundy was settling into his upstairs apartment in one of the older two-story houses along a tree-lined avenue. Shuffling a stack of books out of one of his packing cartons, Ted looked around his new surroundings and decided he would need more bookshelf space.

From Ted's apartment, the University of Utah campus— and the law school where he now was enrolled—was only a few blocks to the east, where the foothills begin to rise toward the Wasatch Front.

Ted felt uneasy, restless, tentative in his new environment.

He was embarking on his second effort at law school. Ted's first experience in law school in Washington State hadn't gone well. He had begun attending night classes at the University of Puget Sound, exactly one year earlier—the autumn of 1973. With some other students who lived in Seattle, he had car-pooled it to Tacoma three nights a week for those classes. Sometimes, even after making the forty-five minute trip to reach the UPS campus, while the others attended their classes, Ted had skipped his. He had gotten only partial credit for those two terms at UPS, but he blamed the school for his lack of inspiration.

"I was just really disenchanted with UPS," he had told a friend a few weeks earlier, just before he moved from Seattle to Salt Lake City. "I'm really looking forward to law school at Utah."

Ted had made application to several law schools, usually without success. His initial application to Utah had not been accepted.

Then, in early 1973 he had reapplied at Utah. His letter of reapplication must have been intriguing for the admissions committee at the law school. It made fascinating reading for those who subsequently came to study the ambiguities of Ted Bundy:

My lifestyle requires that I obtain knowledge of the law and the ability to practice legal skills. I intend to be my own man. It's that simple. I could go on at length to explain that the practice of law is a lifelong goal, or that I do not have great expectations that a law degree is a guarantee of wealth and prestige. The important factor, however, is that law fulfills a functional need which my daily routine has forced me to recognize.

I apply to law school because this institution will give

43

me the tools to become a more effective actor in the social role I have defined for myself.

Ted had folded into that readmission effort a little political persuasion. He arranged that Washington State Governor Dan Evans endorse his admission application at Utah. Because Ted had worked in the 1972 Evans campaign, he had no trouble getting the governor's signature affixed to a letter of tribute:

> I first met Ted after he had been selected to join my campaign staff in 1972 [said Governor Evans' letter]. It was the consensus among those of us who directed the operation that Ted's performance was outstanding. Given a key role in the issues, research, and strategy section, he demonstrated an ability to define and organize his own projects, to effectively synthesize and clearly communicate factual information and to tolerate . . . strain and sometimes critical situations.
>
> In the end it was probably his composure and discretion that allowed him to successfully carry out his assignments. These qualities made his contributions to strategy and policy dependable and productive. . . .
>
> I strongly recommend the admission of Ted Bundy to your law school. You would be accepting an exceptional student.

Although the letter was signed by Governor Evans, Ted was the primary author. Obligingly, the governor signed it as a routine gesture of political appreciation to a bright young man who had faithfully helped in the reelection.

Although the University of Utah had accepted Ted for admission in the autumn of 1973, he decided at the last minute not to enroll then. After his acceptance, he had written to the school, saying he would be unable to attend that fall because he had been seriously injured in an automobile accident. That wasn't true. Instead Ted had begun his rather unsuccessful session of night classes at the law school in Tacoma.

Now in Utah, Ted missed Seattle. He had always enjoyed the city and felt especially at home around the University of

Washington campus and its University District, alive with the sights and sounds of young people. There was a pulsing excitement, he thought, along the strip of bookstores, drugstores, coffee counters, apparel shops of University Way and its cross street, 45th. "I really love the District," he said. "It's a place of constant vitality, of beautiful people. My special place." Now that was 900 miles distant.

Ted also missed Cas, the young woman who had become the closest, most comfortable person in his life. They had known each other—and been going together—for five years. Cas had found Ted to be a considerate, understanding man and a helpful counselor during a difficult period in her life. A rather plain, though not unattractive, woman with an angular face and light brown hair, Cas had just gone through a difficult divorce in Idaho when she first met Ted. Cas lived alone with Becky, her small daughter, near the University of Washington campus, not far from Ted's apartment.

As they spent more time together, their thoughts and talk had turned to marriage. In fact, during that autumn of '74, they still talked about that—marriage—perhaps around the end of the year.

Inwardly, though, each sensed it would not occur. As she thought about Ted, Cas was prone to extreme emotional upswings and downswings. In many ways, she thought, she still loved him. Yet she had developed some nagging doubts about him—doubts about his integrity, some of his actions, and, especially, his fidelity.

Yet they remained close to each other, bound by a mutual dependence. Now that he was in Utah, Ted was grateful for the telephone. His calls to Cas—and he dialed her number often—helped take the edge off his loneliness, caused by being so far from Seattle.

Cas, daughter of a prominent Mormon family at Ogden, had attended college in Utah and had encouraged Ted to enroll at the University of Utah. Her parents, George and Mavis Brimner, had warmly invited Ted to come visit them at their comfortable home whenever he chose. And that was only forty miles from his apartment.

Ted's half brother Glenn had helped him move his belongings from Seattle to Salt Lake City in the earliest days of September. They had driven an old pickup truck which Ted had bought cheap—through a want-ad from an older man in Seattle's North End—just for that move. Then, less than two weeks after his arrival in Salt Lake City, Ted had flown home to Seattle to finish some budget work for the Washington State Department of Emergency Services—an unfinished dab of business left over from his summertime job.

He had seen Cas only briefly during that trip to Seattle. She seemed to be terribly edgy.

The newspapers in Seattle were full of details about the search being carried out near Issaquah for the remains of some murdered young woman who had vanished from Lake Sammamish State Park the previous July.

Those headlines had been rather grisly: BONES, DENTAL RECORDS CHECKED. And INCH-BY-INCH BONES SEARCH SET.

Ted may have noticed a *Seattle Times* article on September 13 which reported, "So far, police and volunteers have covered a square mile by foot and vehicle. More than 140,000 square feet within that mile have been covered by Explorers in a hands-and-knees, shoulder-to-shoulder search. . . . Yesterday searchers found a piece of rib bone, making it the fifth straight day that remains have been discovered. If nothing more is found over the weekend, the search will be called off."

Ted left Seattle that day, returning to Salt Lake City, alone, driving his Volkswagen.

Indian summer came colorfully to Utah's Wasatch Front. Beginning in the final days of September, continuing long into October, the stands of aspen and cottonwood turned to shining yellows. Clumps of oak became bursts of brilliant red. Their colors decorated the apron of the mountain range and daubed all the canyons with brightness. Then gradually, their colors began to fade in the rains and raw winds of late October.

About fifty miles south of Salt Lake City, near Provo, where the family was living temporarily, Shirleen Aime felt uneasy as she read and heard the disturbing news near the end of October. There were reports that a girl's body had been found up in the mountains, at Summit Park, east of Salt Lake City. The girl had been identified as Melissa Smith, seventeen-year-old daughter of Louis Smith, police chief of the little town of Midvale. Melissa had been found nude, bludgeoned and strangled with one of her nylon stockings—the victim, obviously, of a brutal sex killing. Shirleen felt a chill as she looked at the girl's photograph. Melissa reminded her of her own daughter, Laura. It was a ghastly thought, Shirleen reflected, that someone capable of committing that kind of a crime should be on the loose in this part of Utah.

So, when Laura telephoned that day, Shirleen was especially delighted to hear her voice.

"Hi, Mom, I'm just checkin' in. How's everything?"

"Great, Laura. How'ya doin', hon?"

Laura and her parents had gone through some difficult times in their relationship for more than a year now. Laura had dropped out of school, much to the displeasure of her mother and father. They thought she was running around with a bad crowd. In recent weeks Laura had been living with first one girlfriend, then another in the small towns around Provo.

"Where are you staying now?" Shirleen asked.

"Oh, I'm at Cheryl's place in Spanish Fork," Laura reported.

Shirleen told Laura about the news she'd read, of the seventeen-year-old girl getting killed up near Salt Lake City—about how she had been found nude, strangled, and all beat up.

"Laura, I want you to be careful, now," Shirleen admonished.

"Aw, Mom," replied Laura. "I'm a big girl. I can take care of myself."

Laura, indeed, was a big girl—about six feet tall. She had long, brown hair, light enough to be almost a sandy color. At times her eyes seemed a light hazel, which gave her almost a tawny look. When she was growing up, Laura had been a gangly, self-conscious tomboy. But then she blossomed out of her tomboyhood. Laura was now a tall young woman with long legs and an ample figure, which caught male eyes.

Her father, Jim Aime, a ruggedly handsome man of Italian descent, had worked for many years at the Geneva plant of the United States Steel Company outside Provo. The pay was pretty good. But, raising a family of five children, Jim and Shirleen never seemed to get ahead financially.

BUNDY

For several years, while Laura and her older brother John were growing up and going to grade school, and while the younger girls were arriving in the family, the Aimes lived in an aging farmhouse, its original walls made of adobe brick in Mount Pleasant, on the high Wasatch Plateau south of Provo. They lived with inconveniences. Their only toilet was an outhouse.

Yet Jim considered the hardships—even his sixty-mile drive, each way, to and from his job at the steel works—all worthwhile. It was, he thought, a perfect place to raise kids. The old house, at an elevation of 6,000 feet, was surrounded by quiet farmlands, and there were mountains, some of them 11,000-foot peaks, on every horizon. In and around the outbuildings of the old place, the family kept horses, chickens, cows, turkeys, hogs, goats, dogs, cats by the dozen, sheep, and almost every other kind of farm animal. Even peacocks for a while.

Laura loved the animals around the farm. When a wild deer ventured down out of the canyon, Laura left food for it and eventually coaxed it into becoming a pet. Laura got involved in 4-H, especially the horsemanship activities. When she was only eleven, Laura loved to climb on Arab, her shining blue Arabian, and gallop at top speed across the fields, her long hair streaming in the wind.

"That's a damned wild horse," Jim once observed, "and Laura makes him even wilder, the way she handles him."

Laura's mother watched the galloping horse and the girl, her upper body arched over Arab's flying mane, and agreed: "Laura has got hell inside her." It was a smiling, loving, admiring assessment of a spirited girl.

One day Laura was tossed from the back of the galloping Arab into the barbed wire of a fence. Her dad hurried her to a doctor who stitched the awful, extensive gashes of Laura's ring finger and the inside of her left forearm and upper arm.

For years Jim and Laura's brother, John, would tell and retell the story of the time Laura, when she was eleven, helped her father bag his trophy deer and win the grand prize in the Utah hunting contest.

One day, during the hunting season of 1968, Laura, dressed in boots, jeans, red sweatshirt, and red hat, trooped into the mountains with her dad and John—up into the steep, rocky Fairview Canyon not far from their home place. It was a place avoided by less dedicated hunters, because of its steepness. In places they had to grab protruding roots of small trees to hoist themselves up vertical rock walls. On a pine-dotted ridge, Jim got a shot at a buck. He thought he hit it, but the deer had bounded up a draw and over a ridge, out of sight.

They all searched for some sign of the animal and it was Laura who eventually found the spots of crimson, "Hey, Daddy," she shouted. "There's a blood trail over here."

For more than three hours, Laura was their stubborn tracker, leading her dad and brother through the mountains. At last, near dusk, they sighted the wounded animal. Jim raised his Remington 30.06 (a rifle he'd earlier won on a fifty-cent raffle ticket; Laura always teased him about that), sighted through the scope, and pulled the trigger. The big buck dropped.

When they reached the deer, they were astonished by its size and its antlers. "Damn," said Jim. "That's gotta be a trophy."

John laid the rifle across the tips of the horns. "This rifle's forty-eight inches long," John said, "and it just barely covers point to point."

"Oh, Daddy! Oh, Daddy!" Laura squealed in happy excitement, clapping her hands. "You and your fifty-cent rifle!"

Jim's prize for that trophy was a new four-wheel-drive International Harvester Scout. Even before she was old enough to have her driver's license, Laura was allowed by her proud dad to drive the Scout on the farm roads.

Because of her height, Laura always felt conspicuous in the small high school at Mount Pleasant. Some of the other kids teased her—with nicknames like "Wilt the Stilt"—and it hurt her inside. Jim was convinced that was the reason Laura dropped out of high school.

Shirleen worried about Laura's casual attitude toward hitchhiking. In their late October telephone conversation, the mother had said, "Laura, I really would appreciate it if you'd promise not to hitchhike anymore. I know this sounds like nagging, but I just don't want you taking any chances."

"Aw, Mom . . . "

"I don't want you going with anyone you don't know. Promise?"

"Aw, Mom, I'll be okay. Don't worry."

They said their good-byes. Laura promised she'd be calling or coming to the house in a day or two.

A few days went by, and Laura didn't call.

Shirleen wondered if that girl who'd been murdered— Melissa Smith—had been hitchhiking. According to the newspaper, the girl had last been seen on State Street, a main business drag out of Salt Lake City, in the suburb of Murray.

During the early evening of November 8, Carol DaRonch, a pretty, seventeen-year-old brunette, guided her car through a misting rain, off State Street into the parking lot of the big shopping center in Murray.

She chose a parking space in front of Sears, one of the many stores in the Fashion Mall. It was the largest, busiest shopping mall in the Salt Lake City area. Carol got out of her maroon Camaro, locked it, and strode toward the Sears doorway. Tall and slim, wearing a jacket with white fur trim and dark, tight-fitting pants, Carol could have been a fashion model, with the naturally slinky, graceful way she walked. But it was not an affectation. Carol was a fresh, natural, and rather shy teenager.

Carol passed through the doors of the Sears store, browsed at a couple of counters, then entered the mall which connected several shops, boutiques, and department stores. By coincidence, she encountered her cousin, Joanne, who was there shopping with a friend. They talked for a few moments. Then Carol resumed her stroll. She paused to look at the window display of Walden's bookstore.

"Excuse me, miss." The man's voice came from behind her. Carol turned to see a rather good-looking, dark-haired young man in jacket and necktie. He politely introduced himself as a police officer and asked, "Did you just park your car out in the parking lot?"

"Yes," Carol replied, nodding hesitantly.

"We have a problem out in the parking lot," he said. "We think there's been an attempted burglary of your car. I'd appreciate it if you'd go with me out to your car to identify a suspect my partner is holding out there."

"Okay," said Carol, with a shrug.

It was Carol's habit, because of her natural shyness, not to look an older person directly in the eye. So, as they stood at that moment in the lights of the indoor mall, she didn't study his face. As they walked together toward an exit leading to the parking lot, she noticed he was wearing patent-leather shoes.

He escorted the girl out of the mall, into the misty, dimly lighted parking lot. When they arrived at her Camaro, Carol noticed it was still locked. "Everything looks okay to me," she observed.

When the man leaned forward to look into the car, Carol noticed he carried handcuffs in an inner pocket of his jacket.

"My partner must have taken the suspect over to the sub office," he said. "We'll have to go over there."

Carol accompanied him back into the lights of the mall, across the flow of shoppers, and through another doorway. Outdoors again, they walked north along a walkway beside the mall building and then, passing beneath a street light, crossed 61st Street South.

"The sub office is right over there," he said, nodding toward a small building ahead of them. Beneath one exterior light on that building, Carol saw an inconspicuous door which bore the number "139." Carol waited at the sidewalk as he walked to the door and unsuccessfully tried to open it. "Hmmm," he said. "It's locked. I guess we're going to have to drive over to headquarters." Carol wasn't aware that the door he had tried to open was the side door of a laundromat.

By now Carol and the man had been walking together for more than ten minutes. He guided her eastward along the darkened sidewalk until they came to a Volkswagen parked at the curb. "Here's my car," he said, opening the passenger door for her. "Get in."

In the dim light from a distant street lamp, Carol noticed it was a rather ratty-looking car. There were blotches on its side and front fender. She summoned the courage to ask to see his police identification. With a light chuckle of understanding, he drew out his wallet and opened it to show her a police badge. In the darkness she could barely see it, but she was satisfied he had a badge.

As Carol slid into the seat of his car, she caught a glimpse of a conspicuous tear along the top of the rear seat upholstery. Once again, she thought it was a crummy car for a police officer to be driving. Her escort, settling in behind the steering wheel, told Carol, "Buckle up your safety belt. I'm a real nut on safety." She thought she smelled alcohol on his breath.

Carol looked down in the darkened car and sensed that the belt was crumpled and dirty, apparently unused. She refused to snap it around her. The man started the car and sent it lurching into a sharp U-turn, into and across the street, eastward. He made a quick stop at the first intersection and then turned left.

It happened quickly. When he jammed on the brakes and swerved the steering wheel to the right, the VW bounced to a stop with its right wheels up over the curb in front of a darkened school building. With his right hand he grabbed Carol's arm and, in an instant, his left hand snapped a handcuff on her wrist. She recoiled, screaming, "What are you *doing?*"

"Shut up or I'll blow your head off," he snarled reaching for her other wrist. Terror jolted Carol into a frenzy. Screaming, she struggled away from him. The other handcuff clicked onto the same left wrist, as Carol's right hand clawed for the door handle and found it. Then the door was opening, and she was falling, screaming, outward. He was lunging toward her, across the passenger's seat. In the darkness Carol could see a metal bar in his hand—a metal bar, raised to strike. She struggled against the blow, reaching up, gripping the steel. In a blur of terror, Carol wrestled free and went screaming, stumbling around the rear of the Volkswagen and out into the wet, dark street, into the headlights of an approaching car.

When the running girl loomed in the headlights, Harold Walsh slammed on the brakes. For an instant his wife, Mildred, was afraid to open the door and let her in. But the girl who'd run in front of their car, and was clutching the outside handle of the door on Mildred's side, was obviously terrified. In the next moment, Carol had opened the door. She fell into their car, collapsing in Mildred's arms, trembling violently. The older woman could feel the girl's heart pounding as she whimpered and sobbed, "I can't believe it. I can't believe it."

"What? What's wrong?" asked Mildred.

"I can't believe it," Carol sobbed. "He tried to kill me. I can't believe it."

In that instant of confusion, the Walshes didn't see a Volkswagen pull away from the opposite curb in the darkness.

They took Carol to the Murray City Police Department headquarters. It took a while to calm her down enough so that she could describe what had happened. Sergeant Joel Reit was called in to interview her. Whatever had happened, Reit sensed when he first saw her, it must have been something godawful. She couldn't stop trembling and crying. Reit noticed she had lost one of her shoes in the scuffle. There were some flecks of blood on the white fur trim of her coat. Reit wondered if she had scratched the man when she fought him off. Reit decided to clip some of those blood specks for possible evidence.

While Carol was being calmed and interviewed in the Murray police headquarters, an audience of moms, dads, and kids settled into their seats in a high-school auditorium about half an hour's drive north of Murray. The curtain was about to go up on *The Redhead,* a comedy presented by students of Viewmont High School in the quiet residential community of Bountiful.

Sitting with her parents, Debbie Kent, a cherub-faced, seventeen-year-old brunette, grinned and waved at classmates seated with their families in other parts of the auditorium. For many parents, the school play can be a dreaded obligation. But for Dean Kent the evening was an occasion of special happiness. A balding man in his late forties, a good, family-loving Mormon, Dean had just recovered from a severe heart attack. He enjoyed feeling well again, being with his wife and daughter among friends in his community. An official of a petroleum company, Dean Kent was a well-liked and respected man in Bountiful. Debbie's younger brother, Blair, was at the roller-skating rink. They planned to pick up Blair at ten o'clock, after the play ended.

But there were delays getting the show started at the eight o'clock curtain time—the usual delays backstage, tinkering with sets and lighting, plus some last-minute costume adjustments. In the lobby, Raylene Shepherd, the drama instructor, an attractive woman in her early twenties, was hurrying toward some of the student dressing rooms when a young man stopped her. "Excuse me," he began.

She stopped.

"I wonder if I could get you to help me for a minute with my car out in the parking lot," he said. Raylene studied him with interest for a moment. He had long, brown, wavy hair and wore a mustache. The man, who appeared to be in his late twenties, was *quite* attractive, the teacher thought. But she explained she was awfully busy at that moment and didn't have time to help. She excused herself and hurried away to the needs of her young cast.

The auditorium lights dimmed. The play began.

Because of the delay at the start, the final act of *The Redhead* hadn't ended as ten o'clock approached. In their seats, Mr. and Mrs. Kent and Debbie bent heads together for a whispered conference. Someone had to go pick up Blair at the roller arena. Debbie volunteered to leave the play before the final curtain and drive the family car to pick up her brother. "I'll be back to get you," she whispered to her parents.

One of the funny lines of the play produced a laugh from the audience, as Debbie rose and quietly walked to an exit.

About half an hour later the show ended, and as happy applause filled the auditorium, the cast members of *The Redhead* took their curtain calls. As the auditorium lights brightened, Dean and Belva Kent joined the rest of the audience in moving up the aisles to the lobby. While waiting for Debbie, they talked for a while with passing friends. Everyone agreed the comedy had been enjoyable.

Several minutes elapsed, and while they waited, Dean Kent wondered why Debbie hadn't returned yet with her brother. When he walked into the nearly empty parking lot, he made the puzzling discovery that the family car was still there, right where it had been parked originally. It looks like Debbie never reached the car, Dean frowned with the thought. He knew his daughter well enough—her high sense of responsibility—to know at once that something must be wrong.

After they were notified, the Bountiful police began a search that night—around the drive-ins and other places where the teenagers were congregating, and along some of the main streets of town. With flashlights and searchlights, they examined the area around the school building and the fields near the Kent home.

Next morning, in daylight, the search intensified. In the school parking lot, not far from the wall of the high-school building, one of the volunteers picked up a rather odd-looking key. Officer Ron Ballantyne recognized it as a handcuff key.

As the search widened, townsfolk of the good Mormon community turned out to help police in the block-by-block search of Bountiful. The search spread to the surrounding fields, farmlands, and side roads. In four-wheel-drive vehicles they scoured the foothills and canyons of the Wasatch. From a helicopter, sometimes hovering as low as twenty feet above ground, Sergeant Ira Beal and others eventually covered hundreds of square miles around Bountiful by air—all the way from the Great Salt Lake and its marshlands, off to the west, then eastward up into the mountains; from Salt Lake City, to the south, northward to Weber Canyon and beyond.

At the Bountiful Police Department headquarters, Ballantyne was on the telephone with Sergeant Paul Forbes of the Murray Police Department. Together they pondered the fascinating coincidence. Carol DaRonch had escaped a kidnapper that Friday evening, with a pair of handcuffs dangling from her wrist. Then a handcuff key had been found where Debbie later disappeared in the high-school parking lot a few hours later.

The high-school drama teacher, Ballantyne reported, had seen a strange young man at the school the evening of Debbie's disappearance. The teacher had encountered him twice in the foyer of the school. The first time, when he asked her to go out to the parking lot with him to help start his car, it had been a few minutes before eight o'clock. Then she had seen him and walked with him later, while the play was still going on. He was still looking for someone to help him with his car in the parking lot.

She noticed him once again, later, sitting in an aisle seat at the rear of the auditorium, about the time the play was ending. "He seemed to be breathing kind of heavily," she had said. In fact, she remembered that some people sitting nearby appeared to be distracted by the sound of the man's labored breathing.

When the officers of Bountiful and Murray compared descriptions of that man with Carol Da Ronch's memory of her assailant at the shopping mall, they concluded it could have been the same man—a man in his twenties, rather well groomed, mannerly. The teacher at Viewmont thought his mustache was rather full. Carol thought she remembered a neatly trimmed mustache. The stranger at the school had well-combed, wavy brown hair. Carol thought his hair was "kind of dark and slicked back."

There appeared to be one flaw in the theory that it had been the same man at the shopping mall and later at the high school—the time element. According to the time logged on Carol Da Ronch's report at the Murray Police Department, the man would have to have driven about twenty-six miles in perhaps fifteen minutes to reach that high-school auditorium at Bountiful at eight o'clock—a virtual impossibility.

Still, there was that strange possibility that one man, foiled in an attempt to kidnap Carol earlier in the evening, had driven north on the freeway, past Salt Lake City, taken the Bountiful exit, driven through some of the city's business district, found Viewmont High School, and abducted Debbie.

Later, in Salt Lake City, detectives of Bountiful, Murray, and Salt Lake County, met to review their cases. Salt Lake County detectives Jerry Thompson and Ben Forbes, who were working on the October murder of Melissa Smith, had a hunch they might all be looking for the same man. "These cases are all different," said Thompson. "We've got a murdered girl, a missing girl, and a girl who got away from a guy. But there sure are similarities." The victims were all young, brunette, and pretty, noted Thompson, and each girl, wearing her long hair parted in the middle, resembled the others.

Another teenager of the same description was missing. Nancy Wilcox, a pretty high-school cheerleader, had disappeared from the Salt Lake City area in early October, too. But Salt Lake County juvenile authorities had jurisdiction over that case, and considered Nancy a runaway. Nancy had quarreled with her parents before her disappearance.

The investigators at Salt Lake City had never heard of Laura Aime. Worried when Laura hadn't telephoned again, her mother had fearfully reported that she was missing. But the Utah County sheriff's office at Provo dismissed Laura as a runaway.

Much to the despair of the ski-resort operators, Utah's November 1974 was mild and wet. There were days of cold rainfall and some freezing. A few flurries of snow whitened the mountains and the canyons leading into the Wasatch. But then came warm rains to melt the snow.

Wednesday, November 27, was another chilly, overcast day. In American Fork Canyon, north of Provo, Raymond Ivins and Christine Shelly, two Brigham Young University students, were hiking along a trail beside the stream tumbling out of the mountains, looking for rocks and fossils which could be helpful in geology class. But mostly they were enjoying each other's company. It was about nine o'clock in the morning.

From where they paused, at the edge of the stream bed, it was about forty feet to the opposite bank. Christine gasped, "Oh, God! There's a dead girl over there!"

Ray described it: "I looked and I thought, you know, it was a deer or something and . . . it was a girl. . . . It looked like she had been . . . she was dead. It was really grotesque. There was blood around her neck and breasts and she was naked and lying on that hill and it was a freak-out and I lost it. I thought maybe the guy was still somewhere around and I just panicked, worrying about my girlfriend . . . and we ran down the trail. . . . Came down and ran right through the creek and got in the car and just drove like a maniac, I guess as fast as I could, down to the ranger station and I reported it."

The body had been found on a bank on the south side of that stream, in the Timpanogos Cave National Park, a summertime recreation place where thousands of visitors hike, picnic, and visit the natural caves. Usually, it is snow-covered by late November. The discovery had been almost a fluke.

From Provo, Utah, County Sheriff Mack Holley hurried to the scene to join officers of the Utah Highway Patrol and the federal rangers who were already there.

When Shirleen Aime heard the news that a body had been found, her heart leaped to her throat. Fearfully, she dialed Sheriff Holley's office.

"This is Laura Aime's mother," she told the officer who answered. "I want to know if the body they've found up in American Fork canyon could be Laura."

"No, ma'am," replied the voice at the sheriff's office. "It's not your daughter."

"You're *sure?*"

"Yes, we're sure. It couldn't be your daughter."

There was, of course, little else that a sheriff's office radio dispatcher could say in such a situation. There would be no point in telling an anxious parent there *could* be such a possibility. Besides, it had been immediately presumed that Debbie Kent had been found. The search for Debbie had been headline news across Utah for nearly three weeks, since she disappeared from Viewmont High School. No one in Sheriff Holley's office attached any importance to the pleas from the Aime parents that something had happened to their daughter.

That evening the Provo newspaper, the *Provo Daily Herald,* carried a photo of Sheriff Holley, a Utah highway patrolman, and two forest rangers carrying the shrouded body up out of the canyon. Shirleen had studied it, then handed the paper over to her husband. "Jim," she said, "I'm just scared to death. I've got a feeling that's Laura." The canyon was too nearby.

"Well, dammit," Jim said, after he examined the photo and the accompanying story, "the cops sure in hell must know what they're talking about when they say it isn't Laura. They couldn't make a mistake about that. Laura's a tall girl. Almost six feet tall." And right there in the newspaper, they were quoting one of the officers saying, "There's a real good possibility that the body may be that of the Bountiful girl who disappeared Nov. 8 from Viewmont High School."

Before dawn the next morning, Shirleen had a telephone call from her mother, urging her to read the description in the morning *Salt Lake Tribune.* It was a report that the dead girl's height and hair color suggested the body was not Debbie Kent's.

Once again, Shirleen called Sheriff Holley's office and pleaded with the person who answered the phone: "I've got to know about that body. I think it's Laura. I just know it is."

The telephone voice at the sheriff's office said it couldn't be. He assured Shirleen that the body was that of an older woman, not Laura.

About an hour later, though, the sheriff's office called back, asking how they could locate Laura's dental records. Chilled by the question, Shirleen gave them the name of Laura's dentist in Spanish Fork. Next came a phone call from the sheriff's office, asking if Jim and Shirleen could be ready by ten o'clock that morning. Sheriff Holley would come by then and take them to the morgue in Salt Lake City to help in an identification.

For the Aimes, it was a long trip, in cold silence, to the morgue—traveling with the sheriff whose office had been so unresponsive.

Many officers waited at the morgue in Salt Lake City, including Thompson, the Bountiful officers, and others who'd initially thought the body could be Debbie Kent's. At the inner door of the morgue, Jim Aime said softly, "If it's okay, I want to go in alone. Just me. I don't want my wife to have to go in there." The officers nodded. Of course that was okay.

Jim Aime was a leathery man, who could handle himself in any tough situation. But he wasn't prepared for that gut-heaving experience.

Trembling, his eyes smarting, Jim looked at the body and really couldn't be sure. The sickening damage to her head had been so massive, he couldn't tell whether it was Laura or not. She was unrecognizable. "I . . . I . . . just can't be sure," he whispered. "I can't tell."

Jim turned to leave the room. Then he had a thought. He returned to the table where she lay and asked to have the girl's arm raised so that he could see the inside of the ring finger and the inside of the forearm. He had remembered scars which had been left there after her horse had tossed Laura into some barbed wire—scars which had mostly faded.

Outside that room, where she paced in fear, Shirleen heard her husband's scream. She knew that it was Laura.

That was Thanksgiving Day, 1974.

While making arrangements for the funeral, Shirleen remembered something Laura had said—something that had come like a bolt out of the blue only a few weeks earlier: "Mother, at my funeral I don't want to be buried in a dress."

"Laura, what in the world are you talking about?" Shirleen had exclaimed at the time. "You've got your whole life ahead of you."

"I'm serious, Mom," Laura had said. "I don't want to be buried in a dress."

Shirleen had shrugged in puzzlement when Laura had said that. Now, as she planned her daughter's burial, Shirleen decided that Laura would be buried in a warm, white flannel nightie and fuzzy slippers.

At Murray, Detective Paul Forbes continued to show photographs of possible suspects to the kidnap victim, Carol DaRonch, but as the dark-haired teenager patiently looked at them, one after another, she was unable to make an identification.

To the north, around Bountiful, the search for Debbie Kent continued until the December snows persisted and finally covered all the mountains and canyons along the Wasatch Front. The men could search no more.

Belva Kent spent many nights sleeping on the daveno in the family living room. "I wanted to be there, just in case Debbie came home," she explained.

At the Midvale Police Department, Chief Louis Smith sorrowfully watched the days pass, reaching the conclusion that the person who had so savagely killed Melissa would never be caught.

Anguish and anxiety settled into the Aime home Shirleen; quit her job so that she could be around the house all the time to protect her other daughters. Jim Aime brooded at the thought of Christmas approaching. And Laura gone. He checked into a hospital for treatment of his acute depression.

Jim Aime never again had the heart to drive the four-wheel-drive Scout which Laura had helped him win on that hunting trip. He left it parked there at the side of the old farmhouse, to collect the snows of the winters and dust of the summers.

That caved-in place at the rear of the Scout—the dent put there by Laura when she was first learning to drive—was a reminder of her.

As the airliner circled the Salt Lake City airport, Cas Richter stared from a window at the gloomy December fog and concluded that the weather matched her inner feelings.

With her young daughter, Cas had flown from Seattle for a holiday visit with her parents at Ogden.

And to see Ted. That troubled her.

For weeks Cas had been on an emotional roller coaster when it came to Ted. Increasingly, she was plagued by awful thoughts about the man whom she'd thought of marrying.

When her girlfriend first teased her about *her* Ted and his Volkswagen and *the* "Ted" with a Volkswagen at Lake Sammamish, where the girls disappeared, Cas had grinned at the coincidence. But as time passed, suspicion had festered within her.

There were too many dark places, she thought, in Ted's behavior. She thought of that day when she noticed a package of plaster of paris in his apartment. At the time he had laughed it off. But the memory gnawed on her when she read about the "Ted" suspect at Lake Sammamish who wore a sling and pretended to have a broken arm.

Because of those thoughts, Cas had actually summoned the will to telephone the King County police in Seattle, to tell them about her Ted—Theodore Bundy—who drove a Volkswagen. Afterward, full of remorse, she had cried. And the tears, the anxiety recurred, colliding with her recurring waves of love for Ted. Can I be wrong? she wondered. I must be wrong.

Then all the turmoil within her worsened when she learned of the murders of some girls in Utah—beginning about the time Ted had moved to Salt Lake City.

The jetliner touched down on the runway and, with the reverse-thrust roar of its engines, slowed and made a lumbering turn toward the Salt Lake City airport building.

Cas began to gather her belongings from beneath the seat. She had decided that, soon, she'd have a long heart-to-heart conversation with her father about Ted. Meanwhile, she knew, Ted would be there at the airport to meet her—with his engaging grin and a kiss.

FIVE | Taylor Mountain

A late February wind whipped across the campus of Central Washington University, sweeping the dry snow along the ground and rattling the windows of the small frame building of the campus police headquarters.

At his desk, Al Pickles, the campus security chief, leaned back in his chair and, with arms folded across his chest, stared through his window at some students, bundled in parkas and knit caps, bending into the cold wind on the campus pathways. For the five-thousandth time, it seemed, he had Susan Rancourt on his mind, the coed who disappeared from that campus ten months earlier.

"I just can't think of another damned thing that we might have done," he sighed. Pickles' words were directed to Bob Miller, the university's dean of students, sitting on the opposite side of the chief's desk. It had become routine for the dean to stop in now and then to see how things were going in the search.

Pickles swiveled in his chair and leaned forward to his desk, reaching for a file folder. "We had a meeting of law-enforcement people over in Seattle Thursday. Everyone was there, comparing everything they had, on all the missing girls. Seattle P.D. King County. Thurston County. The Oregon State Police. No one had anything new. Except . . ."

The chief opened the file folder. "Except that, down in Clark County, down around Vancouver, they found a couple of skeletons last month up in the hills."

Miller listened as he read from his report: "Carol Valenzuala, age 18, disappeared August 2, 1974. Her skeleton was found in a high valley, a heavily wooded area, by a couple of hunters. Right nearby there was another skeleton. An unknown female, white, 17 to 23 years of age, 125 pounds, 5-5 to 5-7. Long dark hair. They don't have her identified."

"You don't suppose . . ." Miller began.

"No," Pickles shook his head. "It's not our girl." They checked the teeth against the dental charts of all the others, including Susan's, and there was no match. Just an unidentified skeleton of a girl.

Pickles—and he had become accustomed to the grins and gags his unusual name inspired among the kids around the campus—was a veteran law-enforcement man. His Bronx accent betrayed his boyhood in New York. He had started out as a motorcycle cop for NYPD, then later migrated west, serving on the police force of a series of small towns through California and Oregon. For a while, until a political clash put an end to the job, Pickles had been police chief at Leavenworth, Kansas. He liked his job at Ellensburg. As campus police chief at Central, Pickles often explained with pride, "I've got the responsibility for the peace and order and security of a community of 7,000 good young people."

Pickles had taken Susan's disappearance personally. He had been on the telephone often with Susan's parents in Anchorage and had developed an almost fatherly interest in her. And a vexing wonderment about where she'd gone. Susan, Pickles remembered, had been one of the kids who turned out every morning before class for the informal jogging club to which Pickles also belonged. He vaguely remembered her. She had also been one of the volunteers who sewed shoulder patches on the uniforms of the new campus police auxiliary.

"Y'know, Bob," Pickles told the dean, "I wake up every damned night with the thought, Is there something we've missed? Maybe there's something there that's so obvious. And we don't see it."

"Al, I don't know what else could be done."

"God knows we haven't spared the time or money trying," said the chief. "I'll betcha we must have had contact with nearly every state in the country. . . ." He opened one of the loose-leaf notebooks on the Rancourt disappearance and began skipping through its pages, reading.

"There's a Susan look-alike who's supposed to have been seen in Mobile, Alabama, with two guys in a car with Florida plates, heading for Hattiesburg, Mississippi. A nice, helpful campus officer down at Northeast Louisiana State University says he saw a girl who matches Susan's description there, carrying a green suitcase. . . . Some old guy insists that a girl working in a massage parlor in Portland looks like Susan, some girl using the name of Crystal. . . . Susan's sister, over at La Conner, the brother-in-law, the boyfriend, no one can give us a single idea. . . .

"There was one kind of crazy nut we interrogated and he looked good for a while. But we could place him somewhere else at the time Susan disappeared. And he tells us, 'She will be found under water in the gates at the end of the canal system.' Of course we checked there. We've checked everywhere.

"They found a nude female body in Palm Beach County, Florida, and so we got Susan's dentist in Anchorage to send a copy of her dental charts down there. Susan's got—or Susan *had*—really distinctive teeth. Ceramic crowns, a bridge, numerous fillings. She had really pretty teeth in front. Well, anyway, that didn't pan out. A long pass—from Anchorage to Palm Beach—but no completion."

Pickles closed the volume. Dean Miller sighed.

"I'm starting to worry that we're never going to find her," conceded the chief.

Every thread of possibility, in each of the cases of the vanished girls, seemed to fray to nothingness.

And everyone involved was willing to try anything. "Well, why not?" said Bill Harris when he heard the idea. "Why not a water witch? We've tried everything else." The campus security chief at Oregon State University had run out of all the conventional ideas in his search for Kathy Parks. Benton County Sheriff John Dolan, whose office had been cooperating with OSU campus police in the search, mentioned the witch. Polk County Sheriff Woody Jones had told Dolan about the witch—an older man up at Monmouth, Oregon, who had quite a knack for finding underground water and, sometimes, finding bodies which were under water. Not long before, Dolan had heard, the Monmouth water witch had helped locate the body of a dead child.

When they finally located Charlie Bowman, the witch, he said he was more than willing to help. He drove to Corvallis immediately. A leathery old rancher and slightly deaf, Charlie made it clear, right off, though, that he didn't want them calling him a water witch. "Mention the name water witch," he told the officers, "and right away it spooks people. Call me a diviner."

"First of all, I'm going to need something that the girl wore, something of hers that no one else could have worn." Harris retrieved one of Kathy's boots which had been locked away since her disappearance.

Charlie Bowman's technique was simple and, he said, "ain't no magic in it." His body, he had discovered, contained its own unique chemistry and sensitivity to magnetic impulses. In his gnarled hands, Charlie held his homemade divining rod, which consisted of two brass rods welded together in a V. "It doesn't have to be brass," he explained. "Y'can use barbed wire if y'wanna. Stick of wood'll do just fine if you can't find nothin' else."

During that first day of divining, they tried all around the Corvallis area, then headed east to the corridor of Interstate 5. Harris and the other campus officers always thought that Kathy at that point might have gone—or been taken—southward to California, her home state. "Nope," declared Charlie. "She's way off to the north." He removed his one hand from Kathy's boot and took up his divining rod. The impulses were being transmitted in a circuit through his arms now. "Left hand's the negative," he explained softly. "And the right hand's the positive."

"Nope. She's lots further north. Maybe Portland."

Next day they started driving early. Along with Harris and Charlie was Chris McPhee, Kathy's distraught boyfriend. He had traveled to Oregon from his job in Louisiana to help search for the pretty girl he hoped to marry. Charlie's divining that day took them north to Portland and then eastward, across the northern edge of Oregon, until they reached Umatilla. By late afternoon, they had crossed the Columbia River into eastern Washington State.

When they turned toward the Cascade Mountains, Charlie said, "Nope. Nope. It's all wrong." He had been bothered by a confusion of impulses. "It's the boot," he concluded. "I can tell some other girl's had her foot in this boot, some girl besides your Kathy." It was after midnight when they got back to Corvallis that night. Harris was glad for the cover of darkness. He felt a little awkward about it all.

Charlie Bowman wouldn't give up. "By golly," he said stubbornly, "I'm just gonna find out where she's at." Next day he and his friend, Shorty Fisher, who ran a gas station at Monmouth, went out on their own. Again, Charlie's divining led them northward, into Washington State. There, though, he lost the vibrations. Over a three-day period, Charlie had traveled nearly 1,200 miles in the search. At some roadside places, he'd picked up a sardine can and a couple of beer bottles which he was certain gave off impulses of Kathy or someone who had been with her. Charlie was absolutely certain of one thing: "She's up north there somewheres."

Low and softly rounded, Taylor Mountain has almost motherly contours—in contrast to the steeper foothills further east. Taylor is seldom noticed by motorists driving along Washington State Highway 18, which curls between several small towns in rural King County, south and east of Seattle.

To the east, the high Cascades were whitened by snow on that first day of March 1975. The Saturday morning was heavily overcast, and the dense forest covering Taylor Mountain was glistening wet from the previous night's rain.

Two forestry students from Green River Community College were slowly working up one side of Taylor, picking their way through silent, dripping stands of second-growth Douglas fir, red alder, and the pesky vine maple. As a class project, Alex Kamola and Larry Sharie, dressed in rain garb, boots, and hard hats, were cruising an eighty-acre tract there on Taylor, running their line and compass course. Methodically, they worked to the top of the mountain, stopping frequently to take their readings and log locations.

During the late afternoon, they were working their way down the opposite side, when Alex reached a low place at the foot of the mountain. In a swampy area thick with sword fern, maple, and little cottonwoods, he stopped, startled.

Lying in the wet grass, near a rotted log, was a human skull.

"Hey," he shouted to Larry. "There's a skull down here."

"Be right down," Larry shouted back.

Alex sat on a log and examined the skull. He could see that some of the upper teeth had fillings. Curving around the side of the skull bone was a jagged fracture. There was no jawbone.

Larry arrived. "Ugh. Bizarre," he muttered. "Let's mark the spot and finish up."

They left an orange streamer used for timber marking and went to telephone the police.

Speeding toward the scene of the call, King County Detective Bob Keppel was driving past Issaquah on Interstate 90 when his eye turned automatically toward that steep hillside on his left, the place where the Lake Sammamish girls' skeletons had been discovered five months earlier. I wonder, he thought. I wonder if . . . Keppel glanced at his car's mileage reading. Taylor Mountain, the place to which he had been called, would be another ten miles to the east, higher in the foothills. Keppel was thinking about pieces of that third skeleton—still unidentified—which had been found there near Issaquah.

I wonder if a coyote or bear could have carried that damn skull ten miles, all the way out to this Taylor Mountain.

No, he reasoned, whatever had been found, it was a new victim.

When Keppel, Detective Roger Dunn, and the others gathered at Taylor Mountain, it was late, too dark, to begin an immediate search. They'd developed a better plan following the Issaquah search, which had been a nightmare, with reporters and curiosity seekers constantly invading the discovery area. The lone dirt road leading to the flank of Taylor Mountain was sealed off that night. Keppel scanned the mountain, with its dense timber and tangled underbrush, and estimated, "It's gotta be a million-to-one shot that a skull would ever be found here. Amazing."

The officers lifted the skullbone into a plastic bag, sealed it, labeled it, and dispatched it to the medical examiner's office in Seattle.

Keppel, a police-science graduate of Washington State University, was a scholarly looking, soft-spoken detective who was recognized as one of King County's—and Seattle's—brightest and best investigators. Before his transfer to the homicide and robbery detail of the county police force in early 1974, he had been working on a missing-persons case—the disappearance of twenty-two-year-old Brenda Gail Ball. She had last been seen leaving the Flame tavern, in a suburb southwest of Seattle, around two o'clock the morning of May 31, 1974. Brenda did part-time secretarial work. She wasn't a college student. So, at first, her disappearance had not been related to the missing coeds. But Keppel had concluded that the date of Brenda's disappearance, her age, her physical appearance, other circumstances, all added up. It was a case similar to the others.

Late that night, Keppel received the medical examiner's identification of the skull. Dental charts left no doubt. It was Brenda Ball.

Keppel was back out on Taylor Mountain early the next morning. Again, it was chilly and wet. Drooping from the low overcast, gauzy strands of fog interlaced the tall firs. Search volunteers had been summoned and were still en route when Keppel climbed across the face of the mountain, seeking a boundary marker which had been placed the day before. As he waded through the thick underbrush in a slippery place, Keppel's boot caught in a web of maple roots. He fell—heavily—landing on his hip and one elbow in the thick carpet of rotting leaves.

His eyes were riveted to the sight. Five feet from where he lay, at eye level, was another skull.

Christ, he thought. That's gotta be the Rancourt girl from over at Ellensburg.

He recognized the pretty white teeth across the front, which appeared unattached to the skull bone above. Through months of work on the cases of vanished girls, Keppel had memorized characteristics of the missing girls, including their dental charts. Al Pickles and his campus police over at Ellensburg, perhaps seventy miles or so eastward across the Cascades from this point on Taylor Mountain, had stressed the uniqueness of Susan's teeth. She had ceramic crowns and distinctive bridgework.

At the base of the mountain the search volunteers had begun to arrive. Some handlers were already on the mountain with their search-and-rescue German shepherds. As a dog approached him in the woods, Keppel's eye noticed that the animal's paw, stepping in the thick leaves, turned up a human jawbone.

"Everybody get back out of here," the detective shouted. "Everyone out! Watch where you step! Walk straight back. Everybody the hell out of here." Whatever grisly deposits might lie in that thick tangle of forest, brush, and marsh on the mountainside, it had to be preserved if ever the investigators were to reconstruct what had happened.

Later that day, the Air National Guardsmen, the young Explorer Scouts, and the other searchers assembled around the county police truck at the foot of the mountain. Keppel, standing on the tailgate, addressed them: "We're going to search the area first on hands and knees, shoulder to shoulder." He held up a large map of the mountainside, which had been divided by grid lines. "Now, if there is any discovery, everyone stops right where he is. Then we mark it and plot its location on the map." On the mountainside, orange streamers outlined the initial search zone, an area about the size of nine football fields, on the face of the mountain.

It proceeded like a combination slow-motion military maneuver and painstaking archaeological dig. On hands and knees, the searchers on the mountain moved inch by inch, their fingers lifting one leaf at a time. Slowly they crept through the ferns, the blackberry vines, and huckleberry shrubs around the tangled trees.

First news reports of the discovery and search on Taylor Mountain shocked the region. A platoon of news media people assembled around the search base at the foot of the mountain to report developments.

As the search inched down the mountainside, the keen eyes of Explorer Scouts picked up the almost-invisible strands of long human hair which had become entangled in the bushes. It was a path of human hair. As he logged the discoveries on the map, Keppel shook his head. It appeared that predators —coyotes, perhaps wildcats—had been at work on the bodies, scattering the remains. A jawbone was found. Another day of searching passed. Another skull was found. Then another jawbone. Each discovery was logged, charted on the map, packaged, and rushed to the medical examiner's office.

Anxious parents awaited the ominous news reports. Dale Rancourt heard about it in Alaska and was on the telephone with Ellensburg, begging Al Pickles, the campus police chief, for any news: "Al, have they found Susan on that mountain?"

"I don't know, but I'll find out for you," Pickles replied.

He telephoned Seattle, in an effort to reach Captain Nick Mackie, chief of the investigation. He was told Mackie wasn't taking any calls and wasn't returning any calls.

Pickles exploded in frustration and anger: "I've got a father who's going out of his mind, and I've promised him we'd let him know as quickly as there's any information. I've turned over to Mackie and his boys every damned piece of information in our investigation, trying to cooperate. What the hell kind of cooperation is this? Mackie won't even return a telephone call."

In Olympia, Thurston County Sheriff Don Jennings and his officers were having the same trouble. "Can't get a thing out of Mackie," snapped Jennings. The feeble sense of cooperation among the police agencies was falling apart.

Eventually Mackie made the announcements to the press, as the bones were identified. The skull with the pretty teeth, he confirmed, was that of Susan Rancourt.

When the mountainside search was in its fifth day, two detectives arrived at the Bellevue home of Mr. and Mrs. James Healy. Lynda's parents had been waiting for—and dreading—some word for thirteen months, ever since Lynda vanished from her basement apartment. The somber-faced detectives told them there could be no mistake. The teeth of the jawbone matched Lynda's dental records.

Later, Lynda's mother spoke bravely to news reporters: "We still had some hope that maybe she would show up some day, that maybe we would have her home again. But if it's impossible for that to happen, I guess we're glad to know. It's kind of a relief in a way. She was a wonderful girl. Maybe I was just lucky to have had her for twenty-one years."

On Taylor Mountain, in a tangle of wet brush, about 350 feet from an animal trail which crossed the search area, they found the fourth skull.

Keppel studied it, noticing its slightly different, slimmer

shape. He thought about all the photographs of missing girls which were posted in the detective's room in Seattle where he and the others had spent so many months working. One photo leaped to his mind as he studied the skull—the photo of Kathy Parks. "I've got a feeling that's the Parks girl from Oregon State," Keppel told a fellow detective. "She's the one with the really slender face."

"But, God, that's hard to believe. This mountain is more than 250 miles from where that girl disappeared."

Two days before the forestry students had made their initial discovery on Taylor Mountain in Washington State, Kathy's parents, in Lafayette, California, had sorrowfully observed the twenty-first birthday of their missing daughter. When Kathy had been born February 27, 1947, in Lakewood, Ohio, she was premature, weighing two pounds, nine ounces. Doctors had placed her immediately in an incubator, and the whole family prayed for their little "preemie." Slowly, the infant gained weight and eventually grew quite healthy. The only indication of her premature birth was a slightly elongated skull, the result of having lain quietly on her side during those early weeks of life in that incubator. As a young woman, the slenderness of her face gave Kathy a rather dramatic look of fragile beauty.

Her parents had missed sharing her previous birthday with her, too. That year Kathy was away from home, in college at Corvallis. Her father had preserved their exchange of correspondence at that time. Charles Parks had written to his daughter, "My dearest 20 yr. old daughter. It sure doesn't seem like 20 years have gone by since I was looking at you in an incubator at Lakewood Hospital in Cleveland." Her father urged Kathy to take practical courses at the university with an eye on her eventual financial independence. He had closed the letter, "In any event, all my love, good luck and study hard. Have some fun with the attached check or buy some shoes or a dress.—Love, Dad."

Kathy had been affected by the rare letter from her father. She had replied, "Dear Dad: I was touched by your letter to me, so I thought I'd like to sit down and write a letter to YOU—Just for you." She poured out her affection for her dad and suggested they erase all memories of those father-daughter frictions which had occurred when Kathy was in her rebellious teens. "Well," she had concluded. "I could write pages on the whole subject, but I've got a class in 10 or 15 minutes, so it'll just have to wait. I just wanted to tell you I love you and I'm proud of you, too. Hi to Mom and I'll see you soon. Take care. All my love.—Kathy."

The Parkses never had a chance to see Kathy again, though. A few weeks after she wrote that letter she disappeared.

The slender skull and a jawbone were x-rayed in the crime lab in downtown Seattle, and lab chief Kay Sweeny, comparing it with Kathy Parks' dental records, was virtually convinced the remains were hers. But there had been severe damage to the skull. Blows of some kind had caused multiple fractures. Most of the upper teeth had apparently been broken away by a blow or blows.

Sweeny wanted to be certain. He placed the skull and jawbone in a foil-lined paper bag, sealed it, checked out a Cessna 182 from his flying club, and flew south from Seattle to Oregon. Bill Harris, the OSU campus security chief, met him at the Corvallis airport and drove him to the office of Kathy's dentist.

After his own examination, the dentist confirmed Sweeny's conclusion. The skull and jawbone were the remains of Kathy Parks.

For Harris, like Pickles on his campus up in Washington State, the search for "his" girl finally was over. By coincidence, Bob Tucker, an FBI agent, was on the OSU campus that day, and Harris asked him, "Is it possible for the FBI to come in on this?" It was possible, Tucker confirmed. He explained that federal agents could come into the case of Kathy Parks if there had been an abduction.

Harris called the Parks family in California and broke the bad news to them. "But we may be able to get the FBI in on the case now, because she was found in another state," Harris told Charles Parks.

"Oh, that would be wonderful," replied the father. "We'd really appreciate that very much."

Tucker, sitting in Harris' office, joined in the telephone conversation. He informed the father he'd do whatever he could to bring the FBI in on the investigation. (Eventually, though, Tucker's superiors decided the FBI had no grounds to enter the case. There was no proof that Kathy had been alive—and thus a kidnap victim—when she was transported across the Columbia River into Washington State. In fact, the damage to her head suggested she might have been attacked almost immediately after she encountered her killer, on or near the OSU campus that spring night.)

For days, the search continued on Taylor Mountain until there were no more discoveries. A mountainside had been covered, inch by inch, and it was not practicable to go on forever. Keppel and others, some using German Shepherd dogs, did a walking search over several miles around the intensive search area.

Four skulls and jawbones had been found, and the identifications were certain: Lynda Ann Healy, twenty-one, vanished from her bedroom apartment in the University District; Susan Elaine Rancourt, eighteen, from the campus at Ellensburg; Roberta Kathleen Parks, twenty, from Corvallis; and Brenda Carol Ball, twenty-two, last seen leaving the Flame tavern.

Still unaccounted for were Donna Gail Manson, who vanished on her way to the jazz concert in March 1974 at the Evergreen State College campus, and Georgann Hawkins, the girl who vanished in June from the University of Washington's Greek Row.

Keppel and the other detectives theorized that the unidentified skeletal remains found at the Issaquah site, with the Lake Sammamish victims, had probably been Georgann. The officers speculated that the abductor-killer had used Taylor Mountain as a dumping ground for his victims through the first five months of the year 1974. Then, for some reason—perhaps he had been spooked, fearful the site might be discovered—he had chosen a mountainside location near Issaquah, beginning in June. Georgann, who vanished June 11, would have been the first victim to be placed there.

The investigators were convinced that, although no trace of her had been found, Donna Gail Manson, the victim from Evergreen, had probably been transported about 100 miles northward and left on Taylor Mountain, too—exactly one year before the discoveries. Her bones had apparently all been carried away by animals.

Tenderly, Paul Barclift, the Thurston County detective,

talked it over with Lyle and Marie Manson. "Even though there was no trace of her found there, it sure looks like Donna was up on that mountain, too," said the detective.

Quietly, the mother and father accepted their lifetime sentence of doubt. They'd read and reread news articles about the man named Ted—his ploy of an arm in sling, seeking help. And they'd think of Donna, walking to a jazz concert, crossing the campus in the darkness. Marie Manson opened a scrapbook containing some of Donna's writings and her attention went to an impromptu, almost poetic, list of "things to give" which Donna had written while she was in high school.

> *Things to give to people:*
> —Smiles
> —Songs
> —Touches
> —Kisses
> —Things you create
> —Experiences
> —God's love
> —Sunsets, etc.
> —A string of beads
> —A taste
> —A rose
> —An ear
> —A hand to help

A region reeled under the impact of the stunning news—that all those missing girls had, indeed, been murdered.

Detectives of the Seattle Police Department were assigned to assist the King County police in a joint investigation—a rare and ill-fated experiment in cooperation between two (sometimes rival) agencies. Captain Mackie was placed in charge. "You just don't think that something this bizarre is real," mourned Mackie. "It's the most frustrating mystery we've ever seen in the Pacific Northwest."

No clues—just bones—had been found on Taylor Mountain. No clothing of any of the girls was found. There was nothing new for the investigators to go on, except the probability that one man was responsible for all the crimes—the Lake Sammamish abduction-killings and all the others revealed by the Taylor Mountain discoveries. The connection was seen in the Rancourt case. Two Central Washington coeds had an encounter with a man whose arm was in a sling on that campus. That matched the MO of the "Ted" at Lake Sammamish. The fractures of the victims' heads, the mountain location where they were left, added up to one killer.

As a massive new phase of the investigation opened, the team of city and county detectives appealed anew for information about men named "Ted," who drove Volkswagens and who might speak with a clipped accent, a British accent perhaps. Once again, police telephone lines were flooded with calls from the public. On the wall of the crowded detectives' room in the downtown King County courthouse, someone posted the simple reminder: "Get Ted." The task force became known as the Ted Squad.

Keppel and the other investigators began reworking all the disappearances and speculating on the eeriness of the individual crimes. Lynda Ann Healy, perhaps bludgeoned in her bed and then taken—unconscious? dead? how? clothed?—out of her basement apartment while a roommate slept nearby. From that apartment, Lynda would probably have been taken on a forty-minute drive in the night, eastward to the mountain. The most logical route for that trip would have been via a busy freeway corridor, through the bright lights of downtown Seattle.

And Kathy Parks. Taken in Oregon, she would have been transported, 250 miles or more—alive? dead?—to the mountain. If her killer had taken her there directly, officers calculated he would have been depositing her body on Taylor Mountain around dawn the morning of May 7. Had someone seen a car there? And if the killer was the mysterious "Ted," driving a Volkswagen, how did he manage it? With a ten-gallon tank, he would probably have needed to add gas to the tank somewhere between Corvallis and the Seattle area. But at a gas station? With a living kidnap victim in his car? Or a dead body?

Some of the detectives believed there must have been a "slaughter-house" somewhere—a place where the killer might have kept the victims for a while. Perhaps there was some ritualism involved in the killings. "Where are all the other bones on the mountain?" asked Captain Herb Swindler, chief of homicide for the Seattle police. "With four girls up there, maybe more, you should have hundreds of bones." Increasingly, Swindler was drawn to a theory that a believer in some "demon cult" might be involved. Even Mackie, his counterpart captain in the county, conceded it was possible the skulls on Taylor Mountain could have been the result of decapitation.

Keppel, among others, disagreed. He theorized that the bodies had been placed on the mountain intact. Then, the detective reasoned, through the following months, the predators of the mountain had carried away all the other bones. Eventually, a "subtask force" of consulting anthropologists and zoologists, after a study of the locations of the skulls and the predator life on the mountain, confirmed Keppel's belief.

The Taylor Mountain discoveries cleared one suspect—James Edward Ruzicka. A convicted sexual psychopath, Ruzicka had escaped from Western State Hospital near Steilacoom, forty miles from Seattle, the day Lynda Healy vanished in Seattle. He had been reported in the University District, not far from Lynda's apartment that night. Eventually, Ruzicka was charged with rape murders of two West Seattle girls. In March 1974 Ruzicka was finally captured in Beaverton, Oregon, where he was charged—and convicted—in the rape of an Oregon girl. Because Lynda Ann Healy's murder had been associated with the other Taylor Mountain victims, Ruzicka was cleared. He had been in jail at the time of the Ball, Rancourt, and Parks disappearances.

Weeks of intensive investigation had also cleared another once-promising suspect. During the autumn of 1974 an orange Volkswagen had been seen parked in the Issaquah foothill area not far from where the remains of Janice Ott and Denise Nasland had been discovered. The vehicle's registration led to a commercial fisherman, a young man serving aboard a fishing vessel. Investigators' interest surged when they discovered that he was about the same weight, height, and age as the "Ted" described in the park, and his boat had docked in Seattle the day before the Lake Sammamish crimes.

Their suspect had gone to sea again, and so police put his residence under surveillance until the ship returned to port. It was his hair—extremely long, worn in a queue which fell onto his back—which cleared him. That hair would have been much too long on July 14 to have matched the "Ted" description. The fisherman also had a sheepish alibi for the fact that his Volkswagen was seen in a remote area near Issaquah—that's where he tended his illicit marijuana patch.

When the hundreds of telephone calls clogged police switchboards during the Ted Squad investigations, there may have been occasional fumbles.

Maria Ackley, a Seattle writer-photographer, became concerned when she noticed that her pretty young woman shopping companion was being followed by a strange young man with his arm in a sling. Mrs. Ackley watched the man follow her friend, an out-of-town visitor, from place to place in Seattle's Pike Place Market, and concluded, he looks exactly like the "Ted" in the police sketch. Unnoticed, she hurried to a telephone in the market and dialed the police emergency number, 911.

When the Seattle Police Department operator answered, Mrs. Ackley said excitedly, "I'm at the Pike Place Market, and there's a strange man here, with his arm in a sling, following a young woman. He looks exactly like the 'Ted' you're looking for. Can you send a policeman here right away?"

The police operator told her no officer was available at the moment. And besides, Mrs. Ackley was told, the "Ted" case was King County's, not Seattle's.

She banged the receiver into its cradle. From that pay phone she frantically watched the man stalking her friend from place to place in the market.

Quickly Mrs. Ackley dialed the private number of her husband, Norman Ackley, a King County Superior Court judge. A bailiff summoned the judge to the telephone, and when he heard his wife's excited pleas, the judge recessed court, summoned a detective, and drove hurriedly to the market.

The man had disappeared into the crowd of shoppers.

In October 1974, Al Bricker and his fourteen-year-old son had been riding a motorcycle across a mountainside between their home at North Bend and the Issaquah area. Along a power-line road, heavily used by motorcyclists and jeep drivers, Bricker noticed a cardboard box, which had been placed, apparently to hide it, beneath a small maple tree. Bricker parked his bike and, with his son, bent to open the carton and investigate its contents. On top were some women's blouses, pants, and a swimsuit.

"Let's not touch anything," Bricker told his son. Bricker had read the news that some murdered girls had been found near Issaquah a month ago, and that police were looking for clothing as possible clues.

Not far away from that maple shrub, Bricker and his son discovered a brown paper bag which contained, all neatly folded, several white cotton brassieres. Beneath the bras was a collection of panties.

"C'mon, let's go get the police," said Bricker.

Within an hour, Bricker and his son had left a message at a satellite office of King County police that he wished to talk with a detective. When days passed and there was no response, Bricker tried again. His messages to police went unanswered.

As winter's rain and snow closed in on the mountainside, Bricker returned to the site. He found that the carton and the bag had been smashed, the contents scattered and buried in the mud by tires of passing motorbikes.

"Dammit," he grumbled. "What kind of law enforcement have we got here anyway? Why wouldn't they at least come to take a look?"

Neither Bricker nor the police knew it at the time, but his discovery had been made within a few hundred yards of Taylor Mountain, where the remains of some murdered girls would lie in the woods for months before being discovered.

By mid-April 1975, after months of investigations and the intermittent floods of telephone calls into the Ted Squad headquarters, Mackie reported to the public that 2,247 names of potential suspects had been turned in and examined. Many of them were "Ted." More than 900 cars, most of them Volkswagens, had been checked.

The Ted Squad chief gave the nervous citizenry of Seattle and the rest of the Pacific Northwest a bleak report:

"We have no crime scene evidence, no means of death. It's

the worst case I've ever been on. There's just nothing. . . . We'll need a break on it."

In the deluge of tips which Mackie had mentioned was a call to King County police about a Volkswagen driver named Theodore Robert Bundy. Bundy, who seemed a highly unlikely suspect, had since moved from Seattle to Salt Lake City, where he was enrolled in the University of Utah law school.

The break, which Mackie was hoping for in mid-April, was four months away.

SIX | Quiet Neighborhood

A nice, quiet, churchy neighborhood, thought Sergeant Bob Hayward. In the velvety warm August night, his new un-marked green '75 Plymouth sedan purred quietly along the residential street. In its headlights, he watched the tidy homes, all asleep now, sliding by in the darkness. They were homes of his neighbors.

Hayward, a twenty-three-year veteran with the Utah State Highway Patrol, glanced at his watch. It was two thirty in the morning. Saturday, August 16. Hayward had a half hour to go until he finished his shift. His thick hands rested lightly on the steering wheel. Yes, Hayward thought, he liked this little community of Granger. Close enough to Salt Lake City and yet twelve miles away, far enough to be out of the noisy traffic, away from the city hubbub. Nice place to raise kids. When he could, Hayward always made it a practice to cruise his own neighborhood, watching over the peace in the final minutes before his work shift ended.

With his older brother, Pete, Bob Hayward had grown up in West Salt Lake, in a tough neighborhood. Later, each of the brothers had entered a career in law enforcement. Pete now was captain of detectives in the homicide division of the

Salt Lake County sheriff's office. Earlier in this August night, Bob Hayward, on assignment with the special enforcement crew of the Highway Patrol, had been patrolling roadways for drivers high on alcohol or narcotics, especially along that stretch of Redwood Road where the drunks came straggling out of the taverns, wobbled into their cars, and headed onto the roads, sometimes without headlights. Bob Hayward had arrested some.

Turning the corner onto Hogan, his own street, Hayward idly flicked on the high beams. Ahead, his headlights illuminated a parked tan Volkswagen, which suddenly lurched into motion, starting away from the curb without lights. Hayward grunted a faint *humh* and began to follow. The VW headed north, to the end of Brock Street, then went left on Lehi Drive past darkened houses.

In pursuit, Hayward switched on the red spotlight on the passenger's side of his patrol car—a brilliant airplane landing light. The Volkswagen—its headlights now on—ran through a stop sign, swerved left, and ran another stop sign. It was obviously a hopeless race for the VW driver, and with Hayward's car still close behind, the Volkswagen slowed, pulled off the street into a vacant gas station where it stopped. Hayward radioed his dispatcher that he was now apprehending a driver who'd been attempting to evade arrest.

In his headlights, Hayward watched a young man climb out of the VW and start to walk back toward his patrol car. The driver, long haired, wore a turtleneck shirt, jeans, and white tennis shoes.

Hayward hoisted himself through the door of his car and strode forward to meet the younger man. "I need some identification. Can I see your driver's license?"

"Sure, officer." It was a cordial, respectful reply.

From the rear pocket of his jeans he pulled a wallet. "I didn't know who you were, who was following me," said the driver, handing over his driver's license.

In the circle of light from his flashlight, Hayward read the information of the driver's license: "Theodore Robert Bundy." There was a Salt Lake City address—565 First Avenue. Bundy explained that he was a law student at the University of Utah.

"What brings you to this neighborhood at this hour?"

"I was lost. I'd been over to see a movie at the drive-in. And I just made the wrong turn and got lost over here."

"What drive-in were you at?"

"The—uh—Valley View."

"What show was playin'?"

"The Towering Inferno."

Hayward became suspicious. While patrolling that evening, he'd passed the Valley View. He thought he remembered the marquee was advertising a triple bill of Westerns. Hayward used his car radio to contact a partner, Utah Highway Patrol Sergeant Brent Fowles. He asked Fowles to check and see if *The Towering Inferno* was playing at the Valley View. Within minutes, Fowles radioed back: No, it wasn't *The Towering Inferno*. Nothing even close.

"Mind if I look in your car?" Hayward asked Bundy.

"Okay. Go ahead."

Hayward approached the Volkswagen and, through a window, played the beam of his flashlight inside. He noticed the passenger's seat had been removed and placed on the back seat. In the vacant place beside the driver's seat was a small, open satchel. Hayward opened the door, leaned inside, and shone the light into the bag. Sorting through its contents, he noticed a brown knit ski mask, a pantyhose with some slots cut in it, an ice pick, other items. Behind the driver's seat, lying on the floor, Hayward's flashlight picked up a steel hexagonal pinch bar, about fifteen inches long.

"What's all this stuff?" asked Hayward.

"Oh, just some junk I picked up," Bundy explained.

Hayward didn't like it. True, the young man was obviously courteous and intelligent and had claimed to be a law student. But his dark clothing—the dark turtleneck and jeans—and his loitering around this neighborhood at such an odd hour of the morning, with that strange collection of implements in the car, made Hayward think he could be a burglar on the prowl.

While Bundy stood near the front of the police car, Hayward radioed to ask that a Salt Lake County sheriff's detective be sent to the scene. Two deputies, on routine patrol nearby, heard the radio request and arrived within minutes. Then came Detective Daryl Ondrak, nightduty investigator for the sheriff's office. Ondrak made a more thorough search of the Volkswagen. He noticed a rip along the top of the back cushion in the rear seat. Ondrak poked his hand into the stuffing, probing for contraband. There was nothing inside. When he opened the trunk of the VW, Ondrak found, among other items, a pair of handcuffs.

Hayward meanwhile had placed Bundy in the patrol car. After a quiet conversation with Ondrak, Hayward returned to his car, put handcuffs on Bundy, and told him, "You're under arrest for trying to evade a police officer." Bundy accepted it quietly.

Detective Ondrak came to the window of the patrol car to tell Bundy that the articles out of his Volkswagen were being taken into custody. "Possible evidence," said Ondrak. "If it turns out that they're not evidence of any kind, we'll get them back to you."

Bundy nodded and said, "Okay, officer."

As Hayward drove him downtown to the Salt Lake County jail, Bundy remained courteous and respectful. He showed some nervousness when he was subjected to the booking procedure. Standing in front of the police camera, in his dark turtleneck and long hair, Bundy masked his anger with a thin smile as his mug shot was taken.

In the squad room on the ninth floor of the Temple of Justice building near downtown Salt Lake City, there is a Tuesday morning ritual. The "detectives meeting" begins around 8:30 or so. Police from the Salt Lake County sheriff's office, from the city of Salt Lake, the nearby departments at Midvale, Murray, Sandy, Bountiful, and other towns, plus county juvenile officers, campus police, and sometimes the Utah State Highway Patrol crowd into the room to swap information about new cases in each jurisdiction.

That morning, August 19, 1975, there were mundane reports of car thefts, burglaries, and some new bunko action. Salt Lake County detectives Jerry Thompson and Ben Forbes had nothing new to report in their investigation of the Melissa Smith murder the previous October. No one knew what Utah County was doing in its investigation of the Laura Aime homicide. The Utah County sheriff's office down in Provo wasn't very cooperative with Salt Lake County. At Bountiful there was nothing on the vanished Debbie Kent. The Murray

Police Department was still without a promising lead in its Carol DaRonch kidnapping. The pretty, dark-haired girl had laboriously examined thousands of photos of possible suspects but couldn't identify anyone.

Then the solemn-faced Detective Ondrak, a soft-spoken man, began reciting details of a routine arrest the previous Saturday morning. The man, who had been driving a Volkswagen, looked like a burglary suspect, Ondrak pointed out. Ondrak had brought into the meeting some of the things that had been taken out of the young man's car. There was a steel pry bar. Ondrak produced a satchel and started to sort through its contents. He extracted and held up a ski mask, then an ice pick, a pair of handcuffs, then nylon pantyhose with eyeslits cut in it.

"He claims he's a law student at the university," Ondrak told the others. Ondrak referred to his notes. "Says his name is Theodore Robert Bundy. . . . Moved here last year from Seattle."

Theodore Robert Bundy. When he heard the name, Jerry Thompson's dark eyebrows raised in wonderment. He'd heard that name. From *Seattle*.

Thompson turned to his fellow detective, Ben Forbes. "Hey, Ben," he muttered, "does that name, 'Bundy', sound familiar to you?"

"Yeah, it does. Isn't that the name that Seattle called down on some time back?"

"Yeah. Bob Keppel, it was. Called us on that guy last fall."

As the meeting ended, Thompson hurried to his small desk in the cramped cubbyhole office he shared with three other detectives. There, near the telephone on the desk, Thompson had a metal file spindle onto which had been speared layers of notes, advisories, messages, reminders. His fingers shuffled downward through the pieces of paper until he found it—the message which had come from King County Detective Bob Keppel in Seattle the previous October. Among the names of hundreds of possible suspects who had been turned in on the Washington cases had been the name of Theodore Robert Bundy. By that time, Bundy had moved to Salt Lake City.

"Goddamn." It was a whispered exclamation. "Hey, look here, Ben." Thompson showed the message to Forbes.

Forbes nodded. Now, he remembered it, too. When that routine advisory had come in, Thompson recalled, "the information was that this Bundy guy was well connected in politics in Washington, a friend of the governor, Joe College —too damned goody-goody to be a suspect."

Thompson approached Ondrak. "Daryl, I think it'd be a good idea just to take that bagful of stuff you got from Mr. Bundy down to the evidence room."

"Sure," said Ondrak.

"I think we may wanna talk to the guy. Can you charge him? And bring him in?"

Ondrak replied there could be a charge—possession of burglary tools.

Thompson headed into the office of his chief, Captain N. D. (Pete) Hayward, a graying man whose face had the same gruff appearance of his kid brother on the state patrol. Thompson told Hayward how Bob's arrest had triggered some interesting things. A couple of pieces appeared to have coincidentally fallen in place in their jigsaw puzzle. "I think we oughta go to work on Mr. Bundy real hard," suggested Thompson.

"Go ahead," replied Hayward. "If you need any help, lemme know."

Thompson returned to his desk to telephone Bob Keppel in Seattle.

For Seattle's Ted Squad, there had been a burst of activity after the skulls were found on Taylor Mountain in March. Then, with no fresh information, the activity had slowed.

After five months, only three county detectives still worked at desks in the Ted Squad room (the King County Courthouse)—Keppel, Kathy McChesney, and Roger Dunn. In the crammed file drawers and in work baskets on their desks there still remained the names of 3,000 or more "possibles"—a mountain of chaff in which they couldn't find a grain of wheat. Keppel one day shared a fear with his partner, Dunn: "Ya know what I'm thinking? I'm beginning to wonder if our guy might be dead."

Could be, agreed Dunn. There hadn't been another similar case of murder in about a year now—not since the late summer of '74. Keppel theorized that some nut could have put a bullet through his head in a cheap motel somewhere, taking his secret of all those murders to his grave. Dunn grimaced at the thought.

Keppel and Dunn had come up with an ambitious idea, employing the use of a computer to search for interconnections among the cases of murdered girls. It was elaborate and costly. But Captain Mackie authorized it.

With help from a secretarial staff, the detectives created a computer program which included thousands of names. There were the names of every student who'd ever been in the same class with any of the missing or murdered girls. That included years of class rosters from four universities—even those lecture classes which had 200 or more students. Into the computer also went every name from the address books and correspondence of each girl—names of friends, relatives, and associates. The officers added the names of every patron of the Black Nugget Horse Ranch near Issaquah (where riding trails crossed the mountainside on which the first two victims had been found). They added the more than 3,000 "possibles" whose names had been turned in, plus the names of callers who had contacted the Ted Squad headquarters.

Dunn decided to order from the Washington State Department of Motor Vehicle Licenses a computer printout of every Volkswagen owner in the State of Washington.

"That might get out of hand," said Keppel.

Dunn said he planned just to skim through them.

The printout was delivered—a tall stack of heavy cardboard cartons, in all, 41,000 names. Dunn stared at the stack, overwhelmed.

"Start skimmin'," quipped Keppel.

From out of the computer came some extraordinary "matches." One student, who had been in the same class with Susan Rancourt and Lynda Ann Healy at different universities, also owned a Volkswagen. There were others. Dozens of people turned up, over and over, in some statistical relationship with one or more of the victims. But, when examined, each connection turned out to be nothing more than a chance happening.

Conventional police wisdom suggested that kind of effort

could pay off. Almost always in a murder case there has been some previous contact between killer and victim. After months of vain searching for connections, the detectives became convinced that, although all the victims were similar —young, attractive, long hair parted in the middle—they may also have been chosen by the killer *because* he had never had any earlier contact with any of them.

A deliberate stranger.

It seemed almost as though he had a sense of the steps that police might follow in their pursuit. And so he had avoided leaving the usual tracks. Yet, they wondered, if he were that intelligent, how could he be so foolish as to reveal himself over and over in a crowd of thousands at Lake Sammamish?

By August, Keppel, Dunn, and McChesney had begun a final effort. Out of all their files, they refined a "top 100" list—the reports which had been turned in on men, "possibles" who most deserved an exhaustive background check and personal interview.

The first batch of reports in the "top 100" had been placed in a wire basket on a vacant table in the squad headquarters. Starting at the top, the detectives began their deliberate work, making a detailed check of each of the final suspects.

On August 19, 1975, the name at the top of the stack was "Theodore Robert Bundy."

When the telephone call came from Detective Jerry Thompson at Salt Lake City that day, McChesney handled it, excitedly scribbling the information Thompson had to give— the arrest of Bundy and the strange items in his Volkswagen.

When Keppel arrived in the squad room, McChesney broke the news: "Utah called and said they just arrested Ted Bundy." And with a gesture toward the wire basket, she added, "He's the one we've got on top of our list right there."

Keppel stared at the report on Bundy in the "top 100" basket. He examined the polaroid photograph of the man, a photograph which had been turned in by Bundy's girlfriend almost a year earlier.

Bundy's move from Seattle to Salt Lake City, coinciding with the occurrence of homicides in both areas, was the most intriguing possibility to appear through the long months of investigation. But Keppel and the others had seen high hopes dashed before. Dispassionately Keppel said, "Well, let's take him on. Let's work him."

The detectives went to the King County prosecutor's office to seek a court order to examine Ted Bundy's credit-card purchases, his work records, his banking activities. They would try to establish where Ted Bundy was, what he was doing every day, through those months when the girls were vanishing and being murdered.

Under the circumstance, Jerry Thompson thought, Ted Bundy was being a very congenial host as they sat there together, talking, in Ted's student apartment in Salt Lake City.

"Uh—Ted, how long have you lived here?"

"I moved in here in early September last year," Ted replied. "Not quite a year ago."

Thompson wrote a note on the pad of his clipboard propped in his lap. He studied the casually dressed young man with the long dark wavy hair and clean features. Kind of a sharp-looking guy, Thompson thought. Seems to be really on the ball. Ted's gaze was on Sergeant John Bernardo, who was rummaging through the closet of the apartment.

"And that's when you enrolled in law school here?" asked Thompson.

"Uh-huh."

After the Tuesday detectives' meeting, Detective Ondrak had moved quickly. Ted was arrested, charged with possession of burglary tools, and lodged in the Salt Lake County jail. In handcuffs, Ted had been taken from jail out to his apartment while they searched it. Ted didn't appear perturbed. As a law student, he knew that the charge they'd brought was one of those vague misdemeanors used by police to arrest and hold someone briefly—a "fishing license" for police. Ted knew the charges couldn't stick. Every item found in his car could be explained. He could show them how the pinch bar and ice pick were used in various ways for repairing his Volkswagen. That pantyhose mask, he'd explained, was used as a warm inner liner of the ski mask—to protect the face from the cold winds while skiing Utah's high slopes. Although he thought the charge was nothing more than an excuse for some invasion of his privacy, he was pointedly polite to the officers. He'd even signed the consent for the search.

"And you've been in law school here ever since?"

"Yeah. Well, except for this summer vacation."

Ted continued to watch Sergeant Bernardo, whose search of the apartment moved into the kitchen area.

Thompson glanced at the bookshelf, where Bundy's textbooks were neatly arranged. He browsed through desk drawers, noticing a set of legal manuals on physical evidence, plus some neatly filed records and receipts. Thompson picked up a gasoline credit-card purchase receipt. "Okay if I keep this, Ted?" he asked. Bundy agreed. Thompson tucked the slip into his pocket.

A brochure, titled *Colorado Ski Country*, attracted the detective's eye.

"Ever been over to Colorado skiin', Ted?"

"No, I haven't," Ted replied.

Thompson was fishing. A few months earlier he'd learned of some similar crimes in Colorado during early 1975. A pretty young woman had been murdered near Aspen. Another girl was missing at Vail. Both were ski-resort towns in Colorado.

"Ever been to Aspen?"

"No."

"Or Vail?"

"No."

"I was just thinkin' that, with President Ford goin' into Vail all the time, and you bein' involved in Republican politics the way you are, I just thought you might have gone over to Vail for a little skiin'."

No, Ted replied; he'd never been to Colorado.

In their search of Ted's apartment, the detectives had been looking for a gun perhaps, or a cache of women's clothing—anything that might relate to any of the crimes. Nothing of obvious incrimination turned up. Among Ted's books, Thompson noticed, was a copy of *The Joy of Sex*, an illustrated manual of sex techniques. There was nothing out of the ordinary in Ted's closet, but Bernardo and Thompson took note of some patent leather shoes.

"Would it be okay with you, Ted, if we took some pictures of your Volkswagen?" asked Thompson.

Ted agreed to that, too. While they were in the apartment, Ted's handcuffs had been removed. Afterward, the cuffs were snapped on his wrists again, and they took him back downtown to jail.

Next day, after Ted's release on bond, his newly retained attorney, John O'Connell, informed police he had advised his new client not to talk to them anymore.

With Captain Hayward's okay, Thompson and the other detectives arranged to begin surveillance of Bundy, his Volkswagen, and his apartment.

Examining his clipboard notes and the gas charge slip he'd picked up from Ted, Detective Thompson placed a phone call to Colorado to talk with an investigator in Aspen, to let him know what had been found in Bundy's room.

Ted, meanwhile, was deciding he'd clean up his Volkswagen and sell it.

In those days following the search of his apartment, Bundy sensed the police would be watching him. He was right.

In the driveway beside the apartment house, he reparked his Volkswagen in a place near the sidewalk, then firmly set the hand brake. He got out, looked both ways, up and down First Avenue. He stared at the driver of a passing blue Chevrolet and continued to watch intently as the car disappeared, heading west.

Wearing a light-blue sport shirt and checkered slacks, Bundy resumed work on the front end of the VW, continuing to watch passing cars. It was September 10.

Across the street, beyond a 160-foot parking lot, sat the low and inconspicuous building of the Fireman's Fund Insurance Company. It was the stakeout place. In one of the windows, a venetian blind curled, unnoticed, over the twin lenses of some binoculars. Within the small office, the watching detective dictated an observation to his partner: "Subject seems extremely nervous. Walking up and down the sidewalk. Now back to the Volkswagen."

Ted made it a point to tell all his acquaintances that he thought police were watching him—all because, he explained, of "the junk" which had been found in his Volkswagen when Sergeant Hayward arrested him. Thompson, Forbes, and other detectives thought they should seize the Volkswagen in mid-August, but a cautious assistant county attorney vetoed that, doubting that there was probable cause to make such a confiscation.

So the stakeout officers watched in frustration as Ted carried out a complete cleanup-fixup of the Volkswagen. He scrubbed it, inside and out, including the trunk space, installed a new rear backrest, replacing the one that had the rip along the top, touched up the rust spots, installed a new front bumper, and gave the Bug a thorough wax job, which darkened its color. "Damn," mourned Thompson later. "You just gotta wonder how much evidence he might have cleaned out of there."

After the cleanup of the car, and after the surveillence was called off, Ted sold the VW, through a classified ad, to Brian Seiverson, a teenager at Sandy, Utah, for $700. Ted explained to friends he needed the money to pay off some debts and to help meet the costs of his newly hired lawyer. Ted moved to a smaller student apartment in another, older house on Douglas Street, within easier walking distance of the campus.

During September, Thompson visited the law school to check Bundy's class attendance and grade records and to interview some of his professors. As he moved from place to place in the law-school building, Thompson was aware that Bundy was following him at a distance. "The damnest thing I've ever seen," mused the detective. "Since when does a suspect start trailing the detective who's checking him out?" Then, as Thompson was leaving the building, entering a covered alcove, he heard Bundy's shout from behind him: "Jerry! Hey, Jerry!"

Thompson turned and watched Bundy approach. "I'm sorry to have to put you to all this trouble."

"No, it's okay, Ted," responded a slightly perplexed Thompson.

"But then you get paid for doing your work," Bundy added. "Jerry, you seem to be a pretty good detective. . . ."

"I think I'm a damned good detective," said Thompson soberly.

"But, Jerry, you're just grasping at straws," continued Bundy. There was mirth on his face as he continued, "Just straws, Jerry. But you keep at it, Jerry. If you find enough straws, maybe you can put a broom together."

During that September, Carol DaRonch, who had seen thousands of mug shots, looked at another photo lineup and made a tentative choice of Ted Bundy as her kidnapper. She had also, again rather tentatively, identified his Volkswagen as the car she'd escaped from near the Fashion Mall. By late September the Salt Lake County authorities concluded they had sufficient grounds to summon Bundy to stand in a police lineup so that she could view him in person.

On the afternoon of October 1, 1975, Thompson, with a court order tucked in his inner coat pocket, knocked on Bundy's apartment door. Beside Thompson were Ballantyne and Beal, the two officers from Bountiful. There was no immediate answer. Thompson knocked again. At last Bundy opened the door. Fresh from a shower, he wore only a bath towel wrapped around his waist. His hair, still damp, curled down below the ears.

"Hi, Jerry," said Bundy "To what do I owe the honor of the visit?"

"I've got something here for you, Ted," replied Thompson as he and the other officers entered the small kitchen-living room.

As Thompson extracted the document from his inner pocket, Bundy paled. The officers saw his heart pumping violently against the bare skin of his chest. Thinking he might collapse, Ballantyne moved forward, asking, "Are you all right?"

"Yeah," said Bundy, accepting the document. "I'm fine." He glanced at the court paper, the order to appear in a police lineup the following day. "Oh, is that all?" he asked with obvious relief. "Sure, I'll be there. What's it all about?"

Thompson explained it was mere routine—a lineup at which an eyewitness could examine the appearances of several men. Composed, pleasant, Bundy assured the departing officers he would be there at the appointed hour the next day.

As they descended the stairs, Thompson murmured to the other detectives, "Hell, for a minute there I thought he was gonna pass out." The others agreed.

Alone in his apartment, Bundy checked the time. It was after four o'clock. He'd have time to get to a barber shop and have his long hair cut extremely short.

SEVEN | **Chuggin' Right Along**

Nelson Rockefeller had come to the Western States Republican Conference at Portland during the early days of October 1975, to make the customary plea for party unity and to praise the performance of President Gerald R. Ford. Ross Davis, the Washington State chairman, had traveled to Portland from Seattle with the hope he might orchestrate a little gesture of support for Rockefeller, whose own career was plainly on the wane, urging his fellow state chairmen, most of them conservatives, to support a praise-Rocky resolution. Davis' effort foundered. When the meeting was over, I spotted Davis in the hotel lobby and began making my way through the crowd toward him. I wanted to needle him a bit.

But as I approached, I saw a peculiar look—half smile, half bewilderment—on Davis' face.

"Dick," he said, "I just got the damnedest telephone message from my office. You'll never believe it."

"What was it?"

"Well, we got word that the police down in Salt Lake City have arrested Ted Bundy."

"Ted? You're kidding!"

I remembered dealing with Ted during 1973, that year when he was Davis' top assistant and attended practically all the statewide Republican events. Davis and I had talked often of Ted, speculating about his future in the world of politics.

"What in the world would Ted be arrested for?"

Davis' face still held a half-smile, as though he expected the whole thing might yet turn out to be some bizarre joke—or at least a colossal police error.

"Kidnapping and attempted murder of a young girl."

I laughed. "Aw, c'mon. There's got to be some mistake."

"No, I'm serious. They've got him in jail down there."

Davis' grin of puzzlement faded as he relayed more of the information he'd received. The police, he explained, were claiming that Ted had lured a girl into his car and then tried to kill her.

We stared at each other in silence, sharing a cold thought. *Ted* . . .

"Ted doesn't drive a Volkswagen, does he?" I asked.

"Yes, he does," Davis replied.

Ken Knuckolls, the Washington State Republican National Committeeman and a friend of Davis, arrived to join our conversation. "Ken," said Davis, turning to him, "I think we may be having a little problem we need to talk over."

I left them to discuss it and hurried to a telephone to call my newspaper. Within the newsroom of *The Seattle Times*, and in other newspaper, radio, and TV newsrooms from Salt Lake City to Seattle, there was a flurry of activity, triggered by that first brief wire story out of Utah about Ted's arrest. In a region which had been shocked by the "Ted murders," there was instant speculation over the arrest of a man named Ted who'd driven a Volkswagen and who'd lived in Seattle at the time of the crimes.

By telephone, Lane Smith, my city editor, filled me in on the latest wire-service reports out of Salt Lake City. Ted Bundy was in jail, under $100,000 bail, charged with attempting to kidnap and trying to kill a girl named Carol DaRonch in 1974. The girl had just picked Bundy out of a police lineup, and he had been booked into jail.

"Since you know Bundy," the editor suggested, "why don't you fly over to Salt Lake City and see what's going on? Maybe you can talk to him."

* * *

"Well, this whole thing's just gotten absolutely ridiculous!" Attorney John O'Connell was almost shouting the words into a telephone receiver propped on his left shoulder. The tall, bearded defense lawyer leaned back in his chair behind the desk in his downtown Salt Lake City office.

"They're making Ted out as one of the great mass murderers of all times!" O'Connell sounded both derisive and angry. As I sat across the desk from him, I had no idea who was on the other end of his conversation. On O'Connell's desk, the latest editions of both the *Salt Lake Tribune* and *The Deseret News* had bold headlines about the "Kidnap Suspect," with photographs of Ted. "The reporters," O'Connell continued, "are just running wild." The Salt Lake City news media was speculating about Ted's connection with the Melissa Smith murder and the Debbie Kent disappearance, the Seattle media about Ted's possible connection with all the "Ted" murders up there. The *Seattle P-I* had a summary headline: IS UTAH "TED" THE SEATTLE "TED"?

O'Connell, I had been told, was one of Salt Lake City's most successful criminal defense lawyers—a man with a record of winning the big cases. His partner, Bruce Lubeck, and the Seattle attorney Marlin Vortman, a friend of Ted's who'd also hurried to Salt Lake City following Ted's arrest, were in the office with me, listening as O'Connell continued his tirade into the telephone.

O'Connell began to read into the receiver some of the lower paragraphs of a lengthy *Deseret News* article about Ted. Apparently, said O'Connell, a reporter interviewed the landlord at the apartment where Ted was living and that landlord had said, "The only unusual thing I ever noticed was a two-foot square chopping block he had, the kind you'd find in a meat market. And the way he used shiny metal meat hooks on the ceiling to hold up his pots and pans."

"As though Ted were some sort of a mad butcher!" With an exclamation over the "chopping block" and "meat hooks," O'Connell tossed the newspaper onto his desk and ended the phone conversation.

Apparently O'Connell viewed me with less hostility than he held toward other reporters. Helpfully, Vortman had introduced me as an acquaintance of Ted's from Seattle.

"How's Ted doing in jail?" I asked O'Connell. I assumed he was terrified.

Ted was doing as well as anyone could after being thrown into jail and suddenly, while an innocent person, being portrayed as some sort of a mass murderer, the lawyer replied.

O'Connell rose from his desk and prepared to leave the office with Lubeck and Vortman to go visit Ted in the nearby jail. "I'd really like to be able to talk with Ted if I could," I said.

O'Connell frowned and said he doubted that would be possible. Under jail policy, Ted was only being allowed visits with his lawyers. Besides, said O'Connell, he didn't want Ted generating any more publicity about the case. But, the lawyer hinted, I might later place a telephone call to the visitors' room of the Salt Lake County jail, the place where they'd been having their meeting. Thus, by telephone, I might at least be able to say hello to Ted.

While I waited to make that telephone call, I considered how desperately frightened, how anguished Ted must feel at that moment—to be jailed in an unfamiliar city, to be jailed *anywhere,* facing an ominous criminal charge while everyone engaged in speculation about all those cruel murders. If I were in that situation, I thought, I'd be clawing the walls of the jail, screaming my innocence.

My telephone call into the interview room at the jail was surprisingly quick and successful. It was startling to hear Ted's voice at the other end of the line, saying, "Hi, Dick, how are you?"

"Ted," I exclaimed. I was almost breathless with concern about his plight. "How *are* you?"

"Well," Ted responded calmly, "we're just chuggin' right along."

There seemed to be an almost serene control—even a smile—in his voice.

In an instant of silence, I slowly swallowed what he'd said and the unusual way he'd said it: *chuggin' right along.*

Where was that scream of innocence?

"Dick," he added, "I'm not really sure what we can talk about. You realize that I really can't comment on the charges that are pending." He was precise and lawyerlike as he pointed out how his attorneys had forbidden him to discuss the case. I replied that I understood that. There'd be no questions relating to the charges, I assured him, but I wanted to know how he was feeling, how he was being treated, if he had any message to be delivered to his friends in Seattle.

He replied that his jail conditions were okay. Then he added, "One thing you can write is that I really appreciate the expressions of support and offers of help I've had from all my friends up in Seattle."

For a moment I wondered how, locked away in jail, he could have received so many expressions of support. Perhaps Vortman, the Seattle attorney, had brought that assurance to him.

"One thing that concerns me," Ted's youthful voice continued, "is that the news media interest in me causes harassment of my family and friends."

The ground rules he had set for our conversation limited the scope of my questioning. Soon our conversation ended. I wished him luck. He sounded self-assured as we said goodbye.

About a week later, after I'd returned to Seattle, I received from Ted an "open letter to the public," which he asked be published in *The Times*. I took it to Smith, my city editor, who read it:

I address this letter to my many friends and acquaintances who have offered their prayers, concern and support in my behalf. When time permits, I shall do my best to reply personally to each of you. You are truly beautiful people. Your encouragement is the light at the end of the tunnel.

I think of you constantly. I think of our beautiful state and the incomparable loveliness of our Seattle, the breathtaking vistas, which are, for you, part of your daily life are, for me, mind-woven tapestries which color the gray walls. I envy you.

The law is a curious animal. To a law student it becomes highly abstract and impersonal. To a defendant, in my position, it offers incredible new perspectives. The excesses of the system are slight in comparison to the protections it affords each of us, defendant or not. I have great confidence in its ultimate product: Justice.

God bless you.—TED BUNDY

"If I were in his situation," observed Smith, "I think I'd be screaming my head off that the cops made a mistake."

As I reread Ted's letter, I concluded it reminded me of some political speeches I'd occasionally heard from candidates or officeholders who were in trouble—a salute to the system, with the implicit message that he was innocent and would eventually be cleared. I had a brief fantasy about Ted—how, after all this publicity had made him a celebrity, after he'd proved his total innocence, he'd return home and run for high office.

EIGHT | Reflections

November 24, 1946.

Theodore Robert Bundy's date of birth was the starting point, the initial entry at the upper left, of the expanse of paper, almost twenty feet long, stretched across one wall of the Ted Squad headquarters in downtown Seattle.

· The detectives had taped strips of butcher paper, one above the other, almost floor to ceiling. It was the detectives' visual aid, their battle map, as they made their telephone calls, dug through whatever records they could find, or legged it from interview to interview—"Let's keep this confidential please," they always asked—trying to reconstruct the dates, times, and places of Ted Bundy's whereabouts and movements.

Gradually, through late summer and early autumn, 1975, their findings were translated into jottings across the field of paper.

Detective Roger Dunn, a young investigator with the burly build of a fullback, was given the unlikely appointment of "project art director."

Across the top, from left to right, were written the years. Then Dunn had lined the sheets with horizontal stripes of color. Easier to cross-reference that way, he explained—with colors. An orange line was *Employment*—places and dates of Bundy's employment through the years, and his daily work records, if they could be found. A yellow line for *Republican Party*—those meetings, conventions, appointments of any kind that placed Bundy somewhere in some party activity. *Gas slips,* a green line—records of charges made to Bundy's gasoline credit card, gas purchases, and repairs to his Volkswagen. *Friends,* a purple line—the record of dates and places and times when he was known to be with other people at some place at a social event.

At the far right sector of the chart, Dunn had assigned a magnified scale to the year 1974, the year of the crimes. Each of the year's months had its own ample vertical column to record Bundy's daily movements.

Above, in the 1974 section, in jolting red capital letters, were the names of the victims: CLARKE 1/4 . . . HEALY 1/31 . . . MANSON 3/12 . . . and the others.

Dunn walked from his desk to the 1974 section of the chart, twisted the cap from the tip of a black marking pen and, on an orange horizontal line for Bundy's *Credit cards,* lettered a new entry under May:

"5/14 bought Adidas tennis shoes at Nordstrom's Northgate."

Dunn stepped back to study his lettering. Then he moved left to the column for March '74, bent down to the green line for *Activity,* and lettered a new entry:

"3/27 picked up unemployment check."

From his desk, Keppel examined the product of their work and sighed over the gaps.

Dunn folded his shirt-sleeved arms and joined Keppel's contemplation of their wall chart, especially the red-capital-lettered names of victims.

CLARKE—the girl attacked, brutalized as she slept in her downstairs bedroom. Beneath her name was the notation of Bundy's residence at the time: "Lived four blocks away."

Just right of CLARKE, at the top, HEALY—Lynda Ann Healy, vanished from her apartment, subsequently found on Taylor Mountain. Below the name was the notation of Bundy's residence: "Lived 15 blocks away."

Atop the July column of 1974 stood the double entries, in red: OTT AND NASLUND, 7/14.

Below, on the intersecting orange line, some entries, circled, leaped toward the eye: "Absent from work." Employment records at the Washington State Department of Emergency Services, Bundy's place of employment that summer, revealed that Bundy had, without excuse, missed work July 11 and 12. That was the Thursday-Friday before the Sunday Janice and Denise walked out of Lake Sammamish State Park with "Ted." Bundy also missed work July 15 and 16, the following Monday-Tuesday.

Keppel's eye fixed on the column for May 1974. "He's buying gas there on May fourteenth."

Dunn grunted. "Yeah. He's doing lots of driving."

Bundy had made two credit-card gas purchases on that day—the day Kathy Parks disappeared from Oregon State University, about 250 miles south of Seattle. But there were no gas charges, no trace of him in southwest Washington or Oregon that day. Bundy's two gas charges had been made at Seattle stations, not far from where Bundy lived.

If Bundy's Volkswagen was averaging twenty-eight miles to the gallon, a full ten-gallon tank would allow 280 miles of driving—just about enough to drive one way from Corvallis to Seattle, perhaps to Taylor Mountain east of Seattle.

"He's got checking-account activity that day," mused Dunn, nodding toward another entry on the chart. Bundy that day wrote two checks to cash on his account—one for fifteen dollars, the other for five dollars.

"So if he had to stop somewhere and buy gas, he had the cash to do it," Keppel concluded. "And the girl had cash in her purse, too."

The detectives were being overtaken by frustration. They had not found a trail of facts that would place Bundy at or near the scene of a crime at the time it happened. Nor any that would put him, in time and place, away from any of the crimes.

Along their chart's horizontal line of *Activities* were sprinkled the entries of some social events where Bundy was known to be present—a dinner at Susan's house in March . . . a trip to the Ellensburg area for river rafting on a June afternoon . . . an evening with some friends in Olympia. . . .

But no one had come forward to report he was with Ted Bundy in Seattle at ten o'clock the night Kathy Parks was disappearing in Oregon. Or the night Susan Rancourt was vanishing at Ellensburg.

"The only one who can answer our questions, I guess, is Mister Bundy," sighed Keppel. And Ted Bundy, in jail in Salt Lake City, was following the advice of his attorney and not talking to the police.

Publicly, Captain Mackie sought to take a cool position about Bundy's possible involvement in the crimes. Looking drawn and exhausted, Mackie held a news conference in Seattle in early October to announce that six women who'd seen "Ted" at Lake Sammamish fifteen months earlier had failed to identify photos of Theodore Bundy as the man they saw there.

Pointedly, Mackie declared, "There is no concrete evidence of any type that this man [Bundy] is our Ted." Technically, Mackie was correct. There was nothing concrete. Two of the eight Lake Sammamish witnesses had picked out Bundy from a photo lineup, identifying him as the Ted, the man with his arm in a sling, at the park that day. Mackie was trying to cool the news media's hot rush toward Bundy and protect his witnesses.

In the stampede to interview associates and friends of Bundy, reporters produced a stream of reaction reports during that October. From nearly every source, from his friends and associates, came recollections of Ted filled with warm praise. SUSPECT "SUPER NICE" SAY ACQUAINTANCES—the headline was typical.

Supervisors and co-workers at the Washington State Department of Emergency Services remembered Ted as a valuable employee during the summer of 1974. He had been assigned to do budget work—to write the factual narrative which would accompany the agency's biennial budget request which would go to the governor and to the legislature.

"His desk was just across from mine," said one young woman. "He was a great friend to me at a time when I desperately needed a crutch." For her, the 1974 summer was a period of deep personal upset. She was experiencing the pain of a difficult divorce. And Ted "guided me through that summer . . . got me going again. He was the sort of person I would have trusted my life with."

There was an irony in the fact that Ted had been thrust into the news with a charge that he committed a crime against a young woman in a shopping mall in Utah. The first time Ted Bundy's name appeared in the Seattle press was because of his heroics on behalf of a woman in a shopping mall in North Seattle. *The Seattle Times* on January 10, 1973, reported:

> Ted Bundy, 26, who was assistant director of the Seattle Crime Commission . . . caught a man who had snatched a woman's purse in the Northgate Mall parking area Monday night.
>
> Police said Bundy chased the man on foot on First Avenue Northeast and caught him as he was stuffing the purse into a garbage can. The suspect was turned over to the police and is being held on suspicion of robbery.
>
> The suspect, police said, grabbed the purse of Darlene M. Covey as she walked toward her car with her two children. Police said Bundy recovered from the suspect the $34 that had been taken from the purse. . . .

For Ted, a man who publicly allied himself with law enforcement, the clipping was a treasure to be folded and carried in his wallet.

In Salt Lake City, a Mormon missionary, enthused that Ted, who had been baptized in the Church of the Latter Day Saints on August 30, 1975, had impressed him as an intelligent, very earnest young man. The missionary, with beaming confidence, told a reporter, "I wouldn't hesitate to line him up with my sister."

That quote would be used and reused often as the news

media reported the diversity of impressions of Ted. The missionary recalled how Ted had explained that his interest in Mormonism had begun with academic curiosity, then flowered into a positive personal faith in the Church. Ted had participated in a Latter Day Saints retreat late that summer at Bear Lake, a spectacularly scenic place of mountains and woods and water in north Utah, and there was no doubt in the minds of the Mormons who met Ted that he was destined for a shining future in the Church. Soon, they knew, Ted would be a missionary, then, no doubt, an elder.

Among the persons who began trying to raise money for Ted's bond and legal costs was Marian Duvall, a longtime activist in a Washington Republican women's organization. The Seattle woman had known and worked with Ted during the 1972 campaign for governor and had come to love him as though he were a son. She cried over what they were saying about Ted in the media.

"I just feel so sorry for Ted, I can't express it," she sobbed. "I just can't understand how the police could do such a thing to such a wonderful boy. And the hell that his poor mother must be going through."

Seattle Times reporter Paul Henderson seemed to share my misgivings about our late October interview with Mr. and Mrs. Bundy. As we drove toward the Bundy home in Tacoma, Henderson reflected, "I've never before had to ask a mother, 'How does it feel to have your son in jail and suspected of being one of the great mass murderers of all time?'"

Henderson guided the car to a stop at the curb of the 3200 block on Twentieth Avenue South in Tacoma, in front of a neatly groomed, compact two-story house. It was in an orderly, quiet neighborhood of middle-class homes and small yards, lined along a concrete sidewalk, which was heaved up gently here and there by the nudging of old tree roots. The Bundy home had the sturdy livable look of many Northwest frame houses built in earlier decades by careful Scandinavian carpenters. Louise Bundy greeted us at the door with a pleasant smile. She was a tiny woman, with light brown hair and light blue eyes, almost birdlike in her movements. "Come in," she said, leading us into a comfortable living room.

"This is my husband, Johnnie Bundy," she said brightly. With a shy smile, the diminutive, mostly bald man with dark-rimmed glasses, stepped forward to shake our hands. He appeared not much taller than Louise.

Louise offered us places to sit in the grouping of comfortable furniture in front of a fireplace.

We thanked the Bundys for allowing us into their home at such a turbulent time. With a determined smile, Louise confessed she harbored some unkind feelings about most people in the news media. Those others, she said, "seem to be just as determined as they can be to say all kinds of awful things about Ted. Without ever questioning whether or not they have the facts!"

Henderson and I nodded our heads in understanding.

As I examined her, I concluded Mrs. Bundy's face bore a remarkable similarity to Ted's. She had a much more fair complexion. But the brow line, the alert look in the eyes, the forehead, the slender nose, the cheeks, rounded by a smile, were very much like Ted's. There was a reminder of Ted, too, in her fixed smile of composure.

"Mrs. Bundy. Uh—to begin . . ." said Henderson. "How would you describe the kind of son Ted has been?"

"Oh," the mother replied, "Ted has always been just the best son in the world." Her words came out almost lyrically, and her clasped hands almost bounced in her lap. "He was just always a very thoughtful person. At times I wondered if he would forget Mother's Day, because of the busy schedule in his life. But he always showed up with a gift on Mother's Day. Once it was a big fuschia plant. Another time it was a geranium." Her hands flowed in a circling gesture, to illustrate the size of the plant.

She recalled the fondness Ted always showed toward his two brothers and two sisters and how they, in turn, adored and respected him. She talked about his boyhood years, his paper route, his boy-scout days, and his involvement in Methodist church activities. "Ted always liked school, and he always did real well in school," she went on.

Johnnie sat in the background, leaning forward listening to his wife.

She remembered, too, how Ted's interest in politics and the law had begun and grown. "He'd always wanted to be a policeman or a lawyer. And Ted just loved politics. He was always talking politics. And he had his heroes. He was a Rockefeller man. He worked for Rockefeller. And, of course, Governor Evans was his special."

Louise's voice bubbled with the happy memories. "When Governor Evans grew a beard, why, of course, Ted grew a beard, too. . . ." She grinned, wrinkled her nose, and gestured to indicate she hadn't liked Ted's beard.

At one time, Louise remembered, Ted was keenly interested in the People's Republic of China, especially the possibility of restored relationships between the United States and China. Ted had begun his work at the University of Washington as a major in Chinese studies, and at one time, he'd gone to California for a summer session of Chinese studies at Stanford University.

"Ted would come home here, and he'd start speaking Chinese to us. You know, this sing-song sound . . ." Louise laughed at that memory, too. Ted was very good with accents and dialects.

"Ted was a very hard worker, always on the go."

My eye moved across the living room. It was extremely tidy and, though small, quite comfortable. Around the white-painted wood mantel of the fireplace were small leaded-glass windows. In some glassdoor cabinets were the usual ceramic knickknacks which a family would collect. Near the entryway, at the front door, rose a staircase which led, no doubt, to upstairs bedrooms. As inviting as the house was, I somehow had expected Ted's family home to be larger, more lavish. Ted had always impressed me, and others, as a young man who had come from a well-to-do background.

Johnnie Bundy was employed as a cook at Madigan Army Hospital, part of an Army-Air Force military complex south of Tacoma. Louise worked as a secretary at the University of Puget Sound, a few blocks from their home.

"How long have you been married?" Henderson asked.

"Twenty-four years," Louise replied.

Thinking of Ted's age at that time—twenty-eight—Henderson asked, "So this is your second marriage, Mrs. Bundy?"

She nodded, smiling.

I glanced at Johnnie in the background, conspicuously out

of the conversation. He watched and listened passively. It was apparent that Louise was the dominant force in the household.

Louise told us about Ted's girlfriend—Cas, a nice girl, Louise added, whom Ted had been dating for years. She was a Mormon. "And Ted joined the Mormon Church, you know. They were planning to be married in December."

Again, Henderson and I nodded in silent unison, showing our compassion for those whose lives and plans now had been so disrupted.

There was always a closeness in the Bundy family, Louise continued. Ted had many friends and often brought them home. When Ted went off to the University of Utah, Louise recalled, his brother Glenn helped him move. "Ted had bought this old pickup truck to move his things down to Salt Lake City. Just an awful old broken-down thing. I didn't think they'd ever make it all the way to Utah in the thing. But off they went. . . ."

Again she laughed lightly with a happy memory.

Henderson and I turned the conversation as gently as possible toward the tender question of the murdered young women and the police suspicions of Ted. Louise's smile remained on her lips, but abruptly her eyes cooled.

"Well, I just know my son," she began. "And I know he could never do any harm to anyone."

Louise's face was rigid with determination. She remembered one time, during 1974, when there was news about all the disappearing girls, Ted had been visiting home one evening when he noticed his younger sister, Sandra, preparing to go out on a date. "And Ted said to me, 'You know, Mom, she looks like all those other girls.' Her hair was kind of long and parted in the middle. She was nineteen at the time. And Ted said, 'Mom, I hope you know where she's going and who she's with.'

"He was always very protective."

Never, never, Louise insisted, was there any hint that Ted was anything other than a model son—certainly not the type of person who committed all those murders. Why, she wondered, didn't the police, instead of wasting all this time, massing all their investigation against Ted, "go out and catch the *real* criminal?"

"My son drove a Volkswagen, and his name was Ted. But I know it wasn't him."

In the background, Johnnie nodded in solemn agreement.

Henderson asked her if there were any way she could conceive of Ted committing such crimes.

Her response came slowly, thoughtfully, evenly: "Unless he looked right at me and said he did it, I would not believe it."

Our interview was ending. Henderson and I had risen and were thanking the Bundys for their hospitality. In a fumbling way I tried to offer some comfort to Louise. "Mrs. Bundy, y'know . . ." I began. "There are all those dates when—uh—all those girls disappeared. Now, if there's any way you can, by thinking back, come up with any dates—any date—when Ted might have been here with you, or anywhere else that you know of ... . You know, some date that would put Ted somewhere else on that date, just let us know and we'll go after it." I said it almost imploringly. It would be a relief to be able to disprove the police theory, to lift the burden of pain from this little woman. Besides, I thought, it would be a great news story—to come up with a clean alibi for Ted. Perhaps he was at the family home, watching TV, on a night when one of the girls disappeared miles away.

Ted's mother, quietly, directly, returned my gaze. She said nothing.

I thought I sensed a nod of understanding behind her look. But she had no suggestion to offer.

Once outside in the car, as Henderson eased away from the curb, we released long sighs. I reflected how Ted's mother had seemed almost mechanical in her responses to us, as though she had rehearsed, carefully, the memories she would relate to us.

"Paul," I said, "I get a little feeling, talking to her, that Ted's mother has had a bone-deep feeling for some time that her son might not be the All-American boy."

Henderson shrugged. "Maybe so."

Louise was a demure twenty-two-year-old single woman, living in Philadelphia, when she became pregnant in early 1946. Little was ever known outside the family about the father of the child, except that he was a man who had been in the military service.

The day was yet to come when, in a working-class Philadelphia neighborhood, a single girl could comfortably remain at home to have her baby. Louise went away to Vermont, to the Elizabeth Lund Home for Unwed Mothers at Burlington, where her baby boy was born on November 24, 1946. In all, she had spent sixty-three days at the home when Louise returned with her baby to her Philadelphia home.

"He was always just a wonderful baby," she would remember. He was named Theodore Robert Cowell, "Cowell" being Louise's maiden family name.

Ted grew into toddlerhood at the home of his grandparents. Louise's little boy was four when she had his name legally changed to Theodore Robert Nelson. Soon thereafter, Louise accepted an invitation from her brother and his family to move west, to Washington State, to their home in Tacoma.

At Tacoma, a Puget Sound harbor and mill town, Louise and her little boy were welcomed by her relatives and were accepted lovingly into the circle of fellowship of the Methodist Church. It was through church activities that Louise met Johnnie Bundy, a thirty-year-old native of North Carolina, a gentle, retiring man with a soft Carolina accent who worked as a cook at the nearby Madigan military hospital.

After Johnnie and Louise were married May 17, 1951, Louise's young son took his third and final name: Theodore Robert Bundy. During their first three years of marriage, the Bundys lived in an older house in an aging neighborhood in Tacoma where Ted entered the old Stanley Elementary School.

Later the family moved to a compact frame house on Skyline Drive, in a suburban area of Tacoma, not far from the regionally famous Narrows suspension bridge, a graceful span which crosses a narrow, tide-churned saltwater stretch of lower Puget Sound. The little house on Skyline would be Ted's home through the remainder of his public school days, at Geiger Elementary School, Hunt Junior High, and Woodrow Wilson High School.

Not long after their marriage, Louise began having Johnnie's children—first Linda, then Glenn, then Sandra, and eventually Richard. So, while Ted was going through the grades of school, his mother was at home, caring for her new babies.

Ted's fourth-grade teacher at Geiger remembered him as "neither one of the good ones, or the bad ones. He seemed like a happy, well-adjusted child . . . always eager to learn." Mrs. Bundy was active in the Parent-Teacher Association. One teacher recalled, "She was a hard worker. They didn't have a lot of money."

In high school, where most of the other students came from more comfortable homes, Ted earned above-average grades and attracted some attention from girls. He was a serious boy with sharply defined dark brows and close-cropped wavy hair. "My girlfriend had kind of a crush on him," one young woman remembers of those days at Wilson High. "But he never seemed to be very interested." "Nice and polite" . . . "Kind of quiet" . . . "Not a troublemaker"—those were the rather uniform recollections of him among the Bundys' neighbors who lived in the other small houses along the Skyline.

Ted graduated from Wilson in 1965 with a B-plus average, found a summertime job doing warehouse work for Tacoma City Light, the municipal electric utility, and bought his first car, a 1933 Plymouth coupe. His first year of college was spent, near home, at the University of Puget Sound, a conservative, stolid institution on a tree-covered campus not far from the Bundys' small house. At UPS, where the student body was comprised of high achievers, most of them from well-to-do homes, Ted felt ill at ease. During that period, he later confessed, he "had a longing for a beautiful coed," but simultaneously, he acknowledged, "I didn't have the skill or social acumen to cope with it."

After a lonely year at UPS, Ted decided to move away from home and enroll at the University of Washington in Seattle, about thirty miles to the north.

There Ted met a striking, dark-haired young woman and entered into, as he put it, "my first real involvement." Diane came from a wealthy California family, was further ahead in college than Ted, drove a bright red Mustang, and often provided the money for their dates. Although he felt inferior in many ways and once conceded they were "worlds apart," Ted and Diane's relationship would persist for several years.

Ted's performance in the classroom was erratic. After the first quarter of 1967, having received several incompletes, Ted acknowledged he was having emotional troubles, withdrew from school, and traveled to visit relatives in Philadelphia and Arkansas. Eventually he reentered the University of Washington and in 1972 received his bachelor's degree in psychology.

Ted's involvement in politics became a source of new self-confidence. When he first worked in the 1968 Rockefeller campaign, then later that year in the campaign of Republican Art Fletcher for lieutenant governor of Washington, he felt a sense of belonging and accomplishment.

Simultaneously, Ted had developed a close relationship with a new woman, Cas Richter, a divorcée he had met in a chance encounter at a bar one evening. A rather plain-looking, vulnerable woman, Cas was in her twenties, holding down a job, living alone with her young daughter not far from the University District. "He was very sympathetic, very understanding, very tender," said Cas—at a time when she needed sympathy, understanding, and tenderness. They began spending more and more time together, and while Ted still remained personally fascinated by the beautiful Diane, his relationship with Cas persisted.

After he received his bachelor's degree in psychology, Ted took a part-time job as a counselor at the Crisis Clinic at Seattle's Harborview Medical Center, an around-the-clock telephone counseling service for callers experiencing emotional troubles. Ted made friends among his co-workers, but at least one of them sensed he found the work boring and depressing. "Ted," reflected one woman, "always seemed to respond to the callers with sort of a cold lecture, telling them they should learn to discipline their emotions, to take charge. He didn't seem to have . . . the compassion, the understanding that these people were unable to take control."

In an aside, she recalled Ted once saying, "We've got chronic schizos calling in here, and we're supposed to deal with them. We don't have the training or the background to handle these kinds of cases."

Ted threw himself wholeheartedly into Governor Dan Evans' reelection campaign of 1972—the race against Democrat Al Rosellini. Keith Dysart, who was serving as Evans' campaign manager, recalled, "I told Ted that all I wanted him to do was keep track of what Rosellini was doing and saying on the issues. But there was just no controlling Ted. He was always coming back with memos that were too long to read, too much information."

With help from one of his former professors, Ted landed a staff job on the Seattle Crime Prevention Advisory Commission, a short-term, federally funded agency. Despite its prestigious name, Ted reflected, "it was a nothing organization. No money, no real power or function. All the other cities had a crime commission and so Wes Uhlman [Seattle's mayor, a Democrat whom Ted disliked] thought we ought to have a crime commission, too."

Later Ted set himself up as a consultant in the field of law enforcement, securing a contract with the Republican administration in the King County courthouse to carry out a criminal-justice study, funded by a federal law-and-justice planning grant. Ted signed the contract as "T.R.B. Associates"—a little flourish, suggesting that he had a consulting organization.

Through several rewarding months of 1973, Ted served as assistant to Ross Davis, chairman of the Washington State Republican party—a job which enabled Ted to travel extensively across the state, meet new people, add another bright star of experience to his résumé. "Ted was just a super bright guy," Davis recalled. "And an effective worker." Ted was still living in his University District apartment on Seattle's Twelfth Avenue Northeast, and because the party headquarters then was near Olympia, Ted frequently stayed overnight at the Davis home. "We just all loved Ted," remembered Ross' wife, Sarah. Frequently, Ted served cheerfully as the Davis babysitter, caring for their two young daughters.

All the accolades, all the praise-filled remembrances of Ted fell into place to form a portrait of a bright young man of accomplishment, warmth, and sincerity.

Yet, from some who knew him, there came memories that produced dark shadows.

Mrs. Flora McGregor, a dignified woman in her sixties, had enjoyed a comfortable life until she was widowed in 1962. In the late 1960s she found herself working as a pastry cook at the Seattle Yacht Club. There, in 1966, she met the new busboy, Ted, a handsome, curly-haired university student with a ready smile and a flair for conversation.

Once in a while Ted would knock at the front door of her small house, near the edge of the University District. Mrs. McGregor would invite him in and sometimes fix a snack for him. "He was always borrowing money from me," she recalled.

Years after it happened, Mrs. McGregor angrily remembered that trip Ted took in 1967.

"He was going back to that uncle of his in Philadelphia, and he wanted to borrow a hundred dollars from me. He said the uncle would make it good. So I loaned him the hundred dollars to take the trip.

"And then that morning he was going to go, he telephoned me and wondered if I'd take him out to the airport. First I told him no, but then, well, I did. I went over and picked him up. He was all packed and everything. He had some skis, all wrapped up in a fancy leather case with a zipper and everything. . . . He had on a new coat with a big fur collar and all interlined and all. And new trousers which looked like they were tailor-made. You could tell he had too much money. . . ."

While she was driving Ted to the airport, he told her that, on his flight to Philadelphia, he planned to stop off at Aspen. Mrs. McGregor frowned at that. Then, after she'd left Ted off at the airport, she began to seethe. Why should she be lending *him* money—poor as *she* was—so that he could stop off at Aspen and have a fine old time? Aspen, she knew, was an expensive place.

So Mrs. McGregor telephoned Ted's mother in Tacoma to complain about what Ted was doing. "I told his mother, 'He owes me a hundred dollars.'

"And his mother said she didn't know anything about what he was doing. She said, 'He never calls home anymore. We never see him. He's over there in Seattle, but we don't know where. We never see him.' His mother said she didn't even know what his telephone number was."

When Ted returned from that trip to Aspen and Philadelphia that year, he once again came knocking at Mrs. Mc-

Gregor's door. "He showed up just as big as life," the woman recalled. "He said he didn't have my hundred dollars for me, but he promised he'd get it. He was a regular visitor again. Once he wanted to borrow my best china and good silver settings, because he was preparing a fancy dinner at his apartment for that girlfriend of his who had come up from San Francisco."

Mrs. McGregor lent him her dinnerware. Ted described to Mrs. McGregor his plans for that dinner and, she remembered, demonstrated how he would dress for the occasion—in a waiter's jacket and satin-striped black trousers. "He looked like a real smart-looking waiter, all right. And he even had a clever English accent which he'd use during the dinner service to really impress the girl."

When Ted was arrested and charged in Utah, Larry Voshall's memory was jogged. "I'd known Ted only casually," explained Voshall. "We'd met around the legislature a few times." Voshall, a former newspaper reporter, was serving in 1974 as a public information specialist in the Washington State House of Representatives.

"It was June, and Ted invited me to go on a river-rafting trip with him over to the Yakima River. Ted apparently was very much into river rafting." Eventually their plans grew to include a foursome. Susan Reade, a mutual friend, was invited to go along, and she in turn suggested that her girlfriend, Becky, go along, too.

They left Seattle in two cars, Becky riding with Ted in his Volkswagen, Susan traveling with Larry in his sedan. "Neither girl knew how to swim very well," Voshall recalled, "and they were both a little apprehensive about river rafting. So we all stopped off at a sporting goods shop and bought some lifejackets for the girls."

After the two-hour drive across the mountains, they stopped beside the river where Ted and Larry placed the rubber raft in the water. "Even before we started," said Voshall, "Ted's mood seemed to change. I'd always thought of him as being a rather cheerful person, usually in a good mood, but I got a new look at him that day.

"We started down the river, with three of us in the raft and the fourth person in an innertube tied on behind the raft."

The Yakima meanders through farmlands and forests, then sometimes drops into swift white-water rapids. Susan and Becky squealed with beginner's fright through the first stretch of rough water.

"Well, all at once, Ted, who's behind Becky, unties the string of her halter top. The halter top fell off, exposing her breasts. We were all just flabbergasted, embarrassed. You know, we didn't really know each other at all. Ted seemed to get some strange kick out of that.

"Later on we were in a pretty swift current, and Becky was behind the raft in the innertube. Ted reached for the rope and said, 'What'll you do if I untie this rope?'

"Well, Becky's screaming. Just scared to death. And I looked at Ted's face, and I couldn't believe it. He had a look on his face as though he was *enjoying* subjecting her to that terror—hearing her *scream!*

"He had untied the rope. And I really got upset. I got hold of the rope and tied the innertube back to the raft. And I told him we'd better be more careful because the girls can't swim. But Ted was in this grim mood, as though he was angry at all of us. . . .

"Later Susan and I talked about it, and we both agreed we'd seen a side of Ted we never knew was there. I'll never forget how he seemed to enjoy subjecting that girl to terror."

Voshall placed the date of that river-rafting trip as late June 1974, two or three weeks before the Lake Sammamish disappearances.

NINE | Summit Conference

The stern-looking men crossing the lobby of Aspen's Holiday Inn conspicuously did not belong among the skiers or other seasonal fun seekers who check into the high-priced lodges of this fashionable Rocky Mountain resort. They were law-enforcement men, wearing casual clothing, carrying brief-cases and notebooks. They passed the registration desk, striding purposefully toward a meeting room, trying to ignore the news reporters who buzzed around them.

"Excuse me," said a reporter to one of the passing men. "Where are *you* from?"

"Uh—Grand Junction," replied the plainclothesman without slowing.

Thirty detectives and prosecutors had come to Aspen in mid-November 1975—it was the off-season, and only a foot of snow covered nearby Buttermilk Mountain—for what was officially the Intermountain States Law Enforcement Conference. News reports about the event would use the catchier name "Aspen Summit Conference." In the bar, over drinks, the waiting reporters kiddingly referred to it as "the Bundy huddle."

Theodore Bundy, in jail in Salt Lake City, had become a hot suspect in an increasing number of crimes in a widening zone of the West. The lawmen came together to compare dozens of similar, unsolved cases of murdered girls and young women in several states—California, Oregon, Washington, Utah, Colorado. It intrigued the news gatherers that Captain Edwin (Butch) Carlstadt had flown in from northern California for the session.

For years Carlstadt had been at the frustrating task of tracking California's so-called Zodiac killer. One after another, Carlstadt had investigated murders of girls and young women in northern California—fourteen or more between December 1969 and December 1973—in which the victims, often hitchhikers, were found nude, without clothing or other belongings. Near the bodies was found an elaborate witch-craft symbol of twigs and rocks.

Aspen's Carroll Whitmire, sheriff of Pitkin County, sought to quiet the mosquitoish reporters who swarmed around the gathering of lawmen. In his cowboy hat, Western suit, and boots, the sheriff assured the visiting newsmen: "You're sure welcome to visit Aspen. But I'm afraid there won't be anything for you to report out of this meeting. We're not goin' to have anything to announce for you."

"What's the purpose of the meeting, sheriff?"

"We just want to put all these cases into one basket. . . . Perhaps something can come out of this." He conceded the obvious: "We'll be discussing Theodore Bundy, sure, but not just Bundy alone."

Inside the closed meeting room, the officers, getting acquainted with each other, took places around tables, spread out notepads, uncapped pens, and took a fraternal vow of secrecy about the proceedings. A guard was posted at the door to prevent eavesdropping. (In fact, more than a year would elapse before any of the proceedings were leaked.)

Detective Keppel of Seattle, opening some of his file folders, positioned himself at the speaker's stand to begin describing how Seattle's Ted Squad, through the previous eleven weeks, had investigated Bundy.

"Things were rather sketchy about his early life, his early years," Keppel began, "mainly because the crucial people we talked to—his cousin, his mother—have this particular image of him where he could do no wrong.

"At age thirteen—we ran across one individual who knew him then—he was rather naive about sex at that period of time in his life. When, any time, anyone would mention sex, he would shove, push, run, go away, whatever was appropriate.

"He's left-handed, and he's left-eyed, whatever that means."

At the tables, dotted with coffee pots, cups, ashtrays, briefcases, and legal pads, Keppel's audience scribbled notes. It was to be more than the usual rundown on a conventional suspect. Some Seattle psychiatrists, enlisted to advise the Ted Squad, had urged Keppel and the other detectives to seek out details of Bundy's early years, his relationships with others, his sexual proclivities, any other clues to his psychological makeup. Keppel's presentation stabbed into some of those zones.

Keppel hadn't come to Aspen to praise Bundy. In tones dripping with dislike, the detective proceeded to sketch a consistently unflattering portrait of the suspect.

"Up through the fifth grade he was constantly displaying babyish activities. He was rather a loner, didn't want to get involved with too many people at the time. He liked to do superior work when he did it. That doesn't mean that he did do superior work. He just liked to pass this on in school—this impression that he did do superior work. His character was such that he was too good for any sort of discipline. I don't know whether this led from his mother's emphasis or what."

Try as they might, the Seattle detectives had never been able to discover any proof of homosexual tendencies or activities in Bundy's life. That would, in their view, have been an expectable characteristic in a man suspected of violence against women.

But Keppel had some revelations for his audience about Bundy's heterosexual relationships—vignettes which had been divulged, with reluctance and fear, by the women in Bundy's life. One was a vivacious brunette whom Bundy dated during the time he was cheating on Cas. "He used to take her on various trips, and he seemed to be very, very familiar with areas east of Seattle that we are interested in. They drove on specific roads where our bodies were found. . . ." said Keppel.

"We finally drug out of her that they went to a little picnic down on the beach in Washington, and the beach was overcast. So they went back farther inland where the sun was and went to a place he knew about. . . . She was more or less tainted by alcohol."

Their sexual intercourse, the young woman had said, "'was more of a slam-bam-thank-you-ma'am sex act.' But what she could remember about it was that she couldn't breathe," said Keppel. "He had his forearm right across her neck. And she kept yelling at him that she couldn't breathe. And finally, when he was finished, he pulled it off. But he had no knowledge what he was doing at the time."

That had occurred in 1972. The listening detectives jotted down the date.

Outwardly, Keppel explained, Bundy gave the appearance of an energetic, skillful, bright young man, moving from job to job, gaining his education, moving upward in life. But Keppel drew an otherwise portrait—of a young man who dipped into petty thievery, used his boyish good looks and charm to exploit and manipulate others, and who seemed to lack an inner discipline to finish any major task. Bundy's brief career in law classes had been flawed by absenteeism and unfinished work.

Keppel recalled some vague suspicions which arose around Bundy when he had his part-time job at the Olympic Hotel in downtown Seattle. "He worked there for about a month. The people were kind of skeptical, because they were experiencing thefts from lockers. And so they let him go. There were no official charges drawn up against him. There were no official accusations. They just thought it better that he leave. So he left."

Keppel reviewed Bundy's jobs with law enforcement, beginning with the crime-prevention commission, followed by his contract with King County as "T.R.B. Associates" to study recidivism among criminal offenders.

"His specific duties were to study recidivism rates among offenders in the King County jail. To do this he had to delve into police reports. . . . The main thing about it was that he knew about offenders and how screwed up our system was in keeping track [of crimes and criminals]. He is very familiar with problems of police jurisdictions. He had constant talks with people about this when he talked about sexual assaults on women—with the problems of police agencies, just down the line [which] would have a sexual assault on a girl and then wouldn't ever even contact the [next] police agency. . . ."

Keppel allowed the implication of that to fall heavily on the ears of the lawmen in his audience, the notion that they were considering a man who understood police jurisdictions and boundaries, who was familiar with their vulnerability—their imperfect exchange of information with each other.

None of the detectives wished to talk about—even think about—those months during which crimes were being committed while both Seattle and Salt Lake City had Ted Bundy's name among the suspects in their files.

Cas Richter's initial telephone call to the police had been one of hundreds. Her voice was one among a chorus of fear and suspicion during the panic and chaos of late September 1974, after the Lake Sammamish victims had been found—a nervous voice which communicated more vagueness, jealousy, and perhaps flakiness, than solid fact.

* * *

When interviewed by police following Bundy's arrest, Cas had been nervous, fearful, vacillating. "Oh, God, I just don't know," she had said. "I sometimes think I must be all wrong about Ted." Her thin face was drawn, her eyes circled by signs of strain. With wringing hands she had answered their questions for a while, revealing her suspicions of Bundy. Then her mood would change, and she would rise to defend him. "It was tough on her," reflected Keppel. "She still cared for him. He was calling her regularly [from jail], and he had a way to swing her loyalty back to him."

For the men in the Aspen meeting room Keppel re-created the evolution of Cas' suspicions during 1974. It was really an accumulation of happenings that might have been ignored—Ted's unexplained absences, particularly during the middle of the night, and his habit of sleeping during daylight hours. Ted had an unnerving game, said Cas—hiding in the bushes near her house at night, then jumping out to frighten her.

Cas had made some unsettling discoveries. Once she had found a pair of surgical gloves in one of Ted's jacket pockets. That was explainable, she reasoned. He had worked as a deliveryman for a surgical-supply firm.

But another memory caused a chilling focus of all of Cas' vague feelings—the time she discovered Ted had brought home a package of plaster of paris. It was a package of the product used by surgeons in fashioning casts. Cas had remembered vividly the news media's references to the "Ted" suspect at Lake Sammamish State Park—the man who was described as wearing a sling, perhaps a cast, on one arm.

It had been around the end of 1973, Keppel told his audience of lawmen, when Bundy "started experimenting with various sexual moves and methods" in his and Cas' sex relations. "He had asked if it was all right if he tied her up." Cas had consented. Keppel went on: "So he immediately goes over to where he has her nylon stockings. Of course, she doesn't think that he knows anything about where her clothes are. And he just reaches right in the drawer and picks out a nylon stocking and comes over and ties her to the bedposts and does his thing.

"He did this three or four times, and then she cut him off, because she didn't like it.

"She recalls him actually, physically, on one occasion—

while she was tied up—strangling her. And she actually had to awaken him out of this sexual involvement. This is when they terminated their tying-up activities.

"That brings us up to about January of 1974. And that's when our troubles started," Keppel reflected.

A few days later, Sharon Clarke was attacked as she lay sleeping in her basement apartment.

Keppel shared with the other investigators the efforts and failures to make one solid tie between Bundy and all the disappearances of the girls in the Pacific Northwest. Ted Bundy and Lynda Ann Healy had taken some of the same psychology courses at the University of Washington. But never were they placed together at one time. They lived in the same neighborhood and shopped at the same Safeway store. He could have seen her often, said Keppel.

Bundy could be placed at the Evergreen State College from time to time. He and a friend, Tom Sampson, often used the racketball courts at Evergreen. But no gas-charge receipt, no witness, no fact of any kind, could place Bundy on or near the Evergreen campus when Donna Gail Manson disappeared.

"He had been strolling around libraries a lot. We've got a lot of people that have seen him around libraries. But it gets kind of funny. He's not carrying any books. And when he stops to talk to these people, he always says that he's been studying in the library. Here he is, just wandering and meandering around the libraries at night, both at the University of Puget Sound library and the University of Washington library. So he likes libraries."

Keppel's soliloquy came to the double disappearances of Janice Ott and Denise Naslund on July 14, 1974.

"Bob, what about your witnesses at the state park that day the girls went out?" The question drifted out of the Aspen audience.

"Of course we have him [Bundy] positively ID-ed by two of our witnesses so far," Keppel replied. "And the third has a tentative ID on him as being the one who snatched Janice Ott. . . ." But the other witnesses were uncertain. The problem, Keppel reflected, was the variability of eyewitnesses. His fellow investigators murmured, understanding. King County's witnesses at Lake Sammamish had differing memories of the man's height, build, and hair color. "We've had a lot of difficulty in investigating the case. . . . A lot of people were interviewed in the beginning and [when they were asked if they recognized Bundy] they just can't remember back that far—a year and a half previous."

Janice's yellow bike never was found. Keppel believed it had been abandoned somewhere, then stolen.

Cas had assisted the Seattle investigators with information about Bundy's whereabouts during part of that day, July 14, 1974.

"In the morning hours," said Keppel, "He was dressed in shorts and a T-shirt. He'd gone over to her house, and they had some sort of argument about what they were going to do that day." She wanted to go to nearby Green Lake in Seattle. Bundy disdained the idea and went his own way. "So the last time she saw him was about ten o'clock in the morning. And she didn't see him again until six or six thirty that night. . . . He had her ski rack on his Volkswagen. He also utilized the ski rack to take his bicycle places. . . . When he got back [to her house that evening], he claimed he was feeling real bad. And they still went out to dinner that night. But before he went out to dinner, he made the effort to change the ski rack over from his car to hers."

Keppel's presentation to the other investigators coasted to an inconclusive finale. It had been an intriguing symphony of circumstances, but it lacked a finale. There was no hard evidence.

A few more questions came from the audience: "How about clothing? Any of the victims' clothing ever found?"

"We didn't find any clothing. No physical evidence at all. We didn't find any flesh. All we had was bones.

"Just bones."

Keppel's voice held a sigh of finality.

"Just bones," echoed the next speaker at the rostrum of the Holiday Inn meeting room.

Chuck Brink, investigator for the Clark County sheriff's office at Vancouver, Washington, delivered his report on two more 1974 Washington State homicides which had received less media attention. Hunters had found the skeletal remains on a remote wooded hillside in late 1974, in southwest

Washington State, more than 150 miles from Seattle. One of the skeletons, said Brink, was identified as the remains of dark-haired, eighteen-year-old Carol Valenzuala, a girl who had vanished from downtown Vancouver on a Friday, August 2, 1974. That was a little more than two weeks after the Seattle victims disappeared at Lake Sammamish.

"We've never been able to identify the other skeleton," said Brink. A medical examiner concluded the second skeleton was that of a young woman who was apparently killed at about the same time. "So again," reported Brink, "it looks like we've got maybe a fellow that has an affinity for the same dumping grounds for his bodies.

"The similarity between our killings and Seattle's is just uncanny," said Brink. But all he had, again, were bones. No clues.

(Note: Two weeks following the Aspen conference, there would be one development possibly related to those Clark County mysteries. At Evergreen State College, near Olympia, campus security chief Mack Smith would discover an obscure report in the campus complaint files. An Evergreen coed, Joni Dadarion, had reported that a strange man had surprised and terrified her at a dormitory laundromat late at night, August 1, 1974. She was alone, removing laundry from a machine, she said, when he "suddenly appeared behind me. I can't explain how scared I was. He was real schitzy, real wild looking." By chance, another woman student showed up at that moment, and the man had fled. Later, in late November 1974, when the campus chief and Thurston County Sheriff Don Jennings showed the young woman a photo lineup, she held onto a photo of Bundy, looking at it, muttering, "I don't know. I can't be sure. The guy that night was so wild looking." She thought the time of the incident could have been after midnight, making it August 2. "Her identification wasn't positive," the sheriff said, "but it was pretty good." Both the sheriff and campus chief were convinced the "schitzy-looking" man had been Bundy and that he had stopped off at Evergreen, prowled for a while, then continued driving into southwest Washington where the Valenzuala girl had vanished the following day in Vancouver.)

* * *

121

Thomas gave the other officers an update on the investigation of Bundy and the Utah cases—the DaRonch kidnapping, the murder of Melissa Smith and the disappearance of Debbie Kent. Just as had Keppel in his investigation of Bundy's life in Seattle, Thompson had concluded that Bundy, in his life and dealings with people in Salt Lake City, had been "a loner" who always seemed short of money, and a "leech." Thompson recalled an interview he'd had with Cas's father. "He said he [Bundy] at times seemed like a nice guy, but, in his opinion, he was a schizoid. . . . He was very moody."

When Thompson began a review of Bundy's gasoline credit-card purchases through the early months of 1975, it was a cue for investigators from Colorado towns, one after another, to report on their strangely similar cases of murders and disappearances, many of which now seemed to have a "Bundy connection." From Salt Lake City, Bundy apparently had begun travels into Colorado in early 1975. Caryn Campbell, a Michigan nurse, vanished from a ski lodge near Aspen January 12, and her nude body had been found in a remote mountain pass in February. Not far away, at Vail, Julie Cunningham, an attractive ski instructor, vanished from her apartment complex during the early evening of March 15. Then Denise Oliverson, a twenty-five-year-old, disappeared three weeks later while riding her bike at Grand Junction. Neither of those young women had been found. Melanie Suzanne Cooley, eighteen, who disappeared in mid-April from the small mountain town of Nederland, about fifty miles west of Denver, had been found murdered about two weeks later in a canyon. Shelly Robertson, an effervescent brunette, disappeared from the Denver area June 30; her nude body was found in August inside a mine shaft at the foot of Berthoud Pass.

Initially, those had been nothing more than a series of unsolved crimes which seemed only to have a vague geographical connection occurring at places along the east-west corridor of Interstate 70, between Denver and Grand Junction, near the Utah border.

Suddenly, after Bundy's arrest, several of those cases took on a common focus. Bundy's Chevron gas card had been used for gasoline purchases at times and places which conspicuously coincided with the crimes. Two card charges were made at Glenwood Springs January 12; Caryn Campbell vanished from the nearby Aspen area that day. There was a gas purchase at Dillon March 15; Julie Cunningham vanished that day from Vail, about 30 miles away. Gas was purchased on the card April 5 at Grand Junction, the same day and place where Denise Oliverson vanished. To all the investigators of those cases the coincidences were tantalizing, but there was nothing else to connect Bundy with any of the crimes. "We've yet been unable to put Bundy physically in Aspen," said the Aspen investigator, Mike Fisher, as he detailed for fellow officers the Caryn Campbell homicide.

As they swapped information, the investigators began to eliminate Bundy from at least one of the Colorado murders. Melanie Cooley, whose body was found partially clothed, with the hands tied with green nylon cord, her skull fractured by the blow from a large rock, offered a sharply different MO.

Carlstadt, the California investigator, in reviewing the Zodiac killings, conceded to the other officers, "Mr. Bundy has been eliminated from our cases." Seattle's investigation had placed him in Washington State at the time of at least two of the California crimes.

By midday, November 14, the investigators were folding their notebooks, agreeing to further exchanges of information. Each of the men had assimilated an enormous volume of information about Ted Bundy, but none was any closer to the solution of any of the dozens of homicides.

King County Detective Nick Mackie had decided on one last desperate effort. He resolved to stop at Salt Lake City, en route home to Seattle, to request a personal interview with Bundy about the Washington State homicides—a gambling attempt to extract a confession.

Everyone, even Mackie, sensed that would be futile. Thompson had told the other officers, "I asked O'Connell, Ted's attorney, if other agencies could talk to Ted." The defense lawyer, Thompson explained, "said, 'We're not going to talk with anyone.'"

As the detectives at Aspen said their good-byes, one of the Colorado investigators summed up the frustrations of the proceedings with a glum comment to the men from Salt Lake

City. "It looks like the only hope any of us has for tying down Mister Bundy is your kidnapping case there in Salt Lake City."

"Yeah," sighed Thompson. "And the Carol DaRonch case is no cinch."

TEN | Dinner and Conversation

There was a bounce in Ted's stride, and he obviously felt chipper as we walked together in the sunshine up Main Street in downtown Salt Lake City.

After eight weeks in the Salt Lake County jail, he was finally free on bail. Ted's freedom had come almost as a gift for his twenty-ninth birthday which was approaching November 24, 1975. His bond was posted November 20.

"Well, Ted, how does it feel to be out?" I asked.

"There's just no way to discuss freedom, no way of understanding it, unless you've had it taken away from you," said Ted solemnly. "Just the feeling I have now, the ability to walk where I want to walk, is indescribable."

Ted explained he had been treated well in the Salt Lake County jail. "I learned that I can cope. I learned a lot. It's just as though I've received an eight-week course, paid for by the county, in the criminal-justice system."

He sounded as if he were a student who'd been doing research for a thesis. "I've learned a number of ways to improve the system."

"Where would you start?" I asked.

"Well," he grinned, "I'd start with changing the bail-bond system."

We laughed together at that. There had been colossal snags in the raising and posting of his bond. The prosecution had played a tough game, resisting the lowering of his bail. Then, even after the bond had been lowered and his mother had secured a loan and wired the money to Utah, there had been further red-tape delays.

Now Ted was involved in some preliminary court hearings, during which a city-court judge considered whether or not there were grounds to bind him over for trial on charges of the attempted kidnapping and murder of Carol DaRonch. The hearings were closed to the public, but, after one closed-door session that day, Ted had buoyantly told reporters in the corridor, "I welcome a trial. I want to clear my name. I want it all out in the open. I want it aired."

Those hearings were, in effect, a preview of the state's case against him, and Ted said he'd wished they were open to the press. His lawyer, John O'Connell, had successfully moved to have the sessions closed. "Some of the things in that trial will blow your mind," Ted told me. He sounded confident that the prosecution's circumstantial case against him would fall apart and that his defense had a solid attack on the procedures used by police in securing Carol DaRonch's identification of him.

"Where do you want to have lunch?" I asked.

"Well, we can go up here to Lamb's. It's right up in the next block," said Ted.

"Fine."

As we walked along the busy street, Ted's bright eyes were active. He studied the faces of passersby, took in the sights of the street, looked over displays in store windows. It seemed to me his hair was darker than I'd recalled. His skin was much paler, the result of his weeks in jail. He wore a checkered sport coat, slacks, and open-collared shirt.

"I'm pretty impressed by O'Connell," I observed.

"Oh, yes. He's a very effective lawyer. And Bruce Lubeck is very, very, bright, too. They make a good team."

"You seem confident."

"You bet. I've got every reason to be confident."

We turned into the small, rather homey restaurant in the heart of downtown Salt Lake City. In a front booth, two young women looked up, smiled brightly, and greeted Ted. "Well, hi," he replied. They were obviously friends from the university. I left Ted to talk with them and walked to the rear of the restaurant to find a table and to wait for him.

Ted stood at the booth in an animated conversation with the young women. To some of the students at the University of Utah, Ted Bundy had—through all the bizarre, speculative news stories, and the charges—attained almost folklore status, an example of a young person victimized by excess zeal of the system. Ted shared a hearty laugh with the girls. He was handling his celebrity status rather easily.

When Ted joined me at our table, I pushed a menu toward him. "Order whatever you want. I'm picking up the check."

A matronly waitress in a blue nylon uniform arrived to take our order. "Well," Ted told her pleasantly, "I'll start with a double order of potato salad and a glass of milk. And while you bring that, I'll study the menu." She beamed at the handsome young man and hurried to get his potato salad.

While we talked through lunch, I also suggested to Ted that we have dinner that night. Ted seemed to be famished, and I knew he had little or no money. He agreed that dinner was a fine idea.

"We could go up to Park City," Ted suggested. "There are a couple of good restaurants up there, and it's pretty." Park City was a historic old mining town in the Wasatch Mountains, which had been restored in recent years and turned into one of Utah's more popular ski resorts.

"Sounds good," I said. I had a rental car, a Gremlin, and I asked Ted if he'd like to borrow it that afternoon after our lunch.

"Sure," Ted responded. "That'd be a help. I've got a lot of errands to run. I want to pick up some jeans. And I have to go to the law library."

Our ground rules of conversation forbade my pumping him about the case, the evidence, the legal issues involved. But Ted seemed to want to talk about it.

"David Yocom is supposed to be a pretty good prosecutor," said Ted. "But I think the state's got real trouble with this case, and they know it." He sounded confident, combative.

"When they brought me into that lineup," Ted continued, "and the DaRonch girl identified me, I was the only one there who wasn't a policeman. Every other man standing in that lineup was a *police officer.*"

"You're *kidding.*"

"No, I'm not. All those other men standing there were police officers. When they walked out on that stage, into those lights, they could act really confident. And then I walk out there. I'm obviously different. Anyone in a situation like that is going to act nervous. So you appear different from all the others.

"And they're all older than I am. I'm the one who looks like a college student. And Carol DaRonch was sitting out there in the audience. She'd been shown my photograph. She knew I'm a law student. She knew who she was looking for. And that's their whole case. *Her* identification of me."

I sighed. Ted, I thought, had grounds to contest the key element in the state's case—Carol DaRonch's identification.

When I lent Ted my Gremlin that afternoon, we agreed he would come by the Travelodge to pick me up around 5:30.

He was punctual. So, in the darkening late November afternoon, we left Salt Lake City on the Interstate highway, heading eastward, climbing upward in the mountains. "I love to drive," said Ted, relaxing at the wheel. "It's really restful, just having the countryside pass you by."

Ted was an entertaining, informative tour guide. As he drove, he told me all about the Wasatch Front, the mountains, some of the history of Utah, some of the things to do around the Salt Lake City area. "I've really enjoyed it here," he said, leaning back in the driver's seat. "But I do miss Seattle. No doubt about that. And I miss my friends up there." We reminisced about Seattle's newest restaurants, the night life, and about mutual friends in the political world there.

"Y'know, Ted," I told him, "I've always thought of you as a candidate for office one day. And a pretty good candidate, I'd guess. But now . . ." I fumbled for words to describe his new situation. "What happens in your life now? How do you see your future?"

Ted was guiding the Gremlin through a gentle, sweeping leftward curve of the highway. He smiled and sighed and raised one fingertip to an arched eyebrow. "Well, I always had about three goals in my life," Ted began. "One, to be married and have a family life. And, second, to become a lawyer. And then, maybe, to be in politics—to try to do something through the political system. Now, I guess, I can see they're all out of the question."

"Yes," I sighed. "You may be right. But not necessarily. We don't know what'll come of all this."

It was troubling to consider that such a young man, still innocent in my view, the victim of such outrageous circumstance and suspicion, could have his life ruined by such events. I had compassion for Ted. Yet I was puzzled by the rather mechanical way Ted had clicked off his life goals—one, two, three—as though his response had been rehearsed. Ted's top priority goal in life, he had said, was marriage. I waited for him to volunteer some expression of tenderness and love for Cas, but he said nothing further.

Ted turned the subject to skiing. "Utah has some really fine places to ski," he said.

"I gave up skiing," I replied. "It's getting to be just too damned expensive. It costs hundreds of dollars or so just to get outfitted nowadays, and the tow tickets are so high, I get a nosebleed before I reach the lift."

Ted chuckled in agreement. He remembered the fun he used to have when he was "fourteen or so. I remember fixing up my own skis," Ted recalled. "Old wood skis. You know, working on them, putting the base on them, waxing them. That was fun skiing. Up there on the hills, wearing my old blue jeans." He smiled at the memory.

As a kid, that was the way I skied, too. And I hated it. On my heavy old, hand-me-down wooden skis, I remembered resenting the other skiers on the hills who could afford high-fashion ski clothing and their expensive new lightweight skis. I wondered if Ted might not have had some of the same resentments, but I kept the question to myself.

As we drove higher in the mountains, I thought about Melissa Smith. Whoever killed her must have traveled this highway to the point where her body was dumped at Summit Park, using a turnout which the Gremlin was passing on the right.

There was a sense of enormous latent energy within Ted, I thought. For a moment I noticed his hands on the steering wheel. They were rather slim hands, almost bony. Now they were a pale ivory color, the result of the jail time he'd served. But they were strong hands.

He was a poor driver. The Gremlin seemed to drift within the lane, slowly, from one stripe to the other and back again.

Darkness was falling as we approached Park City, driving past new condominium developments mushrooming at the outer edge of the development. Ted drove around the small town perched on its mountainside, to point out some of the old mining-camp buildings remaining from Park City's boom days. Then he parked the Gremlin on the narrow, sloped little main street of the village. A few snowflakes were beginning to appear, floating in the cold, black night.

November was the off-season, so Park City's ski slopes weren't operating. As Ted and I began strolling along the sidewalk, past the restored fronts of a tavern, an antique shop, the other businesses, there was almost no one in sight. Suddenly I was aware that Ted wasn't walking beside me.

"Aha!" The sound of his voice came from behind me. I turned.

Ted had stopped on the sidewalk and stood at the curb, admiring a Volkswagen parked there. "A *Volkswagen!*" he exclaimed. Ted reached out with one hand to pat its top, and turned his face toward me, smiling.

He seemed to have struck a pose just for me, a perfectly staged cameo I'd be able to photograph in my mind. Against a black night background, Ted, wavy haired, smiling, and a Volkswagen.

"I just love Volkswagens," he laughed.

He held the pose for another long moment.

I didn't know quite how to react. It was obvious he wanted my memory to be inscribed with the sight of and thought of Ted Bundy and a Volkswagen.

With a playful grin, he jauntily rejoined me as we resumed our stroll along the line of shops.

I suggested we step into the Purple Onion, a little art gallery. Ted shrugged and followed me. I browsed slowly, looking at some fair metal sculpture and wrinkling my nose at some mediocre oil paintings. They were Sunday artists' work mostly—for the tourists. Ted seemed wrapped in a mood of boredom. I guessed he had little interest in galleries. I moved to an artist's display which covered most of one wall. It was a grouping of unusual framed works of wood inlay. The pictures had been created by a Salt Lake City artist, who had meticulously cut, then fit together, pieces of wood of different species and colors, to create outdoor scenes, mostly Bambilike deer, forests, mountains, and streams. "I don't think much of the art," I murmured, peering closely at one, "but the craftsmanship's good."

Off to my left a few feet, Ted sounded suddenly interested.

"Aha," he exclaimed. *"Here's* one I *really* like!" Ted was examining one of the wood-inlay works I hadn't yet reached. I moved to see what had caught his eye.

It was a picture of a bird's nest in the crotch of a tall pine tree. In the nest, two innocent, frightened baby birds looked upward, where, wings spread, an evil-eyed hawk swooped toward them, its talons reaching to snatch up the babies.

Ted enthused: "I *like that* one!"

I stared at the picture. The hair of my neck prickled. I glanced over my shoulder. Ted stood, his arms folded across his chest, grinning broadly at the portrait of the predator.

He gave me a sly glance, obviously seeking some reaction.

The symbolism was so obvious, so precise. Ted was playing an enigmatic game with me, delivering a tantalizing hint of guilt.

I decided to finesse. "Let's go have dinner," I suggested.

Only one other table was occupied as we ordered prime ribs and baked potatoes in the rustic frontier dining room of the aged Claimjumper Hotel. I ordered a glass of burgundy. Ted preferred milk. We talked about all the publicity that had descended on Ted in recent weeks. His eyes kept moving around the mostly vacant room, seeming to expect that he would be recognized. But no one—neither the hostess, the waiter, nor the other people at the red cloth-covered tables—recognized him. He talked about the superficiality, the near-hysteria of reporters and their news coverage of him. Ted seemed to exclude me from guilt. I was, after all, a political writer, not a crime reporter. And he knew I was operating on a strong presumption of innocence.

Everywhere there is a missing girl, Ted mused, "someone's now got to try to connect her disappearance with Ted Bundy."

I nodded. I told him, "I remember telephoning John O'Connell the other day, and before I could even get out the first question, John shouted, 'It's a false, malicious rumor. Ted Bundy did *not* take Amelia Earhart.'"

Ted chuckled.

"Well, when this is all over and I'm exonerated," Ted said matter-of-factly, "I'll expect equal time and space for the stories of my innocence."

Later, after dinner, as we drove in the darkness down the lonely highway from the mountains toward the lights of Salt Lake City below, Ted began talking about the cops.

"Y'know, they had this big meeting over at Aspen—of all the police from all over. And Captain Mackie, head of the King County investigation, stopped off here on his way home. And he wanted to interview me. I guess he expected me to confess everything in sight. Well, John O'Connell just laughed at him and sent him on his way.

"I don't know how much in taxpayers' money was wasted on that meeting with all those officers over there. Of course, one feels sorry for the families of all those poor, unfortunate victims. But as long as the police keep trying to hang every one of their unsolved crimes on me, as long as they keep their heads in the sand about me the way they are, there are going to be girls disappearing and turning up murdered all over the place."

He continued to refer to the Washington State investigation. "They're not going to find any evidence there," he said emphatically, "because there's no evidence there to find."

I studied Ted's profile, softly illuminated in the light of the dashboard. It was a good profile—the wavy hair, well-shaped nose, good chin. He had the good looks to be an actor. In what role? Perhaps, I thought, casting him, he'd be one of those handsome young good-guy cops on a television show.

Ted talked again about the police lineup procedures used in his case, plus the evidence that had been found in his car when the state patrol sergeant had arrested him the previous August. "They made a big thing out of the fact that I had a pair of handcuffs," Ted snapped. "I don't know what's so unusual about that. Heck, I was in law enforcement. You know, I was with the Seattle crime commission. . . ."

Ted's trial was not imminent. He would be free on bond until after the holiday season. He was planning to revisit Seattle, he told me. (That experience was still ahead of him.

He would discover that Seattle and King County police would trail him wherever he went. And Ted, recognizing them, would taunt them, hide from them, and, occasionally, walk up to the surveillance men and begin conversation with them. Sometimes he would playfully tail the men assigned to follow him.)

As the Gremlin entered Salt Lake City, I asked Ted if he had found any good nightlife in the city.

"Oh, sure," he replied. "I've found some fun places. There's a place over in Trolley Square that I've gone to a lot. I love to find a place with music where I can—y'know—get down and boogie."

I told him that I had some work to do that night. So, assuming he might want to be able to get around and see his friends, I offered him the overnight use of the Gremlin.

"Sure, that'd be fine," he replied.

Perhaps, I thought, it wasn't very wise to be lending Ted my car, yet there was a quality about Ted which evoked a desire to help him. I knew he had little or no money, and he no longer had his apartment. Most of his possessions had been stored. He'd said he'd be spending the night at the home of Salt Lake City friends, where he'd toss a sleeping bag on the floor.

Ted let me out of the car at the Travelodge. I almost—but not quite—gave him a parting shot: "Ted, I'd just as soon not read in the morning paper that some girl mysteriously disappeared in a Gremlin. So watch it, okay?"

He probably would have enjoyed that kind of a needle. But I didn't have the audacity to say it. Ted was better at games playing than I was.

ELEVEN | On Trial

"Dave, you're prosecuting the wrong guy," said the dark-haired young woman television reporter. "Ted Bundy can't be guilty of anything."

Barbara Grossman was grinning as she said it, kidding Dave Yocom. She stirred her vodka tonic and watched for a reaction from the prosecutor across the table.

"What makes you think we've got the wrong guy?" asked Yocom.

"Ted's just too cute," she explained. "A sharp, good-looking law student. Hell, Ted doesn't have to go around kidnapping girls. He can have all he wants. The first time I ever saw him I said to myself, 'Wow, all he'd have to do is ask me to go with him and I'd go.'"

"Yeah, Barb." Yocom forced a chuckle through his sigh. "Stick around for the trial. Maybe we can change your mind." Around them, in D. B. Cooper's, a small, private basement club, the tables and bar stools were already filled with the early-evening crowd of media people, lawyers, and others from the nearby courthouse. Despite the Mormons' influence, Salt Lake City had a few watering holes—licensed private clubs—and D. B. Cooper's was one favorite in 1976.

Nearly everyone in the place recognized Yocom, assistant Salt Lake County attorney, a longtime newsmaker. A gregarious, well-liked man, Yocom was known as an effective prosecutor, who prepared his cases well, was assigned the big ones, and usually won. And he was usually good for a quip and a quote afterward. Yet Yocom sensed that, in the crowd around him, and in the city, there were doubts and misgivings about the Bundy prosecution. Barbara Grossman, in a light-hearted kidding way, had made a point. Many people, even Yocom's close associates in the legal fraternity, wondered if the police and prosecution hadn't reached too far to charge Ted Bundy. The charge of attempted murder had been dismissed during pretrial proceedings. Now it was down to a charge of aggravated kidnapping.

Covering the case for KUTV, Grossman had met and interviewed Bundy occasionally during his court appearances. She had found Ted to be consistently cheerful, charming, photogenic, and newsworthy—good footage. Most reporters, viewers, and newspaper readers had difficulty reconciling the appearance of that attractive, articulate young man with the allegations against him. Yocom knew this. It would be a key prosecution problem in the courtroom—the defendant didn't look like a criminal.

"Barb," said Yocom, leaning forward, taking a sip of his drink, "I've got an offer for you."

"What?" asked the young woman.

"If we convict Theodore, I'll see if I can get him released to your custody for a while."

"It's a deal," she replied, laughing.

It had been nearly five months since that day when Carol DaRonch had chosen Ted from among the six other men in the police lineup and written his number, 7, on a slip of paper. Even though Ted had had his long hair cut short, hours before the lineup, and altered the part in his hair, she had identified him as the man who kidnapped her from the Fashion Mall November 8, 1974. Besides Carol, two other young women, watching the police lineup that morning had identified Bundy. They recognized him as the strange man who had been seen later that same night, nearly 30 miles to the north, at Viewmont High School where Debbie Kent had disappeared. There would be no prosecution in that case. Debbie had not been found. For a while, Yocom had toyed with the notion of trying to shore up the kidnapping case against Bundy by attempting to introduce some of the circumstances—the handcuff key and the eyewitnesses' identification—from the Debbie Kent disappearance. However, the prosecutor dropped the idea. It would have seemed an act of desperation, and those circumstances had little chance of being admitted into the DaRonch case, anyway.

The prosecution lacked hard physical evidence which could

directly connect Bundy to Carol's kidnapping. While Carol had been walked toward the Volkswagen the night of the crime, her abductor had handled the doorknob of the laundromat across the street from the shopping mall. But the Murray City police had been unable to lift a fingerprint from the knob. No latents, either, could be found on the handcuffs left dangling from Carol's wrist. The handcuff key found at Viewmont High School next morning, after Debbie Kent's disappearance—was useless as evidence. No microscopic proof could be found to show that key had ever been used in those handcuffs. In fact, that common key could fit any number of inexpensive cuffs.

Yocom was going to trial without a fingerprint or "smoking gun" or otherwise piece of conclusive evidence. There were photographs of Ted's Volkswagen, taken before he cleaned it up, replaced the seat cushions, and sold it—photos taken in August by Jerry Thompson. Those photos, which showed some exterior rust spots and a tear along the top of the rear seat, matched Carol's memory of her kidnapper's VW. Carol had remembered the man's patent-leather shoes. Thompson had seen some patent-leather shoes in Bundy's closet during that August 21 search of Bundy's apartment, but a subsequent search of his new apartment yielded no such shoes. Flecks of blood found on the white trim of Carol's coat were Type O. Bundy had Type O blood. So did tens of thousands of other young men in the State of Utah.

Circumstance.

Yocom's best element in the case—and the most uncertain —was Carol.

The shy, passive teenager, the prosecutor knew, could not be counted on as an unshakable witness.

O'Connell was derisive of the police investigative steps which led to the girl's identification of Ted. Her initial photo identifications had been uncertain, and then, he noted, "She was so psyched before the lineup that it was just a contest to see if she could pick the guy whose picture she'd picked out and which the police patted her on the head for picking out."

O'Connell employed a last-minute, pretrial stratagem which came as a surprise both to Yocom and, especially, to Judge Stewart Hanson, Jr. Ted, O'Connell advised them, was waiving his right to trial by jury.

Judge Hanson, a capable, sincere jurist, winced at the thought. He had been handed the unenviable task of sitting as both judge and jury in a trial which had raised passions all the way from Salt Lake City to Seattle. In the weeks following Ted's arrest, the court had been flooded with letters about Ted Bundy. One friend of Ted's had expressed outrage over the "apparently reckless excesses of the law enforcement system . . . and the tragedy of a young man whose life and career may now be ruined." In Salt Lake City, the missionaries of the Mormon Church stood loyally with Ted. One of them said, in a gentle voice of hope and confidence, "We just know that the trial will clear away these awful doubts which have surrounded Ted."

There were hate-Bundy letters, too. A woman in Seattle, upset by Ted's release on bail, had written the Salt Lake County court to ask, "Why is it that our courts allow a murderer like Theodore Bundy to run around free on the streets?" During a December trip home to Seattle, Bundy had triggered a flurry of consternation when he showed up at the University of Washington law library to check out some Utah statute books.

A panicked library employee who recognized him had telephoned police to ask, "Did you know that Ted Bundy is running around loose out here at the library? Ted Bundy, that *murderer!*"

During the Seattle visit, Ted had met John Henry Browne, a public-defender lawyer who would eventually become a regular, trusted adviser—Ted's "Seattle counsel." They discussed the surveillance of Ted by Seattle police and had a few laughs over it. As he had in Utah, Ted played games with the investigators who were shadowing him around Seattle. At one point, Ted had walked up to a police stakeout car, leaned in to greet the detectives, and suggested, "Would you like to give me a ride downtown? It'd be a good way of keeping an eye on me, having me right there in the car."

When Captain Mackie learned that Browne was advising Bundy, the chief of Seattle's Ted Squad telephoned the Seattle lawyer. Mackie wanted Bundy to take a lie-detector test. And he asked Browne what information Bundy had shared with him during their conversations.

"Well, Captain," Browne replied, "you know that anything

Ted and I talk about is a privileged attorney-client communication. I can't tell you what we've talked about. And you know that!"

"These crimes are too enormous," Mackie sputtered in response. "Your attorney-client privilege doesn't apply in a situation like this."

After a surprised moment of silence, Browne laughed.

The police, he concluded, had reached a point of desperation when it came to Ted.

On the morning of February 23, 1976, in a hushed, expectant courtroom of Salt Lake City's Metropolitan Hall of Justice, the trial of *Utah* v. *Theodore Robert Bundy* began.

At the defense table, Bundy, looking dapper and serenely confident, listened with his lawyers as Dave Yocom delivered an opening statement, reciting how the state would show he was the man who led Carol DaRonch away from the shopping mall, then tried to kidnap her in his Volkswagen. "The state, at the conclusion of this case," said Yocom, "will request this court, in its powers as both judge and jury, to find this defendant guilty as charged of aggravated kidnapping."

From the defense table, Ted's eyes skipped briefly around the crowded courtroom, pausing here and there to recognize familiar faces of friends—some former neighbors from the district locally known as "The Avenues," some young people from the Utah law college. Ted's eye quickly passed over two faces which directed long, cold stares toward him. Belva Kent, Debbie's mother, couldn't resist coming into the Salt Lake City courtroom to study the man who was the prime suspect in the apparent abduction of her daughter nearly fifteen months earlier. Louis Smith, police chief of Midvale, Melissa Smith's father, had been drawn to the courtroom too, with feelings of pain and anger about the unsolved murder of his daughter. There was extra security for Bundy during his trial. Obligingly, Louie Smith permitted the guards to search him, to assure them he carried no weapons.

O'Connell's opening statement for the defense was a concentrated attack on Carol's identification.

"At the outset," O'Connell told the court, "I think this trial is going to be somewhat anticlimactic to all the hoopla. I think it's kind of like a Whoosits comedy a few years ago—an awful lot of excitement, but when it comes down to it, there's not much here. An awful lot of smoke, but not much fire.

"In viewing the evidence, I would ask the court to pay particular attention to the personality type person that Carol DaRonch is. I believe you can do this from observing her testifying, her actions on the night of November eighth and then her various statements. And I think it will become apparent that this is a rather immature young lady.

"I believe she appears to have lived a rather sheltered life, is relatively unsophisticated. I think it's also apparent that she's relatively unobservant. I think it will become apparent that she has a malleable memory. I think it is apparent that she's submissive to authority. She's the kind of person that really does not look at somebody, particularly somebody who is an authority figure, somebody who is somewhat over-whelming her, that she spends a lot of her time looking down. And that is why the only thing she really remembers about the individual, at least on November eighth, were his shoes and pants.

"She thought initially the man had a mustache. A couple days later she decided he didn't have a mustache. Then later she decided that he did.

"There was a great deal of police activity immediately following this incident. As Mr. Yocom said, the young lady was shown thousands of photographs. We believe that the viewing of these photographs, picking out of the look-alikes, affected the original image that she had of the individual."

O'Connell referred to Carol's first tentative identification of a photograph of Ted Bundy shortly after Ted's initial arrest. After she had examined a new series of photographs, which included one of Bundy, "she made the statement, 'He's not in there.' And Officer Thompson said, 'Well, what about that photograph?' He was referring to one she casually had with-held and cradled in her hand at that moment. 'Why did you take that out?' And she said, 'Well I don't know. I suppose it looks more like him than other photographs I have seen.'"

From that moment onward, O'Connell told the judge, the police worked with Carol DaRonch, almost subliminally suggesting that Ted Bundy was the man.

By the time Carol, on October 2, 1975, sat down in the police lineup room, O'Connell went on, "she's seen the man's picture, she's associated in her own mind the pictures and the automobile, she knows the officers know that this is really a hot suspect and so she . . . of course has no difficulty in picking out the individual."

"This is solely an eyewitness case," declared O'Connell. The eyewitness was fallible, he suggested, and thus so was the state's case.

The state opened with routine testimony and introduction of evidence—the handcuffs and the flecks of blood, taken from Carol's coat, by the Murray police officer who first interviewed her that night. It was Type O blood, but not a sufficient sample to produce more precise blood classification.

Mary Walsh testified how, that night, she and her husband had encountered the terrified girl as she fled from her kidnapper. "Terrible," said Mrs. Walsh. "She was absolutely . . . well, I have never seen a human being that frightened in my life." Yocom wanted Mrs. Walsh's words to register on the courtroom and the judge. That intense fear supported the state's contention it was an *aggravated* kidnapping, as opposed to the lesser offense of simple kidnapping.

Yocom called Carol to testify. When the slender, dark-haired young woman walked into the courtroom, passing the prosecution and defense tables, the attentive spectators and reporters—and Judge Hanson—noticed that her eyes were cast downward. Solicitously, Yocom had her describe the series of events that night in the mall—the approach of the "police officer," their walk to her car, then later to his Volkswagen on the darkened street, and a few moments later his attack.

Carol testified about the photographs she'd looked at and the other steps which led to her identification of the man who kidnapped her.

Yocom asked his climactic question: "Is that man present in the court today, Carol?"

"Yes," she replied, her voice nearly a whisper.

"Where is he seated?"

Slowly, almost reluctantly, Carol for the first time turned her eyes to the defense table. Without real eye contact with the defendant, she nodded toward Bundy. "Right there."

At the defense table, Bundy, his eyebrows raised, stared at Carol—an unblinking, unemotional gaze.

139

It was obvious that Carol, weary, nervous, apprehensive, was on the brink of tears when the prosecution's questioning ended. As the cross-examination began, so did her tears. O'Connell asked Carol if she had cried when she had given testimony behind closed doors during preliminary hearings.

"No," she replied, her soft voice quavering.

"Is it the crowd here that is making you nervous?"

"Yes."

O'Connell questioned her at length about the steps through which police had taken her in identifying Bundy's Volkswagen as the car of her abductor—even though, at the time she saw it, the ripped back seat had been repaired and the exterior of the car had been altered.

O'Connell asked how Carol had identified the Volkswagen after it had been so changed in appearance. "It looked completely different," said Bundy's lawyer, "but you identified it anyway, isn't that true?"

Carol nodded. O'Connell brought out that when she had gone to see the Volkswagen with Detective Thompson, she assumed it was the same vehicle she had seen earlier in the photograph, at the time when its rear seat was ripped and its rust spots and other blemishes were conspicuous. Quietly, Carol conceded she understood from conversations with police that it "was *supposed* to be the car in the picture."

O'Connell paused. There was quiet. He was satisfied. He had shown how totally trusting Carol had been of police officers.

In his redirect examination, Yocom sought to prop her up, to emphasize Carol's final certainty when she had selected Ted Bundy in the police lineup that October.

"When you saw him in the lineup, could you tell?"

"Yes," Carol replied levelly.

"Seeing Mr. Bundy at that lineup when he first walked into the lineup room, what did you associate that with, Carol?"

"When he first walked in was the way he walked on that night."

"What night?"

"November eighth."

"Did you know immediately?"

"Yes."

"And you are positive today?"

"Yes."

Yocom hoped he had persuaded the court that, as uncertain as Carol might appear in many elements of her testimony, she was positive about that moment when she sat in the darkened audience and Ted Bundy walked on stage, along with the other men.

Bundy's defense was allowed to offer the testimony of an expert on the human memory—Dr. Elizabeth Loftus, a University of Washington psychologist.

She gave technical testimony about experiments dealing with the fallibility of the human memory. Various conditions alter and impair the reliability of a person's memory, she testified, especially the span of time between the original incident and the subsequent attempt to identify the person involved. Accuracy of recall, too, is lessened, according to the degree of stress which was imposed on the eyewitness.

The implication was clear: Carol DaRonch had been under extreme stress that night. And nearly a whole year had elapsed from the kidnapping until the police lineup.

Judge Hanson posed a question about a changing situation in which there were both—a nonstress circumstance, which later became stressful. "Let's assume, then, that you have a time continuum as represented by a straight line. At one point in time there is no stress whatsoever. As that continuum line proceeds, the stress begins to build. . . . The victim begins to suspect that the victim might be a victim. And then at a point further down in the continuum line, the victim becomes assured of the fact that there is a real problem.

"Now, at all times on that line of continuum . . . the victim is able to observe the perpetrator of the offense.

"How would stress, in your judgment, affect eyewitness identification under those circumstances? . . . Would the victim be more likely to be able to identify the perpetrator under those circumstances than in a situation where there was a sudden violent event, like a breaking-in through a door or a window?"

"Well, although that particular experiment hasn't been done," Dr. Loftus said, "my guess is that the sudden event would produce a less accurate identification, because the whole experience would be while the victim was in an extreme state of stress."

It passed as an almost academic exchange between the judge and the witness. Yet Judge Hanson had logged a conclusion in his mind. The violent situation in which Carol DaRonch found herself in the Volkswagen, struggling for her life, may have impaired her memory during those moments. But there had been that earlier period, walking with her abductor during unthreatening minutes, when her memory might not have been impaired.

Through all the months since his arrest, Ted Bundy had been publicly silent about the accusations around him and about the charges. Understandably there was anticipation among the reporters and spectators when, on Thursday, February 26, the defendant at last was called to the witness stand to testify.

As Bundy stood, taking the oath, with a faint smile of self-assurance, Yocom, pen and legal pad in hand, studied him. He had a feeling that, if he could put the right kind of pressure on Bundy, the young man's composure could be shaken.

O'Connell asked Ted where he was on the evening of November 8, 1974, at the time when Carol DaRonch was being kidnapped. "I'm not going to fool anybody," Bundy said with a grin. "It's hard to think back ten months, twelve months . . . sixteen months now." He did remember, he said, that his Volkswagen had been acting up about that time. So he believed that he had gone to a movie and later to a favorite hangout, The Pub, had had a beer and then gone home. "The only time I can fix definitely in that evening is I know I must have been home by eleven-fifty that night, because I made a phone call to a girlfriend of mine in Seattle. And I told her at that time that I'd been to a movie."

Listening, Yocom tightened in a reflex of anger. He knew that the detectives, checking Bundy's telephone records, had determined that each night a girl disappeared in Utah, Bundy had telephoned Cas in Seattle. It seemed to police to be almost ritualistic. Bundy's telephone call, at 11:50 P.M. that night, November 8, had been used in the search for Debbie Kent's body. If Debbie vanished from Viewmont High School just after ten o'clock, and if Bundy were at his apartment in Salt Lake City, about thirty minutes away, at 11:50, placing a telephone call, police speculated that the high-school girl should be found somewhere within forty-five minutes' drive from the place she disappeared at Bountiful.

"Did you go to the Fashion Mall on November eighth, 1974?" O'Connell asked.

"No, I did not," Bundy replied.

"Did you have any contact with Carol DaRonch that day?"

"No, I did not."

O'Connell's questioning elicited from his client an explanation of the items, especially the handcuffs, which had been found in his car when the state-patrol sergeant had arrested him the previous August.

"In the early part of 1975, in the course of doing work for my landlord," Bundy testified, "I took things to the Salt Lake City dump. And I found them [the handcuffs] in a box of odds and ends there."

Initially, he carried the handcuffs away from the dump in his old pickup truck, the one he'd bought in Seattle for his move to Salt Lake City. Later, Bundy said, he tossed the cuffs into his VW. He said he'd never had a key for them.

There was one conspicuous lie which lurked in the record of Ted's statements—that explanation he gave to Sergeant Hayward the night he was arrested in the suburb of Granger. He had said he had driven, lost, into the neighborhood after seeing *The Towering Inferno* at a drive-in movie. O'Connell began a line of questioning by which Bundy could explain that away.

Earlier that night, Bundy testified, he had worked at his job as a University of Utah building watchman until eleven o'clock. Then, he said, he went home, bathed, and decided to go for a nighttime drive. "I just decided to, as is my habit on occasion, to drive until I felt tired enough to come home and go to bed."

There was an expression of mild chagrin on his face, as he admitted he had smoked one marijuana joint early in the evening. Then, while he was parked on that quiet residential street, in the darkness of early morning, he said he lighted up another. Then came the state trooper's car. And the pursuit began.

With a sheepish grin and gestures of embarassment, Bundy described it: "All of a sudden I became frightened, paranoid. I can't describe to you the feeling. But I knew that what I was doing was definitely illegal. That is, smoking dope. And, also, you know—I have always been paranoid about doing it because I was a law student. I mean, quite panicky . . . I just wanted to make sure I got rid of this stuff as quick as I could and air out the car, just in case it was the police."

It was an understandable reason for lying when he told Sergeant Hayward he had lost his way into that nice quiet Mormon neighborhood after being at a drive-in movie. He was avoiding detection as a pot smoker.

O'Connell tied it all up: "Why did you tell them that you had gone to a movie rather than just driving around?"

"At the time it seemed like a plausible explanation."

"When did you get around to telling *me* what really happened, Ted?" It was a gently understanding question from his defense lawyer.

"Well, a couple of weeks ago. The whole thing seemed so absurd to me. I don't want to be argumentative, John. But its relationship to this particular case, to me, was not such that I felt that it was something I had to get into."

When he at last began cross-examination, Yocom had an unexpected defense position to challenge. The All-American, young defendant smoked a little pot and had—perhaps understandably—invoked a fib as a cover when he had been nearly caught.

Yocom began his questioning with some long-planned questions about Bundy's whereabouts on the date Carol was kidnapped. Bundy had testified his car had not been running well on November 8. Yocom produced gas slips, signed by the defendant, which indicated he had purchased a total of twenty-three gallons of gas in a four-day period during late October.

"In fact you were running the wheels off it, weren't you?"

"I can't recall."

Yocom asked how many miles of travel Bundy had put on his VW during those four days. "Can you tell me just generally, in your head, how many miles you traveled on twenty-three gallons of gas?"

"Well, no."

O'Connell objected. "This is a math test?" he asked. The objection was overruled. There was silence.

Yocom: "Have you computed that yet?"

Bundy: "Oh, I'm not really thinking about it, Dave. I thought you made your own conclusion. I'm not here to do mathematical problems."

Bundy's eyes smiled with self-satisfaction.

Yocom fumed privately for an instant. He resented Bundy calling him Dave from the witness stand.

When the court went into its midday recess, with Bundy still on the stand, Yocom retreated to his desk at the county attorney's office, tossing his briefcase onto his desktop in anger. Damn it, he thought, I haven't cracked him. I haven't even dented him. Yocom reflected on Bundy's testimony to that point. It had been controlled, a detailed alibi for everything. Yocom had the feeling that, whatever he asked Bundy, the response was a carefully rehearsed speech.

When he resumed questioning that afternoon, Yocom had vowed to rattle Bundy out of this well-orchestrated performance. The prosecutor asked Bundy to go over details of his early-morning arrest by Sergeant Hayward, beginning with the smoking of that marijuana cigarette when the state-patrol car approached. "So you lit up and started driving," said Yocom. "And that is when you saw Officer Hayward's car. Is that correct?"

"That was when I first saw a car which later turned out to be Officer Hayward's car."

"How fast were you going?"

"I couldn't tell you. Fast enough to try to air out my car."

"When did you roll down the windows?"

"When I determined that someone was following me. Which was after . . . I made the second left-hand turn."

"So you were in a residential area, making numerous turns, saw a car two hundred yards behind you, then rolled down both windows."

"I believe I rolled down the driver's side window. I may have slipped open the window on the other side. I couldn't reach over too well."

"And at the time you were going at a high rate of speed?"

Bundy acknowledged he was speeding.

Gradually, his composure had begun to disintegrate.

Bundy seemed unsure of himself, unsettled by Yocom's rapid-fire questions.

Yocom pressed for explanations—detail after detail—about how Bundy was getting rid of his marijuana evidence as he fled the pursuing officer.

"When you threw out the Baggie of marijuana and, I take it, the cigarette you're smoking, I assume you also threw out the cigarette papers."

"I got rid of the paraphernalia—quote—so to speak."

"Driving the car, rolling down the windows, and making turns at high rates of speed—you were able to do all of this?"

"Well, yes, I was. Like I say—"

"Where did you keep your Baggie?"

"I was rather panicked at the time trying to find it. It was in the glove compartment. Then at some point in time it may have fallen on the floor. I was hunting around for it while I was traveling out of the area."

"So you were driving a car at high rates of speed, making turns, trying to find your Baggie of marijuana, cigarette papers, all at the same time rolling down the windows?"

"Well, it really is not as impossible as it sounds. It can be done rather easily, I would imagine."

Yocom had elicited an implausible picture of Bundy, speeding from his pursuer while performing acrobatic feats within his car. Sergeant Hayward had testified that, when he arrested Bundy, there was no aroma of marijuana in the car.

Yocom sought to take care of another loose end—the mustache question. Carol had vacillated, but she believed the kidnapper had a mustache. The prosecutor asked Bundy if it were true that, while he was involved in Governor Dan Evans' 1972 campaign in Washington State, he had worn a false mustache in his spying on the other candidate.

"I wasn't spying on anyone," Ted replied, almost angrily. "I never wore a fake mustache during that period." He acknowledged that, years earlier, while he was visiting Philadelphia, he did own a fake mustache and had worn it. But, he said, it seemed absurd, so he got rid of it.

Yocom had to deal with one other loose end of circumstance in the state's case—the patent-leather shoes Carol had noticed. The defense had provided testimony to the court from acquaintances of Bundy that he had never been seen wearing patent-leather shoes. Yocom called to the stand Charles Shearer, a young man who had resided for several months with his wife, in apartment 4, at the house on The Avenues where Bundy lived.

"Now, Mr. Shearer," asked Yocom, "did you have occasion . . . to observe Mr. Bundy in a . . . dressed-up manner?"

"Yes." Shearer explained he often saw Bundy dressed up in a suit or sport coat on Sundays.

"Did you have an occasion to observe the type of shoes that he was wearing?"

"Yes."

"Would you describe that for the court?"

"Black patent leather. Shiny black."

"Is there any particular reason why you would notice that, Mr. Shearer?"

"I don't like the shoes," replied the young man.

"What?" Yocom grinned inwardly.

Shearer replied emphatically. He hated patent leathers, so he really remembered Bundy's.

For his closing argument in the case, Yocom had decided to group together all the elements of circumstance in a charted graph of mathematical probability. "Assume, as a base, we are dealing with the population of all males in Salt Lake County between the ages of twenty-five and thirty," said the prosecutor—the age of the man whom Carol DaRonch had identified. "Consider those twenty-five-to-thirty-year-old males who have Type O blood—about thirty-five percent of that population."

Systematically, he narrowed the population of possible suspects—males, twenty-five to thirty . . . who have Type O blood . . . who have dark hair . . . who are about six feet tall . . . who drive Volkswagens . . . who drive older Volkswagens . . . who drive older Volkswagens with a rip in the back seat . . . Volkswagens with chips and rust spots on the right front fender and body, as Carol described. . . . Males twenty-five to thirty who possess all those characteristics, who drive such a Volkswagen, who also carry a crowbar in the VW . . . who also carry handcuffs in their car.

Yocom continued to suggest that the mathematical probability of Carol's kidnapper being someone other than Ted Bundy was virtually zero.

At the defense table, Bundy glared at the prosecutor. Along with some other observers in the courtroom, Judge Hanson had noticed during the week that the defendant's physical appearance seemed almost to change with his mood. Bundy's skin, the blueness of his eyes, seemed somehow to pale at that moment of upset. His hair, at other times almost sandy in color, appeared darker as he leaned into an angry, animated conversation with his lawyer.

During his closing statement for the defense, O'Connell brushed aside the prosecutor's pseudo-mathematics of probability. Yocom's last-minute use of that graph had bothered the defense. Now, said the defense attorney, the key consideration before the court had to be the presumption of innocence of Ted Bundy—a promising law student, "a young man trying to get ahead in the world," who had become the victim of zealous police suspicion and rampant publicity. The prosecution, suggested O'Connell, had parlayed all that into a portrayal of Ted as "a monster." And the suggestible kidnap victim, while well-intentioned, had become the central actress in a tragic drama of misidentification of an innocent man.

The closing statements ended on Friday, February 27. When Judge Hanson summoned the principals back to the courtroom the following Monday afternoon, there was already a sense of what was to come. The judge had asked for extra security and so a special guard of deputy sheriffs had been posted around the courtroom.

There was tomblike silence as the judge pronounced the verdict. "I find the defendant, Theodore Robert Bundy, guilty of aggravated kidnapping, a first-degree felony."

Ted's face was impassive. From behind him came the sound of Louise Bundy's gasp. Her tears began. Johnnie Bundy reached to comfort her. So, too, did Cas Richter, who had come, with troubled emotions, to be there.

John O'Connell swallowed hard.

The weight of the decision and the deliberations which had gone into it showed on the weary face of Judge Hanson as he looked down at Bundy. It had been a difficult role for him, sighed the judge. "I cannot say that there weren't any doubts," he confessed. But, he added, there were no reasonable doubts based on the evidence.

Ted Bundy stood as a convicted felon, a stoic look masking his inner anger. "I wonder," he asked flatly, "if I could have a couple of minutes with my parents?"

The judge agreed to that. There would be an extensive presentence examination prior to any decision on probation or prison sentence, he indicated.

In the explosion of activity, reporters swarmed after O'Connell for comment.

"The turning point was when you people started bringing in other cases," O'Connell told the newspeople. There would be an appeal, there was a presentence investigation pending, so O'Connell was saying nothing further. Privately, though, he was furious. If the defendant's name had been different—something other than "Ted," the highly publicized Ted Bundy —he fervently believed, the verdict would have been innocent.

"Dave," shouted a reporter at Yocom, who was leaving the building through a lower-level corridor, "when did you know you had a conviction?"

Yocom muttered he'd make no comment. Afterward, though, Yocom confessed the answer in a quiet aside to Paul Van Dam, the county attorney walking beside him. "I didn't know I had a conviction," Yocom grinned, "until I heard the word 'guilty' from the judge."

TWELVE | Murder in the Rockies

Caryn Campbell's brother Bob would well remember that evening in Dearborn and the small dinner party at Caryn's apartment. It was January 10, 1975—the last time he ever saw her, less than forty-eight hours before her murder.

"Gee, I did the dumbest thing today," Caryn had confessed with a laugh to her brother and the other guests that night. She described how, in a burst of housecleaning zeal, she had removed the six smoked-glass chimneys from the chandelier in her dining area and put them in the dishwasher.

"I was going to make them extra sparkly clean. And *look* at them." She gestured toward the overhead lights. "Most of the tint came off."

Her brother examined the cylinders of glass. The heat from the dishwasher had melted the plastic coating which had created the smoke tint. Now the glasses were a mottled mess, partly smoky, partly clear.

"Well, Caryn," he teased, "as I remember, that's about as clean as you ever got the glasses when you washed dishes at home."

"Aw, be quiet, you rat," she laughed.

It had always been natural for Bob to tease Caryn. She was the baby of the Campbell family—a good-natured, cheerful, energetic girl. Her brother would never acknowledge it verbally, but as he watched Caryn hovering over the table, serving the dinner that evening, Bob reflected what a beautiful young woman she was. Caryn, twenty-three, had an appealing, animated face, sparkling brown eyes, and long brown hair which fell onto her shoulders.

Bob hadn't seen Caryn or other members of his family for a year, not since he had moved from Michigan to Florida, to his new job as an officer on the Fort Lauderdale Police Department. He had saved three weeks of vacation for this early January trip home to Dearborn.

"Well, Bob, how do you like being a policeman?" asked Caryn.

"Really good," he replied. "I like Fort Lauderdale a lot. But, after Michigan, that Florida climate takes a little getting used to."

Caryn was conspicuously proud of her brother. So was the whole family. Bob made a good-looking officer, they all thought—a tall, slender young man, with dark good looks.

Bob felt especially pleased watching Caryn and Ray Gadowski together. She and her handsome young physician boyfriend were obviously in love. Caryn, reflected Bob, seemed to be in the most promising phase of her life. Caryn had confided to the family that she and Ray planned to be married, perhaps that spring. Everyone approved, especially Bob. Caryn's brother thought that Ray was a mature man, with an excellent career, who seemed very caring and considerate with Caryn—a man who could give Caryn a good life.

The dinner conversation turned to Caryn and Ray's planned trip to Colorado, to a ski resort near Aspen. Ray explained he would be attending a cardiovascular seminar for physicians there, a combination of profession and pleasure.

"While Ray's at his meetings, the kids and I can go skiing and pal around together," Caryn added brightly. Ray, recently divorced, had two children—twelve-year-old Gregory and nine-year-old Jennifer.

"Sounds like a pretty nice trip," said Bob. "When do you leave?"

"We'll have to get away early tomorrow morning," Ray replied.

"And I'm still not packed," Caryn sighed.

After dinner had ended, as they said their good nights, Bob told Caryn, "Now don't go breaking a leg skiing. Nurses aren't supposed to be hobbling around on crutches."

January 12, in her final hours of life, Caryn was skiing with Ray's children on a dazzling bright expanse of snowfield in Colorado's high Rockies. She absorbed the beauty around her—the brilliant blue of the sky behind the craggy mountain peaks above, and below, the snow-frosted village of Snowmass and the lodge, the Wildwood Inn, perched on the mountainside.

Caryn stayed close to Jenny, who frequently tangled her skis and fell in the snow. Patiently, Caryn had helped the little girl up, laughed with her, and steadied her for another try. By early afternoon, Caryn and the kids were becoming weary, so Caryn suggested, "Let's go down and see your dad."

They made their final run down the gentle slope, unhooked bindings, removed their skis and returned to the Wildwood

Inn. The midwinter sun vanished abruptly, and the deepening blue-gray shadows fell quickly down from Elk Mountain, to envelop the lodge and the rest of Snowmass basin in darkness. By five o'clock a long cold night had begun, and Caryn's life was nearly ended.

They had an early dinner together—Ray, Caryn, the children, and a physician friend from Michigan, Dr. Brian Sternoff—at the little Stew Pot restaurant in the village immediately below the lodge. Caryn drank a glass of milk, but didn't quite finish her beef stew because, she said, her stomach felt slightly queasy. It was shortly after six o'clock. They finished their meal and left the restaurant.

Stepping outdoors, they all felt a sharpened bite of cold in the night air. As they turned uphill toward the lodge, Caryn snuggled into the warmth of her new sheepskin jacket. "Brrrr," she said, putting an arm around Jenny. "It's really getting cold."

The five of them paused and entered the village drugstore to browse for a while. Ray and the children went to the display of toys and games. Caryn and Sternoff stood at the magazine rack where they leafed through some of the photo mags. Sternoff opened a *Playboy* foldout and chuckled in admiration. "I think I'll buy this one," he said.

"No, wait," countered Caryn. "I've got that magazine up in the room. Why don't you buy a *Viva?* And then I'll trade you for the *Playboy* in the room."

Sternoff agreed. He selected the *Viva* and paid the young woman clerk at the cash register. They left the drugstore and strolled uphill the few more steps toward the Wildwood Inn, past the rock pillars of the entryway and into the small lobby.

"Do you want to go up to the room and get the magazine?" Caryn asked Ray.

"No, why don't you go get it," he answered. "I'll wait here in front of the fireplace with the kids." He handed Caryn the key to their room, 210.

Caryn walked past the front desk toward the elevator door. When Jenny and Greg began to follow, she paused and, with a trace of impatience, shooed them back. "You guys stay here with your dad, okay? I'll only be a minute."

She entered the elevator alone. The door closed behind her.

On the level above, the Wildwood Inn's heated outdoor swimming pool, surrounded by wings of the sprawling lodge, emitted a glowing cloud of steam in the night air. A few swimmers were soaking in the warm water. It was *aprés ski*—that special early evening hour for cordiality, relaxation, a sauna, a soak in the pool, or conversation over a cocktail. Groups of people moved noisily along the outdoor wooden walkways and steps interconnecting the rooms, wings, and levels of the lodge. On the walkway of the second level a party of doctors and wives talked and laughed as they headed toward a cocktail party.

Just as they reached the elevator at the second level, the door opened, and Caryn stepped out.

"Hello there," said Ina Yoder, a physician's wife who recognized Caryn.

"Hi," Caryn replied with a smile.

"Are you going to the cocktail party?"

"No, we're not planning to. I'm just on my way to the room to pick up something," Caryn said. "Maybe we'll see you later. 'Bye."

The others walked on toward the cocktail party. Caryn turned from the elevator door and started in the direction of Room 210. To Caryn's left, slightly below the walkway, in the blackness, was the glow from the pool.

From the elevator door, Room 210 was about twenty dimly lighted steps along that open walkway.

There, on January 12, 1975, Caryn disappeared.

Waiting in the lobby, Ray Gadowski had settled into a comfortable chair, glancing through a magazine, in front of the rock fireplace; Sternoff had strolled up to a small mezzanine area, just off the lobby, into a TV-viewing lounge.

When more than a half hour elapsed and Caryn hadn't returned, Ray went to Room 210, looking for her. He discovered to his puzzlement that she had apparently never reached the room. Caryn's purse and the magazine she had gone to retrieve were still there. He looked for her around the lodge and searched village shops, then with rising fear, finally telephoned the local sheriff's office for help.

After they arrived, the two Pitkin County deputy sheriffs

took a sketchy report and, with Ray's assistance, began a search in the numbing cold night.

Next day, Detective Sergeant Bill Baldridge called in Michael J. Fisher, investigator for the local district attorney's office. Every room of the lodge had been checked, as many people as possible had been questioned, but there was no sign of Caryn, Baldridge told Fisher.

"I don't like it at all," said Baldridge as the two men retraced the steps Caryn had taken, walking toward Room 210. Gesturing toward the other wooden walkways fronting on the wings of the lodge, Baldridge explained, "There were people all over the place at that time of the evening. But no one saw or heard anything unusual."

Fisher, a skilled investigator, didn't enter a routine police case unless there was some sign that a major crime might have occurred. "I don't like this one at all," he muttered. "It doesn't smell right."

The two men paused on the wooden walkway outside Room 210. "Something must have happened right along here," observed Fisher. "She must have met someone here on this walkway."

"If she went off with somebody . . ."

Fisher's eyes followed the walkway to the end of that wing of the lodge. There, some stairs led downward to a roadway and, beyond, the lodge's parking lot. Silently Fisher wondered if that "someone" had somehow gotten the girl to walk willingly to the parking lot.

Beginning with Dr. Gadowski and Dr. Sternoff, the detectives began a night-and-day questioning of all the guests of the Wildwood Inn, none of whom could shed light on the disappearance.

Some of the guests had checked out before they could be questioned, noted Fisher. "We'll have to catch up to them later on," he grumbled, "but they're gonna be scattered all the way from Hawaii to Maine."

When Caryn's frantic fiancé telephoned her family in Michigan, to break the news that she had vanished, Caryn's brother decided to fly to Aspen to join in the search. After his arrival, the distressed Bob Campbell pumped Fisher for information about his sister's disappearance. "What does it look like?" he asked.

"Not good, Bob, not good at all. There's nothing to go on. Usually, we have a good handle on what goes on around here. In Snowmass, in Aspen, in Glenwood, anywhere around here," Fisher continued, "if some drunk cowboy picks up a girl in a bar, we know about it. Fast. We've got good grapevines. But on this thing we've got zero."

But, Bob wondered, how could Caryn disappear in such total silence, out of a crowded lodge?

"I think someone just walked her out somehow. Maybe using some kind of ruse."

Bob Campbell had a private thought about that. He wondered if his sister might have been approached by someone posing as a policeman. Later he would reflect, "I'm a police officer, and I'm her brother. Caryn always has respected the police. She wouldn't ever go off with just anyone. But if some guy had shown her a badge and said he needed her assistance . . ."

Venting his frustration, Bob conducted his own personal search, retracing Caryn's steps—dozens of times—asking questions, looking in cars. He kicked away the snow cover to search the village garbage dump for anything—perhaps some article of his sister's clothing. By Saturday, six days after Caryn's disappearance, her brother had to give up and fly home to Fort Lauderdale to return to his job as a patrolman.

Fisher, a short, wiry man, with light-colored hair worn long to the collar, and a mustache which curled downward at the corners of his mouth, had specialized in cases of white-collar crime and narcotics trafficking common to the booming, affluent Aspen area. This kind of investigation was new to him, yet Fisher had immediately been fascinated by the circumstances of Caryn's disappearance.

During his hours of questioning guests at the Wildwood Inn, Fisher had turned up one intriguing lead. Dr. Edward Brown, one of the visiting physicians, remembered that, while he was soaking in the swimming pool that evening—when the rising steam of the pool would have obscured his view of the walkway where Caryn had walked—he had talked briefly with a young man who was also there in the pool. Dr. Brown told Fisher he thought the man had said his name was Michael. "And I think he said he worked here at the lodge."

Fisher spent weeks interviewing employees of the lodge,

checking work applications, seeking former employees, but was unable to locate the "Michael" described by Dr. Brown.

A fluke period of balmy weather visited the Rockies in mid-February. Snow melted in the warm afternoon sunshine, and nighttime low temperatures hovered above freezing, softening and shrinking the mountain snowpack. On the morning of February 17, a car climbed through the curves, up from Aspen, along the slushy Owl Creek road, toward Sinclair Divide. At the summit, between Aspen and Snowmass, the woman driver, en route to her office job at Snowmass, noticed, off to her left, a flock of magpies fluttering above a snowfield. Perhaps, the woman thought, the big black-and-white birds were pecking on the carcass of a deer. Curious, she stopped the car, got out and strode to the edge of the roadway.

From there, through a screen of bare scrub-oak branches—perhaps seventy-five feet distant in a snowfield—she could see the birds were feasting on a human body. She ran to her car to drive to a telephone to notify police.

Within an hour, the officers' cars and trucks had converged at the summit of the road, and the photography and crime-scene work began.

When the noisy magpies had been scattered into the nearby pines, Fisher and the other men could see that the body, face down, with one arm raised, was now mostly skeletal above the upper back.

If it was Caryn, Fisher reasoned, she had probably been brought by her killer directly to this remote summit, 2.8 miles from the lodge. Perhaps she was already dead by the time she had been dumped, pushed, or rolled over a roadside snowbank.

After being covered by snow, the body had been partially exposed by the February thaw. And then, obviously, the coyotes had reached her. "You can see she's been dragged out onto that snowfield," Fisher grumbled. Faint drag marks showed in the blood-pinkened snow between the body and the roadway.

The remains were placed in a body bag, then taken in a pickup truck to Aspen. From there Fisher telephoned ahead to Denver, to Dr. Donald Clark, a deputy coroner who arranged to perform the autopsy as soon as the body arrived in Denver.

Fisher had promised to telephone Caryn's brother, Bob Campbell, in Florida as soon as anything turned up in the case. But while Fisher waited in Aspen for word from the coroner, the information leaked to the news media in Denver. The body was that of Caryn Campbell.

Dr. Clark said he couldn't be absolutely certain what actually caused death. Damage to Caryn's skull from some crushing blows could have been fatal, but she had been dumped into the snow nude, in severe subzero temperatures, so that death could have actually been caused by exposure. There was evidence of at least three separate blows to the head—obviously heavy blows from some object which seemed to have had some sharp surface. One blow had fallen along the lower jaw. A rear molar had been broken away below the gumline.

About 40 cubic centimeters of rather well-preserved food had been found in her stomach. The material, said the examiner, was "consistent with that of stew and milk"—the food which she had for dinner that night. It was an indication to Fisher and Baldridge that, as they suspected, Caryn had been killed shortly after she disappeared.

Not enough tissue had been left on the upper body to determine what kind of damage might have occurred at the throat. The Ranan acid-phosphate test, an indicator of semen residue, was negative in the anal area, positive in the vagina.

But there could be no conclusion whether or not her killer had sexually attacked Caryn.

Fisher and Baldridge's investigation intensified. Now it was a certain case of murder. The two Colorado detectives flew to Michigan to make a thorough investigation of the two doctors who had last been with Caryn. The two men were cleared of any possible involvement.

In March, about one month after the discovery of Caryn's body, Fisher and Baldridge heard that another young woman, about the same age and physical appearance of Caryn, had disappeared from Vail, another ski resort town about a hundred miles from Aspen. Although the Vail police department was strangely reluctant to give information to the Aspen police, Fisher learned that the vanished girl, Julie Cunningham, twenty-six, was an attractive brunette ski instructor, who had last been seen near her apartment during the early evening hours of March 15, perhaps around six o'clock.

"Hell, that's about the same time of the evening Caryn went out," snapped Fisher. "And she sounds awfully similar to Caryn."

When Fisher and Baldridge went to Vail, they met a surprising lack of interest in the similarities from the Vail police chief, Gary Wall. Wall explained that Julie Cunningham was being handled as a routine missing person. There was no evidence of foul play and no body.

"But, Gary, it's almost identical to the way our girl went out—on a weekend, at about the same time of the evening," argued Fisher.

Wall explained that the small Vail police force was overburdened with work. President Gerald Ford and his family had chosen Vail as the place for the First Family's ski vacations, and the Secret Service had been placing heavy demands on the local police. In fact, Dave Bustos, the Vail officer assigned to the Cunningham case, had spent most of that day on Vail's streets, busy with skier traffic, performing patrol duty.

"Well, if you're short of manpower," Fisher replied, "we'd be glad to come in and help. These cases are too much alike."

Wall declined the offer. It appeared to the visiting detectives that the Vail chief wasn't anxious to have the publicity of a murder investigation in his town at a time when the President of the United States and his family were regular visitors.

A month later, in April 1975, Fisher and Baldridge went to Salt Lake City to confer with Salt Lake County detectives Jerry Thompson and Ben Forbes, and to compare their cases of look-alike murders, nearly 400 miles apart, in Utah and Colorado. In a darkened room they sat at a conference table, examining color slides being projected on twin screens—the autopsy photos of the bodies of Melissa Smith and Laura Aime, the girls murdered in Utah, and the remains of Caryn Campbell.

The detectives discussed similarities of all the cases. Never, they noted, at any of the scenes where the bodies were found, had a scrap of physical evidence been found. Each victim was found totally nude. No clothing was ever found. Each of the victims had last been seen moving from one place to another in darkness. The place where each girl was killed remained unknown, but the bodies were placed in a similar location—rural, mountainous, lightly traveled areas.

Even the physical damage to the victims was similar, the detectives concluded.

"Christ, that's almost identical. You've got the same kind of fracture patterns of the skull."

"Yeah. Even the same kind of jaw damage. And the ears."

"A lot of violence there. It's something heavy. Like maybe a tire iron or a lug wrench or something like that."

"Melissa was strangled with a stocking. So was Laura Aime. It was violent strangulation. Knotted tighter 'n hell."

"Well, of course we don't know about strangulation in Caryn's case. We didn't have enough tissue left to tell. There's a girl missing out of Vail, too. But we can't get a goddamn thing out of the police down there about her case. So we don't know."

"Well, it looks like we have a similar problem."

"That's for sure."

By late summer, seven months had elapsed since Caryn Campbell's murder. Although scores of possible witnesses were interviewed around the United States—people who had been at Snowmass in January—the persistent investigation had turned up nothing. Meanwhile some other strange happenings had visited western Colorado—events which had Fisher and Baldridge wondering. Besides Julie Cunningham's disappearance at Vail in March, a pretty young brunette, Denise Oliverson, twenty-five, had vanished at Grand Junction April 6. She had been bicycling that spring afternoon. Later her yellow bike was found beneath a bridge near the Colorado River, but weeks had elapsed, and no trace of her had been found.

In late June, Shelly Robertson, another young woman, had vanished from the Denver area. Now she was considered a possible murder victim, too.

Each of these disappearances, Fisher noted, had taken place not far from Interstate 70—the route which extends from Utah into and across Colorado. Sitting at his desk in the district attorney's office behind the Aspen courthouse, Fisher reexamined reports of Utah's murdered girls and contemplated the theory of the California investigator, Butch Carlstadt, that someone could be moving from place to place, always into a new police jurisdiction, systematically killing girls.

On Fisher's desk, heaped with file folders, investigation notes, and reports, the telephone rang. He reached across the paperwork to lift the receiver.

"Hi, Mike, this is Jerry," said the voice of his caller. "How y'doin?"

Fisher recognized the voice of Detective Jerry Thompson in Salt Lake City. "Fine, Jerry. What's up?"

"We just picked up a guy here who looks kind of interesting in our cases," Thompson reported. "Name of Theodore Robert Bundy."

Fisher wrote the name on a yellow legal pad. Thompson continued, giving details about the suspect—twenty-eight years old, white, male, a law student at the University of Utah. Moved to Salt Lake from Seattle in the fall of '74. Bundy had just been arrested a few days earlier, August 16, near Salt Lake City, driving a Volkswagen.

"Hmm, a Volkswagen, huh?"

"Yep," agreed Thompson. Both the detectives had become well informed about the Washington State cases, especially Seattle's "Ted" suspect with the Volkswagen. Thompson gave the Colorado investigator other details of the arrest—the handcuffs and other paraphernalia which had been found in the Volkswagen. Handcuffs, emphasized Thompson. There were handcuffs in the DaRonch kidnapping.

"I'm going to try to interview him," Thompson went on. "We're going to try to make a search of Mr. Bundy's apartment."

"Well, if you do," replied Fisher, "see if you can pick up anything that could put him in Colorado."

Thompson agreed. Five days later, Thompson called again to report to Fisher on the search of the suspect's apartment.

"Mike, this Bundy's a real cool guy," said Thompson. "He was real nice and pleasant when we searched his place. I did find a brochure in there—a pamphlet called *Colorado Ski Country*. I asked him if he'd ever been to Colorado, but he said he never had been there. Never to Aspen or Vail. But in this brochure he had at his place, there's a little check mark beside one of your resorts down there. Name of—uh—the Wildwood Inn."

"You're shittin' me, Jerry," Fisher growled. *"That's* the place where our girl went out! What else did you get? Any credit cards or anything like that?"

"Yeah. I picked up a receipt for a gas charge. Bundy's got a Chevron card."

"Got the number?"

"Yep. It's—ahh—Number 769-002-2475. Chevron."

Fisher jotted it down. "I know a guy at Standard Oil," said Fisher. "I'm pretty sure I can get a run on the card charges. . . . We'll find out if he's ever been to Colorado."

Thompson explained that Bundy would probably be put under surveillance in Salt Lake City.

"I'll get back to you on the gas charges," Fisher promised.

It took a while, but Fisher's pleading and pestering speeded the process. Ray Nordquist, Fisher's helpful Standard Oil Company source, notified Fisher that a computer printout of the gas charges was available in Standard's Denver office. When Fisher arrived at the office, Nordquist handed him a neatly stacked and stapled bundle of slips.

Fisher grabbed them. When his eye fell on the top slip, the reaction seemed to leap out of Fisher's belly: "KEEEE-riist!"

That slip on the top of the stack was for a gas purchase, on Bundy's credit card, January 12 at Glenwood Springs. "So he's practically right next door to Snowmass on the day Caryn disappeared," Fisher breathed.

Startled by Fisher's reaction, Nordquist pleaded, "I want a subpoena."

"You'll get it," Fisher promised, hurrying out of the office.

As his fingers shuffled through the slips, Fisher's eye paused on another charge: 3/15/75 . . . eight-plus gallons of gas, $4.02 . . . Golden, Colorado. That would place Bundy, or his card, right near Vail the day Julie Cunningham disappeared there.

Another slip: 4/16/75 . . . a $3.16 charge at Grand Junc-

161

tion. The day Denise Oliverson disappeared in Grand Junction.

Fisher ran to a telephone to inform Baldridge, his partner in the Campbell investigation. Then he drove to Boulder to share the new information with Bob Demming, the investigator in the disappearance of Shelly Robertson. Together they placed phone calls to Salt Lake City and other places to inform Thompson and other investigators of the credit-card "matches" with dates and places of Colorado crimes.

There had been two Chevron gas purchases on Bundy's card at Glenwood Springs, near Snowmass, around the time of Caryn Campbell's murder—one at Clayton Brothers' station, near Interstate 70, where the freeway enters Glenwood from Utah; the other at Adair's, at the south edge of Glenwood, along the highway leading toward Aspen and Snowmass.

The two investigators went first to Adair's, to interview the station owner, hoping they might be able to find someone who could "eyewitness" Bundy as the gas customer that night.

At Adair's, the station owner, a burly man in coveralls, studied the gas slip which Fisher handed to him. Then he shrugged. "Of course, I wasn't here that day," he said. "That was a Sunday, wasn't it?"

"Right. But," said Fisher, pointing to the slip, "you've got these initials on there. It's kinda hard to make out, but it looks like someone initialed the sales slip. Like 'T.M.' Would that be the attendant who sold the gas?"

"Yeah," nodded the station owner. "That would have been Tom. He would have been working alone that Sunday. He was always real faithful about putting his initials on a charge slip."

"We'd sure like to talk to Tom," replied Fisher. "Where can we find him?"

"You won't."

"Why?"

"Well, I heard he committed suicide in a motel over at Denver last February."

"Goddammit!"

Fisher and Baldridge sought and found and interviewed men who had worked at both gas stations, but no one could remember, among hundreds of cards and drivers, selling gas to Bundy. There was no eyewitness at either gas station.

Studying the gas-card charges, conferring by telephone with Thompson and others checking Bundy's activities in Seattle and Salt Lake City, Fisher began to construct a theory that Bundy's spasms of travel could have something to do with the man's emotional condition.

"Somewhere on his drives—on some of those long stretches of lonely highway between Utah and Colorado—it was obvious he sometimes paid cash for gas. But there are enough credit-card charges to figure it out. On the tenth of January—that's the Friday before Caryn goes out—he's gassin' in Salt Lake City. But he's putting on lots of miles. He's making gas purchases the equivalent of 420 miles of driving in one day! All in the Salt Lake City metro area. Ted's trolling. [That became Fisher's visualization of Bundy driving, driving, moving, looking—Ted, the troller, "fishing" for a victim.] Then on the next day, the eleventh, he's coming in here to Colorado. He gasses at Glenwood on the twelfth and Caryn goes out. On the thirteenth we have him buying gas over at Green River, Utah, on his way out. And next he's buying gas in Salt Lake City. And it's quiet for a while.

"It's like clockwork. He starts out with a lull, then builds to a peak of activity, in his driving, over a period of approximately, but not quite, thirty days. And he hits that peak. Then, ZOOM! On the March trip it's Julie Cunningham at Vail.

"Then it's quiet again, without a great deal of driving activity for a week or two. Then it starts to build up. And he's back driving again. Prior to the departure there's a great deal of driving activity around Salt Lake City.

"And then, ZOOM! Back into Colorado, and we have Denise Oliverson out of Grand Junction."

After Bundy had been charged and jailed in Salt Lake City, the Aspen detectives were hosts for the November 1975 "summit conference" on the cases of missing and murdered girls in the Western states. Fisher reported to fellow investigators on all the gas slips which pointed toward Bundy as the suspect in the Colorado cases. But neither Fisher nor anyone else had anything solid to tie Bundy to a murder. The FBI laboratory had been asked to examine vacuumings from the man's Volkswagen, but the analysis—and comparison with body traces of the murder victims—would take a while.

January 1976, almost exactly a year following Caryn's disappearance, found Fisher still working on the case, still locating and interviewing people who had been at the Wildwood Inn the evening of the crime. Two California doctors and their wives returned to the Wildwood that month for another vacation stay together—in the same place they'd registered for the 1975 cardiovascular seminar. When he learned that Dr. and Mrs. Harold Brown and Dr. and Mrs. Richard Harter were at the ski lodge, Fisher decided to reinterview Dr. Brown. It was Dr. Brown who had remembered the mysterious "Michael" in the swimming pool around the time Caryn vanished.

When Fisher arrived at Dr. Brown's room, he carried with him a large white envelope which contained mug shots of a photo lineup. One of the photographs was that of Bundy. After their greeting and handshake, Fisher quietly spread out the photographs on a desk, saying, "Take your time, Doctor. Just look them all over carefully."

Dr. Brown examined the pictures, one after another, shaking his head, saying, "No" . . . "No" . . . "No." So it went through the entire selection of photos. Finally, Dr. Brown told Fisher the "Michael" he remembered was none of the men in the photos. He had passed over the photograph of Bundy with no sign of recognition.

When it was over, Fisher grinned and shrugged. "Well, thank you anyway, Dr. Brown." Fisher hadn't expected anything else. Dr. Brown's original description of the "Michael" in the swimming pool had never been very close to a description of Bundy anyway.

Moments later, the others, Mrs. Brown and Dr. and Mrs. Harter, entered from the adjoining room. "Hello there, Mr. Fisher," said Mrs. Brown. "Nice to see you again. It's been almost a year now, hasn't it?"

"Hello," replied Fisher. "Yes. Just about a year." Dr.

Brown complimented the mustached investigator on his persistence in trying to solve the crime.

"Well, you gotta keep tryin'," Fisher explained to the others. "I just came here today to have Dr. Brown take a look at some photographs."

Mrs. Harter's eyes turned toward the white envelope. "May I see the photographs?" she asked.

"Okay," said Fisher. He took the photos from the envelope and handed them to the middle-aged California woman. She took one from the stack and, in an urgent tone, asked, "Mr. Fisher, how tall is this man?"

"Why do you ask, Mrs. Harter?" Fisher kept his voice low, calm. She was holding Bundy's photograph.

"Well, he's the strange man I saw by the elevator."

"What strange man, Mrs. Harter?"

The doctor's wife recalled something she'd never mentioned before. That night in January 1975, about the time the girl disappeared, Mrs. Harter had walked from her room to the drugstore below the lodge. She recalled she needed to buy some Pepto-Bismol. She'd seen that strange man standing near the elevator. She remembered him particularly, she explained, because he seemed so out of place. "He wasn't in ski clothes—just a jacket and pants. And bareheaded. He wasn't wearing ski boots."

Fisher contained his excitement. "Mrs. Harter," he asked quietly, "would you please put your initials and the date here on the back of this photo to indicate you identified this one?"

Lizabeth Harter obliged. On the back of the photo she wrote, "L.B.H. 1-9-76."

After a full year of work, Fisher had put together a few pieces of his puzzle. There were the credit-card slips, the Colorado ski brochure found in Bundy's apartment by Jerry Thompson, and now an eyewitness who could actually place Bundy at the Wildwood Inn the night Caryn disappeared.

It wasn't enough for a case.

The next scrap of potential evidence came in early 1976 as Ted Bundy was going to trial in Utah for the DaRonch kidnapping.

The FBI forensic specialists had completed their examination of vacuumings from Bundy's Volkswagen, and made their comparisons with samples from murder victims' bodies. The report caused a stir in the investigations in both Utah and Colorado.

A pubic hair vacuumed from the trunk of the Volkswagen owned by Bundy was found to be "microscopically indistinguishable" from a pubic hair specimen removed from the body of Melissa Smith, the girl found murdered in the mountains above Salt Lake City in October 1974.

At the same time, Robert Neill, the FBI's veteran expert on hair specimens, notified Fisher that Specimen PC-L 6351 —hair samples taken from the head of Caryn Campbell during her autopsy at Denver—had been found to be "microscopically indistinguishable" from one hair vacuumed from the front floor mat of the Volkswagen and a second hair vacuumed from the trunk of Bundy's Volkswagen.

That kind of a hair "match," unlike a fingerprint, isn't proof of identification. But in a telephone conversation, Neill assured Fisher there was a strong indication that the hairs taken from the Volkswagen could have come from Caryn Campbell. By at least fifteen microscopic criteria, Caryn Campbell's hair was identical to the hairs in Bundy's car, said Neill.

Fisher thought it might be time to talk with Ted Bundy.

On March 1, 1976, Judge Stewart Hanson had, in that tense moment in the Salt Lake City courtroom, pronounced Ted Bundy guilty of the kidnapping of Carol DaRonch. While a presentence investigation began, Bundy was in the Salt Lake County jail.

A few days later, Fisher and Baldridge arrived in Salt Lake City where, after some preliminary negotiations with Dave Yocom, the assistant Salt Lake County attorney, and John O'Connell, Bundy's lawyer, it was agreed that the Aspen investigators could meet and talk with Bundy. Bundy's and O'Connell's willingness for such an interview had come as a surprise. Until then, Bundy had resisted talking with police about anything.

Fisher guessed that Bundy was willing to talk with him in an effort to find out some information for himself. Through leaks to the news media, there had been widespread publicity about Bundy's credit-card purchases in Colorado. More recently, the Salt Lake County sheriff's office had leaked word of "some new physical evidence" in the Caryn Campbell murder —a reference to the still-secret FBI report on the hair specimens. Fisher anticipated that Bundy might spar his way through an interview, seeking to find out as much as he could about the Colorado case.

Bundy met the Colorado investigators for the first time in the late afternoon, March 11, 1976.

Fisher and Baldridge studied the slender, good-looking young man, his dark hair trimmed neatly around the ears, as he greeted them cordially in the Salt Lake County jail.

Fisher motioned Bundy to take a seat at a table, in a chair where his back would be to the steel wall of the visiting room. Fisher sat opposite him, Baldridge nearby. With a trace of anxiety Bundy examined the tape recorder the investigators had set up on the table between him and Fisher.

Bundy's lawyer, obviously wary of the interview, delivered an opening speech for the record:

"I want to start out by saying that, for the last five or six months we have been attempting through the local law enforcement agencies . . . to get information on the Colorado cases. We have been constantly informed . . . the authorities in Colorado refuse to allow them to release any information. And so all the information we have is that . . . leaked to the press . . . Mr. Bundy has been subjected to these Kafka-type interrogations before. . . . I think it ought to start out with—uh—you telling us something about what you're investigating. . . ."

Fisher replied that he and Baldridge were investigating the Caryn Campbell murder at Snowmass, near Aspen, and were interested in Bundy's activities "from, let's say, January tenth, which would have been a Friday, through January twelfth and thirteenth . . . January 1975." Fisher laid an open pack of cigarettes on the table. Bundy seemed to want a smoke. Fisher offered one. Bundy accepted and lighted up. Fisher left the Marlboro pack lying there. "Do you recall—uh —where you were on or about January tenth, 1975? That would have been a Friday," Fisher asked.

"No, I do not. I mean, I've been so . . . 'I really can't remember' would be a more accurate statement. I have no records. I have no records before me, no diary. . . ."

"Okay. During January 1975, Ted, were you ever in the State of Colorado?"

"Possible. Uhhh—it's—it's possible. Uh—I can't say for sure, okay?"

(Fisher had anticipated Bundy might "turn" on that question. When Salt Lake Detective Jerry Thompson first asked the question of Bundy after his arrest the previous August, Bundy had told him he'd never been to Colorado. But, since then, Bundy and others had learned that Fisher had the credit-card receipts in Colorado.)

"If you were in the State of Colorado, do you know where you would have been?"

"Uh—in the general Rocky Mountain area, you know. Like I don't know—recall—names of the routes or the cities. Uh—I don't know the area that well to say for sure."

Fisher asked pointedly about the town of Glenwood Springs and, especially, a gas purchase there on January 12. "Here," he said, handing Bundy the copy of the gas-purchase receipt from Adair's Chevron. Bundy studied it for a moment and quietly replied that he didn't recognize the place. Fisher unfolded a Colorado road map and handed it to Bundy, pointing out Glenwood Springs.

Lighting another cigarette, Bundy studied the map. Fisher noticed that the map trembled slightly in Bundy's hand. Bundy turned to study the gas slip again.

"Do you recall making that purchase, Ted?"

"Well, not specifically. It appears to be my signature and—uh—I certainly wouldn't deny that it's my signature, if you asked me. But I don't remember making that purchase."

"Have you ever been to Aspen, Ted?"

"I recall clearly one time, years ago, first of all. I think it was '69 I was there. And I'm trying to remember if, for sure, I was there at any other time—in January, or last year. And I'm not really sure of that. I know that at some point in time that I passed by Vail, but simply because it's on the main highway. But I can't say for sure."

Fisher made a mental note that Bundy, while unable to remember if he'd been to Aspen in 1975, could remember being there in 1969. That earlier visit to Aspen, Fisher already knew from the Seattle police background check of

Bundy, had been a stop on Bundy's 1969 travels from Seattle to Philadelphia.

"You don't recall being in Aspen in January of last year? Is that right?"

"I can't—uh—I can't say for sure. No. I—I—I'm not denying it. But I still—I still—I still can't recall."

Fisher leaned across the table, moving his face a few inches closer to Bundy's. Then, deliberately, the detective noisily cleared his sinuses. It was a Fisher habit and an unsettling sound. He pressed Bundy to confirm again that the signature on the gas receipt was his.

"Yes," Bundy replied. It was apparently his signature. "I mean—I—my card was not stolen or missing during that period. And I did use my credit card during that period on a trip through—that I may have taken to Colorado."

"Do you recall even the name of the hotel, something like that, you may have stayed?"

"Well, it's hard to separate the one or two trips I've—I made, to Colorado last year. Uh—I remember having slept in my car a couple of occasions, simply because I didn't have much money."

Here, Fisher noted, was a concession. Bundy remembered one or two trips. Deliberately, Fisher leaned his upper body even closer to Bundy's, to invade his body space, sensing that was bothersome to the young man. There was perspiration on Bundy's brow. He mashed a cigarette in the ashtray on the table. Fisher pressed for more specific recollections from that January trip.

Bundy lighted another cigarette and his voice faltered: "I have trouble—uh—recalling that specific trip, separating it out from any other trip that I've had. Mainly I just drove and—uh—just drove off a side road somewhere and—uh—came to a point where I didn't want to go any further, the road got steep or something, and turned around and went back to the main road."

Baldridge stiffened imperceptibly in his chair. That vague description sounded like the road off the Glenwood-Aspen highway, the spur road up into the basin of Snowmass Village, and, perhaps, even the snow-covered Owl Creek pass where Caryn's body was dumped.

Bundy's lawyer, standing, listened in silence. He watched his client intently.

When Bundy raised a hand to his forehead, Fisher noticed that sweat had drenched the underarms of his T-shirt.

"And the purpose of your trip was just to drive, just to get out of Salt Lake?"

"Yeah. Just to drive, relax. See some scenery. Uh—it—uh—to get away from the pressure of law exams. I wasn't really prepared for them at that time, as I recall. I just—uh—it's something to do to set my mind at ease and to think while I was driving—which is something I do quite a lot."

Yeah, I've noticed that, Fisher thought privately. Then, aloud: "Do you recall whether or not you slept in your car on that particular trip?"

"I may have. I—uh—if it was any—anywhere from two to three days, I probably did."

"Yes, we're talking about January the twelfth now. . . . It was a cold part of the year." Freeze-your-ass cold, thought Fisher. Like you'd really remember.

"I can't say for sure. Probably was. I can't say for sure where I would have stayed that night, 'cause I don't remember that day or that evening, January the twelfth."

(Fisher and Baldridge in their months of trying, had never turned up a single witness to place Bundy at any motel along the route the night before or after Caryn was murdered. He'd made a gas purchase back in Salt Lake City on Monday, the thirteenth.)

"Ted, evidently you talked to Detective Jerry Thompson of Salt Lake County sheriff's office. Uh—did you tell him that you had never been to the state of Colorado?"

"Well, okay. The fact is, I have been to Colorado. I think it—this is—well . . . There'd be just no reason why I'd tell another lie."

"I'm going to ask you really specifically, did you meet a young lady at Snowmass-at-Aspen, Colorado, on January the twelfth? That's a Sunday. And it's in the evening. Did you meet a woman anywhere near that area on January the twelfth, 1975?"

There was silence. Breathing heavily, Bundy studied the smoke curling from a cigarette in his fingers. At last he answered, "No, I didn't."

"Huh?"

"Well, I mean I don't recall having been to that area. But—but—if I'd met a young woman, I would remember it."

"On January the twelfth, 1975, did you kill that young lady up there near Snowmass-at-Aspen, Colorado?"

"I certainly didn't kill anyone, anywhere. And I— wherever I was—I didn't kill anyone."

"But you don't recall any of the occurrences that happened on that trip?"

"Well, yeah. Of course I wasn't paying a great deal of attention to specific places or signposts or mileage, traveling. Uh—but one thing you would remember, I mean. . . ." Bundy's voice trailed into a dry laugh. "It's certainly. Almost. I won't say that it's—it's . . . Unfortunately it concerns you very much. But if you . . ." He took a drag from a cigarette. "If you meet someone, you'd remember. Especially if you start up a relationship with them. That was not my intention. Nor did I do that. Uh—and as far as the question 'Did I kill anyone?' I certainly didn't. It sounds absurd to say so, but you'd remember if you've done something like that. I certainly didn't."

The two investigators—and Bundy's lawyer—stared at the young man's perspiring face and his unsteady smile.

Fisher pressed for more of Bundy's recollections about the January trip.

"I can remember having, say, stopped and gotten—got gas. And then maybe taken a—a side road, for—for a short distance. And then just trying to remember, coming back to the main road. Just a sort of nice, exploratory venture."

His voice was low. The end of that sentence almost lyrically: *A nice, exploratory kind of venture.*

What the hell was he saying? Fisher and Baldridge later would contemplate that phrase again and again. Could that be an allegoric reference to killing? A mystical allusion to murder?

"Can you describe the road to me at all, Ted? What did it look like? What was on it?"

"Well, I—I—again, I don't know if it's this particular time or not. I had one road that turned off into—below the city there. There were some gas stations. I remember gas stations driving up. And it went by a lake. And then it went by the ski

171

resort. And I drove up there and stopped for a while. Then drove back to the main road and got some more gas. Another road I can remember. It got really quite steep and very snowy. And I just decided when I got to the summit that I'd turn around and come back."

It was an ambiguous description. It could fit many places in the Colorado Rocky Mountain region. Yet it could describe the drive from Glenwood, off the side road up into Snowmass Village. *And then it went by the ski resort. And I drove up there and stopped for a while.* At the Wildwood Inn? Was he saying that? *It got really quite steep and very snowy.* The Owl Creek road summit, where Caryn was left in the snowstorm that night? The finale of *a nice exploratory kind of venture?*

Bundy enthused that Volkswagens "are just a superior car in the snow." Bundy said he sometimes slept in the VW, so Fisher asked him how he managed to do that.

"You put the back seat down, slide the front seat forward as far—maybe even off the tracks—as far forward as you can. And then that space in the back of the Volkswagen, while uncomfortable, is big enough to curl up in."

Fisher knew from his research in Washington and Utah that sometimes, in the suspect's VW, the passenger seat was in place. Sometimes it was removed. Fisher asked, "Can you recall whether or not the seat was out on that particular trip?"

"I'd seriously doubt that I would take the seat out on that particular trip."

On that particular trip. Fisher paused at that reply, his thoughts racing. What in the goddamm hell did that suggest? Those two coeds who went with the weird-looking man to the Volkswagen on the campus of Central Washington University at Ellensburg, where Susan Rancourt had vanished, noticed the passenger seat was gone. At Lake Sammamish, where the two Washington victims went out the same summer day, the seat was in place. When Carol DaRonch was kidnapped, there was a passenger seat in place. What determined whether the seat would be in—or out—when Bundy began a trip? Fisher decided to leave that question unasked for a while.

When the investigator pressed for more details about

Bundy's Colorado travels, the usual answer was "I don't recall." However Bundy eventually acknowledged some recollections of the towns of Grand Junction and Dillon, in the vicinity of Vail. Those were the places where there had been gas purchases about the times Denise Oliverson and Julie Cunningham disappeared.

Fisher decided to end the interview. After some moments when he appeared rattled, Bundy had rallied and seemed to collect his composure the longer they talked.

The investigators rose from the table. Baldridge punched the "off" button of the tape recorder, and they said their good-byes.

"We'll see you again, Ted," grinned Fisher.

"Fine," replied Bundy with a smile.

O'Connell said good-bye to his client, and the Colorado men left Bundy there in the jail.

Later, when Fisher and Baldridge were alone outdoors, Baldridge summed it up. At least, he said, they had pried some concessions out of Bundy about his travels in Colorado. And he had been locked into a recorded story.

"Yeah," agreed Fisher. "And I dunno if you noticed it or not, but he smoked up nearly all of my cigarettes. I think Theodore's a little worried about Colorado."

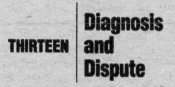

THIRTEEN | **Diagnosis and Dispute**

Dr. A.L. Carlisle, the slender, bespectacled blond psychologist at the Utah State Penitentiary, slid into a chair across the table from Ted Bundy, with a friendly greeting: "Hi, Ted. How are you today?"

"Just fine, Al," Bundy replied levelly. Wearing prison denims, Ted leaned back in his chair watching as the scholarly Carlisle opened his notepad, glanced through some earlier notes, and prepared for another session of questions and answers about Ted's feelings and attitudes.

"Ted," Carlisle began, "I'd like to talk with you some more today about some of your general feelings. And, particularly, I want to go back over some of your early years, the childhood years."

Bundy's expression hardened into a mask of guardedness. "I thought we'd just about covered all that," he said. The cramped interview room, a converted prison cell, felt confining. Ted, who liked Carlisle personally, girded for another session of questioning, more moves in an ongoing verbal-intellectual-psychological chess match. Ted, the psychology graduate, was cooperative even though he grumbled about the subjective nature of the testing, the hours of questioning to which he was being subjected during the court-ordered evaluation.

"The fact is that I am innocent of that kidnapping charge," he had said over and over to his interviewers. Yet, in his view, the psychiatrists and psychologists were determined to produce an analysis of him that would explain, rationalize, his commission of a crime which Ted steadfastly contended he didn't commit.

"Ted," asked Carlisle, "what do you think about life after death?"

"Well, death . . ." Ted paused. "It's inevitable for each of us. I haven't had much experience with it." Ted smiled faintly at the thought. "I don't fear death, I don't fear anyone or anything!" A surge of strength powered into his voice at that thought. He paused, then continued:

"But life after death? No, I don't believe in it. If there's life after death, we will live it and have a good one." Bundy paused again. And he went on, "If not, you will have fulfilled your purpose here. If there's life after death, okay. If not, okay."

Once again, as he had before, Carlisle, a devout, orthodox Mormon, contemplated the commitment which Ted, during his baptism, had made to the beliefs of the Latter Day Saints Church, and how, since his baptism, Ted had continued his smoking, drinking, and other activities with obvious disregard for LDS doctrine.

During the days immediately following Ted's conviction, Donald Hull, a presentence investigator for the Utah Probation and Parole Board, had interviewed Ted about his childhood and adult years. Hull had also contacted police and many of Ted's acquaintances. It was an examination process which customarily was thorough enough to guide a judge in considering the alternatives of probation or sentence, and length of sentence, for most convicted defendants. But, in the case of Ted Bundy, Hull's eventual report had been uncertain, indistinct in its conclusions. Judge Hanson wasn't satisfied.

Thus, when the judge had convened court March 22, 1976, for the scheduled sentencing, he had already decided he wanted a more thorough psychological evaluation.

There continued to be public reverberations over the judge's guilty verdict. "Frankly, I have never seen a conviction in a serious case on less evidence," O'Connell had said. O'Connell had many believers in his contention that all the pretrial publicity about Ted and murders had made its impact. "A lot of people didn't think Ted acted right during the trial," O'Connell told one reporter. "But how are you supposed to act when eight million people think you're a monster?"

So, when Ted, O'Connell, the other lawyers, and a few spectators gathered in the courtroom that day of scheduled sentencing, Judge Hanson, with obvious soul-searching, spoke of the process he had gone through in reaching his verdict three weeks earlier:

"If the Court had had anything to say in the matter . . . I would not have wanted the burden that was placed upon me with regard to Theodore Robert Bundy's guilt or innocence. Nevertheless, that was my job. . . . I suppose you are entitled to know part of what agony I shared with everyone involved on that long weekend. . . .

"I was concerned that trials of a spectacular significant nature . . . may tend to place an undue burden upon the Court . . . to reach a result that the public wanted, as opposed to a true and just result based solely upon the evidence. And after I was confronted with those temptations of human intellect, and after being satisfied in my own mind . . . that I had purged myself of any consideration whatsoever relating to other events, other things hanging in the wind . . . I proceeded to examine the evidence.

"By my nature and disposition, as counsel may be aware, it would have been an easier thing for me to find no guilt in this matter than the determination that I made, which was the harder of the two . . . I think Mr. Bundy and his very able counsel are entitled to know this. . . ."

Judge Hanson's eyes studied the upturned faces at the defense table and the prosecution table—Bundy, O'Connell, Yocom. There was an unmentioned personal coincidence of which the judge and attorneys were all aware. Hanson, O'Connell, and Yocom had all been classmates together during their law-school years at the University of Utah. Hanson resumed:

"To say that there are no doubts of any kind somewhat begs the question. . . . There are always lurking doubts, about, not the defendant, but the ability of the trior of fact to purge himself of all of those things about which he ought to be purged. While I have lurking doubts about my own abilities, I have no reasonable doubts based upon the evidence."

The judge turned to the question of sentencing, saying, "I am not satisfied that I have sufficient information to make the determination which it is now my duty to make. Accordingly . . . I am going to order that the defendant be committed to the custody of the Division of Corrections for a period not to exceed ninety days for a diagnostic evaluation."

Thus, in late March, Bundy had been transferred from the county jail to the state penitentiary south of Salt Lake City. Classified as a "high visibility" resident, he was assigned a cell in the medium-security block during this three-month diagnostic evaluation. Ted immediately began writing letters of protest, noting that other "diagnostics" were in minimum security.

Dr. Van Austin, the prison psychiatrist, and psychologists Dr. Al Carlisle and Dr. Robert Howell began an extended examination. After the skull X-rays, electroencephalograms, the computerized thermographic brain scan, and other examinations, they concluded there was no brain damage, no other discernible physiological problems. Then Ted underwent a battery of psychological tests, a process during which his mood seemed to swing from highs to lows. At one moment he was cheerful and cooperative. The next, he seemed absorbed in anger and depression. His IQ score: 122, superior intelligence, though not genius.

To supplement his interviews with Ted, Carlisle continued to conduct telephone interviews with police in Salt Lake City and Seattle, with men and women who had known Bundy. Once again, as during the police backgrounding, there emerged a mixed portrait of the man. From many people who had known him came glowing reports of Ted's stability, his social skills and sensitivity. "I don't think I've known anyone who seemed to have a higher respect for women and their role in our society," said one woman acquaintance.

From others came contradictory impressions that Ted appeared to be "a loner," a person reluctant to open himself to any deep, personal relationships. "I think Ted was always on guard against anyone getting close to him," said a young Salt Lake City woman who had known him intimately, had even had sexual intercourse with him. After their lovemaking, she recalled, "Ted was very quiet, aloof—very distant. He told me afterward he just didn't want to be touched."

A young woman who had dated Ted in Seattle remembered her puzzlement. They knew each other well, yet Ted always refused to go to her home to meet her parents. "It was funny," she said. "Ted was always so self-confident, so sure of himself, but I got the feeling that he felt terribly inferior at times."

Bundy's interviewers discerned a pattern which pointed toward some void, some hostility within the young man, something perhaps rooted in his early years, perhaps in his family relationships.

Another woman Ted had known in Washington remembered the day she accompanied him when he drove on an errand to the Bundy family home at Tacoma, a midday visit when he knew his mother and the others would be away from the house. "I didn't know anything about Ted's family," she recalled, "and while we were driving there, he told me about everyone. Ted said his father was dead and that his mother was an older woman, in her sixties."

When they arrived at the Bundy home, Ted pointed out some family photographs hanging on the wall. "He pointed out the photo of his mother, his older sister, his younger sister and brother." Much later, the woman went on, "I saw a photograph of Ted's mother, and I figured out that the photo Ted had said was his 'mother' was actually his *grandmother*. His 'father' was his *grandfather*, his 'older sister' was really his *mother*. I could never figure that out."

The professionals examining Ted felt convinced that the fact of his illegitimate birth was a troubling psychological dynamic within the man, even though, when asked about it, Ted's standard comment was, "I can't understand why everyone wants to make such a big deal out of that. I don't consider it to be important."

Through his earliest years, Ted had been told that his real father was dead. He thought he had been around thirteen years old when he discovered a birth certificate which listed his father as "unknown." "I think I'd had a sixth sense about it," Ted reflected. "It really wasn't that important." When he discovered that birth certificate, Ted explained, "I didn't feel nauseous or tearful. It just confirmed my inner knowledge. An experience of being bitten by a dog when I was four years old was more clear than finding the birth certificate."

Thoughtfully considering Ted's answers, Carlisle wondered if the words used by Ted in his disclaimer of concern—*nauseous . . . tearful . . . having been bitten by a dog*—might have been a more accurate representation of the actual feelings he had.

No, Ted insisted, he harbored no feelings of anger toward his mother. His praise for his mother sounded mechanical: "She had sacrificed a great deal to have and raise an illegitimate child." His mother was, Ted recalled coolly, a person who "paid all the bills" and who never used force or anger. "She never yelled at me." Otherwise, he had little to say about her.

Ted acknowledged an initial dislike for Johnnie Bundy, the man who married Ted's mother and who fathered the other children in the family, Ted's half-brothers and half-sisters. Again, Ted's description of Johnnie came in words carefully chosen, mechanical, devoid of affection: "He was always busy digging in the garden, rebuilding things. He couldn't sit down." Briefly, during his toddler years, Ted developed memories of his grandfather, the man who came closest to providing a father figure. Ted described him as an "intelligent man, interested in science and technology."

Cas Richter, Ted's onetime fiancée, had gone through another abrupt change in her feelings about Ted. Following his conviction, she had developed a new feeling of hostility toward the police and prosecutors. Conspicuously remorseful about her role in what had happened, she sought to explain away all the suspicions she had once voiced about Ted. "I certainly don't want anyone to think that I truly believe Ted had anything to do with the murders of those girls or that kidnapping," she had said plaintively during one telephone interview.

When Ted talked about Cas, he reflected about their times together, the comfort of her home, the fragrance of cooking in her kitchen, their conversations. She seemed almost to have taken on a motherly role in their relationship. At times, his tears welled as Ted talked about Cas, as he shared the poetry he had written for her. And there was his memory of the time when she had had too much to drink and, Ted later discovered, had a sexual experience with another man. "My world was so destroyed," Ted said tearfully. "That was the last straw. But we got back together and we cried together. . . . That was the only time she was unfaithful."

At every opportunity, Ted forcefully turned his interviews to a diatribe about his conviction. He criticized the evidence, the police techniques, and Carol DaRonch's eyewitness testimony. "Yes I had some handcuffs in my car," Ted snapped. "But I felt they could be useful if I had to apprehend someone. I had a job as a night watchman at the university. And, in Seattle once, I had chased and caught a purse snatcher. I thought at that time it would have been useful to have handcuffs to restrain that suspect."

In late May, Ted wrote to me:

The diagnostic evaluation will be sixty days old tomorrow. The bulk of the time has been spent sitting in a

179

cell, but the staff here has conducted tests and examinations on me that are, by far, more thorough than any one else has been subjected to.

Frustrated, confused and perplexed, the psychologists and psychiatrists have found my responses normal. Of course we all have our idiosyncracies. (So who is truly normal?) Phrased another way, there is *nothing* in the results to substantiate the judge's verdict or to answer the unanswerable question: "Why?"

They repeatedly characterize my case to me as "very interesting," "very complex" and "extremely difficult." This case becomes curiouser and curiouser. The obvious conclusion of my innocence is strenuously avoided.

Carlisle and the other examiners would not disagree that it was, as Ted said, "extremely difficult" to enter the tightly locked doors Carlisle sensed were within the man. Again and again he pondered words Ted had used to describe events and his responses. During that period when his once-exclusive relationship with his mother had been changed abruptly by her marriage to Johnnie Bundy: "Life was not sweet, but not a nightmare." And Ted's recollections of "the buzzing, baffling world of kindergarten." And his adjustment: "I didn't feel like an outcast."

"I had lots of friends," Ted said of his early high-school years. But then, too, he spoke of becoming "less dependent on my friends and more of an individualist." During his crucial formative years, when the young teenager usually seeks new social experiences, Ted fell into a very private, introverted pastime. For hours, he listened to the radio, finding pleasure, he explained, in memorizing voices he heard. "Social relationships were not that important. . . . I just felt secure with the academic life."

There could have been an implication, too, in Ted's aborted interest in entering a fraternity during his first weeks at the University of Washington. He appeared to betray a feeling of inferiority, of some hostility when he explained how he turned away from the whirl of fraternity-sorority life: "I wasn't interested in the social politicking, the emphasis on clothes and parties. It was shallow and superficial." Whether by choice or otherwise, Ted was on the outside, looking in, at the rather exclusive social world, the laughing, beautiful people who resided in "Greek Row" at the edge of the campus.

During his questioning of Ted about his relationships with women, Dr. Carlisle's attention focused on Diane, the strikingly beautiful, tall brunette with whom Ted became infatuated during his first years at the University of Washington. In an interview at her California home, Diane had confided that, at the end of 1973, she had the distinct impression that Ted and she were engaged; that Ted's intention was marriage. But then, she said, he subsequently refused to write or telephone her. When asked about that, Ted coolly explained, "I just wanted to prove to myself that I could have married her."

Dr. Carlisle reflected much later that Ted might have been fearful of entering into a deep relationship with a woman of such extraordinary poise and confidence. Perhaps haunted by insecurities and self-doubts, he turned away, into his loneliness . . . perhaps with bitterness.

(More than a year later, in a personal letter, Ted engaged in some free-wheeling memories of Diane, perhaps betraying his feeling of inferiorities. "All right, so she had a Mustang. . . . And so what if she may have been the most beautiful woman I had ever seen, or have seen since: tall, dark haired, smooth, and oh, so sophisticated. She moved like something out of *Vogue* and anything she wore looked like a million dollars. I, on the other hand, possessed the innocence of a missionary, the worldliness of a farm boy. . . . She and I had about as much in common as Sears and Roebuck has with Saks.")

After twenty hours of interviews, spanning a six-week period, Dr. Carlisle wrote his own preliminary evaluation of the intriguing young man.

Mr. Bundy sees himself as a fairly open person. This contrasted with the strong defensiveness shown throughout all the interviews. He also viewed himself as a person who experiences almost no anxiety, yet he showed definite indications of anxiety at times during

181

the interviews. In general, the scores of the objective tests portray the picture of a person who is happy, confident and very well adjusted. These results contrasted with the results found in the projective tests and in the interview. Even the turmoil he is experiencing because of his present situation did not show up on the objective tests. An intelligent person can answer the questions to place himself in a favorable light, which would help explain the conflicting results. . . . Mr. Bundy is an intelligent person with a good verbal ability. He can present himself well and makes a good initial impression on most persons. Thus he tends to win friends easily. . . .

Mr. Bundy is a "private" person who does not allow himself to become known very intimately by others. When one tries to understand him he becomes evasive. Outwardly he appears confident and reveals himself as a secure person. Underneath this veneer are fairly strong feelings of insecurity. He has a strong need for structure and control, such as in interpersonal relationships and in control of his own emotions. . . . He becomes somewhat threatened by people unless he feels he can structure the outcome of the relationship . . .

With a smile, Carlisle recalled how, during his questioning of his subject, Ted had skillfully managed to attain the role of the superior. Once the psychologist had jotted an analytical marginal note to himself: "He's controlling *me!*"

The constant theme running throughout the testing was a view of women being more competent than men. There were also indications of a fairly strong dependency on women, and yet he also has a strong need to be independent. I feel this creates a fairly strong conflict in that he would like a close relationship with females but is fearful of being hurt by them. There were indications of general anger and, more particularly, well masked anger toward women. . . .

He has difficulty handling stress and has a strong tendency to run from his problems. That his defenses break down under stress is shown by his general instability, both in the past and with his inability in adjusting during his first quarter at the University of Utah. His use of marijuana and the fact that he was a heavy drinker at one time are also indicators of difficulty with handling stress. These correlate with the evidence of anxiety, loneliness, and depression found in the testing.

Passive-aggressive features were also evident. I felt there was a good deal of hostility directed toward me and other personnel even though he would carefully point out that it was not aimed directly at us personally.

The above personality profile is consistent with the possibility of violence and is consistent with the nature of the crime for which he is convicted. A prediction cannot be made as to whether or not Mr. Bundy will show violence in the future as the best predictor is past behavior, and he disclaims any violent acts in the past. . . . However, I feel Mr. Bundy has not allowed me to get to know him and I believe there are many significant things about him that remain hidden. . . .

On June 7, 1976, Dr. Austin, the prison psychiatrist, submitted the final diagnostic report to Judge Hanson. "I do not feel that Mr. Bundy is psychotic," Austin wrote—i.e., he is not a victim of a severe mental illness, such as schizophrenia. "In fact he has a good touch with reality, knows the difference between right and wrong, has no hallucinations or delusions," Austin explained.

Perhaps, the psychiatrist suggested, Ted would be included in the loose diagnostic category known as personality disorders.

He does have some features of the antisocial personality such as lack of guilt feelings, callousness and a very pronounced tendency to compartmentalize and rationalize his behavior. . . . At times he has lived a lonely, somewhat withdrawn, seclusive existence which is consistent with, but not diagnostic of, a schizoid personality. . . .

His denial of memory for the crime is not consistent with amnesia due to a hysterical reaction, alcohol or drug intoxication, or temporal lobe epilepsy. This amnesia seems too circumscriptive and convenient to be real. . . .

In conclusion, I feel that Mr. Bundy is either a man who has no problems or is smart enough and clever enough to appear close to the edge of "normal."

It is my feeling that there is much more to his personality structure than either the psychologist or I have been able to determine. However, as long as he compartmentalizes, rationalizes and debates every facet of his life, I do not feel that I adequately know him. And, until I do, I cannot predict his future behavior.

For weeks, apprehensive of the course of the evaluation by the doctors, irritated by what he considered to be the repetitive, vague, subjective nature of the examination, Ted had written letters of complaint to Judge Hanson. At last Ted had filed his own legal motion—a bold show-cause action to require prison officials to explain why they should not be held in contempt of court for failure to perform an appropriate evaluation. In his letters to the judge, Ted had also argued it would be inappropriate to sentence him to prison. Given his clean record, Ted contended, he and society would be best served by a decision for probation.

On June 30, the day of sentencing, Bundy, wearing plaid shirt and jeans, stood before Judge Hanson for more than an hour, arguing, gesturing, sobbing at times, disputing the conclusions of the doctors in their evaluation. His eyes sometimes brimming with tears, he disputed, point by point, the conclusions which had been reached by Austin and Carlisle.

"Dr. Austin's a very experienced man, practiced years at the state hospital at the prison," said Ted in a quavering voice. "But the conclusion he states—'I feel that Mr. Bundy is either a man who has no problems or is smart enough and clever enough to appear close to the edge of normal' . . ."

Bundy swallowed heavily. He exhaled a sigh and continued, "That's a helluva choice. Your Honor, I think it revealed the basic lack of security, maybe even the pressure that is on these men—that a man with a great deal of experience, an education, is going to make a preposterous, but perhaps honest, statement like that. . . ."

Judge Hanson watched compassionately as Ted, his hands trembling, his heavy breathing pulsing with sobs, turned to other pages of the diagnostic report.

Ted bit his lip. "Summarizing my bad points . . . I was 'defensive, a private person, insecure.' . . ." I was 'dependent on women.' Good grief! I don't know that there's a man in the courtroom who isn't. And if he isn't, maybe there's something wrong with him. Our mother is a woman. . . ."

He attacked Carlisle's conclusion that the "personality profile [developed during the examination] is consistent with the nature of the crime for which he was convicted." "There are probably tens of thousands of people in the city walking around, especially on the university campus here, more or less like me. . . . Those characteristics are not predicted by anyone necessarily, because many people have them and are never violent. And there are many people who are violent who never have those characteristics."

As they watched and listened, the doctors earnestly felt they had done a professional, unbiased evaluation of Ted and had managed some significant and accurate glimpses of the real "inner Ted."

A silent fact worked against Ted and his impassioned arguments that day.

During the days following his conviction, another FBI laboratory report had been belatedly provided to Jerry Thompson and the other investigators of the Carol DaRonch kidnapping. A hair found in Ted's Volkswagen, detectives learned, was a highly likely match for the hair of Carol DaRonch. As he watched Bundy in the courtroom, tearfully pleading against imprisonment, Yocom felt more comfortable than ever. He had convicted Ted Bundy *without* a crucial piece of evidence.

"As I said," Ted went on, red-eyed, his voice still trembling. "This . . ." He held up the several pages of the psychological evaluation. ". . . was written to conform to the verdict."

At last Judge Hanson indicated he was ready to impose sentence, and he allowed Ted a further chance to address the court.

Defeat and anger showed in Ted's body as he addressed the certainty that he would be sentenced to prison. "Imprisonment," he pleaded, "is neither a rational nor a humane alternative. To commit me to prison . . . I can assure you this . . . Some day, who knows when? Five, ten, or more years in the future? When the time comes for my release . . ."

He was sobbing. So was his mother, who sat among other spectators straining to hear his mumbled words.

"When the time comes for my release, I suggest you ask yourself, What's been accomplished? Was the sacrifice of my life worth it all? An eye for an eye, measure for measure, is child's play in comparison to what you are about to do today.

"Yes," he continued, turning moistened eyes toward Austin and Carlisle, "I *will* be a candidate for treatment. Not for anything *I* have done. But for what the *system* has done to *me*."

Then it was time. Ted stood listening as Judge Hanson sentenced him to be confined to the penitentiary for a term of from one to fifteen years.

Ted's face bore a look of frozen hostility as the guards led him out of the courtroom toward a room where he would be dressed again in prison clothes for his trip back to prison and a medium-security cell.

FOURTEEN

Point of the Mountain

Compared with other prisons, the Utah State Penitentiary was regarded as a rather easy, decent joint—a place which had its assaults, rapes, and an occasional inmate murder, but a place which also had the reputation of being well run and secure, relatively free of the overcrowding at other institutions.

Locally, it was known as Point of the Mountain, a name derived from its location, south of Salt Lake City, where the freeway to Provo curls around the toe of some foothills jutting westward from the Wasatch Front. The complex of neatly clustered buildings, ringed by double steel-mesh fences, topped with barbed wire and razor steel, was surrounded by valley farmlands. In early July 1976, Ted Bundy was checked into his medium-security cell there to start serving his time.

Although he was apprehensive about his personal safety, Ted made a deliberate effort to befriend other inmates and, because he had enough familiarity with the law and the skills to write motions, he was accepted as a potentially helpful "jailhouse lawyer." Prison officials and guards assessed him as a respectful, pleasant, cooperative prisoner. Ted settled into a daily routine of morning calisthenics, letter writing, and work, assisting John O'Connell and Bruce Lubeck on the appeal of his kidnapping conviction. Ted routinely accepted his excommunication from the Mormon Church. "I know there was no alternative for them," he reflected. After all, despite the fact he was appealing, he stood convicted by law of a felony. Even so, Ted told Mormon friends, he would continue to attend Mormon church services at the prison.

There were no new developments in Colorado, so far as

Ted knew—nothing since Mike Fisher and Bill Baldridge had interviewed him in early March about the Caryn Campbell murder. "Colorado is a dead issue, no matter what the hopes of the interested parties might be," Ted wrote to me. But despite that kind of public-relations utterance, Ted was concerned about what might be happening in the Campbell murder case. It dangled in his mind as a persistent threat. Ted's guards began to notice that, when he moved through the prison, or while he was at his assigned job in the prison print shop, Bundy's eyes were constantly moving, absorbing the sights around him, memorizing the places, the routine. "He's one to keep our eye on," concluded one of his guards.

Bundy made it a point to gain the acquaintance of Willis Maguire, a lean, dour-eyed prisoner in his mid-forties, a long-termer who had a reputation as an escape artist. In a whispered conversation one day, Bundy proposed a plan to the veteran con. Working in the print shop, said Bundy, it would be possible for him to manufacture phony identification—driver's licenses, Social Security cards, other papers—which could be used to assume new identities. That would be his contribution. Maguire's contribution would be the escape plan itself.

"That's stupid," growled Maguire. "Just goddamn stupid. You start messing around printing stuff like that inside here, and it'll get you into deep shit. ID is nothin'. Who needs it? You can always pick up all the ID you need on the street, once you get out."

Ted tried again. But the older con responded by giving Bundy a lecture: "If you had any goddamn smarts at all, you'd settle down in here and stay clean." At the Utah pen, doing one to fifteen, as Bundy was, parole could come early. "In a couple years you're gonna walk. Why risk it?"

Ted mumbled an explanation—about "a problem I got in Colorado." Maguire seemed bored.

Other inmates began to notice that Bundy, while seemingly adjusting to the prison routine, at times was short-tempered, restless. "You can hear him pacing in his cell at night," muttered a man in a neighboring cell. "Back and forth. Back and forth. He's tight." A prison staff member reported a feeling of uneasiness about Bundy: "I've seen a lot of guys in here, but—it's funny—Bundy's the only one I've ever picked up a sense of real fear from. You can tell he's got a helluva lot of anger inside him." The Utah Appellate Court had rejected Bundy's appeal of the kidnapping conviction, so the next step would be an appeal to the Utah State Supreme Court. That meant months of waiting in confinement.

Among others, the supervisor of the print shop noticed the increasing nervousness, the furtiveness in Bundy's behavior. One day, by prearrangement, Bundy was abruptly summoned from the print shop, where he was working, to a guard station. His supervisor, watching from a distance, saw him slip something into a garbage can before he left. It was discovered to be a facsimile of a phony Social Security card, almost ready for printing.

When guards shook down Bundy's cell, they also found roadmaps, airline schedules, and a false driver's license. For possession of such escape-plan contraband, now considered a "high escape risk" prisoner, Bundy was dispatched into an isolation cell—the Hole—for two weeks. When he came out, he was assigned to the maximum-security block, home of the "heavies"—the prison's most dangerous inmates and the men under sentence of death.

At Aspen, investigator Mike Fisher, still working on the Caryn Campbell murder case, received a cryptic note in the mail from a prisoner at the Utah state prison. Fisher had never heard of the man who wrote, but he was fascinated by the message: "I might have some information for you about a murder case there in Colorado involving Theodore Bundy. If you're interested, contact me—Willis Maguire."

"I'm damned interested," Fisher breathed. He went to Ashley Anderson, a youthful assistant district attorney who had been assigned the Campbell case. Anderson agreed that they needed to talk with Maguire. After their flight to Salt Lake City, Fisher and Anderson discussed the Maguire note with Jerry Thompson, Dave Yocom, and others who had been involved in Bundy's Utah conviction. "What do you know about this guy Maguire?" asked Fisher.

"He's a tough old con," replied Thompson. "From what I

can find out from the guys down at the prison, he's not your usual snitch. If he's got something to say, it might be worth listening to."

"Yeah," said Fisher. "But we've also got to find out what Maguire wants in return."

The Salt Lake County attorney's office, Warden Sam Smith, and the others at the Utah prison offered total assistance to Fisher and Anderson. Whatever Maguire wanted as his end of the deal would be delivered, if at all possible, by the State of Utah. Smith arranged for the Colorado men to see Maguire in an absolutely secret meeting inside the prison.

As they talked, the wily prisoner gradually outlined his side of the deal. Maguire was to be moved to a prison in South Dakota where, he said, he could be closer to some members of his family. Looking into the cold eyes of Maguire, Fisher guessed the man's real motive was to get into a prison where he'd have an easier chance of escape.

"That might be worked out," Anderson conceded.

"Now, Willis, why don't you tell us about Bundy," said Fisher. "What's he told you?"

Maguire repeated the conversation he had with Bundy about Bundy's plans to print false identification papers for an escape. "And I asked him, why in hell he was so hot to get out of here," Maguire went on. "And he said, "Well, the Colorado cops are gonna be coming in here to get me for that girl I killed over in Colorado.'"

Fisher and Anderson exchanged hopeful glances. It sounded like a breakthrough in the case—a confession, even if it was heresay, could be admitted in trial. The wiry little investigator pressed Maguire. "You're not shittin' us are yah?" Fisher asked.

Maguire shook his head. "He said it."

"You know you'd have to testify to that."

"Yeah," said Maguire. "If . . ."

"Okay," replied Fisher. "We're gonna have to find out what we can do with these Utah guys about your deal. And we'll get back to see you."

Later, as Anderson and Fisher talked it over, they had an approval from Utah officials of Maguire's deal. "It'd sure as hell make our case for us," concluded Fisher. "The hair in his car . . . the gas slips . . . Mrs. Harter's eyewitness . . . And now this."

But, noted Anderson, "it's a death-penalty case." With the stakes that high, Anderson and Fisher decided Maguire would first have to undergo a polygraph test.

A day later, Fisher and Anderson returned home to Aspen in deep gloom. Maguire's story hadn't held up convincingly. What Bundy actually told him, they concluded, probably was "The cops in Colorado are gonna be comin' here after me. *They say* I killed a girl in Colorado." There was still probable cause to bring a charge of murder against Bundy in the killing of Caryn Campbell. But the state would have to go with what it had.

On October 22, 1976, Fisher, carrying a warrant charging Bundy with Caryn Campbell's murder, was once again heading toward the Utah prison at Point of the Mountain. He had planned it carefully, hoping to catch Bundy by surprise. Perhaps, thought Fisher, Bundy, caught unawares, might be shaken into some admissions. After that March interview, in the Salt Lake County jail, which had left Bundy upset, perspiring, and rattled, Fisher had developed a theory: "Theodore's always got to be in control of every situation. But if you can catch him when he's rattled, when his defenses are down, when he's not ready for you, when he doesn't have that control, you might shake something out of him." And, Fisher had learned, Bundy's emotional condition had sagged to a deep low in "the max" at Point of the Mountain.

But it was Fisher who was in for the surprise that day. There had been an advance leak of his plan to serve the murder warrant. A television reporter in Salt Lake City had telephoned Bruce Lubeck to ask, "Is it true that someone from Colorado is on his way to Point of the Mountain to serve a murder warrant on Ted Bundy?" Bundy's defense lawyer had driven immediately to see his client at the prison.

When Fisher arrived in the steel-wrapped visiting room in the "max" area at Point of the Mountain, Ted greeted him with a smile. "Hi, Mike," said Ted. "What can we do for you?" Sitting beside Bundy was his lawyer. Fisher's hope for the element of surprise was gone.

"I've got a warrant here for you, Ted," Fisher said quietly, "from the State of Colorado. It's a charge of murder."

Bundy's initial reaction to the Colorado charge was to fight extradition. Meanwhile, as he waited there in maximum security at Point of the Mountain, there was a lively, growing media interest in a man in another cell. The hoopla was over Gary Gilmore, a 35-year-old tough who had served 18 of his years in prisons and jails. He had committed a couple of pointless murders while committing robberies at Provo that July and had been convicted in October and sentenced to death by Utah's firing squad. Gilmore requested a quick execution.

One day when Lubeck sat talking with Bundy in the visitor's room at "max," their eyes turned to another inmate and his visitor: Gilmore, looking casually tough and disheveled, straight, dark hair flopped onto his forehead, was having a conversation with his pale, brunette girlfriend, Nicole Barrett.

Ted Bundy had always been a fervent opponent of the death penalty and now, watching the condemned Gilmore, he was as close as he had ever been to the reality of the planned execution of a human. It made Ted queasy.

"Y'know," he said to Lubeck as they gazed at Gilmore, "if someone doesn't do something pretty soon, they're going to *kill* that guy."

Yes, agreed Lubeck with a sigh; and America would resume its old business of executing people.

Gilmore achieved what he'd asked for. Shortly before sunrise on January 17, 1977, they took Gilmore to an old, unused cannery building on the prison grounds, shackled and strapped him loosely into a chair, placed a black hood over his head and pinned a black target with a white circle to his T-shirt. Firing squad marksmen hit the target, killing him with a fusilade of four slugs through the heart.

For weeks Ted had been wrestling with his Colorado dilemma, especially that state's move to extradite him. Because he was without funds, he had been assigned the services of a Colorado public defender lawyer, Chuck Leidner of Aspen. Leidner, a competent defense lawyer, had scoffed at Colorado's murder case against Ted: "I can't imagine a prosecutor in his right mind bringing a case as thin as this." But Bundy was wary. He was unimpressed by Leidner. And he worried that the wave of publicity about him, which had washed over Utah, had extended to, and prejudiced, Aspen and other places in Colorado.

"Of course," he reflected, "if I fight extradition, I come off in the news media like someone who's afraid of going to trial. And everyone reaches the conclusion, 'See, he must be guilty!'" On the other hand, Bundy told friends, he could encounter in Colorado, as he maintained had happened in Utah, an atmosphere of prejudice which could result in a conviction, regardless of the vacuum of evidence in the state's case. With help from O'Connell and Lubeck, he had initially filed motions resisting extradition. But it was inevitable.

When he appeared in court on January 28, 1977, his ankles and wrists manacled, Bundy waived extradition. It was over in moments. Ted winked and smiled as he left the courtroom, and Lubeck handed out to reporters a carefully structured, confidence-filled statement which Ted had written the night before:

> I would not waive my right to a hearing and voluntarily request removal to Colorado unless I was certain that I will be acquitted of the charges there.
>
> I have postponed going to Colorado these past two months for a number of reasons. First, I wanted to determine what remote connection, if any, there could have been between myself and the tragic death in Colorado. As I suspected, the accusations . . . have proven to be grossly exaggerated, in some instances purely fictitious and totally without merit.
>
> Second, I needed time to check into . . . the legality of the extradition.

He vowed to appeal the kidnapping conviction in Utah which, he said, is "the major, if not the sole justification for the charge against me in Colorado."

A "new" woman had begun to occupy Ted's thoughts during the final months of 1976. Tall, auburn-haired Carole

Boone, a woman in her late twenties, one of Ted's co-workers at the Washington State Department of Emergency Services during the summer of 1974, had been one of the persons who had lavished such high praise on Ted after his initial arrest. She had been married and living in Europe through his trial period but, when she took up residence in Seattle again, newly divorced, she began corresponding with Ted.

"Mostly they were just letters to make him laugh, to keep his spirits up," she explained. Like Ted, she had a wry sense of humor (her letters were sometimes addressed to "Dear Bunny" or "Dear Bun-Bun"). Carole and some other Washington State friends had visited Ted in Salt Lake City, during the spring of '75, when Carole and Ted had gone horseback riding and laughed together—only weeks before Ted's arrest and the beginning of his troubles. Like others among Ted's circle of friends, Carole was convinced of his innocence, and she was derisive of "the flock of gobbling turkeys"—the investigators, the prosecutors, the media people—who, she believed, were responsible for Ted's plight.

Throughout his Utah confinement, Ted had kept busy with his reading (*The Gulag Archipelago*, nonfiction dealing with political subjects) and his writing, which sometimes turned to poetry. In one of his poems, "Nights and Days," he wrote of the boredom of watching daytime television, especially the game shows, with their slick hosts, prizes, and giggling, raucous participants and audiences. One passage in particular would intrigue detectives who suspected Ted in the disappearances and brutal murders of all those girls. It referred to the "perverse pleasure" derived from watching such shows and the tendency of "some neat suburban daisy/To scream and go crazy."

At four o'clock on the morning of January 29, 1977, a Colorado sheriff's car passed through the gates of Point of the Mountain in a freezing fog and turned southward toward Provo, beginning the trip to Aspen. Bundy, the prisoner, handcuffed and his ankles chained, sat in the back seat with Fisher. Pitkin County Deputy Rick Kralicek was driving and, beside him, Undersheriff Ben Meyers kept an eye turned toward Bundy.

It was a secret operation. There continued to be deep concern about Bundy's security. Not only was he an escape risk, he was also a potential assassination target. Fisher knew a number of anger-filled fathers or relatives of murdered and missing girls—or some crackpot—might take pleasure in shooting the man. In the predawn darkness, the car turned eastward where the highway began rising into the mountains toward the Colorado border.

Windblown snow swept the lonely gray-brown plains, with their scrubby sage and dwarfed trees, and the distant flat-topped buttes. Fisher watched as Bundy stared at the passing landscape. "Country look familiar, Ted?" asked the mustached, long-haired investigator. It was, Fisher knew, the same highway Bundy had taken on his trips into Colorado two years earlier, the route along which he had left a trail of credit-card purchases—at Grand Junction, Glenwood Springs, and other places in Colorado.

"Yeah," Bundy replied. "It looks a little familiar."

Slowly, the three police officers in the car became uncomfortably aware that another sedan, following at some distance, was rapidly gaining on them. Kralicek accelerated the police car to eighty-five. Then to ninety. The following car continued to gain.

Meyers lifted the microphone of the police radio to send a message ahead to the Colorado Highway Patrol, to alert troopers of their home state that they were approaching the border. Meyers explained theirs was a Pitkin County vehicle with a high-security prisoner. "And we have an unidentified vehicle coming up on us from behind at a high rate of speed," Meyers added.

The speedometer hit a hundred miles an hour. "Chrissake," muttered Kralicek. "That bastard's still comin' at us like there's no tomorrow. He must be doing a hundred-ten or more."

Bundy had become aware of potential danger. Gradually, Fisher noticed, the prisoner lowered his upper body below the window level and began to slide onto the floor of the car.

The pursuing car passed them on a long, straight stretch of highway dropping down from the plateau toward the town of Grand Junction. Watching the other driver pass, Meyers sighed and grinned. "Hell, he's just a racer. Poor bastard. He's headin' into some kind of a trouble." Ahead the alerted Colorado Highway Patrol troopers waited to make the arrest.

In the back seat, Fisher glanced down at Bundy, who now lay in a hunched position on his knees on the floor of the car. With his wrists cuffed together, he seemed to be in a position of prayer. Theodore, thought Fisher, you really ARE afraid of dying, aren't you?

Utah was behind. They had just crossed the state line. Ted was in Colorado.

FIFTEEN | Taking Control

Only a handful of reporters were waiting when Ted, in handcuffs and leg irons, was brought into the old brick Pitkin County Courthouse in Aspen for his "advisory hearing" on the afternoon of January 31. His on-again, off-again beard was off again. He looked serenely confident and greeted me in the corridor with a quip: "I see I've brought you over to beautiful Aspen."

"Yeah," I said.

"Watch out for the crazy women over here," Ted laughed.

Chuck Leidner, Bundy's public defender, a man whose relaxed expression was distinctly Aspen casual, arose to fire some aggressive defense motions. He asked Judge George C. Lohr for a court order to permit Ted to make his court appearances without handcuffs or ankle restraints and that he be permitted to wear street clothes, rather than jail garb in court. Leidner further asked for a court ban on all photos of his client, in handcuffs, en route to the courtroom. Such photos carry an aura of guilt, Leidner argued.

Lohr, well known as a judge of careful sensitivity to defendant rights, agreed Ted could wear street clothes and be free of restraints when he appeared in the courtroom—despite a plea from the sheriff that Bundy had shown thoughts of escape at the Utah penitentiary. The judge took under advisement the motion to ban photography and a broader defense motion to close all pretrial hearings completely.

Ted eased into the daily routine of the ancient jail in the courthouse basement. Pitkin County deputy sheriffs discovered that their intriguing new prisoner was pleasant, talkative, witty. At Aspen, the jail had an open-cell-door policy. So Ted had a chance to mingle with and talk with the other prisoners, most of them youthful short termers, doing time for drunken driving, thefts, other minor offenses. Ted's only complaint was about the food. "Aspen has some of the finest gourmet restaurants in America," he mused, "so why is it our meals are so bad in here?"

Leidner, however, found Bundy to be a difficult, demanding client, who insisted that his lawyer spend hours with him in interminable conferences about his case. "It's a murder charge," conceded Leidner, "but one of the weakest I've ever seen. Hell, the state's got no case at all." Privately Leidner grumbled that "Bundy just wants a babysitter. I've got other cases to take care of. I can't give him all my time."

Bundy anxiously fretted that "discovery" documents—the details of investigations which had been carried out by police in the Caryn Campbell case and other murders—were coming into the possession of Leidner. Ted wanted those reports in his personal control.

Thus Bundy made a quiet resolve to undertake his own defense, *pro se*. In a penciled letter, on yellow legal stationery, he outlined that proposal to the judge, saying that course of action, handling his own case, "is intelligently charted in my own best interests. . . ." Leidner's reaction to the idea was a miffed shrug of the shoulders. Judge Lohr persuaded Bundy to wait until after the important pretrial show-cause hearings, scheduled for early April, before deciding to undertake the case, serving as his own counsel.

Frank G. E. Tucker, the district attorney, had conceded he didn't have the courtroom skills or time to handle the Bundy murder trial. So he had succeeded in getting two prosecutors assigned to the trial from Colorado Springs—Bob Russel, the D.A. there, and the quietly effective Milton K. Blakey, Russel's assistant. Blakey had already taken on most of the case preparation and had spent hours with Mike Fisher, the Aspen D.A.'s office investigator, familiarizing himself with the evidence.

Critical pretrial hearings began in early April. Under subpoena, Mrs. Harter, the state's key witness, had flown into Aspen from her California home April 3, and that evening, at Aspen's Holiday Inn, she met and chatted briefly during the dinner hour with Fisher, Blakey, and Russel. "I get a feeling something's wrong," Fisher reflected afterward. When she had picked out Bundy's photograph from those Fisher had shown her in January 1976, Mrs. Harter had been an enthusiastic, positive witness. "Now she seems kind of detached and withdrawn," Fisher told the prosecutors.

Early next morning, before the beginning of the hearing, Russel drove Mrs. Harter the few miles from Aspen to the Wildwood Inn where, together, they walked the route she had walked that night—from her room, past the elevator, down the stairs to the drugstore below. She pointed out to the prosecutor the place near the elevator where she had seen "the strange man." Russel concluded she would be a good witness.

Perhaps unwittingly, however, she was about to drop a bombshell on the prosecution when pretrial hearings began. As she took the witness stand the morning of April 4, Mrs. Harter appeared nervous and faltering, even under the gentle questioning of Blakey. She recalled her movements at the ski lodge that evening of January 12, 1975, and remembered that, while she was returning to her room she saw two men near the elevator. She described the younger man, but added that, in the darkness, she hadn't seen him too well. One man was quite close to the elevator and the other was several feet away, she said—near a low woodlath structure which surrounded a refrigeration compressor.

Suddenly Blakey had an uneasy feeling. He was now dealing with a witness who remembered having seen *two* men.

Gingerly, the prosecutor proceeded with the questioning.

198

"Do you see anyone in the courtroom that looks like either of these men?"

"Could I have one of them stand up?" asked Mrs. Harter.

"Certainly."

"The man in the first row," she replied. "Stand up."

Blakey's heart sank. The woman's eyes had swept past the defense table where Bundy sat and had focused on the front row of spectators. Mrs. Harter had pointed to a man sitting there.

"Referring to the man in the blue pants, in the blue jacket?" asked Blakey in an almost forlorn tone.

"Uh-huh," said the woman. "In the blue jacket."

Blakey stared at the man in the blue jacket standing, a sheepish look on his face. It was Ben Meyers, the undersheriff. He was a middle-aged man, huskily built, with sandy brown hair, brown eyes, and a straight nose. Some of his facial characteristics were similar to Bundy's. But he was a heftier man with a distinctly fuller, rounded face.

"Does he look like either of the men?" asked Blakey.

"Similar."

"To the one . . . ?"

"To the one by the elevator."

"The one that was close to you?"

"Right."

At the defense table, Bundy's eyes filled with mirth as he tossed his head back, suppressing a laugh. The few reporters in the room furiously scribbled notes. They had a startling story. The state's chief eyewitness had identified the "mystery man" in the Caryn Campbell murder case—the Pitkin County undersheriff!

It was a crazy moment of confusion and consternation for the prosecution. Blakey did the only reasonable thing. He ended the questioning. It remained possible that some man she'd seen near the elevator resembled Ben Meyers. Perhaps she would remember Bundy as the "strange" man, further away, near the refrigeration unit. But . . . Blakey risked no more questions.

A quiet "goddamn"—almost in unison—rose in the throats of Fisher and Russel at the prosecution table. They studied Mrs. Harter as she left the witness stand and nervously sought the courtroom exit. She had been *so positive* in her photo identification, Fisher remembered. "Somethin's happened to her. But I don't know what the hell it was," the investigator growled.

Later, a disconsolate Blakey vetoed a suggestion that someone talk to Mrs. Harter to determine what had gone wrong. "No, let's leave her alone," ruled Blakey. Perhaps by the time of trial, Blakey hoped, she could be rehabilitated as a witness.

But, for the prosecution, there had been severe damage: EYEWITNESS FAILS TO IDENTIFY BUNDY, said one of the many headlines.

Through the rest of the pretrial hearings, the prosecution produced testimony steadying the other elements of its shaky case. Robert Neill, the FBI hair-comparison specialist, testified about the morphological characteristics of human hair and the range of characteristics of Caryn Campbell's hair which were "microscopically indistinguishable" from the hair found in Bundy's Volkswagen.

Neill pointedly conceded that a hair comparison is not like a fingerprint. It is not a precise method of identification. He recited, too, the comparisons of hairs taken from the VW with the hair specimens of Carol DaRonch, the Utah kidnap victim, and the murdered Utah girl, Melissa Smith.

"Mr. Neill," asked Russel, "in your fourteen to fifteen years of experience, have you ever had the experience before, whereby, in relation to three alleged victims, you would be able to make such a match to one source?"

Neill: "In my experience, I can't recall a situation in which hairs from three alleged victims were microscopically identified from one common source, such as the interior of an automobile."

Fisher's testimony established Bundy's gas purchases near the Wildwood Inn about the time of Caryn's disappearance. There, too, was testimony about the Wildwood Inn notation discovered in the ski brochure found at Bundy's Salt Lake City apartment.

At the end, Judge Lohr ruled there was, at least, legal probable cause. Ted Bundy would stand trial for the murder of Caryn Campbell.

* * *

Even with Mrs. Harter's testimony under a dark cloud and the state's case weakened, Ted was unhappy. It upset him when he was transferred from the easy jail at Aspen to the more secure Garfield County jail, forty miles down the Roaring Fork River Valley at Glenwood Springs. Only a few weeks earlier, the Colorado health department had ruled the aged Pitkin County jail was not suited for holding prisoners on long-term basis.

He forced the issue of serving as his own counsel. Judge Lohr was clearly reluctant, issuing the standard reminder that, "a man who serves as his own attorney has a fool for a client." Yet the judge permitted Bundy to go ahead, to take command of his own case, as a *pro se* defendant. Simultaneously, Lohr ordered that Leidner and James Dumas, a Denver public defender who wished to be involved, serve as Ted Bundy's "advisory counsel."

Ted was exhilarated. He would be in control of his own murder case, defending himself against the massed efforts of police and prosecutors. He took control with gusto.

In his jail cell at Glenwood Springs, Bundy began penciling a flurry of motions to the court—motions requesting access to a telephone, mornings and afternoons, six days a week . . . that he be allowed to receive telephone calls, any time, seven days a week . . . a telephone in his cell . . . access to a law library for a three-hour period, twice a week . . . services of a secretary in the public defender's office . . . a court-appointed investigator to check the investigations of police and develop new defense evidence . . . permission to keep law books and case files in his cell . . . and to have his own forensic hair specialist, to challenge the FBI hair analysis.

Ted also began a series of vigorous actions to improve his jail conditions, his diet, the illumination of his cell. He asked Judge Lohr to order a better jail diet, plus vitamin supplements. With a deficiency of Vitamin A in his diet, "my eyes become sore and my vision blurred," he complained.

"What justification is there for being treated like a dangerous animal, with a big sign over my door saying, *Caution?*" he asked the judge. "I am guilty of nothing in the State of Colorado. The total environment is cruel and unusual. . . . The weight loss threatens my health. My treatment contradicts the notion that I am proven innocent until proven guilty. . . ."

And he demanded periods of outdoor exercise, a monthly haircut, and dental care.

Solicitously, cautiously, Judge Lohr examined each of Bundy's seemingly endless series of demands and requests and granted most of them. Soon Ted had a county-issued credit card with which he could make long-distance calls in his defense preparation. He had use of a telephone in jail and in the law library in the nearby Garfield County Courthouse, where he spent several hours each week.

Cheerfully, Bundy agreed to an interview with Barbara Grossman, of Salt Lake City's KUTV, who had traveled with her cameraman to Glenwood Springs to visit him at the jail.

Barbara and Ted, who liked each other, laughingly reminisced about the Utah happenings. With the lights and camera trained on him inside the jail, Ted discussed with Barbara his decision to direct his own legal defense. "By putting myself in the position of being my own counsel," he said with determination, "I'm using positive psychology. *I'm* going to *do* it!" His speech accelerated, his voice strengthened. "I'm going to do it because I'm right, because the person I'm representing is innocent. . . . I wanted to get involved because I'm such a part of the defense. After all, I'm going to bear the consequences. Why not bear the responsibility of seeking my own acquittal and sustaining my own innocence?

"More than ever," he said, staring hard at Barbara and the camera, "I'm convinced of my innocence."

Several days later, in the KUTV studios in Salt Lake City, Barbara and I together viewed the tapes of her jail interview with Ted. She explained it would be used as a segment of a series KUTV was producing, which also would include interviews of some of the families of the Utah crime victims—especially the families of Melissa Smith and Debbie Kent.

"Sometimes," Barbara confided, "I come away from an interview with Ted thinking I've got great stuff. But then the more you listen to what he says, the more you wonder what he's saying."

We reran the tapes, watching, listening more carefully. Ted

said he was *even more than ever* convinced of his innocence. "What the hell does that mean?" I wondered: Does it mean that at some time he was *less than convinced* of his innocence?

And his line, "The *person I'm representing* is innocent."

"That," I said, "is quintessential Ted—the lawyer discussing his client."

Near the end of May, I had a chance to interview Ted inside the Glenwood Springs jail. I found him rather edgy and hostile. Ted told me he had been displeased with the way the KUTV interview had turned out. "The problem was what they're doing with that interview," Ted complained. "Barbara Grossman was running it with a whole series of interviews and stories on the missing girls. And I mean . . . who do they have sitting there, saying he doesn't beat his wife? Me!

"Here is my interview, saying 'I'm innocent.' And then, 'All right, here we are with all these missing girls, folks.'" Ted's voice quickened and he gestured as though he were a circus ringmaster. "'And here we are, folks, with all the teary-eyed parents! And here are the solemn faced detectives.'

"And Ted Bundy's the one who's put in a position of denying it. Again and again and again. And that doesn't do me any good." Ted's jaw tightened. His eyes showed anger.

I turned the conversation toward his handling his own case. "How is it going, doing the thing you've always wanted to do, practicing law in a courtroom in a major trial?"

"It's not exactly a Walter Mitty trip," Ted said, his mood mellowing, "but it may border on that at times. I enjoy doing it. I'm doing a serious job of it." Ted was brimming with a sense of combat. In Blakey and Russel, he noted, the "State of Colorado brought in two of its top prosecutors. And I'm really holding my own against them."

He predicted he was going to beat that kidnap conviction in Salt Lake City. "I'm not guilty of crimes—the crimes in Utah or Colorado. . . . Or in Washington. I don't care what state you're talking about."

"What about Washington, now, Ted?" I asked. "Let's talk about Washington for a minute. What about those cases up there?"

He avoided my eyes as he prepared his answer.

Ted had learned, through discovery proceedings in Colorado, that there was a cold trail in the murders of the young women in Washington. He knew only a couple of eyewitnesses at Lake Sammamish State Park had identified him as the man in the park that day in July 1974—the man with his arm in a sling and the Volkswagen. He knew the other witnesses had not IDed him.

"I'm not accused of anything in Washington," Ted said confidently. "I've got the problem here. They've got a special problem up there. And I wish them all well in their investigation.

"I can't say that I will ever understand what's happening up there. That's what you have police for. I'm just a citizen looking at a situation you have in Washington as far as I'm concerned."

Ted ended that phase of the discussion. He would have nothing to say about the Washington murders.

He returned to the KUTV interview. "While I thought I was playing to a Utah market, I was obviously spread all over hell," Ted complained. "And they played it up here in Colorado in the *Denver Post*. . . . So it spreads. And I have to deny it over and over. And how am I supposed to act? Confident? Angry? How?

"People can draw their own conclusions, I suppose, from anything I say. Whether I say I'm innocent or whether I say I'm happy or whether I say I'm mad or sad. And they are going to say 'Aha! Well, I knew it!' . . . You know people say, 'Well, he's obviously a sociopath or something. . . .'"

Our interview was being conducted through some bars in a holding cell—really a sectioned part of the corridor at the Garfield County jail. Ted said he was thirsty. I bought him a Dr. Pepper from a vending machine, and we ended our chat with some casual talk about politics.

Later I thought about Ted's conspicuous use of the term "sociopath"—a psychological label I had heard him use more than once. And at times, I wondered if Ted, the psychology graduate, might have focused on that condition, in some form of self-diagnosis.

Among the multiple characteristics of the sociopath, a person who fits into a broad category of persons with antisocial behavior traits, is that he often shows emotional immaturity and an ability to rationalize behaviors, which frequently run counter to accepted rules of society. The sociopath, too, often displays a persistent propensity to get into trouble, without thought of resulting adversity or punishment, consistently rationalizing his behavior as reasonable and rational.

While Ted was at the University of Washington, earning his degree in psychology, one of the available textbooks, *Modern Psychopathology*, by Theodore Millon of the University of Illinois, offered an extensive discussion* of the various forms of sociopathic behavior:

> Despite their disrespect for the rights of others, many sociopaths present a social mask, not only of civility but of sincerity and maturity. Untroubled by feelings of guilt and a sense of loyalty, they often develop a pathological talent for lying. Unconstrained by matters of honesty and truth, they learn with great facility to weave an impressive picture of their superior competencies and reliability. Many are disarmingly ingratiating and charming in their initial social encounters, becoming skillful swindlers and imposters. Their cleverness and alertness to the weaknesses of others may enable them to play their games of deception for long periods. . . . Before long their true insincerity and unreliability may be revealed by their failure to keep "working at" their deceptions or as a consequence of their need to let others know how cleverly deceptive they have been. . . .
>
> Many sociopaths evidence a low tolerance for frustration, seem to act impetuously and cannot delay, let alone forgo, prospects for immediate pleasure. . . . Quite characteristic is a proneness to taking chances and seeking thrills, acting as if they were immune from

---

* From *Modern Psychopathology: A Biosocial Approach to Maladaptive Learning and Functioning,* by Theodore Millon. Copyright© by W. B. Saunders Company. Reprinted by permission of Holt, Rinehart and Winston.

danger. Others jump from one exciting and momentarily gratifying escapade to another, with little or no care for potentially detrimental consequences. . . .

What no one else knew—just Ted—was that he was getting ready, within the next few days, to make a newsworthy, exciting, momentarily gratifying jump.

SIXTEEN | **Jump to Freedom**

In the Ted Bundy murder case there had been so many defense motions, so many preliminary hearings in the courtroom at Aspen, that the one Tuesday morning, June 6, 1977, attracted little notice.

When the sheriff's car carrying the prisoner arrived from Glenwood Springs and parked behind the old courthouse, Bundy stepped into the sunlight, handcuffed, with Deputy Sheriff Rick Kralicek at his shoulder. A waiting Aspen photographer clicked a shot of them entering the courthouse. Bundy curled a faint, preoccupied smile toward the camera.

Although it was a warm day, Bundy wore a bulky knit, tie-around cardigan over a tan turtleneck. He had shaved his beard again.

There was a drowsy atmosphere in the upstairs courtroom during the morning proceedings. Judge Lohr listened carefully while James Dumas, the dark-haired public defender, delivered a well-used defense argument against Colorado's death-penalty statute. Time and again, in courtrooms all around Colorado, defense lawyers had been offering the same legal reasoning in capital-crimes cases. Colorado's death penalty law, Dumas told the judge, was too inflexible, in that it denied judges and juries the freedom to consider a wide range of mitigating circumstances which might have been present during the commission of a capital crime.

Already that argument was before the Colorado State Supreme Court, awaiting a decision.

While his lawyer was speaking, Bundy's glance flicked around the courtroom. From his seat at the defense table, he glanced to his right, beyond the place where the court clerk sat taking her notes, to the large window and the view of the barren base of nearby Smuggler Mountain. During recesses, Bundy often stood there at that window, gazing down onto mostly vacant stretches of brushy, rocky land behind the courthouse. In fact, he had stood beside that window so often, looking out, one of the young women in the nearby clerk's office sometimes had the nervous feeling he was thinking of jumping.

Dumas' legal argument continued. Bundy's eyes turned to his left, examining the few rows of spectator benches, mostly empty, and, beyond, the little law library. The stacks of olive-colored lawbooks there partially obscured the view of the old cathedral windows at the front of the courthouse. Through one of those open windows, Bundy could hear the sound of a passing car on Aspen's main street. It was a languid morning.

At last Dumas was ending his argument against the death penalty. Bundy watched for any expression from Judge Lohr's impassive face as Dumas concluded, "And so we move that the death penalty be removed as a consideration in this case."

Glancing at the clock, the prim judge announced the court would take its midmorning recess. Judge Lohr rose, left the bench, and passed through a side door into the clerk's office toward his chambers. With an empty, clattering sound, the few others left the courtroom and moved into the corridor.

Bundy was the last to leave. He yawned as he passed through the doors, turned into the clerk's office, and approached the service counter.

"What can we do for you?" asked Shirley Dills, the clerk.

"Hi," Bundy replied. "Has the judge filed that written

order yet? The one I asked about the other day?" It was a reference to one of several motions he had filed to improve his jail conditions.

"No, not yet," replied the clerk. "I'll check on it."

Bundy turned from the counter, walked into the corridor outside the courtroom, then circled back to the clerk's counter.

"That order?" he mumbled. "Has the judge signed that order yet?"

Dills shook her head. Perplexed that Bundy had returned to ask the same question, she wondered if he might be ill.

Alone, Bundy reentered the courtroom. As he passed through the door, he noticed his guard was still standing in the hallway, holding a half-smoked cigarette.

The courtroom was empty. Bundy walked a few steps, turned left into the aisle, past five rows of spectator benches, and pushed open the wooden gate which led to the law library. He moved quickly along the rows of bookcases and stepped into the circle of morning sunshine at the big window which was partially open.

There was no hesitation. He'd recall later, "If it had been six stories, I still would have jumped." Bundy raised the window further, and, noticing there was almost no activity in the street below, he jumped, feet first.

How are skydivers supposed to land? His thought scarcely was formed when—*thump!*—he hit the lawn. One ankle turned, and he fell. But he wasn't hurt. He rose, shed the bulky cardigan, dropped his file of papers, and ran.

Ted's only fear was that he might be shot by a guard. But he sensed the odds were against that happening. Most of Sheriff Dick Kienast's deputies, he knew, weren't the kind of old-line cops who shot first and asked questions later. No, he thought, they don't shoot you in Aspen.

He dashed behind the business building next to the court-house, then trotted down an alleyway. Within moments he was at the edge of town, beside a river flowing under a bridge. No one saw him as he ducked and scrambled into a brushy place beneath the bridge.

In the basement of the courthouse, the deputy at the front desk did a slow double-take when she heard the question.

The young man who had just walked into the sheriff's office asked, "Hey, is it kind of unusual for someone to be jumping out of the courthouse window?"

"Oh, Gawd," exclaimed the deputy after a moment. "Bundy! Where's Bundy?"

Deputies scrambled from the basement, up the stairs toward the courtroom, shouting, "Where's Bundy?" Kralicek burst into the clerk's office, asking excitedly, "Is Bundy in here?"

"No," said the clerk. Standing nearby, Judge Lohr stared in disbelief. "He's gone," exclaimed the deputy as he ran from the office.

Dills would recall later the chaos of that morning. One wave of deputies running up the stairs, to collide with another wave of deputies heading downstairs from the courtroom.

"Christalmighty, *Bundy's* gone!" shouted a voice from the second floor. The shout echoed throughout the courthouse.

Within minutes a posse, bristling with shotguns and old military carbines, was beginning to form behind the courthouse. Dills looked down on it all from her clerk's office and muttered to a fellow worker, "The Keystone Kops ride again."

Nearby, Dumas, contemplating the noisy hubbub, reflected on the argument he had just delivered in court, pleading to have the death penalty stricken from the Bundy case.

"Never," sighed Dumas to Chuck Leidner, the other defense adviser, "have I ever had a client show so little faith in my argument."

From the highway bridge, Bundy had walked quickly along the south edge of Aspen, directly toward Aspen Mountain, which rose steeply behind the town. No one recognized him. The alarm had not yet spread. When he had left the jail at Glenwood Springs early that morning, guards hadn't sensed Bundy was wearing an underlayer of clothing—jeans under his tan cords, two turtlenecks under the striped, shawl-collared cardigan. When he discarded the outer layers, the description police would remember from his courtroom appearance wouldn't be valid.

From the sheriff's office, the crackling police radio was spreading the alarm. Deputies from nearby counties were being summoned to Aspen, and roadblocks were being set up along the highway leading out of Aspen toward Glenwood Springs. Police were alerted at various places along Interstate 70.

A team of tracking dogs led the searchers from the courthouse to the Neal Street bridge, into the brush below it, to the edge of Roaring Creek. But there the dogs yelped and circled in frustration.

Bundy was gone.

The political furor was instantaneous. District Attorney Frank Tucker howled in anger at Sheriff Kienast and his men. "I told that sheriff over and over again, we had to have Bundy watched every single minute," Tucker told reporters. "We kept tellin' him 'Bundy's an escape risk!'"

Meanwhile, the sheriff's officers were quietly blaming the judge for the escape. The sheriff and prosecutor, they noted, had argued in vain to have Bundy kept in leg chains, at least during all his courtroom appearances, but Judge Lohr had considered that would be an inappropriate courtroom restraint to be placed on a defendant who was presumed to be innocent.

Possemen in high-country rigs and on horseback started up the mountain roads around Aspen that afternoon and a helicopter began searching the ridges. Meanwhile, Kienast and some of his men studied the wall map in the sheriff's office, debating where to concentrate the effort. To the south and east, up to the 9,000 and 10,000 foot flanks of Smuggler Mountain? That would have been a likely direction from the place beneath the bridge where the dogs had lost the scent. Or to the south and west—Aspen Mountain, and beyond, toward the rugged peaks at the beginning of the Maroon Bells-Snowmass Wilderness area? Or eastward, beyond miles of awesome Rocky Mountain peaks, ranging toward the Continental Divide? Did Bundy have help? A rendezvous with someone in a car?

Night fell. Police cars prowled the streets of Aspen. Heeding radio appeals, most residents locked their doors.

By the second day of the search, Aspen's offbeat sense of humor came to life. One local T-shirt shop was rapidly silkscreening a new item. Your choice, in a variety of colors: A smiling portrait of Bundy and the dark-humor message: "Ted Bundy Is a One-Night Stand."

At the bar of the Jerome Hotel, one drinker began a fund-raising effort to install a bronze plaque on the courthouse lawn where Bundy had landed after his jump from the window. The memorial to police bungling, he suggested, should be inscribed "Ted Bundy Leapt Here."

One Aspen bar quickly advertised its new "Ted Bundy Special"—a shot of tequila, rum, a dash of cascara, and two Mexican jumping beans.

In Aspen Bundy had become a folk hero.

One of the police roadblocks, between Aspen and Glenwood Springs, netted an unexpected catch on the second day. When deputies stopped a dark blue sedan, they smelled a familiar, heavy, sour-sweet aroma. They opened the trunk to discover two bales of marijuana. Another bale was in the rear seat. The burly black man who was driving the car and his well-dressed white companion were arrested for possession. The two men had been making a routine drug run from Las Vegas to Michigan when, after spending the night at Aspen, they encountered the unexpected roadblock.

Later, while he was being booked into jail, Jerris Williams, the black, asked one officer, "Hey, what's the name of this cat you had that roadblock set up for?"

The officer looked at Williams—a well-muscled, 6 foot 4, 280-pounder. "We're looking for a guy named Theodore Bundy," replied the cop. "Why do you need to know?"

"Just do me a favor," growled Williams. "Whenever you pick up this Theodore Bundy, I want you to put him in my cell with me for a while, okay?"

Mixed with Aspen's grins and derision at the Pitkin County sheriff's officers, there was fear and anguish over the escape.

In Salt Lake City police quickly set up protection around the homes of Carol DaRonch, the key witness, and Stewart Hanson, the judge in Bundy's kidnapping conviction.

At American Fork, Utah, where they had just moved into an old farmhouse, Jim and Shirleen Aime, parents of the murdered Laura Aime, seethed at the news of the escape. "Those goddamn stupid cops," snapped the father. "How could they let a thing like that happen? If I could afford it, I'd take off work and go down there and hunt for him myself." Jim bought his wife a revolver and instructed her to stay home and not let any of their other three daughters out of her sight.

In Seattle, Eleanore Rose, the anguished mother of the murdered Denise Naslund, telephoned Aspen repeatedly for news of the escape and search.

Earlier in the year she had written a letter of desperation to Bundy at the Glenwood Springs jail:

Theodore Bundy: I ask myself, "What were Denise's last thoughts? How long did she suffer? How frightened was she? How? Why?"

If you know anything—ANYTHING at all—please let me know. . . . I am so sick at heart and so unhappy. Everywhere I look I see her face. I visualize her walking in the door, sitting here and talking to me— putting her makeup on and combing her hair. . . . Please if you can give me a lead or know anything about anybody, write and let me know.

Her letter had gone unanswered. In terror, Eleanore now locked herself in her small house, alone, fearful of everything around her.

By Sunday, the fifth day following the escape, the search had yielded one trace of Bundy. Searchers discovered that a cabin eighteen miles from Aspen, on Aspen Mountain, had been burglarized. "Bundy had to break a window to get in there," said Mike Fisher, the D.A.'s investigator. "We got some really good [finger]prints out of the place."

Fisher and I sat drinking together in the hot Sunday afternoon sunshine outside the trailer house where Fisher lived at Basalt, a few miles downstream from Aspen along the Roaring Fork River. Wearing a T-shirt and faded denim shorts, Fisher sat with his right leg, the knee heavily wrapped, propped on a camp stool. "Helluva time for this to happen," growled Fisher, pointing to the knee. He had undergone surgery for an old cartilage injury the day of the escape. The knee was painfully swollen.

"I just can't believe those goddamn guards lettin' him get away," Fisher sputtered. "I kept tellin' 'em, 'He's gonna go. He's gonna go.' For weeks we were getting reports from the other prisoners in the jail. Bundy was making them all just nervous as hell. Hour after hour, they could hear him in his cell, jumping. He'd climb to the top bunk and jump to the floor. And do it over again, getting his legs in shape for that jump."

"Mike, where do you think he's gone?" I asked.

Fisher took a long swallow from a can of Budweiser and shrugged as he scanned the surrounding mountains. "Hell, he could be anyplace. But I got a hunch he didn't get far.

"I don't think Theodore is very good in the mountains," the diminutive detective added.

Theodore—when Fisher spoke the name, there was contemptuous anger in his voice and a flash in his mournful, pale-blue eyes. Probably no one in law enforcement had studied Bundy so intensively, for such a long time, as had Fisher. He had spent months assembling and storing all the collected wisdom available on Bundy.

A few years earlier, Fisher had decided to leave, as he put it, "the plastic rat race" of Southern California, where he had been making a prosperous living in sporting-goods merchandizing. Then, through police friends, he became interested in law enforcement. He took a lower paying job as a deputy sheriff in Aspen, a place where he would be surrounded by free, open country—the Rockies—with abundant fishing and hunting. Fisher was that unusual sportsman who, when he hunted deer or other mountain game, preferred to use bow and arrow. Sometimes, though, he would confess, Fisher's prey became of secondary importance as he trekked through the Colorado wilderness, especially during the richly colored Rocky Mountain autumn. "Sometimes y'know, the greatest thing in the world," he would say, "is to get under a stand of those beautiful Quakers [his nickname for the quaking aspen] and just lie there on the ground and look up through those bright yellow leaves shimmerin' against the sun. What a light show. And maybe take a nap."

Because of his feisty, intelligent persistence and his quick understanding of law, Fisher had been chosen to become the D.A.'s investigator in 1974.

Caryn Campbell had been murdered at Aspen in January 1975, and for a year and a half, Fisher had become a determined stalker working nonstop in a deeply personal hunt for her killer.

Each of us finished a beer. I rose and pulled two more cold ones out of Fisher's nearby ice chest.

"I only hope we get Theodore back without another girl getting killed," sighed Fisher. He was staring into the distance, toward a sunlit ridge, its pink-rock face dotted with mountain cedar.

I un-zip-topped a Bud and handed it to him. "Mike," I asked, "do you think Ted's good for all those cases up in Washington and Utah? I've always had my doubts."

"Yeah, most of them," he replied. "Not the California cases, though . . . I don't think. But all the others are just too damned similar." He took another swallow of beer. Then, with a long, rattling snort, he cleared his sinuses. "Ted the Troller," he murmured.

"Mike," I continued, "what do you think *really* happened to those victims? What would have been the MO?"

"Well, first there's the approach. Making the contact with the victim and then, once the girl had somehow been lured into the car or beside the car, I think she was hit pretty quick. We will probably never really know whether or not they were always out of earshot of a witness because, if there was a witness, we've never been able to find one.

"There's just a total lack of other signs of struggle on the body," he added. "No traces you might expect to find, for example, under the fingernails, if a girl had been able to put up a fight. So I think immobilizing the victim was accomplished first. Similar to DaRonch. Like, 'Here comes the crowbar! Bang!'"

"Do you think the victim is killed with that first blow?"

"I don't think that initial blow could have been all that controlled. You couldn't predict that the first blow would kill each victim or only render her unconscious or partially conscious. The lack of clothing also goes against you in trying to figure out what happened. If you never find the clothing, you never know how much violence there was, because you don't know if the clothing was unbuttoned, or cut off, or torn off or . . . Christ, maybe it was eaten."

"Any theory on the clothing? What was done with it?"

"Those garbage bags . . . that damned garbage bag in his Volkswagen up in Utah. You put clothes in a black plastic garbage bag, tie a knot in the top, and toss it in a dumpster. And then *Adios!* We never found one single scrap of those girls' clothes."

"Would it be possible, inside a little Volkswagen, to swing a crowbar with enough of a swipe to really knock out the girl?"

"Oh, yeah. I think once she was in that passenger's seat, if that was the MO at that particular time, it was just down with the hand to pick up the crowbar and then across. And bang! Ten, fifteen inches of metal is a lot of force. Left-handed, or with the right hand. It had to be very quick and it had to be very natural. With the right hand, sort of a backhand wrist snap. WHAP! That first shot had to be enough to bend them over so they could be handled after that.

"Some of the victims could have been killed with the first blow or the second blow. But where, in the sequence of things, the other blows came, I don't know. We have, in just about every case, up to as many as four blows. But they're just about all from about the same quarter. Now I would think that if a guy was going to start hitting with the crowbar during sexual intercourse, or while he's doing whatever he's doing with them, when he's all excited, I think we'd have a great deal more massive violence on all the victims."

"What about strangulation? Where would that occur? At what phase?"

"I think the strangulation came along with the sexual attack part of it. Particularly where there was anal intercourse. Usually you find a pattern of experimenting in the sexual part of it. Always experimenting, which is why you have a difference from case to case. That's part of the profile of the antisocial personality. Experimentation. Anal intercourse could have been part of that and we know that, up in Seattle, he was playing with that. And bondage. And I think the strangulation was part of the sexual experimentation. See, strangulation causes contraction of the sphincter."

Fisher groaned in pain and shifted his swollen knee.

And he reflected on the hours he had spent with the prosecutor, Milt Blakey, examining all the autopsy photos of the Utah and Colorado victims whose bodies had been found. "I'm not expert on all this, of course," Fisher said, "but it sure does appear that the strangulation was coming from the rear. In other words, the ligature was being bound and was being tightened from the rear."

"Do you think that the victim was killed inside the car," I asked, "and then moved into the trunk for transportation to the dump site?"

"Could be. Or the victim could have been bopped on the outside of the car. Let's say her suspicion grew as they approached the car. And maybe a thump and a bump on the outside of the car put her down. Then put her in a big garbage bag and put her under the hood to move her somewhere."

"That would be a helluva lot of dead weight to lift. It'd take a lot of strength."

"Well, in a situation like that, that kind of a personality, all hyped up, all fired up with the excitement of the killing, the beating, has got a lot of adrenaline pumping. You can lift enormous weight. You know this from the preliminary hearing—that in Caryn's case, we found one hair under the floor mat inside the car. And another hair is found in the trunk. That could lead you to two theories. Was she in both places? Or was she just in the front and then her clothes placed in the trunk—in the bag? Where the hair fell off."

"So you come up with the initial knockout, then hauling the victim, either inside the car or in the trunk, to some other place, where you have strangulation, with the intercourse or whatever else there was. Then," I asked, "they're dead when they're dropped?"

"No, I don't think he ever checks them out for any vitals. That's an interesting little ploy he uses. He always leaves them near a road. Right off the road. You know how he rationalizes everything. He can say, 'Now, if she had just gotten up, somebody would have seen her.' Or, 'Somebody was bound to find her. Therefore, it's not my fault.'"

"What the hell is that all about?"

"Well, it goes back to what the doctor up in the Utah pen said. Often a guy will be using that rationalization—that if the victim could have gotten up, or if someone had just come by, she might still be alive today. I can say, 'I'm not the full fault of all this.' "

I thought about that for a while. "So what does that do? Make it possible to say, 'I'm innocent of murder?' "

Noisily Fisher cleared his sinuses again. "Yes. He's got everything pretty well rationalized."

I was intrigued by Fisher's analysis of his prey—Ted, my friend. Fisher understood that Ted and I were longtime acquaintances. I asked if Fisher thought he could ever get Bundy to talk—to confess or to make any incriminating concessions at all.

"I doubt it," replied Fisher, "unless you catch Theodore when he's really down. When he's all in pieces, ragged as hell. Now that could happen. If, y'know, he gets caught here—without being shot—and he's all exhausted. He'll be really, really down. Maybe then."

Fisher confided that he had gotten a promise from Sheriff Kienast. "If Theodore's caught, then the first thing that happens is I'm gonna hit him with questions. Not about his goddamn escape, because that's what he'll be expecting. We're just going to talk about Caryn Campbell's murder.

"I think he's still up those goddamn mountains somewhere," Fisher continued, shifting his knee again. "And he can't handle those mountains. They're just awesome if you're not familiar with them. When we get him, he's going to be pitiful. He's gonna be way down. And we'll just talk about that murder."

During the five days since his jump, Ted had never really gotten much beyond Aspen Mountain. After he circled the edge of the town, he reached the woods at the foot of the mountain and made a lung-tearing run to the top—past the 8,200 foot level, then above 9,000 feet, then higher.

He had no real plan. In his pocket he carried a sparsely detailed map of the Aspen area mountains and some vitamins he had saved from his extra jail ration as prescribed by court order.

When Ted reached the top of the mountain that first day, exhausted, he became confused about the best route to take from there. Had he turned toward his left and followed along the crest of some forbidding ridges, he would eventually have crossed into the Gunnison country—or eastward, the Continental Divide.

Instead, he turned in the opposite direction and began moving in befuddled circles. That night a cold rain and snow pelted the mountain, and Ted, wet and shivering, returned to a vacant cabin he had noticed earlier in the day. After long thought about the dangers, he broke into the cabin. Inside he looked for food, but found only some brown sugar. He slept for a while. Through part of the following day, he lay in the cabin, listening to the sounds of the searching aircraft overhead.

Carrying a .22 rifle he had taken from the cabin, Ted tried to find an escape route, but in whatever direction he tried, he encountered awesome, sheer, frightening rock mountain faces, which seemed to stretch for miles.

Always Ted would retreat, tired and confused, limping on blistered feet, toward the cabin. His hands had become bloodied as a result of falls on the sharp, merciless rocks. As each long night and terrifying day passed, Ted felt smaller, weaker.

By Saturday he discovered traces the searchers had been at the cabin. Ted shivered in the nearby woods that night. On Sunday morning, the helicopter hovered to a landing on an open ridge near the cabin to discharge a searcher and a dog. From his wooded cover 200 feet away, Ted watched, his heart pounding. But the dog didn't pick up his scent.

That night, exhausted, limping, befuddled by the high altitude, Ted made his way back down the mountain into the Castle Creek drainage, even though he knew the route led back into Aspen. He tossed the .22 away. Carrying a rifle, he might be shot.

In the middle of the night, just outside town, Ted crossed the Glenwood Springs highway and slipped into a darkened Aspen residential area. In front of one house, he found an unlocked Cadillac with the key in the ignition switch.

Well, he thought wearily, let's just give it a go.

He was recaptured shortly after two o'clock that morning. Deputy Sheriffs Maureen Higgins and Gene Flatt, driving in their patrol car, noticed the oncoming headlights of the car on Highway 82, entering Aspen from the west. The car weaved slowly toward the right shoulder of the road. "Probably a drunk," said Flatt, turning the police spotlight on the light-colored Cadillac. The driver appeared to slump down in his seat and turned his head away from the light.

When the car was stopped, Flatt at first didn't recognize the driver. He wore a plaid shirt, an old yellow fishing hat, and some wire frame glasses he had found in the car. And he'd applied a Band-Aid over his nose.

Bundy—emaciated, exhausted, confused—was ordered out of the car and told to spreadeagle on the roadway while Higgins radioed for other officers. Minutes later one of the deputies, shining a flashlight in his face, grinned, "Hi, Ted, welcome back."

Two hours later a crowd of deputies and news reporters clustered around the counter at the sheriff's office. In a back room Bundy was being interrogated about his escape by Sheriff Kienast and Deputy Don Davis. Leaning against a nearby wall, propped on his crutches, Fisher was alone in anger.

The look on his face told it all. The sheriff had reneged on the promise. Fisher wasn't getting first crack at questioning Bundy—about murders. The sheriff was draining all the details from Bundy about his escape. That was the sheriff's political priority at the moment.

In the interview room, the sheriff's people provided Bundy with coffee and food and some medication for his scraped, blistered feet. Smiling, talking, Ted gathered his composure, and he told his attentive questioners, over and over again, the details of his jump from the courthouse and his race up Aspen Mountain. "I just ran right straight up that mountain without stopping," he laughed with pride.

"And when I came back down off that mountain, I knew I was going to get caught," he said. "But I was just . . . I dunno . . . I just didn't care. It was a funny thing. My body was strong, but my mind was weak." He chuckled—weakly— at the thought.

The sheriff's office cranked out news releases for the

waiting reporters, detailing the recapture. Two hours elapsed before Fisher was given his chance to talk to Bundy, who now was fully composed and in command.

When the investigator entered the interrogation room, Bundy noticed he was on crutches. "Gee, Mike," he said solicitously, "I hope I wasn't the cause of that."

"No," growled Fisher. "Ted, I want to talk with you about the Caryn Campbell murder."

Bundy smiled. His eyes were confident. Fisher knew that the fleeting moment when Bundy might be caught with his defenses down had passed.

Next day, exhausted, gaunt, and disheveled, resembling an animal which had been run to ground, Ted was taken— shackled and barefoot—into court again. He faced a mass of new charges—escape, auto theft, burglary. Judge Lohr's mood had changed. Sternly he warned Bundy, "It's possible that consecutive sentences could be proposed." And that, Lohr warned ominously, could add up to 90 years. Hollow-eyed, Ted had no reply.

Later, in the basement cell of the courthouse, Ted had a visit with John Henry Browne, the Seattle lawyer, a tall man with long hair and electric dark eyes. Browne, a trusted counselor, had been one of the first people Ted telephoned after his recapture. Sensing there were now storms of crisis around his friend, Browne had flown immediately to Aspen.

"Ted," said Browne, "I think you'd better give up this idea of a *pro se* defense." Now, confronted by the new charges, there would be no way Bundy could handle it all, Browne told him.

The exhausted Bundy, slumped on a jail cot in jail coveralls, his bare feet bandaged and bleeding, listened as Browne emphasized that a murder conviction could mean the death penalty.

Browne produced a pamphlet he had recently obtained—a booklet issued by the Team Defense Project, Inc., legal organization in Atlanta. Headed by Attorney Millard Farmer, it was, Browne explained, a group which was fighting the death penalty in all states. "You might want to get in touch with Farmer. He could be a lot of help to you in your case here," Browne suggested. Ted accepted the pamphlet.

"What's going on with executions now?" Ted asked. "Where are most people likely to be executed now?"

"I suppose it might be Georgia," replied Browne. "No," he corrected himself. "It'd probably be Florida now."

"Florida?" repeated Bundy.

Browne explained there had been a U.S. Supreme Court ruling which had clearly upheld the constitutionality of Florida's death-penalty statute.

"Florida's probably where they'll start executing now," said Browne.

"Florida," murmured Bundy, "Florida. Hmmh."

SEVENTEEN | Similar Transactions

There was a kaleidoscopic aftermath to Ted Bundy's freedom leap at Aspen.

Pale, weak, and skinny after his ordeal in the Rockies, Ted managed some gaunt grins, when he heard how he had become a full-fledged Aspen celebrity—with Ted Bundy T-shirts and the Bundy-inspired cartoons lampooning the Pitkin County sheriff's office. One Aspenite named her newborn quarterhorse colt Ted Bundy, saying, "It'll know how to run." Bundy had made the cops look silly, and that, in the view of the habitués of the Jerome bar and other Aspen hangouts, was a beautiful trip.

Ted added to the festival of comment with his dry question: "Did anyone see who it was that pushed me out that window?"

There was an investigation of the sheriff's department's lapse of security in the courtroom. There were some resignations and firings (some of them more political than escape-related), but Sheriff Kienast emerged, predictably, unscathed.

For Chuck Leidner, the public defender, Ted had been a

troublesome, argumentative, demanding client. Now, because Leidner and Jim Dumas had been in the courthouse and thus would be potential witnesses to their client's escape, a crime, the defenders were excused as Ted Bundy's advisory counsel.

During his brief visit in Aspen, John Henry Browne, Ted's Seattle counselor, spurred Bundy to accept new court-appointed counsel to represent him on the escape-related charges, as he was urging his friend also to consider giving up his *pro se* murder defense. Ted had seemed contemptuous of his public-defender lawyers, perhaps because they were *public* lawyers, whose practice usually involved indigents, usually petty-crime defendants. Browne and Bundy were conspicuously pleased when, during a postescape hearing, Judge Lohr appointed Stephen (Buzzy) Ware, a brilliant Aspen lawyer, a private-practice specialist in major-crimes defense, to represent Ted. Named as Ware's associate was Kenneth Dresner.

Later, when I met with Ted in his cell at the Garfield County jail at Glenwood Springs, I found him enthusiastic, almost euphoric, about his new lawyers. "They just left the cell here a few minutes ago," Ted told me cheerfully. "We had a couple hours together. Our first meeting. And I was really impressed. It went awfully well.

"Dick," he continued, "I'm *so* impressed with their imagination. Not only their ability to comprehend this case as quickly as they have—it's just incredible—but their imagination. It just runs rampant! Just like my own!

"I always appreciate people that have that kind of creativity."

Ted continued in a rush of praise for Buzzy Ware. "And Buzzy . . . Just great! It's the silver lining to the whole thing. Who would have thought that, coming to Colorado, that not only would I be in the driver's seat in my own case, but [that I'd have] *my own* investigator, *my own* hair expert, *my own* pathologist, *my own* very first-rate attorneys. I'm far better off than I was in the Utah thing."

"Sounds great," I replied. Despite new problems, Ted was brimming with confidence. New security restraints had been placed on him over at Aspen. He'd have to wear leg irons during his courtroom appearances, and the Pitkin County guards watched him more carefully. Judge Lohr had ordered tighter rules on Ted's use of a telephone. But Ted still was a *pro se* defendant and maintained his telephoning and other privileges, including regular trips from the cell where we were visiting to the nearby law library in the Garfield County courthouse.

When I had come to Glenwood Springs to see Ted there that day, I had been surprised at the casualness of the Garfield County jailers. I hadn't been searched. Instead, the obliging deputy had taken me directly to Ted's cell and locked me inside with him. Occasionally I glanced at the small window of the solid steel door, but there was no guard to be seen. (Eventually, after an hour, Ted and I would have to pound on the door to get me out.)

His jump, Ted said, was probably triggered by his lengthy isolation and confinement—"in a six- by twelve- by six-foot-high cell, where people are ordered not to speak to me." He lifted both hands toward the walls and ceiling of the steel box where we stood, each of us leaning uncomfortably against the upper cot.

"Well, since the escape," Ted grinned, "I've gotten lots of mail." He gestured toward a box of letters and envelopes in the mounds and boxes of legal documents and books stored on the top bunk. "I got one very charming little note from a girl. She's ten or eleven or twelve years old, I don't know. Complete with her picture. Neat little girl . . . She's the only girl Golden Gloves boxer. . . ." We both began to shake with laughter.

"A *girl* Golden Gloves boxer?"

"True," said Ted, almost giggling. He explained: "She was a big media favorite in Utah. You know why? She and Gary Gilmore were very close. He gave her a bicycle. He wrote to her constantly from prison, and she wrote to him. . . . I've got her letter somewhere here."

Ted rummaged through his correspondence and pulled out her letter. "And I disagree totally with the Gary Gilmore trip, right? But she was really into it. Anyway, she says, 'He fought for his right to die and he won his fight.' "

"Yeah, Gilmore won, I guess," I observed. "If that's how you define victory."

"He sure did," said Ted. "And she says, 'I was hoping you would win your fight for freedom. And I believe you're innocent.' Y'know," Ted concluded, folding the girl's note, "it was a nice letter, and I wrote back to her."

I asked Ted how he felt about the whole new array of charges facing him—the murder charge and now all the other charges of escape, car theft, and the others. It was obvious now there would be delays in the murder trial. "How will they proceed with all these other charges? What'll be the scenario?"

"Well, how about this for a scenario?" Ted began. "I am not only found innocent of the murder charge, but I am given a new trial in the DaRonch case. And I'm found not convicted of anything. But I would stand faced with the escape charges."

He stood in the middle of the cell, delivering that prediction, like a speech, with intensity. "And," I replied, "the escape charge just would never be prosecutable if it involved a man who'd been jailed but not guilty?"

"Exactly right," Ted said.

In his initial appearance on Ted's behalf, Ware had begun to dissect the escape-related charges. The burglary of the cabin might not have been a burglary at all, Ware noted, because the cabin technically wasn't a "dwelling." And, in the taking of the Cadillac, there was no evidence of theft, "merely joy riding."

Stephen Arnold Ware, thirty-four, had an impressive, extensive private law practice. Sometimes he flew his own plane to distant courtrooms to represent wealthy clients in major racketeering and narcotics cases. In appearance, Ware was a blend of the urbane and rustic—quick witted, wry, lively eyes peering through thick glasses, and a shock of blond hair topped by a cowlick. He had a penchant for speed—by plane, car, or motorcycle. On the early morning of Thursday, August 11, 1977, only a few weeks after he began representing Bundy, Ware crashed his motorcycle at high speed into a rock wall beside a highway near Aspen. Ware's wife, Pamela, was killed outright. Ware's face and skull were smashed. A helicopter whisked him to St. Anthony's Hospital in Denver where he remained in a coma for days.

"God, it's a tragedy," said Ted as we discussed the accident later by telephone. "Just awful." Ted choked in tears. Eventually Ware would make a long, slow recovery, but he would be of no further help to Bundy.

Bundy's soaring confidence and his cheerful belief in "the silver lining" he'd found in Colorado turned abruptly to dark anger. The prosecution served notice of its intent to introduce "similar transaction" evidence in his trial. Milt Blakey, the prosecutor, moved to have the court consider in the Caryn Campbell case the facts and circumstances involved in the Utah murders of Melissa Smith and Laura Aime, the disappearance of Debbie Kent and the kidnapping of Carol DaRonch. Under Colorado law, it was possible to introduce into one case evidence of "other, similar acts or transactions of the defendant."

If testimony about the Utah cases could be introduced in the Colorado trial, it would be a substantial bolstering of a thin case, which had almost been fractured by Lizabeth Harter's failure to identify Bundy in court.

Bundy told me he was thinking about complaining to the Colorado Bar Association about, what he called the "unprofessional and unethical conduct of the prosecution" in seeking to introduce those other cases. "They're just goddamn desperate," Bundy snapped. Here he was, holding his own, punching holes in their weak murder case, he grumbled, "and now they're talking about three homicides, a missing person, and a kidnapping. And I don't think it's right."

You know," said Mike Fisher, the Aspen investigator, "they're just absolutely identical."

Milt Blakey, the prosecutor, sitting in Fisher's Aspen office, nodded in agreement. For hours he and Fisher had been going over the case reports from Utah, comparing the autopsy photos and reports on the murdered Melissa Smith and Laura Aime, with the autopsy and photos of Caryn Campbell.

There should be little trouble, Blakey reckoned, in getting the Carol DaRonch kidnapping into the case. It would be worth the effort too, to attempt to introduce the Debbie Kent disappearance as a "similar," considering the handcuff key found at Viewmont High School where Debbie disappeared, plus the two witnesses who placed Bundy at the high school that night.

"There's a possibility, too, in the Smith case," Blakey added. Melissa's autopsy, her cause of death, the damage to the skull and jaw were like the damage to Caryn Campbell. And there was the other wispy link—the hair specimens, comparable to both Caryn's and Melissa's hair, both found in Bundy's Volkswagen.

"Now in the Laura Aime murder," Fisher explained, "we got a lot of trouble. Her murder's identical. A carbon copy. She goes out right after they find Melissa's body. And look at the strangulation and skull damage."

Blakey nodded, again studying the autopsy photos.

"But," continued Fisher, "the trouble is, we cannot get one goddamn bit of help out of the Utah County sheriff up there in Provo. I don't know what's going on. But they're absolutely uncooperative."

"About the hair in the Volkswagen . . ." Blakey began. Fisher nodded. Both men had the same thought: What if there still remained, undetected in Bundy's Volkswagen, a hair which would match the hair of Laura Aime?

Bob Neill, the FBI specialist, had already testified he'd never before encountered a situation where hair samples, all found in one car, "matched" the hair of *three* different victims.

Both Fisher and Blakey wondered if there might be *a fourth* to be found—Laura Aime's.

"They've vacuumed the hell out of Theodore's car up in Salt Lake," said Fisher. "But I'd like to have our guys at the CBI [Colorado Bureau of Investigation] lab really tear the goddamn thing apart."

"Worth a try," said Blakey.

Once again, the tireless Fisher hit the trail—to pick up the largely stripped Volkswagen from the Salt Lake County impoundment garage, load it into a van, and haul it to Denver to the CBI laboratory. Already the seats and everything removable was gone from the interior of the VW, the result of the searches and vacuumings by Jerry Thompson and the others in Salt Lake County.

At the Denver lab, Fisher waited while lab specialists stripped away the headliner, the side panels and dug into tiny crevices of the floor, especially the well beneath the emergency brake, vacuuming, testing for any more trace evidence to be submitted to examination.

Completing his thousand-mile marathon, Fisher drove the van, carrying the skeletonized Volkswagen, back to Salt Lake City.

Through the months of 1977, a strange political law-enforcement feud had been going on in the Utah County Courthouse at Provo, in Utah's Mormon heartland. Sheriff Mack Holley and most of his men had quickly concluded, after Laura Aime's body was found in November 1974, that her death was unrelated to the crimes in neighboring Salt Lake County. And Holley had pointedly informed the Salt Lake investigators to stay out of his case.

Later, however, Utah County had an aggressive new county attorney, Noal Wootton, who brought into his office a well-trained investigator, Brent Bullock. As he studied the Salt Lake County crimes, talked with the investigators, Bullock concluded, "Hell, this Laura Aime case is like theirs. It sounds to me like it was the same guy."

But Holley and Sergeant Owen Quarnberg, the sheriff's initial investigator, stubbornly disputed that. Despite the doubts of Laura's parents and some other deputies who'd been involved, the Utah sheriff's department had taken the position that Laura had been a runaway, a hitchhiker, who had probably been living somewhere, or held somewhere, for several days between her October 31 disappearance and the time her body was found twenty-seven days later in American Fork Canyon.

It was a chance conversation that day in early '77. Sitting in his office, discussing the Aime case with Dick Smith, a sheriff's deputy, Bullock uttered a thought: "I just wonder if we could ever place Bundy down here in Utah County around that time."

"Shit, yes," replied Smith. "Didn't anybody ever tell you?"

"Tell me what?" asked Bullock.

"Well, way back, after Bundy was picked up and charged, I came across a girl who identified Bundy as the guy who'd been hanging out over at Brown's Cafe, at Lehi, where Laura Aime disappeared."

"WHAAT?" Bullock bolted forward in his chair.

No one else in the sheriff's department seemed interested at the time, though, complained Smith. "And I was just a lowly deputy."

On his own, getting some help from Smith, from Fisher at Aspen, and from the Salt Lake County detectives, Bullock began pushing a reinvestigation.

From Smith's witness, Marin Beverige, a girlfriend of Laura Aime, came a startling new version of the case.

Marin told Smith and Bullock that an older, good-looking, wavy-haired man, who said he was a university student and who drove a Volkswagen, had first appeared at the small town of Lehi one day in September 1974. Marin remembered that she and Laura were sitting together in sunshine with some other teenagers on the grass of a high school. He joined them. When a boy teased Laura by putting some grass down her halter top, the "college guy" objected. "This guy came unglued and told him [the boy] Laura was his," Marin said.

"He was really weird," Marin continued. She recalled the man kept reappearing in Lehi, always looking for Laura. One night at Brown's Café on the main street of the small town, Marin recalled, "He came in and was sitting there talking and I got up. . . . When Laura said, 'I'm ready to go,' this guy said, 'You can't. I'm going to rape you.'"

"Laura just laughed and pushed him away."

Marin told her interviewers she had seen the man again and again, once driving his Volkswagen past Marin's house when Laura was there. One night he came to the house and called Laura outdoors where they held a private conversation. Afterward, said Marin, "Laura was really shook up. But she wouldn't say what happened."

Laura had vanished the night of October 31, 1974, and Marin had a totally new version of what happened that night—different from the conclusions which the Utah County sheriff's office had recorded in its case reports. Laura, Marin, and several other teenagers had gathered at Marin's home for a Halloween party. The boys had brought an abundance of vodka, and Laura had had a lot to drink. "It was about midnight or so, and she was pretty well drunk," said Marin. "And she wanted me to walk downtown with her to get some cigarettes." Marin declined. But, she said, she watched as

Laura began to walk in the darkness, toward Brown's, the all-night restaurant, one block away.

That was the last she saw of Laura. "Around three or four o'clock some of us went to town to look for her," said Marin, "but we couldn't find her."

When shown a photo lineup, Marin chose the picture of Ted Bundy.

"Will you take a polygraph test—that's a lie detector—to verify what you've told us?" asked Bullock. Marin agreed. She passed the test.

A woman employee of Brown's Café made a similar identification.

Bullock calculated it. From Brown's Café on Lehi's main street, it was a quick drive along old highway 89 to American Fork and there, after passing the business district, a left turn would have put the killer and Laura on an easy, quick route to the American Fork canyon where her body had been found.

Bullock's findings were exciting, encouraging news to Fisher.

"Y'know," said Fisher, "there's always been something about that Aime case—that one in particular—that's bothered Theodore. When several case files were given to Bundy in his jail cell, under the discovery procedure," said Fisher, "the first one he went for—and he really tore into it—was the Aime case."

Together Bullock and Fisher were developing a strange theory. "Maybe," guessed Fisher, "our man departed from his usual MO just once. In every other case, the victim became a victim because she had never had any contact with Bundy. Maybe this was the *one* time where there had been some previous contact with the victim."

The time frame was right, the investigators noted. The sightings of the man with the Volkswagen had been in late September and during October 1974—a time of stress for Bundy, when he was skipping his law school classes and running up miles on his Volkswagen.

For weeks, Fisher tried in vain to get Sheriff Holley to provide the evidence gathered at the Aime crime scene and autopsy—especially the specimens of head hair and pubic hair taken at the autopsy. In frustration, Fisher eventually called

Bullock. "Brent," said the investigator at Aspen, "we can't get any response from the sheriff there. We keep getting told it'll be sent but we never get the stuff."

"Mike," replied the Provo investigator, "I got this eerie feeling that the sheriff may have *lost* the evidence."

"Oh, Christ," sighed Fisher. "That's all we need. . . . Here we are with a whole bunch of new hair vacuumed out of that goddamn Volkswagen. And we need a sample from Aime for comparison. And those SOB's *lost* it?"

In October 1977, Randy Ripplinger, Provo bureau chief for Salt Lake City's KUTV, dropped a bombshell on the station's nightly newscast. The Utah County sheriff's department, he reported, had lost or thrown away some or all of the evidence it had collected in the Laura Aime murder investigation less than three years earlier.

In his telecast, Ripplinger reported that at least two sources within the sheriff's department had confirmed the loss which had occurred while the sheriff's people were moving into a new office. The television newsman quoted one of the sheriff's officers as saying, " 'To be quite frank, I believe I threw it out. I got tired of moving it around.' "

Next day, an irate Sheriff Holley, sensing political troubles, confronted the county attorney and his investigator, demanding to know who leaked the information to Ripplinger.

"Mack," asked Bullock levelly, *"is* the evidence lost?"

The sheriff had a lame reply. It wasn't really evidence—it would have become evidence only when admitted in a trial. But, yes, he acknowledged, Laura Aime's hair specimens and other trace evidence collected at the autopsy and at the crime scene were gone.

For nearly three years, his frustration had continued to eat within Jim Aime. In the Aime's century-old, weathered farmhouse, outside the town of American Fork near Provo, Laura's father sat brooding at the kitchen table. And for perhaps the five-thousandth time, he cursed and banged his fist on the table top. "Dammit," he exclaimed, "it's bad enough to have your daughter murdered, but to think that those goddamn cops don't know what the hell they're doing . . . or they don't care . . ."

Standing nearby, idly wiping the top of the kitchen range,

Shirleen Aime agreed in a dry voice: "Well, they *don't* know what they're doing."

Never, in all the weeks following their daughter's murder, did the Aimes believe that the sheriff's office had investigated the case thoroughly enough. Sheriff Holley said he didn't have the manpower to assign anyone full time to the investigation. The Aimes had pleaded with Holley to allow Salt Lake County detectives to enter the case. They were capable and anxious to help. But Holley had refused the outside help, Bullock told the Aimes.

"Brent Bullock's the only one who seems to know what the hell he's doing," said Jim. "But what can he do when the sheriff won't help?"

It was almost the third anniversary of Laura's murder, and her parents were in for another shock. When Brent Bullock came to visit them, he explained he was heavy-hearted. "I've got something really difficult to ask. Can we sit down?"

Jim and Shirleen nodded toward the kitchen table, where they all sat down together. Bullock explained to the parents that, in Colorado, there was an important hearing coming up in the murder trial of Ted Bundy. The Aimes nodded. They knew all about Bundy's trial there. The Aimes had absorbed every bit of information they could about the man they strongly suspected had killed their daughter. He haunted their lives. Shirleen had once gone to the Salt Lake County courthouse to view Bundy in the courtroom. From a cousin who lived in Bountiful, Shirleen had learned that police there were ready to charge Bundy with the murder of Debbie Kent, except that Debbie's body had never been found. So Shirleen had sought training in psychic methods, placed herself in a trance, and had spent hours searching the mountains near Bountiful, looking for the remains of Debbie, another mother's murdered daughter.

"Yes, we know all about it," said Shirleen.

Bullock told them how the Colorado prosecution was trying to relate Laura's murder to the Colorado case. "Now they've vacuumed some more hair out of Bundy's Volkswagen," said Bullock. "And they'd like to make some comparisons, to see if one of those hairs might match Laura's."

Bullock gulped and issued a deep sigh. He saw that the Aimes anticipated what was coming. They had heard the rumors that Sheriff Holley's office had lost all the evidence, including the hair samples which had been taken from Laura.

"So we need a sample of hair," Bullock continued. "And that means we're going to have to ask you if Laura's body could be exhumed. Now the odds are less than fifty-fifty that they'll find a match, but . . ."

Tears welled in the eyes of the mother and father as they exchanged glances. There was agreement.

"Oh, God, God," whimpered Jim Aime, elbows propped on the table, his rugged hands clutched to his forehead. Tears again poured onto his lined cheeks. "You might as well go ahead. They can't hurt her any more than she's already been hurt."

EIGHTEEN | Oh, the Rose Bowl Game

In Utah, in early November 1977, almost exactly three years after they happened, the murders of Laura Aime and Melissa Smith and the disappearance of Debbie Kent were being intensively reinvestigated by the men from Colorado.

At Aspen, Judge George Lohr was considering Prosecutor Milt Blakey's argument that there were similar threads of circumstance which ran through those crimes and the Carol DaRonch kidnapping, "which, taken altogether, comprise a common fabric, a pattern of conduct," and that included Caryn Campbell's murder. And interwoven with it all was Ted Bundy.

On November 3, Blakey, in a closed-door hearing in Judge Lohr's chambers, had made an offer of proof on that argument. Bundy, now being assisted by Aspen attorney Kevin O'Reilly, argued vehemently. "The *dis*similarities of all these transactions," Ted said, "are just overwhelming."

Hours later, Blakey, Mike Fisher, and George Vahsholtz, the district attorney's investigator from Colorado, were scurrying from place to place in Utah, interviewing witnesses.

"All we've got to do," Blakey wryly told Fisher and Vahsholtz, "is solve three unsolved murders to bolster our own case."

At Bountiful, local police opened their files on the Debbie Kent case to Fisher and Vahsholtz who went through the investigation records and began reinterviewing witnesses who had known Debbie or who had been at Viewmont High School, November 8, 1974, the night she left the auditorium and vanished.

In the Bountiful police station, Tammy Tingy, a short, black-haired, black-eyed Indian girl, gave some startling information to Fisher. She told him that, the night Debbie disappeared, "I talked with the weird guy who was standing there in the back of the auditorium."

"How close were you to him?" asked Fisher.

"Right next to him," she replied. Tammy, although a shy girl, was certain. In October 1975, she had sat in the police lineup room at Salt Lake City and had chosen Bundy as the man she'd seen that night. But in subsequent police questioning, the subdued Tammy had been questioned less extensively than had been the Viewmont High School teacher, Raylene Shepherd.

"Then when he walked forward, from the back wall of the auditorium up to the brick divider," Tammy continued, "I walked up there, too, and stood next to him."

"From where you were standing, could you—and the man—see Debbie?" asked Fisher.

"Oh, sure. She was sitting just a couple rows in front of us."

"Tammy, would you draw a diagram for me, to show where you were . . . where the guy was and where Debbie was sitting?"

The Indian girl obliged. A terrific witness, thought Fisher. With thoughtful, deliberate confidence, she placed Ted Bundy, standing, watching, fifteen feet behind Debbie Kent just before that moment when Debbie rose to leave the auditorium.

"And did you know Debbie pretty well?" Fisher asked.

"We were locker partners all through high school," Tammy replied firmly. "She was my friend."

Fisher emphasized to Tammy it was important that she be sure of what she was saying, especially her identification of Ted Bundy as the man who stood beside her that evening.

The young woman's response was quiet, emphatic: "*God* knows I'm right."

Fisher's mournful blue eyes studied her earnest face. "Thank you, Tammy," he said.

Afterward, Fisher and Vahsholtz began tracking down another young woman who had been at the high school that night—a girl who had been approached by a man in the parking lot. "She reported at the time the guy came over to her at her car and asked her to come help him hold something on the engine of his car so he could get it started," said Vahsholtz. "She wouldn't go with him."

"Sounds like our boy's MO," observed Fisher.

But, noted Vahsholtz, "she says this guy was wearing glasses."

"And we've never had Bundy wearing glasses," mused Fisher with a shrug. "Huh!"

That night, by telephone, Vahsholtz reached the woman, now a student at Utah State University in Logan. She confirmed that report and gave a description of the man, which matched Bundy. But she insisted the man in the parking lot that night had been wearing glasses—"with lenses that had kind of a graduated tint."

"Well, maybe I should make a run up to Logan to talk to her anyway," said Fisher.

Over breakfast next morning at the Tri-Arcs Travelodge in Salt Lake City, Blakey, Fisher, and Vahsholtz were talking over details of their simultaneous reinvestigations—at Provo in the Laura Aime case, at Salt Lake City in the Smith murder and DaRonch kidnapping, and at Bountiful.

An attractive, well-dressed young woman had joined them for breakfast—Judith Strachan, the young woman who had occupied an apartment near Bundy's on The Avenues. She had been a close friend of Bundy and had provided much background information to Fisher and the other investigators. She had come to have deep suspicions of Bundy.

"How's everything going for you?" asked Fisher, opening

idle conversation. "Oh, fine," she replied. During breakfast they continued their small talk. Opposite them, Blakey was talking business with Vahsholtz, figuring how to deploy their lone rental car that day. "And Mike," said Blakey, "needs to get up to Logan to talk with the girl about the guy with the glasses."

"Oh, *glasses*," said Judith. "That reminds me! Did I ever tell you about the glasses?"

"No," said Fisher, taking a bite of hotcake, "what glasses?"

"Well," replied the young woman, "Ted always had a couple pairs of glasses which he used to wear once in a while."

Fisher choked on his hotcake. Startled, Blakey dropped a cup, clattering onto the saucer, spilling his coffee. "Tell us about the glasses," said Fisher, still choking.

"Well," she began, "he had one pair, black rimmed, with just plain glass lenses, which he called his lawyer glasses. Then there was this other pair. They had kind of shaded, tinted lenses. Ted said he wore those because they made him look *cool*."

Fisher finally managed to swallow. He, Blakey, and Vahsholtz exchanged stares. "So Theodore *did* have some glasses," he muttered.

"And shaded, tinted lenses," Vahsholtz added. "We better talk to the young lady at Logan."

Later that day, in a mood of triumph, the Colorado men and Brent Bullock, the Utah County investigator, began a jubilant conversation over cocktails in the Thirteenth Floor, the dimly lighted lounge of the high-rise Travelodge.

"I think we've got somethin' going at last," enthused Fisher. After weeks of work, he had solidified the facts of the Melissa Smith murder, tying in similarities to the Caryn Campbell murder. And now, new witnesses, new breakthroughs in the Debbie Kent case.

"Hell," said Bullock, "if Debbie's body could ever be found, we'd have a case there."

The others nodded. "Any word yet on the Aime hair samples?" asked Blakey.

"No, I'm afraid it'll be a while," replied Bullock.

After the recent exhumation of the body, Bullock explained, Laura's hair specimens had been sped to the FBI lab. "They promised to put a 'rush' on it, but nothing so far."

Bullock had become an active part of the Colorado team putting together the Bundy prosecution there. "Y' know, I've worked on the Laura Aime case for so long, I feel like I'm married to it," said the hefty investigator. "I dunno if I'll ever get Laura—or Bundy—out of my belly."

"Guess we all feel that way," sighed Fisher. "Lotta incredible effort's gone into all this." Fisher and Bullock, in fact, had recently flown to Toronto to interrogate a former Salt Lake City friend of Bundy, to check one witness's statement that Bundy and that friend had been together once at Brown's Café at Lehi, where Laura Aime had been. They'd struck out. Bundy's friend denied ever being in Lehi. "Lotta goddamn frustrations," Fisher reflected, "but maybe our luck is finally turning."

As they ordered another round of drinks, Blakey excused himself to find a telephone. "I've got to return a call from my office," he said.

"This little Tammy Tingy," Fisher told Bullock, "is just a fantastic witness. A quiet little gal, kinda plump, soft-spoken, and dead serious. Put her on the witness stand, and she'd be just powerful."

"Great," said Bullock. "Damn, I'd like to get Bundy put away. Maybe we're on the way."

"I'll drink to that," said Fisher. When the three investigators raised their glasses in a toast, Blakey returned to the table.

His somber expression erased the mood.

"Guys," said Blakey, "I hate to throw a damper on the party. . . ."

"What happened?" asked Bullock.

"I just got the message. Judge Lohr threw us out on the similar transactions in the Aime and Kent cases. We're through."

The investigators froze. Their months of work had all been in vain.

"Sorry, guys," Blakey told Fisher and Vahsholtz. "But I guess we pack our bags and head home."

At a table in a far corner of the lounge, some drunks were

singing a raucous, happy song. "Looks kind of peculiar," sighed Bullock, "for us to be sitting over here sobbing."

At Glenwood Springs, in his jail cell cluttered with files and books, Bundy was jubilant. "You know," he told me in a telephone conversation, "*I* wrote the briefs on the Kent and Aime transactions! And I think anyone would have to admit they were damned good legal arguments.

"I'm feeling very good about the case," he went on. He predicted that Judge Lohr would also throw out the state's effort to bring in the Melissa Smith murder as a similar transaction.

"So now," said Ted, "we've got the hearing November fourteenth on the motion to suppress the other Utah matters." That would be the final pretrial hearing—an effort by Bundy, helped by his advisory lawyers, to block the admissibility of Utah testimony about his August 15, 1975, arrest and his subsequent conviction of kidnapping.

Meanwhile, with the state's case badly weakened, Blakey was confiding privately, "The best thing we've got going for us now is Ted Bundy." The thoughtful prosecutor, along with Fisher, had studiously examined Bundy's background and watched his appearances in court. "As long as he's functioning as a lawyer, everything's real cool with Ted," Blakey observed. "Then when something reminds him that he's the prisoner, you sense these flashes of anger, hostility. He's always got to be the superstar. But he's only good in the first quarter of whatever game he's in. Then something happens."

"Something's gonna blow. Something's gonna happen," agreed Fisher. "I gotta feelin'."

In mid-November, the Utah witnesses—principals in Bundy's conviction at Salt Lake City—began appearing in the Aspen courtroom. Among his other avenues of attack, Bundy sought to show that his Volkswagen had been illegally searched the night Bob Hayward arrested him and that his credit-card slip and the Colorado ski brochure—the items which triggered the Colorado investigation—had been taken unlawfully during the search of his apartment.

But personally Ted Bundy, acting as his own counsel, was most anxious to have his crack at questioning his nemesis—Carol DaRonch.

That morning, watching Ted in the courtroom, his hair long and his beard again fully grown, ankle irons visible beneath the cuffs of his jail coveralls, I made a marginal note on my legal pad: "Ted looks more disheveled today." He was awaiting Carol DaRonch's appearance on the stand.

During the midmorning recess that day, Ted, with a sudden movement, began to approach the prosecution table to examine a document. Don Davis, a strapping deputy sheriff, gruffly ordered him back. Ted erupted in anger and turned toward the guards. There was an instant of scuffling. Crisp sounds of leather, bodies colliding. Three guards grabbed Bundy and swept him out of the courtroom and down the stairs to the jail.

"They whipped him down three flights of stairs and his feet didn't touch one goddamn stair," said a courthouse worker who'd watched it. "And Bundy's face was pure fury."

Court was delayed for more than an hour, as they left Ted in a cell to cool off. Alone, he mischievously tucked one link of his leg chain into the crack of an open steel door. When he swung the heavy door, it snapped the chain. He was grinning when guards applied new leg chains.

When court resumed that afternoon, Ted Bundy, the counsel, stood at a lectern, smiling, seemingly composed, and began his questioning of Carol DaRonch. "I'll ask you to please relax," he told the slim brunette woman, now a twenty-year-old. "There's nothing more that can occur between us right now."

It became a long, slow, deliberate question-answer replay of all the events that night of November 8, 1974—Carol's stroll through the Fashion Mall, the subsequent attack in the Volkswagen, her eventual identification of Bundy in the Salt Lake City police lineup.

"Did you identify me at that lineup?" asked Bundy.

"Yes."

"Will you please describe what I looked like."

"I don't remember exactly," Carol said softly.

"Be very careful here. 'I don't remember' is not an excuse for not answering a question. . . . Could you have recognized me in that lineup from seeing my pictures?"

"I don't know."

Judge Lohr's quizzical eyes watched Bundy, in jail coveralls, asking the questions, with his occasional tense smile, and the nervous, soft-voiced girl as she replied.

After more than two hours, it came to an end. "You're not sure about who your abductor is," said Bundy in a statement-question.

"Yes, I am," the young woman said. Carol, level and calm, directed a stare at Bundy. "You can't change your face."

Bundy stared back at her. Coldly, slowly he said, "Miss DaRonch, I feel very sorry for you. But you've made a mistake."

Blakey objected. Judge Lohr sustained. The statement was stricken from the record.

Later, as we visited again in the jail at Glenwood Springs, Ted reflected buoyantly on the significance of what had occurred during the hearings. "Prosecutors won't be able to bring in the Melissa Smith murder as similar transaction," Ted went on. "Where is the similarity? I defy anyone to find a common uniqueness between the two. . . . The only case where we have detailed operation of the MO is DaRonch. In the Smith transaction nothing is known as to how she disappeared, what the method of death was. So we know what happened to DaRonch. We don't know what happened to Smith. There's just nothing."

"Ted," I asked, "how'd it feel to be questioning Carol DaRonch?"

He grinned boyishly. His reply was an analysis of Carol. "I thought Carol was fairly relaxed under the circumstances. I did my best to be charming as I could. I enjoyed it—the opportunity to speak to her again."

"And what in hell was that fracas all about—that uproar with the guards?"

Ted laughed. "Well, it was just a minor conflict." He said he'd merely been walking toward the district attorney. "I was doing legitimate work." Then his expression turned cold as he talked about the guards. He was fed up with the tight security he said, the restraints on him. "I'm not going to do what *the man* tells me to do."

Ted explained how he'd been able to break the leg chains after they'd tossed him in the basement jail.

And, he chuckled again, "I could have made it very

239

dramatic, you know." After snapping the ankle chain when no one was there, "I could have used a paper clip to put the chain back together again." Then, when he was back in the courtroom, getting hostile testimony from Carol DaRonch, "I could say, 'That makes me MAD!'"—and he demonstrated for me, grabbing the steel chain and theatrically snapping it with his bare hands.

We shared another laugh. It would have been great show biz, I told him.

As the end of 1977 approached, Bundy's legal position was strengthened. The Melissa Smith murder had also been ruled out by Judge Lohr as a "similar transaction."

Despite the advice of his Aspen lawyer, O'Reilly, Ted was determined to seek a change of venue. Aspen, with its liberal, easygoing social attitudes, O'Reilly told him, was "probably the best place in the whole state of Colorado to go to trial."

But Bundy was stubbornly determined. "I want to get a public-opinion survey of Aspen," he had said, "to see how much they know about Ted Bundy, to see what the mood is." In Seattle, his friends began raising money to finance such a survey, asking for contributions of fifty dollars or more. The survey never got started. Ted filed his motion for a change of venue.

During the hearing in the courtroom that Tuesday before Christmas 1977, Judge Lohr announced he would grant the motion. Ted's face brightened with triumph. Beside him, Kevin O'Reilly sighed inwardly. O'Reilly sensed Bundy was making a colossal error.

After a brief recess, Judge Lohr returned to the bench to announce that arrangements already had been made for Ted Bundy's murder trial to commence in its new location: January 9, 1978, in El Paso County.

Bundy looked puzzled. "Where's El Paso County?" he asked O'Reilly.

"*The Springs*, you dumb shit," snapped O'Reilly in a stage whisper.

Colorado Springs. Of all the places in Colorado a defense lawyer didn't want a murder case tried, it was Colorado Springs. At that moment five men were on Death Row in the

Colorado prison. Four of them had come from courts in Colorado Springs.

And, Ted knew, Colorado Springs was the home base of his prosecutors, Blakey and Russel.

Ashen-faced, trembling, Bundy leaped to his feet. His guards took a step toward him. Stabbing an angry gesture toward Judge Lohr, Bundy shouted, "You're sentencing me to death!"

The judge ignored the remark. Seething, Bundy was returned, handcuffed, in leg irons, in the sheriff's car back to the jail at Glenwood Springs.

"He's boilin'," noted Fisher. "They'd goddamn sure better watch him now." Blakey began plans to have Bundy transferred from the Garfield County jail to the county jail at Colorado Springs some time after the holiday season—probably January 3 or 4.

When Ted and I next talked by telephone, on December 28, I asked him about his angry outburst in the court. He laughed it off. "What's so tough about Colorado Springs?" I asked.

"I guess it is true that Colorado Springs is probably the easiest place in the state to death-qualify a jury." Ted said he'd learned the Springs had a fairly heavy military population, a high concentration of middle-income working-class residents, and generally a strong law-and-order feeling. "It is more conservative, shall we say, than other parts of the state."

Ted had some good news that day. Judge Lohr had ruled in favor of the defense argument. Colorado's death-penalty statute, the judge held, was unconstitutional. "I'm hoping that the Supreme Court will review that before we go to trial," Ted told me. That could mean months of delay before trial.

We talked about his Christmas. "No big deal," said Ted. "We had only one other prisoner here in the jail. It was real quiet." Ted said he'd been losing weight. We talked about Seattle happenings. "Of course the big excitement here," I told him, "is the Rose Bowl game. I suppose you'll watch it on TV."

There was a pause. Ted had no reply. "You know," I told him, "your old alma mater [the University of Washington] plays Michigan in the Rose Bowl."

Still Ted was silent. It hadn't seemed to register with him. Washington versus Michigan in the Rose Bowl January 2 would, I thought, be something Ted would really be looking forward to. "Will you have a chance to see it on TV?" I asked.

"Oh, the Rose Bowl game," Ted replied. "Yeah," he said. "I suppose I'll see it." I thought there was a strange vagueness in his voice.

What I didn't realize was that Ted's phone call that day was his "good-bye" conversation with me. He didn't plan on being in jail when the Rose Bowl game was played.

For weeks, Ted had been planning the escape. A steel plate above the light fixture in the ceiling of his steel cell, he discovered, had been imperfectly welded. It was loose. By prying and some hacksawing (carefully done when there were other loud jail noises, especially the kitchen clatter during meals preparation), he had fully loosened the fixture and the plate. When they were pushed upward, Ted had a foot-square hole in the ceiling. Ted's dieting had taken his weight down to a slim 150 pounds. He was thin enough to wriggle through that hole.

Above the ceiling, Ted made test explorations during the nights preceding his actual escape. Hoisting himself, scraping his hips, twisting his body upward through the hole, he emerged in the pinched attic space above, beneath the flat roof of the one-story building.

There, crawling in the darkness and dust—stifling his need to sneeze—Ted had looked for a way out. Once he almost crawled onto a wobbling section of plasterboard, through which he could have crashed into the jail kitchen. One night, by chance he noticed a shaft of light in the attic. Below, in a jailer's apartment, someone had opened a door to a closet. Ted had discovered his eventual exit.

That afternoon, December 30, Frank Perry, an elderly guard, talked with Ted in his cell. "I'm not feeling too well," Ted told him. Later that evening, Perry looked through the window of the cell door and saw the prisoner sitting on his bunk, reading. Next morning Perry knocked on the cell door, to offer breakfast. There was no response. Through the window it appeared Bundy was still asleep. It was nearly noon when the discovery was made. Beneath the blanket, mounded to resemble a human body, were books, papers, and clothing. Ted Bundy was gone.

All hell broke loose. Police radios broadcast the alarm. A police dragnet was set up around the whole Rocky Mountain area. Fury came down on the Garfield County officers, especially Sheriff Ed Hogue.

"We're just sick about it," said the forlorn Hogue. "We knew that the steel box up above that light fixture in the cell was loose. We'd been trying to get a welder in to fix it. I kept asking the county commissioners for a surveillance system, with television and all, so the guards could keep an eye on all parts of the jail. But they said they didn't have the budget for it."

Undersheriff Bob Hart was issuing information about the escape to other law-enforcement agencies and the news media that Saturday. "We know Bundy probably got out of the jail sometime after eight-thirty this morning," Hart said. He explained it appeared that Bundy had crawled across the attic, then broken through the plasterboard downward into a closet of the guard's apartment. "The guard and his wife had gone out shoppin' for groceries," said Hart. "Bundy'd probably been layin' up there listenin' for them to go out. Then he went. We think he had about seven dollars on 'im.

"Everything in that closet was okay around eight o'clock or so," Hart continued. "Near noon, they came back and found the closet all torn up."

It was erroneous information.

At midday, Saturday, December 31, while police hurriedly set up roadblocks, while the first frantic alarms were being broadcast, Ted Bundy was in Chicago.

Theodore really set 'em up in that jail," grumbled Fisher. Despite all the reminders that he was a constant escape risk, Ted had made friends with the Garfield County jail guards, had observed their movements, and learned, through friendly chitchat, that just one elderly guard would be on duty that New Year's weekend. "And he knew," added Fisher, "that within about three or four days, he was gonna be transferred to Colorado Springs. He had his plan. Time was running out. So he went."

"Funny thing," Fisher went on, "Theodore had everything goin' his way in the case. All the similars were being tossed out. I didn't think we'd ever get the Utah evidence in. It turned out we never made a match on Laura Aime's hair. He was winnin' everythin' in sight."

"Where do you guess he's gone?" I asked.

"Well, my guess would be north. To Canada. There's a lot of places up there where they have kind of American communes—gathering places for the guys who ran from the draft . . . Ted would fit in really well there."

"I dunno," I replied. "There's a really mean winter storm all across the Midwest right now. Colder'n hell. I doubt he'd head that far north."

"He might go south, but I don't think he'd go to Mexico," said Fisher. "Too much of a cultural change."

On January 3, at Fort Lauderdale, Florida, Police Officer Bob Campbell was served with a subpoena from Colorado. Issued one week earlier and delivered to Campbell's home by a local officer, the subpoena ordered him to appear at Colorado Springs to testify in the trial of Theodore Robert Bundy for the murder of Bob's sister, Caryn Campbell. "Forget it," snapped Campbell. "I hear those jerks out there let him escape."

The FBI had entered the case on the presumption Bundy had become an interstate fugitive. Police in Colorado and Utah were pleading to have him placed on the Ten Most Wanted list (an action which finally came on February 10). Dave Yates, the FBI agent at Glenwood Springs, telephoned me that first week of January. He was interviewing all of Bundy's friends and acquaintances, asking for information or hunches about Bundy's whereabouts.

"Where do *you* think he might be," Yates asked.

"I really have no idea," I replied. "At first I thought he might head for Southern California—LA, maybe. But then, of course, LA's hot with police activity right now, with the Hillside Strangler down there. Ted knows that."

Yates agreed. We talked about Ted's supply of money.

Officials at the Garfield County jail still were reporting he had only about seven dollars with him when he escaped.

"So," I said, "I'd guess Ted would have to hole up somewhere, get a job and pick up some money. If he hitched a ride to Denver, I'd start looking around Denver University, maybe around the edge of the campus there.

"Ted," I told the FBI man, "really likes being around the edge of a campus."

NINETEEN | Chi Omega Murders

Around the edge of the Florida State University campus at Tallahassee, the fraternity and sorority houses, the student residence halls, the drab old houses along oak-lined streets, were quiet, mostly asleep that cold, black early morning, January 15, 1978.

It was an unusually chilly winter in north central Florida.

Across the street from the campus, a coed and her date returning from a party at one of the frat houses, passed under a street lamp, then turned in at Chi Omega sorority house.

It was late, almost three in the morning.

At the side door, Nita Neary dialed the combination of the security lock, said good night to Steve, her boyfriend, then tiptoed inside. Some of her sorority sisters, she noticed, had left the lights on in the recreation room and the living room. As she began flipping off the switches, Nita heard a loud *thump!* Perhaps, she thought, Steve had fallen on the steps outside. She peered through a window, but saw nothing. Steve was gone.

Then, from the upstairs hallway, she heard the sound of hurried footsteps.

When Nita approached the foyer, she saw the man. For only a moment. He was moving from the foot of the stairs toward the front door. His body was slightly hunched forward as he reached for the front door knob. In that instant, Nita saw he wore a dark knit cap, pulled down, and a dark jacket. In his hand, he carried a log, or a club, with bark on it. Then he was gone. Nita was startled.

The upstairs area, where all the girls slept in their rooms, was off limits to males. Perhaps, Nita thought, one of the girls had sneaked a man into her room. But the man Nita had seen had somehow frightened her. He seemed older.

She ran upstairs to rouse Nancy Dowdy. "Nancy," she told her drowsy, red-haired roommate, "I just saw a guy go down the stairs and leave the house. Who'd have a guy up here? It's three o'clock in the morning."

Together, they went to waken Jackie McGill, the Chi O president. The three of them—Nancy and Jackie in nighties and robes—stood in the brown-carpeted hallway, as Nita described what she'd seen. "I just saw his profile. He was reaching for the door. . . ."

Nita's sentence was cut short. One of the nearby doors opened. A girl staggered out into the hallway, her upper body bent forward, her hands clutching her head. "It's Karen," exclaimed Nancy. "She must be sick."

Karen Chandler turned, wobbling, falling toward the hallway wall. Nancy ran to her. "Oh my God . . . Blood! She's bleeding!" Blood was soaking Karen's hair.

Nita and Jackie tried to steady her, help her. In the next instant Nancy discovered Karen's roommate. Kathy Kleiner sat in her bed, groaning. Blood poured from her nose and smashed lips.

"God! Someone call the police. We need medics!" Nancy shouted.

Within minutes—at 3:23 A.M.—Tallahassee police officer Oscar Brannon and two Florida State University campus officers arrived on the run at the front door of the Chi O house, "Upstairs!" shouted a girl in the entryway. "They're upstairs." The FSU men raced up the stairs.

Brannon stopped at the front door. "Can anyone give me a description of the guy?"

"I can," Nita said. Hurriedly she gave the description of the man she'd seen at the front door. White, male, maybe 5 feet 8. Slender . . . large nose. Waist-length dark coat. Dark knit cap down over the ears . . . light pants . . . "He was carrying a club or something in one hand. It was rough, like it had bark on it. He had some cloth or something wrapped around the handle."

Quickly the information was translated into a police-radio BOLO: "Be on the lookout for . . ."

At the top of the stairs, Officer Ray Crew bent over Kathy Kleiner. Blood was pouring from her mouth and head. "Broken jaw," he concluded. A sorority sister held a plastic pail under the girl's mouth, to catch the streaming blood.

Medics, other police, began swarming through the front door and racing up the stairs. "Take care of her," Crew shouted at a medic. He pointed to Karen Chandler, who lay on the floor, her head bleeding.

Crew, a mustached young officer, began checking other rooms. Jesus, he thought, what's going on here? He reached for the knob to open another room along the hallway. "That's Lisa's room," the house mother told him. "Lisa Levy."

Crew opened the door. In the semidarkness, he saw the girl's form on the bed. She lay on her right side, face down. A sheet was pulled to the top of her head.

"Lisa, wake up," said Crew softly. She didn't respond. Then, with the lights on, Crew saw all the blood. "Get an EMT," he told the house mother. (It was police parlance for the Emergency Medical Technicians.)

Crew touched the girl's wrist to seek a pulse. There was none. He began to lift and roll Lisa toward her back. He saw her eyes glazing. Her lips were purpling. Gently, Crew lowered the girl's left shoulder onto the bed again.

When the medics arrived, they lowered her to the floor, to begin frantic resuscitation efforts. Lisa's nightie had been unbuttoned. Her buttocks were bloodied.

Weeping sounds—and wailing—filled the hallway. Girls were spilling out of other rooms, converging in the hall. "Where's Margaret?" one of them shouted. "I haven't seen Margaret!"

Henry Newkirk, a tall slender Tallahassee city officer, pushed open the door to Margaret Bowman's room. He flipped on the light. Entering, he quickly closed the door behind him so no one else could see the bloody mess. The bedspread had been pulled up over her, but Newkirk could see the gaping hole in her skull. "Oh, sweet Jesus," he muttered. A nylon was wrapped so tightly around her throat, it looked like she had been decapitated. The wall was spattered with blood.

Outdoors, arriving at the entryway, George Brand, a tall, husky Leon County sheriff's sergeant, shouted, "What've we got?" "A goddamn mess," a deputy replied.

One ambulance, then another, screamed away from the Chi O house, carrying victims toward Tallahassee Memorial Hospital. Karen, partially conscious, was the first to be taken. Then Lisa. In the ambulance, medics worked over her furiously, trying to get her breathing again.

Brand hopped into his car to follow the ambulances. He radioed a request for every available sheriff's officer—off-duty people, everyone—to turn out.

Hurrying up the stairs of the sorority house, Howard Winkler, veteran crime-scene specialist for the Tallahassee Police Department, shuddered. The stairs, the hallways were filled with weeping girls. Some had blood-covered hands. They'd tried to help the victims. With so many people, so many fingerprints, and multiple crime scenes, Winkler knew it would be an evidence-gathering nightmare.

In Margaret Bowman's room, Winkler photographed the dead girl. Her head was down. Her right arm was at her side. The other hand, palm upward, rested on her back.

"Girls! Everyone! Out of the hallway. Downstairs, please," pleaded one of the officers in the corridor.

The chaos worsened. More police cars howled to a stop outside. Three law-enforcement agencies were on the scene—the sheriff's officers, city police, and campus police. "What a mess. Who's supposed to be in charge?" grumbled a detective on the stairway.

Youthful-looking, black-haired Leon County Sheriff Ken Katsaris had always stubbornly insisted on his legal prerogative as the highest-ranking law-enforcement officer anywhere in his county. A former teacher of police science, Katsaris was clever at politics and publicity, but he had no working police experience to help him cope with the crime-scene confusion, the madness, now surrounding him and his top aide, Captain Jack Poitinger. City Detective Don Patchen and some of the others on the scene concluded at once that no one had taken charge.

"We oughta just get everyone out of here and seal this whole place off," snapped one of the detectives upstairs. "We need Bill Gunter." Gunter, a skilled crime-scene specialist, was a cool, methodical evidence gatherer. But that weekend Gunter was visiting his family in southern Alabama, two hours away. Katsaris failed to call in Gunter.

"Goddammit, any evidence we might have is gonna be ruined in this confusion," Patchen grumbled. Patchen tried to restore sanity. He ordered fellow officers to guard the front door, so no more curiosity seekers could enter the place. But the sheriff's people countermanded Patchen's order.

Meanwhile, at Tallahassee Memorial Hospital, Dr. Mark Goldberg was fighting, but losing, a battle to save the life of Lisa Levy. She had arrived in the ambulance with no vital signs. No blood pressure. No pulse. No respiration. Goldberg tried chest massage. And drugs to stimulate heart activity.

"Large amount of swelling under both jaws, extending down to her neck," he'd report later. "A laceration over her right nipple . . . some bleeding in her eardrum . . . severe head injury . . . Also some evidence of some rectal bleeding."

Lisa was dead.

It was as though a tornado of violence had touched down at the Chi Omega House. Then the tornado touched down again, an hour and a half later, six blocks away.

In a small, dilapidated frame duplex on Dunwoody Street, Nancy Young was fast asleep. But her roommate, Debbie Cicarelli, dozing on a mattress on the floor, was roused by a sharp, staccato sound, as though someone was pounding on the floor with a hammer.

Bang . . . bang . . . bang. It went on, Debbie thought, for ten seconds. Maybe more. She sat up, her ears straining to hear.

Through the wall, from the other unit, Debbie could hear the girl's voice, whimpering, moaning. *Something's wrong with Cheryl,* Debbie thought. Cheryl Thomas, a friend, a pretty, graceful FSU dance major from Richmond, lived alone in the adjoining apartment.

Debbie roused her sleeping roommate. "Nancy! Something's wrong over at Cheryl's." Together, they listened to the whimpering sounds. Debbie reached for the telephone.

After she dialed Cheryl's number, they could hear the telephone ring beyond the thin wall. There was an eruption of sounds. A bump. The thumping of running feet. A crashing sound in Cheryl's kitchen, as though the table were banged into the cabinets. Sounds of someone running.

After five rings of Cheryl's telephone, Debbie hung up. She dialed police. Instantly, the duplex at 431 Dunwoody Street and its neighborhood was swarming with police, dispatched from the nearby Chi Omega House.

Tallahassee City Patrolman Wilton Dozier raced in the darkness toward the duplex with Officer Mitch Miller. "The guy might still be around," yelled one of the other officers who were arriving, carrying shotguns.

Inside, Dozier and Gerald Payne found Cheryl semiconscious, lying on the bloodied bedsheet. An ambulance was on its way. "Are you okay?" Dozier asked the girl. Cheryl tried to mumble something through the blood, the groans. "She's still alive," Dozier exclaimed.

Most of the bedclothes had been pulled from her bed. Atop the wadded blanket and sheet on the floor, Dozier noticed pantyhose. Nearby was a long piece of wood, a two-by-three.

Soon paramedic Gary Mathews was bending over Cheryl. He'd just made one ambulance run to the hospital with the badly injured Kathy Kleiner. Now he was examining the newest victim. "Possible neck injury . . . Maybe a fracture," he murmered. The pretty, brown-haired girl had suffered crushing blows to the head. Already there was severe swelling of her face and neck. Cheryl's eyes stared blankly at the ceiling. Matthews and the others lifted her gently onto a special stretcher bed, to guard against any further damage to her spinal column. She was a talented dancer.

Then they rushed her to Tallahassee Memorial Hospital.

Upstairs in the Chi O house, Winkler was dusting for fingerprints on the door of Lisa Levy's room. Nearby, Carroll

Hurdle, his partner, was dusting the door of Margaret Bowman's room. The crime-scene men were doing their best. "God, I wish someone had taken some control over this," said Winkler. He could only imagine all the crime-scene contamination that had been permitted to happen. "But who am I to tell the sheriff what to do?"

Then came another sheriff's order. Winkler was to abandon his work at the sorority house and head to the morgue. "Dammit," Winkler told two nearby officers, "let's at least seal these rooms up." As ordered, he left for the morgue.

Dr. Donald Woods was completing the autopsy on Lisa Levy's body, which lay on a slotted metal examining table. Body traces were taken. Hair specimens. Fingernail scrapings. Winkler photographed her upper body. One nipple had been nearly bitten away.

When she was turned over, face downward, they saw the streaks of blood which had streamed from the vaginal and anal areas, covering the buttocks. When that was swabbed away, Woods and the others noticed, on the left buttock, the marks of human teeth.

"Chrissake," breathed one of the officers in the room. "The son of a bitch bit her." Winkler winced. The attacker would have left saliva residue with that bite. But the swabbing of the blood had swept away any saliva trace. Lost evidence.

The medical examiner's camera was malfunctioning. So, while the sheriff and others watched, Winkler focused his Pentax .35 millimeter camera on the bite marks.

Steve Bodiford, a sheriff's detective, interrupted. "Think we should have some kind of scale there, like a ruler?" he asked. Winkler concurred. He waited, camera in hand, while Bodiford went to a desk drawer and found a yellow plastic ruler. That was laid beside the bite mark. Winkler snapped the strobe-lit photo.

He thus recorded, in one photo, the circle of bruises, beneath the skin, which had been left by the killer's teeth.

Bodiford's thought—putting the ruler there—would eventually prove to be crucial.

Dr. Woods excised a section of skin and tissue, containing

the actual bite mark, for possible evidence. It was placed in a saline solution. Days later it would be learned that the solution had ruined it for evidence.

Winkler was horrified when he learned that Sheriff Katsaris, perhaps in his overexcitement, had prematurely ordered Margaret Bowman's body to be taken from the sorority house to the morgue.

(If attendants handling the body had worn gloves, if it had been processed properly, there could have been found on the body a fingerprint of the killer. That wasn't done. The crime scene was being bungled. "I should have hollered, 'Whoa!'" mourned Winkler afterward. But Katsaris and his man Poitinger were running the show.)

Chunks of bark were found in the beds and in the hair of the victims. The attacker apparently had entered the Chi Omega house through the side door, with the combination lock. Often that door failed to latch securely. He'd gone from room to room, attacking the girls with an oak club—perhaps taken from a stack of firewood outside the sorority house. On the carpet, inside that door, was a trail of oak-bark particles.

For hours, police searched the streets, sidewalks, yards, and garbage cans around the Chi Omega house, seeking the murder weapon. Hundreds of limbs and chunks lay beneath the old oak trees of the neighborhood. None was found with blood on it.

At midmorning, police began forming a joint task force to investigate the killings and attacks.

In the foyer of the sorority house, one after another, the Chi O's were being fingerprinted and interviewed. Nita Neary stood, advising an artist who sat sketching, re-creating the profile of the man she'd seen at the door.

It was instant national news. The "Chi Omega murders," at a quiet, sedate college campus, near the Florida state capitol. Two girls were dead: Margaret Bowman, a slim, twenty-one-year-old beauty with long dark hair, an art history major; and Lisa Levy, twenty, an effervescent, cheerful blonde, a fashion-merchandising major. Coincidentally, both were from St. Petersburg.

Each had died of violent strangulation. Margaret's skull

had been damaged by savage blows. Lisa's body had bite marks—on the buttock and one nipple.

Karen Chandler, twenty-one, of Tallahassee and Kathy Kleiner of Fort Lauderdale had been brutally beaten. They were undergoing extensive surgery. Each would live. Cheryl Thomas, horribly beaten an hour and a half after the Chi Omega attacks, would barely survive.

When the wire-service report reached the newsroom of the *The Seattle Times*, it caught the eye of Paul Henderson. He handed a copy to me with an attached memo: "Sounds like 'Ted.' A campus. He loves a campus. Girls the right age. And the guy's ballsy enough to go into a sorority house, filled with girls, like he'd go into a state park with 40,000 people to take two girls."

"Nah, Paul," I replied. "I just don't see it. Even if you give all those others to Ted, this one sounds too sloppy. There's gotta be evidence and fingerprints all over the place down there. He's too careful for that."

In downtown Seattle Bob Keppel, veteran of the King County police's old Ted Squad, was on the telephone to Florida. "You might want to look for a guy named Ted Bundy," Keppel told Captain Steve Hooker of the FSU police. "He's a multiple-murder suspect from up here who goes for young women."

Hooker replied, "We're getting thousands of calls like this." But Hooker also asked Keppel if he could provide original sets of Bundy's fingerprints. "You probably could get 'em from Mike Fisher in Colorado," Keppel replied.

Already, Fisher was on the telephone to Tallahassee, telling Patchen, the Tallahassee detective, and D. Phillips, of the sheriff's office, "Look for a guy named Ted Bundy."

At Fort Lauderdale, police officer Bob Campbell read the news of the Tallahassee murders, then folded the paper and had a private thought: Strange as hell, but I got a hunch Bundy's in Florida. One week earlier, Bundy would have been going to trial in Colorado for the murder of Bob Campbell's sister.

In Tallahassee, late that Sunday, Virginia Ellis, state capitol bureau chief for the *St. Petersburg Times*, had a telephone conversation with her mother, Virginia Riley, who lived at the far corner of the continent—on Whidbey Island, in Washington State.

Mrs. Ellis explained to her mother that, instead of covering government and politics that day, she had been out gathering facts at the scene of a horrible murder. "It was gruesome, horrible," she told her mother. Two pretty girls had been molested and murdered as they slept in the sorority house.

"Do they have a suspect?" asked Mrs. Riley.

"No," replied the Florida newswoman. "And they don't think they'll ever find him. They have so few clues."

"I'll bet I know who should be their suspect."

"Sure you do," said Mrs. Ellis, chiding her mother.

"Ted Bundy," said the Washington State woman.

"Who?"

"Ted Bundy."

"Who's Ted Bundy?"

Ted Bundy was living in a new place—in a cramped, bleak apartment in Tallahassee, Florida, on West College Avenue, about a block and a half from the FSU campus. He had assumed a new name, "Chris Hagen."

Inwardly, Ted occasionally glowed with the memory of that wild, exciting adventure which had taken him cross-country, from a jail cell in Colorado that cold, snowy night, to his new anonymity in the far corner of America, in Florida.

That evening of December 30, 1977, he had lain in the attic of the Garfield County jail, above the jailers' apartment, listening until the jailer and his wife left to go to a movie. Deliberately, as quietly as he could, he had broken through the plasterboard and shelving, lowered his body down into the closet, then slipped through the outer door of the unoccupied apartment.

Beautiful . . . beautiful . . . beautiful. That's how it felt, he rejoiced. *Freedom.* Walking into a lovely snowy night in the Rockies. Giant snowflakes were drifting down in the blackness as he walked to a neighborhood of Glenwood Springs where, other jail inmates had told him, there was a good chance to find a car with a key left in the ignition switch.

Ted found an aged, snow-covered MG Midget. He cramped his body into the small seat, nursed the engine to turn over, then wheeled the small car, its engine coughing and sputtering, across the Colorado River bridge to the freeway and turned toward Denver.

Before he reached Vail, though, the small car was overheating, gasping its last. Ted abandoned it against a snowbank beside the highway in the blizzard. He was offered a ride by a motorist bound for Denver. After the sedan passed Vail, the weather worsened. At a mountain tunnel between Vail and Denver, state troopers were halting traffic and directing motorists back—toward Vail. Ted had a sinking feeling, as his Samaritan drove him back the way they'd come. "I'll just get out here at Vail," Ted told the driver. "Thanks for your help."

Then Ted, still not knowing if his escape had been detected, took a gamble. He went to the Trailways bus depot at Vail. He caught a bus to Denver. Because of the snowfall, other traffic was being turned back, but the bus was permitted to go on—all the way to Denver. At the TWA counter in the Denver airport, he paid cash for a ticket to Chicago. Late Saturday morning, December 31, his flight was landing in Chicago—about the time the panic-stricken jailers at Glenwood Springs were reporting his escape.

He was heading for a campus—the University of Michigan at Ann Arbor. "I always loved trains. There's something romantic about trains," Ted would recall later. "So I thought, Why not?" From Chicago, he traveled by train to Ann Arbor, passing the time in a club car, sipping Scotch, making cheerful conversation with fellow passengers.

At Ann Arbor, with the few hundred dollars he still carried, Ted walked through the snow and numbing cold to find the YMCA, where he took a room for the night. Next day, Monday, January 2, he recalled later, "I sat there in a bar in Ann Arbor, Michigan, watching Washington, my alma mater, beat the pants off Michigan. Great game!"

Washington, a gambling underdog team, won 27–21. "And I was there, getting a little drunk, cheerin' my head off for Washington. And surrounded by Michigan fans!" He was living dangerously and enjoying it.

Unprepared for the harsh Midwest winter, he decided to seek a warmer climate. At the University of Michigan library, Ted said later, he leafed through college catalogs until his eye fell on Florida State University. At a place called Tallahassee.

He didn't know where that was, but on the map, it appeared to be closer to the ocean—the Gulf—than did the University of Florida at Gainesville.

When he stepped off the bus at Tallahassee a few days later, Ted sucked in a breath of "that soft, sweet, warm southern air." And he began walking toward the Florida State University campus, looking for a place to live. In his pocket, he had only about $160 left from his original roll of $700 or so. As he walked through neighborhoods around the FSU campus, Ted was disappointed by his new surroundings. There were a few palm trees but little else to suggest the warm, tropical Florida he'd expected. Along the streets were small, unpainted old houses, perched on blocks, their porches sagging.

On West College Avenue an "Apt. for Rent" sign caught his eye, and he turned into a narrow, aging, two-story frame building huddled under a massive old oak tree. The weary-looking apartment house bore a hand-lettered name: "The Oak." Inside, Larry Winfield, the student manager of the place, asked for advance rent and had him fill out a lease. As he signed it, Ted became "Chris Hagen."

Chris moved into Room 12, a tiny upstairs room, with a bunk bed, a chest of drawers, an old desk, and a Formica-topped table. With other occupants, he'd have to share the upstairs bathroom. Slowly, he got acquainted with the other tenants—some students, a young working woman, and a rock musician, whose high-decibel rehearsals with his band shook the old building.

To most of the others, Chris seemed friendly enough, although sometimes standoffish. As days passed, he began carting into the apartment a few possessions—a sleeping bag, a bicycle, a small TV, some other items.

"He gave me the impression he was a law student, that he'd gone to Stanford," said one of the tenants. Now and then there were impromptu, middle-of-the-night gatherings of some of the young people, sitting in the hallway, smoking, drinking, talking. A couple of times, Henry Polumbo, the musician, recalled, Chris seemed to be very drunk.

Tina Hopkins, who lived two doors away from Chris, puzzled over the fact that the quiet, aloof new resident of Room 12 seemed to have a changing physical appearance.

She'd remember later, "He always looked different. . . . I don't know, sometimes he just didn't even look like the same person at all. His face—sometimes it would be real sunken. Sometimes he'd be healthy looking. Sometimes, you know, his hair would be perfectly straight. Sometimes it would be real curly.

"And his face, his whole face, even his eyes, you know . . . he would just look real different all the time." Tina noticed that Chris sometimes wore tortoise-shell glasses; at other times he wore wire-rimmed glasses.

Henry and his pal, Rusty Gage, the sound man in Rusty's rock band, hadn't heard about the crimes at the nearby Chi Omega house when they arrived at The Oak shortly before five o'clock that morning. They had been at Rusty's place listening to records. In the predawn, at The Oak, they encountered Chris, standing alone, staring up the street, toward the fraternity and sorority houses.

"Hi, how's it going?" asked Henry.

Chris didn't reply, Henry remembered. "He was just staring off."

The crimes dominated conversations around The Oak. Henry thought he recalled Chris once saying, "It was a pretty professional job. Whoever did it has done it before."

Tina had a taunting, offbeat sense of humor. Once, when she encountered the solemn-faced Chris on the stairway, Tina grabbed his arm, stared at him menacingly and whispered, "I'm the murderer, and I'm going to *kill* you!"

Chris' response was a mirthless stare.

In early February, Chris was late with a promised rent payment, and he was out of money.

On the morning of February 11, the *Tallahassee Democrat*, still heavily playing news of the Chi Omega crimes, printed a "psychological profile" of the Chi Omega killer. Prepared by an FBI psychologist, it portrayed the attacker as "a loner," living in the Tallahassee area, "but [who] is not a student.

"He has had an emotional problem ever since his childhood," it went on, "which was deeply influenced by a dominant mother . . . who probably lives by himself and who definitely does not live with a woman."

Earlier that week, Chris had been away from the apartment, on a trip somewhere for a couple of days. That Saturday, February 11, one of his neighbors remembered that Chris borrowed a copy of the *Democrat* and read it. Soon after that, around February 12, a little over a month after he'd moved in, Chris slipped out of The Oak.

That night, in a nearby neighborhood, a young man named Rick Garzaniti discovered that his car had been stolen from its parking place on East Georgia Street. It was an orange Volkswagen.

TWENTY | **Talks in the Night**

A salty, chilling, Gulf Coast breeze added to the rawness of the cold February which gripped Florida's Panhandle. It was well past midnight, so the streets of Pensacola were quiet, almost deserted. Patrolman David Lee, an unsmiling young cop with stern dark eyes and eyebrows and a brooding black mustache, turned his patrol car onto Cervantes Street, in a slow cruise.

It was about one thirty in the morning, February 15, 1978. The headlights of Lee's police car briefly reflected off a bright orange Volkswagen, which was moving slowly along an alleyway behind Oscar Warner's restaurant. Lee knew the place had long since closed for the night, and he didn't recognize the VW as one of the restaurant employees' cars. No reason for that car to be prowling there so slowly, Lee thought. He kept driving, past the restaurant—a police deception—keeping his eye on the rear-view mirror, watching the VW.

When the little orange car turned west, in the opposite direction, Lee made a U-turn and began to follow. The VW picked up speed, made a left turn, then another turn. Following, Lee switched on his patrol car's blue pursuit light and radioed for an "NCIC"—a "stolen" check on the license of the car ahead.

Gradually, the tempo of the chase accelerated. Lee noticed his speedometer had reached 55, as they traveled north beyond the Pensacola city limits. "Subject vehicle," said the voice on his police radio, "reported stolen by Tallahassee P.D."

Finally the Volkswagen slowed and came to a stop at the roadside in a darkened area. Gun drawn, Lee emerged from his police car and approached the driver's window of the car ahead.

"What's wrong, officer?" asked the voice of the driver in the Volkswagen.

"Get your hands up where I can see 'em," Lee ordered. Lee thought he saw a form, perhaps another person, in the passenger seat.

"What's the problem?" the driver asked.

"I want your hands up." Lee opened the Volkswagen door and ordered the driver to get out and walk forward, into the lights of the car. "Now, down on the ground, spreadeagle," he ordered.

With a wary glance back toward the VW, where he still thought there might be someone else, Lee knelt to snap on the handcuffs—first, on the driver's left wrist.

It happened with cat quickness—the swing of the man's legs, then his lashing body movement. As though hit by a football block, Lee was knocked from his feet, and the sinewy man was scrambling up, running. Lee's gun discharged. Cursing, the policeman leaped to his feet and started pursuit, firing a warning shot in the air. Ahead, the man ducked into Scott Street, looking back over his shoulder. From a quarter of a block away, Lee saw a glint of metal—the dangling handcuff—and, thinking it was a gun, he fired directly at the man. He missed. But the man dropped, as though hit. Lee ran and pounced on the man's body.

There was a kicking, gouging, wrestling battle on the ground until Lee, after rapping the man's head with the butt of his revolver, had his captive, hands cuffed behind him.

"Let's go, goddammit," ordered the cop. Lee marched the young man back to their cars. In the beam of his flashlight, Lee could see that the Volkswagen interior was piled with possessions—the "passenger" he'd thought he'd seen.

Ted Bundy felt empty, numb, too tired to even protest, as Lee put him roughly into the patrol car. Ted's head hurt. Blood was seeping through the messed hair at the back of his head and dribbling down his neck.

Driving toward the police station, Lee studied his morose prisoner. He had a scruffy mustache and mussed curly hair. "I wish you'd killed me," said the prisoner in a voice muffled by fatigue.

"What'd you say?"

"I wish you'd killed me back there," Bundy repeated.

I did my damndest, Lee thought. Lee had been shooting to hit this guy, whoever he was, but he'd missed. Goddamn gun doesn't shoot straight.

For Bundy a forty-six day blur of freedom had come to an end in an unfamiliar Florida town near the Alabama border. At the desk of the Pensacola city jail, he was booked as "Kenneth Misner"—the name on the driver's license he carried. It was a name he had fully researched to use as his new identification. While his fingerprints were being rolled, Ted wondered how long it would take for these small-town police to discover the prize they had caught that night.

As exhausted as he was, he couldn't resist tweaking their interest. He asked Lee what police rank he held. Lee replied he was a patrolman. "You'll make sergeant for this," the prisoner murmured, cocking one eyebrow.

Pensacola Detective Norman Chapman had been summoned to the police station in the predawn to question the man Lee had captured. Already the police had compiled an inventory of suspicions about him. Within the Volkswagen was stuffed a bicycle frame, a portable television, some stereo equipment, clothing, a sleeping bag, a brown leather notebook filled with the identification of Kenneth Raymond Misner of Tallahassee. In his possession and strewn inside the car were more than twenty credit cards bearing a wide variety of names, plus several photographs of girls and young women.

Chapman, a plump man with a soothing Southern accent, opened the questioning:

"Would you state your full name, please?"

"Kenneth Raymond Misner."

"Where do you live, Mr. Misner?"

"Presently I live in Tallahassee. Nine-eighty-two West Brevard."

"Okay. How old are you, Mr. Misner?"

"Twenty-nine."

"How much education do you have?"

"I have a bachelor-of-science degree in education."

(Bundy had initially stolen a student identification card belonging to Misner, a onetime member of the Florida State University track team. Systematically he had begun developing other documents of identification with the eventual plan of *becoming* Kenneth Raymond Misner. He had applied for and received duplicate copies of Misner's university diploma and Misner's birth certificate from North Carolina.)

Chapman asked about the Volkswagen and the credit cards with all the different names. The answers came freely. He'd stolen them in Tallahassee. Where in Tallahassee?

"Well, let's see. Ah . . . Can't tell you the street. Ah . . . Oh boy . . . Okay. About two or three miles from campus I guess."

The word "campus" registered. Everyone in Florida, probably, knew of the murders just one month earlier near the FSU campus.

Chapman was simultaneously suspicious and intrigued by the man he was questioning. An intelligent, respectful, almost friendly manner came through the man's obvious fatigue. Chapman was beginning also to learn that he'd try never to lie to his questioner.

"Okay. You also had in your possession—uh—some identification cards and a number of credit cards. Uh—would you tell us where you received this identification?"

Those things, said "Misner," had been stolen from purses. "Took the small stuff . . . uh—from . . . uh. They were in taverns. Well, the purses were in taverns, you know—in the Tallahassee area—I'd just take the pocketbooks out."

"Was there any specific tavern that you took them from?"

asked Chapman. (Police of North Florida and elsewhere knew that, before the murders, some of the Chi Omega girls had been at the disco taverns Sherrods and Big Daddy's.)

"No. No specific tavern."

The interview was being tape-recorded. Chapman asked, "Has this statement been made voluntarily and of your own free will so that the truth may be known?"

"Yes," replied the obliging "Misner."

"Would you like to make any corrections, or add to, or take away from, this statement at this time?"

"Well, let me see . . . uh—I just want to make it clear. You know . . . I guess technically, under the law, it's assaulting a police officer . . . But I'd just like it to be known that I . . . the intent was not to hurt the police officer. All I did was run away." Chapman nodded acknowledgement.

The suspect also conceded the TV in the Volkswagen had been stolen at Tallahassee.

The interview ended at 4:33 that morning and later, back in his cell, exhausted and tense, Bundy noticed he was being watched by a special guard outside the steel door. Ted contemplated how he'd handle the eventual revelation of his identity. He wanted control over that. And he wondered how long it would be until they'd be questioning him directly about those Chi Omega murders over in Tallahassee. He knew he'd be a suspect.

Chapman quickly telephoned the Tallahassee Police Department, where he reached Don Patchen, one of the officers of the Chi Omega murders Task Force. Pensacola's strange new prisoner sounded highly interesting, Patchen agreed. By late morning Patchen had been in touch with Steven Bodiford, a Leon County detective, and by midday they were driving toward Pensacola.

Later that day, Thursday, February 16, Bundy was being questioned by the officers from Tallahassee. This time he dropped the "Kenneth Misner" identification.

"You wish to remain anonymous, as far as a name goes at this time, is that correct?" asked Patchen.

"Yes, sir." During this interview Ted would be John Doe.

Patchen, a pleasant, blondish officer, had "John Doe" go over the thefts of the credit cards. Patchen read names and numbers of the cards—the Sun Oil, Mastercharge, Gulf, Bankamericard, Shell charge plates.

"Do you recall where you took these from?"

"I really can't tell you."

"Did you steal these cards?"

"Yes, I did," he replied with a sigh.

"Where?"

He couldn't remember. There were times when, at a shopping mall or a supermarket, he said, he'd pick up a wallet from an unwatched purse in a shopper's cart. His collection of stolen documents included numerous student ID cards from men and women FSU students, plus other papers from many wallets. There were indications that "John Doe" had been very, very busy around Tallahassee in January and early February.

Patchen and Bodiford had been deeply involved in the Chi Omega murders. Both had worked in that bloody crime scene that night. Bodiford had been the detective who thought to place the ruler on Lisa Levy's body for that autopsy photo. But the two men were approaching this suspect—their hottest suspect thus far—carefully.

Listening to Patchen's questioning, Bodiford reflected on some peculiar, seemingly unrelated happenings a few days earlier. He had received a report from a Jacksonville police officer about a strange man who was driving a stolen white van with the license 13-D-11300. The man had tried to pick up the officer's fourteen-year-old daughter. That had been in Jacksonville February 8. On February 12, in Tallahassee, Leon County Deputy Sheriff Keith Daws had been questioning a young man about a license plate found lying in a car the man was entering—plate number 13-D-11300. Suddenly, the man had run away from the deputy, leaving the plate behind. That incident had happened very near the Dunwoody duplex where Cheryl Thomas had been attacked.

Patchen asked "John Doe" if he remembered—"somewhere around the twelfth"—being stopped by a deputy sheriff and being asked about a license plate.

"No. Nothing . . . L' . . . Let's not talk about it . . . I . . . [sniff]."

"You're not denying it, is that right?"

"I don't want to discuss it."

Bodiford asked, "What about a white van?"

The prisoner seemed to recoil at the question. He said he knew nothing about it.

Later, though, he freely talked about stealing the Panasonic TV out of a car, even stealing cards from, among other places, Sherrods, the disco next door to the Chi O house: "Uh—well, they'd be in . . . like purses would be under a desk . . . a . . . a table or bench or something. And there'd be a large crowd of people, and I'd just take the pocketbook out of the purse."

Weary, with a dry, lonely ache in his belly, Ted groped disconsolately toward the inevitable. "I would," he told the detectives, "like to call . . . uh . . . an attorney friend of mine in Atlanta to . . . to d-d-determine just how and when I should reveal my identity . . ." Patchen and Bodiford nodded their agreement.

Bundy had decided he'd first talk with Millard Farmer, the lawyer in Atlanta with whom he had developed a long-distance telephone relationship during his jail months in Colorado. Farmer was chief of the Team Defense Project office at Atlanta, a fighter against the death penalty.

That was Thursday morning. It would be a day of flurrying activity. During their telephone conversation, Farmer asked Ted about his arrest, the interrogation and the crimes Ted had admitted—the thefts of cars and credit cards. Farmer advised him not to say anything more to police until one of Farmer's associates, Alan Holbrook, could reach Pensacola to talk with him later that day.

When Ted was taken, heavily guarded, to the Escambia County Courthouse, for a first appearance before Judge Jack Greenhut, he remained a mute "John Doe," being charged with possession of stolen property, auto theft, and assaulting an officer. But already the Florida detectives had learned, through his telephoning, that the man's name was Theodore Bundy—a name which, for the moment, meant nothing to them.

Bodiford telephoned Tallahassee, to report to Leon County Sergeant George Brand. "This guy they've got over here at

Pensacola," said Bodiford. "We found out his real name is Theodore Robert Bundy."

"Damn, that's familiar," replied Brand. "I think we've got that name in our files." Four weeks of frantic investigation by the Chi Omega Task Force at Tallahassee had produced a mass of reports on suspects. Within the files were reports about Bundy from investigators in Seattle, Salt Lake City, Aspen, and other places. Mike Fisher had provided a complete packet of information about Bundy.

Meanwhile, Patchen was shipping to Tallahassee from Pensacola, by air, a polaroid photograph of Bundy, a set of fingerprints, and a list of all the stolen credit cards. Those items would trigger some nonstop work among the Chi Omega investigators and other lawmen across North Florida.

In a meeting at the Pensacola jail late Thursday, an agreement was worked out among Holbrook, Farmer's representative, Pensacola public-defender lawyers, Bundy, and the police: the public announcement of his identity could be made at a news conference the following morning. Meanwhile, Ted was permitted to make a series of telephone calls.

His first thought was of Cas Richter in Seattle. In his telephone call to her, Ted's words came in rambling sentences, punctuated by frequent breakdowns, weeping. Initially Cas had difficulty understanding where he was, what he was saying, what had happened. Peculiarly, Ted apologized for his behavior that Sunday—that one memorable day, July 14, 1974, that hot summer day in Seattle. "I really was awfully sick that day," he told her in plaintive, mumbled words, barely above a whisper. He reflected his mood had been foul; he had spoiled their dinner together that evening, but Cas was remembering particularly that that was the day those two girls vanished at Lake Sammamish State Park. And (police determined later) Ted murmured tearfully to Cas, "I want to make it right with all the people I've hurt." She was tenderly, sympathetically encouraging.

Ted made his other telephone calls—to John Henry Browne in Seattle, to his mother, to others. Ted was allowed a visit by a Catholic priest because the regular Pensacola jail chaplain, a Protestant, was ill that day. Police wondered if Bundy, a non-Catholic, was making confession.

From the Far West, news-media people, responding to "leaks" that Ted Bundy had been recaptured, were beginning their rush toward Pensacola. From Aspen, Mike Fisher placed an excited call to Tallahassee, where he reached investigator William Dewitt (nicknamed D.) Phillips, one of the detectives working nonstop on the Chi O murders. "What the hell's going on?" asked Fisher.

"I don't have all the details," said Phillips. He explained the man had been captured at Pensacola, about 200 miles west of Tallahassee. Phillips explained that Bundy seemed anxious to talk to the detectives there, "but no one here knows anything about Bundy."

"Well," said Fisher, "if you're gonna get anything out of that guy, you're gonna have to get it *now*—when he's flat on his ass . . . When he's *down*."

Phillips puzzled over that. *Down?* Fisher explained his theory. "Right now Theodore's probably down, right at the bottom. . . . He's emotionally at an all-time low. If you ever let him come out of that, if you ever let him up, you're not gonna get it out of him."

"Just a minute, Mike, I've got Steve Bodiford on another line." Phillips put Fisher's call on "hold" and relayed the information to Bodiford at Pensacola. "Mike Fisher's on the other line, from Colorado," Phillips told Bodiford. "And he says that if you're gonna get anything from this guy, you've got to do it now."

"I think it's going to work out," replied Bodiford. "He told us he wants to talk to us tonight, and he told us to bring plenty of tapes."

Phillips repeated that to Fisher. "Well, if that guy ever starts telling all, they'll be listening for a long, long time," said the Colorado investigator. "I'll help any way I can," said Fisher. He and Milt Blakey were preparing to leave immediately for Pensacola.

A compelling urge, a lonely need churned within Ted that midnight when he sent word he wanted to talk with the detectives. Chapman, Bodiford, and Patchen wearily—but hopefully—sat down again with Bundy in one of the offices at the jail.

Setting the tape recorder in operation, Chapman established that Ted had earlier talked with Holbrook, the lawyer, and also the local public-defender attorneys, Isaac Koran and Terry Terrell, and "you desired to talk with us . . . without these individuals present. Is that correct?"

"Yes," Ted agreed. "I approached you."

It was one thirty in the morning. The interview began. Although Ted appeared ragged, unkempt, and his face was marked by a raw cheek abrasion suffered in the scuffle with Lee, his bright blue eyes appeared alert—more alert than the drowsy eyes of the detectives. As had happened after his recapture at Aspen and as at other times, Bundy's energy level seemed to be rising in the middle of the night.

Chapman, a gentle, hefty man, assured Bundy, "Any time you get tired of seeing our wornout faces, tell us so. And we'll take you back to the cell."

"I feel like I'm in charge of the entertainment tonight," Ted responded with a grin.

"Whatever you want to talk about," Chapman assured him, leaning back in his chair.

The detectives wondered about his escape in Colorado. Bundy obliged, enthusiastically describing in elaborate detail how he worked his way out of that cell in Glenwood Springs.

"I can't reveal too much [of what] was involved there, but it simply involved cutting a plate out of the ceiling of my cell. And I knew the jail layout. I knew the place inside and out. I knew the place better than the people that worked there."

For more than an hour, Bundy, sometimes laughingly, regaled his interrogators with anecdotes and details of his cross-country flight after the escape.

Bodiford asked the question which would long puzzle Mike Fisher and other of Bundy's Colorado pursuers: "Where'd you get that money from?"

"Well, man," said Bundy, his eyes fixed on the ceiling of the room, "there's other people. Other people are in it. It was not . . . uh . . . let me put it this way, it was not given to me for the purpose of escaping."

(Months earlier, while he was in jail in Colorado, Bundy had proposed to Seattle friends that they raise a $700 or $800 fund for him, which would be used to finance a public-opinion survey of the Aspen area. The survey was to have been used in his argument for a change of venue. I pledged fifty dollars, which was never collected. Seattleites who were principal fund raisers had refused to say how much money was provided to Ted—or how, or if, it was delivered.)

As the interview went further into the early morning hours, Bundy's rambling turned to the joys of his brief freedom: "Walkin' without chains . . . playing racketball." Sometimes the memories came with tears, in a trembling voice. "There are certain places and certain things, Ted, when you start thinking about, that you start crying," Bodiford noted quizzically.

Bundy: "I think it was part of . . . I think . . . I don't know. Hold the phone. Well, it may be tearful. Not sobbing or crying . . . Anyway . . . No, it was just so good to be around people. And just so good to be a part of people. Not to be looked at differently. And . . . it was just college students. People are great anyway, but college students are beautiful people. *Good looking* people. *Healthy* people. *Exciting* people. Right? . . . Uh—and it was good to be back amongst them."

Patchen noticed he was shaking, his head down. "You still feeling all right, Ted?"

Bundy raised his eyes. "Oh, I'm feeling fine." The officers poured more coffee for him. Bundy went on, reminiscing about his need during freedom, to acquire little things "to make life more comfortable." He talked freely about the thefts of credit cards and the things he bought with them— clothing, meals, books. The Tallahassee detectives prodded him about the wallets he stole at Sherrod's, the popular disco, a student hangout right next door to the Chi O house. (Some FSU coeds had reported encountering a "weird looking" man there the night the murders occurred.) Bundy emphatically denied ever being in Sherrod's during January.

He detailed how he stole two Volkswagens and a Mazda at various times in Tallahassee. Patchen asked about fingerprints. Did Ted wipe away prints in the cars?

Bundy: "Well, I didn't wipe my prints out. I wore gloves."

Patchen: "You wore *gloves*? Every time did you wear *gloves*?"

Bundy: "When? In the car? Most of the time. Just leather gloves."

The hours wore on toward dawn. While the officers tired, Bundy seemed eager to talk, even though his words occasionally were broken by sobs, and he appeared overtaken by depression. Steadfastly, he refused to talk directly about the Chi Omega murders. But, at one point, which was unrecorded, the detectives remembered Ted told them, "The evidence is there. Keep digging." It was no confession, only a tantalizing encouragement to the detectives—just as he once, in Utah, exhorted Jerry Thompson to persist in the search for straws, to make the broom, in the Carol DaRonch investigation.

Watching, listening, Patchen and the others had a distressing thought: Here we are with probably the biggest thing in the nation right now. And we really don't know what we're dealing with.

Bundy began talking about the difficulties he'd had during his law-school days. During that period, he said, "My problem arose again." This "problem," wondered the detectives —what was this "problem"?

Ted's eyes moistened. His voice became distant. His words went unrecorded, reconstructed only by the memory of the detectives. "Guys," he said, "remember this. It's important." He began to recall an event from an earlier year, an unspecific happening. He'd seen a girl. She was riding a bicycle. "I saw her and I knew I had to have her. I had to possess her"— those were the words, as recalled later by the detectives. He said he had followed the girl, but nothing had happened. It was then, he indicated, that "the problem" began for him.

(Eventually the detectives reached a common interpretation: Bundy was telling them his "problem" was a need to possess, wholly control, dominate girls or women. They also concluded that Ted long had been, as Chapman put it, "a voyeur," who furtively watched, savored, coveted unsuspecting young women.)

Hours passed. The detectives' bodies began to ache. They stood, walked around the room. They drank more coffee. "You guys getting tired?" asked Bundy. "No, we're fine," Bodiford replied. "How're you doin', Ted?"

Ted, although he looked ragged and was smoking heavily, replied he was fine. He revealed he was most alert during the nighttime. "At times I feel like a vampire," he mused.

With the constant, unspoken thought of the Chi Omega killings on their minds, Bodiford and Patchen encouraged Ted to recall some of the crimes out West in which he had been a suspect. He defensively recounted that first arrest of his and "the satchel of things" the Utah officers had found.

"Uh—in the satchel there . . . was all kinds of stuff . . . It was sort of a junk bag I carried around in my car. There was rags, and there was rope in it . . . There was pantyhose in it with the eyes cut out. There was . . . ."

Bodiford and Patchen suppressed their reaction: *Pantyhose. Pantyhose at the throat of Margaret Bowman. Pantyhose at the Dunwoody house. Pantyhose.*

"Okay," said Bodiford a little later, "so then, in Aspen, Colorado, uh . . . a woman was kidnapped. Is that right?"

"Again," replied Bundy, "there's only speculation as to what happened." It was the Caryn Campbell murder.

"In what manner was she murdered?" asked Bodiford.

Bundy's faltering reply: "Well, I—I—I had the misfortune of seeing the autopsy photographs and uh—uh . . . a combination of uh—blunt trauma and strangulation." (To Steve Bodiford, a thoughtful, husky man with dark, curly hair, a thorough, perceptive detective, came vivid memories—his memories of the Tallahassee morgue, at the autopsies of Lisa Levy and Margaret Bowman, both victims of blunt trauma and strangulation.)

Clearing his throat, Patchen asked, "Back in Tallahassee, did you—did you ever go and visit any of the sororities, or been in any of them?"

"No," said Bundy.

Next day, the news media were out in force—reporters and cameramen from Seattle, Salt Lake City, elsewhere—when Bundy, handcuffed, heavily guarded, returned to Judge Jack Greenhut's courtroom. Public Defender Isaac Koran was visibly upset as he protested the prolonged police questioning of the defendant. "Just what is my access to Mister Bundy?" he asked. Koran complained he and other defenders had problems getting into the jail to see the man. And, he said, referring to Bundy, "He's tired. He's worn out."

Bundy was obviously uninterested in the public defender's words. The silver-haired judge ruled the defenders could have access to Bundy from early morning until 10 P.M. daily. Then Bundy, a strange, aloof look in his eyes, was taken away past the photographers to reenter a police car and return to jail. He didn't recognize me. His face wore a dour, *goddammit* look of boredom.

He wanted to talk with the detectives again that night. There were heavy thoughts on his mind. Again together with Chapman, Bodiford, and Patchen, he told them he was tired of the public attorneys' meddling. Lying in bed in his cell earlier that evening, he said, he had some of his own thoughts:

"I—I thought I came up with something I thought was very comfortable. Uh—which as I lay there in bed . . . It is, I said to myself . . . going to be easier than the dickens. And it would all come out. I mean not—and again I know what you want—but I'm interested in the whole thing. I'm interested in everything. Okay? And it's the whole . . . it's the whole ball of wax. And it's—it's got to be dealt with."

Chapman: "In other words, you're interested in clearing up everything?"

"From Seattle all the way down to Florida and . . ." Bundy said.

There were gentle, delicate offers, urgings, from the three interrogators, who now sensed a final breaking through. "Uh—just exactly, you know, do you want to handle it?" asked Patchen.

"Now . . ." Bundy began. There was another pause. "If I had my choice . . . I can't force anything. But if I were to sit back and think about how I would like the thing to resolve itself—everybody being satisfied to the degree they would be satisfied [in] getting all the answers they want to all the questions they want to ask . . . Then, after that was all over, I would like to be back in Washington State . . ."

Bundy's voice choked. He cleared his throat. "Because that's where my mother is, that's where my family is. And that's where I'm from.

"Now, I—I—I—I imagine that is a lot involved there, to say the least." There was a long silence. "That's where I started out thinking about . . . answering all these questions."

Chapman interpreted, "In other words, what you're trying to tell us is you don't mind answering the questions about anything you've done, as long as the end result's you're back in Washington State so that you'll be in an institution close enough to where your mother can visit you?"

Bundy: "That's what I'm saying."

Chapman: "Is that your way of asking for some kind of deal?"

Bundy: "Let's turn off the tape recorder."

The visible tape recorder was turned off. But a surveillance tape recorder was operating, picking up, with some garbles, the subsequent talk of "deals."

In vague ways, the men talked about the complexities of jurisdictions, of prosecutors, of political conflicts, of finding a course, as Bundy put it, which would "be very satisfying [to] all parties concerned."

His words sometimes inaudible, Ted went on, "Okay. Ted Bundy wants something out of this. And maybe that's not right. And maybe he doesn't deserve it . . . But still, I mean . . . I've got to take care of—of . . . survival . . . Ted Bundy wants to survive, too."

Chapman noted there could be a problem, dealing with all the police jurisdictions. But he added, "There's a lot of people who are heartbroken . . . because of missing people they don't know what happened to. And they don't know where they are . . . And if we could, you know—you could ease a lot of people's minds. They're going to be heartbroken anyway, but at least their minds would get eased. At least they'll know. And at least they'll be able to make, you know, decent burials and so forth. And set things right as best you can."

Chapman hammered on that theme of conscience. Bundy replied he was seeking "a way that's satisfactory to me . . . I still place a value on myself."

Patchen: "Let me ask you this, if you can answer, of course . . . How many states we're going, you know, to be concerned with—so we know how wide a range we are looking at to get things in—uh—perspective."

Bundy: "Well . . . well, I think you'd be talking about—investigations [in] six states."

"That's *six* states?"

Bundy: "I'm not sure about that."

Patchen: "Uh—it'd be around that number, more or less, huh? Whew! *Six*," he sighed.

Bundy: "Some of them don't even know they're involved."

TWENTY-ONE | # The Valentine Girl

Possessive of his celebrity criminal, now the highly publicized prime suspect in the Chi Omega murders, Ken Katsaris, the publicity-conscious Leon County sheriff, arranged to have Bundy whisked suddenly out of Pensacola that Saturday night, February 18.

While reporters and cameras waited in a floodlight-illuminated entry of the Pensacola jail, Bundy was removed through a dark side exit and placed in a Leon County sheriff's car, which sped the 200 miles along Interstate 10 to Tallahassee.

There Katsaris' office had tipped other reporters, other cameramen, about the impending arrival, so that they could get their photos and footage of the suspect in Katsaris' home county. "It's amazing," Bundy would recall later, "how easy it is to form such an instant dislike for Ken Katsaris."

The following day, Sunday, Ted's eye fell on a page 1 article of the *Tallahassee Democrat*. It was splashed with photographs of Bundy, taken through the years. The article extensively quoted Katsaris' description of Bundy and the three nights he'd spent, under questioning, at Pensacola. "We're changing the rules now," Katsaris was quoted as saying. "We've played his game until now. A change in jails might make a difference. We'll establish when we'll talk to him and under what conditions."

Bundy bristled when he saw that. He resolved, in his later words, to get "stronger and stronger and stronger and stronger . . . And harder, harder, harder . . . guarded." Whatever rapport had developed during his interviews at Pensacola with Chapman, Bodiford, and Patchen had now been marred. When they read those Katsaris words, the detectives' hearts fell, too. They sensed that whatever hope they might have had of eliciting confessions from the evasive subject now might be fading.

Square-jawed John Rudd, a man with close-cropped hair and the leathery look of a North Florida outdoorsman, went to see Bundy at the Leon County jail for a preliminary hearing. The tough chief criminal judge of Florida's Second Judicial Circuit, a man famed for his quick wry humor and stern judicial conduct, was coolly curious about the former law student whose name and face had been page 1 news in recent days. They met at a jailhouse hearing room.

Judge Rudd wasn't surprised when Bundy told him that, on the initial charges being filed against him—grand theft, auto, and burglaries—he'd like to proceed *pro se,* acting as his own legal counsel. Rather boastfully, Bundy told the Florida judge that he had been conducting a *pro se* defense while he was in Colorado, prior to his escape, and that he thought he'd been conducting it well. Frostily, Rudd suggested Bundy might not be as clever an attorney as he thought. Said Rudd slyly, "You've just made an admission to commiting a felony [escape] and this is a judicial proceeding." Bundy grinned in chagrin.

That same Sunday I was driving eastward, toward Tallahassee from Pensacola, when my eye caught a conspicuous sight beside the freeway. Parked on the grass shoulder was a blue sedan which had hitched behind it an orange Volkswagen. A wiry, mustached man in blue denims was frantically waving his arms for me to stop. It was Mike Fisher.

I braked and pulled over to a stop. "That goddamm

Theodore," Fisher shouted, "look at the mess he's got us in now." Fisher and Milt Blakey, along with Tallahassee City Detective Don Patchen, had been towing the orange Volkswagen to Tallahassee, where it would be impounded. Suddenly one of the VW tires blew out.

"And here we are stranded out somewhere in the Florida swamps!" snorted Fisher. "Damn Bundy."

Patchen had sent word to a service station, asking that a Volkswagen tire be delivered to the scene. "But," said Patchen, "I don't know how long that'll take." They couldn't enter the VW to use the spare. The vehicle was sealed for evidence.

"You'd think that Bundy'd have sense enough to steal a car with decent tires on it," growled Fisher. "Nah," he contradicted himself. "Bundy's too dumb."

As we all sat in the sedan, waiting for the spare tire to arrive, Blakey and Fisher, the men who had pursued Bundy so persistently over such great distances for so long, had some laughs now that their prey was in custody. "Y'know," quipped Fisher, "if Ted had ever learned anything about credit cards . . . and if he'd learned to drive better, we'd never have caught him."

"That's right," said Blakey. Bundy, he noted, first got into trouble driving too slowly in Bob Hayward's neighborhood in Utah. "Then," added Fisher, "the only reason he got stopped in Aspen, that night after his escape there, was because he was driving that Cadillac so damned slow and wobblin' all over the place.

"And he gets picked up in Pensacola, 'cause he's driving dumb again—too slow in a residential area in the middle of the night. If he'd ever learned to drive right . . ."

"If I were the judge," said Blakey . . . And he laughed, pretending to be a judge uttering a solemn verdict: "And now, Theodore Bundy, having been found guilty of murder in the first degree, I sentence you to die in the electric chair. But first! I sentence you to spend thirty days in remedial driver's school!" Rollicking laughter filled the car.

After the tire repair, Patchen, driving the Colorado men's car, towed the orange Volkswagen into a police impoundment at Tallahassee. Inside were dozens of articles Bundy had crammed into it after he stole that car—shoes, socks, shorts, pants, a small TV, a burgundy shirt and other clothing, a sleeping bag, a bicycle frame, and other items.

Eventually, each item would be scrutinized by lab technicians. Some would yield clues to the yet-undiscovered murder of a twelve-year-old schoolgirl.

They were peculiar, seemingly unrelated happenings. Yet they all began to fall together that weekend of Saturday–Sunday, February 18–19, 1978.

It was more than a shot in the dark when Steve Bodiford had, during his early questioning of Bundy at Pensacola, asked about a stolen white van. A few days earlier, on February 9, Bodiford had received a phone call at Tallahassee from Les Parmenter, a fellow detective with the Jacksonville Police Department, 165 miles to the east. Parmenter was angry. "Some SOB tried to pick up my daughter yesterday," said the Jacksonville officer. "Some guy from over your way."

Parmenter described what happened. A man, driving a white van, had approached fourteen-year-old Leslie Parmenter at a shopping mall near her junior high school. When Leslie's older brother Danny showed up, the man was frightened away. Danny wrote down the license number of the van: 13-D-11300. It was, said Parmenter, a plate or tag registered to a Tallahassee owner who reported his tag had been stolen in January.

"Ah'll see what I can find out and get back to you, Les," Bodiford promised. Bodiford, through a call to Captain Steve Hooker of the Florida State University police, learned that a white van, owned by the FSU media center, had been stolen around February 6, but then had just been found abandoned. It was being impounded. But its license number wasn't 13-D-11300. That was obviously a stolen tag, used by the person who had stolen the van.

In the meantime, Deputy Sheriff Keith Daws had an encounter with a suspicious man in the early morning of February 11, at a time when Daws was doing surveillance in the vicinity of the Chi Omega sorority. "When I came up to him, the guy was leaning into this car." When he questioned the man, Daws noticed, lying on the floor inside the green Toyota, a license tag—13-D-11300. Then, while the deputy used his car radio to check the status of the tag, the man bolted away into the darkness.

Bundy's photograph, flown to Tallahassee from Pensacola, was shown to Daws in a lineup with other photos. He identified Bundy as the man who fled from him, leaving that license tag behind.

On Saturday, Detective D. Phillips drove east to Jacksonville with a photo lineup, which included a duplicate photo of Bundy. There he met with the Jacksonville officer, Les Parmenter, and his daughter. The pretty, blonde fourteen-year-old identified Bundy as the strange man who had terrified her that day, February 8—the man driving the white van with license 13-D-11300. "Yeah, this is the one," said the girl, selecting Bundy's photo. She recognized him, even though he had been wearing glasses that day he approached her.

Next, in the town of Lake City, a Florida State Highway Patrol trooper, helping other officers trace the purchases on Bundy's stolen credit cards, parked in front of the Holiday Inn. Inside, interviewing a desk clerk, he discovered one of those cards had been used at that motel the night of February 8. The clerk identified a photograph of Bundy as the man who spent the night there.

Thus, in a flurry of investigation, police reconstructed some movements of Ted Bundy during the earlier part of February. Driving a stolen white van, bearing the stolen plate 13-D-11300, he had apparently traveled across North Florida, from Tallahassee to Jacksonville, then returned, making an overnight stay in Lake City, a small town near the intersection of Interstate Highways 10 and 75.

Lake City.

The trail of investigation led there.

On February 10, the local newspaper, *Lake City Reporter*, had carried an inconspicuous headline: GIRL REPORTED MISSING. "A twelve-year-old Lake City girl was reported missing by her parents Thursday afternoon when she did not return home from school," the story began.

Ted Bundy's trail had intersected on February 9 with the disappearance of Kimberly Diane Leach.

* * *

BUNDY

About all we know right now is that we got a little girl missin'," said G. Larry Daugherty, investigator for the small Lake City Police Department. I'd driven immediately to Lake City to learn what was happening. "Ah dunno nothin' about Theodore Bundy," added Daugherty, "'cept that he's from out your way, isn't he—from Washington State?" I confirmed that and said I knew him. "You *know* him?" asked Daugherty. The square-shouldered young detective seemed interested in that.

He gave me the basic facts about the missing girl. "She'd gone to school, over at Lake City Junior High School, that mornin' . . . February ninth."

During her first-period class, she had returned to her home room in a separate, satellite building to pick up her blue denim purse, which she'd forgotten there. "She left her home room, and no one saw her after that," Daugherty told me. "She just vanished." Probably the girl had taken a short cut to the main school building, an outdoor route across a playfield.

"It wasn't till the afternoon that they discovered her gone," Daugherty said. Kimberly's mother had become frantic. "Kimberly wasn't the kind to jus' take off like that," she had said. H. Morris Williams, the principal, and everyone had searched the school and around the grounds, but found no trace of her. "We checked all the alleys and garages, and the woods, the pine and oaks around the edges of the lakes around here, but we found nothin'," the detective said.

"And it was in broad daylight, with all kinds of cars comin' and goin' around the school. You'd think someone woulda seen somethin'."

Daugherty showed me a photo of Kimberly. My heart sank. She was beautiful, a pretty, shining, gamin face, radiating the beauty of a young-woman-to-be. She had long, brown hair, parted in the middle. Five feet tall, one hundred pounds. When last seen she was wearing jeans, a blue football jersey, with crimson numerals "83," and probably, a fur-trimmed tan coat.

"She'd just been voted first runner-up in the school's Valentine Queen contest," said Daugherty. I silently wondered who in the world could be prettier.

"C'mon into the chief's office," Daugherty told me. "He'd

like to talk with you about Mister Bundy." I followed the investigator into the tiny, wood-paneled office, where I was introduced to the chief, Paul Philpott, Columbia County Sheriff Glenn Bailey, and Dale Parish, Daugherty's fellow investigator.

The officers stared at me intently. I was unaware of anything other than that Ted Bundy had reportedly been in their town about the time the twelve-year-old girl vanished. Now their task was to find her—or her body—wherever she was. They were obviously worried.

"What do you know about Mister Bundy?" asked the sheriff.

"Well," I said, "he's an escapee from Colorado. He was convicted in Utah of kidnapping a girl."

"And he's a suspect in a whole bunch of murdered girls out your way, isn't he?" asked Daugherty. A suspect, yes, I answered—but there was no hard evidence to connect him with the crimes.

They began pumping me with questions about the crimes of which Bundy was suspected—the MO, the approach of the victim, and especially the age of the victim. "The girls in all the cases out West," I said, "were all in their late teens or twenties."

They already had sketchy information about Bundy, picked up from lawmen at Tallahassee and from the FBI. Now they had the task of beginning a search—a search which could cover thousands of square miles of swamp and forestland—for a small body. And they had no idea where to start.

"Where were all those bodies left, in the cases out West?" asked Daugherty. The ones I knew about, I said, were usually on high ground. Mostly in mountainous areas. "Of course," I said, "that won't help you here. Your country's perfectly flat."

"Were any of those victims left in water?" asked the sheriff.

"No, not to my knowledge." Most of the victims out West had been, as Mike Fisher had noticed, left near a rural side road, not many miles from an interstate highway.

"You guys gotta understand, that I'm just a newspaper man," I told them. "I really don't know all that much about these cases. And I'm not sure that Ted Bundy's guilty or innocent of those crimes out West. And I really doubt it in your case here. A twelve-year-old, that doesn't fit those others at all."

"You're sure he never leaves a victim in water?" The question was repeated by one of the officers. No, I replied. Never water. Always high ground. I added, "The guy you should talk to is Mike Fisher. He's the investigator in Colorado, and he knows the most about Bundy."

Later Daugherty led me to a wall map in the police station, a map of Lake City, Columbia County, and its surrounding area—a remote, sparsely populated stretch of North Florida. "Thousands of square miles," he drawled, "an' most of it's pine forest and oak and palmetto and swamps." His hands swept over thé map. "This's all swamp country. Up no'th hea's mo' or less jus' an extension of the Great Okefenokee Swamp, comin' down out of Georgia.

"'N' all around this country, in all these forests, we got them sink holes. Deep, deep black water. Sometime's the hole's only a few feet across. And sometimes y' nevah find bottom, 'n one of them sink holes."

I could understand why they were wondering if the body of the girl might have been dropped in water. "An', y' know," the intense young investigator continued, "there's 'gaters all 'round. And snappin' turtles. They'd take a body fast. An' just leave bones."

Within the next few days, fanning outward from Lake City, there began the largest ground search in North Florida history. Hundreds of men, on foot, in pickup trucks, on horseback, began looking for Kimberly. The Florida Highway Patrol dispatched dozens of its cars and scores of troopers. Overhead were search planes. One of them, flying at night, was equipped with a sensor camera which could pick up "hot spots" on the ground, where there might be a decomposing body.

The Florida Department of Criminal Law Enforcement,* a highly professional investigative agency, was asked by the sheriff to coordinate the effort. George Robert (Bob) Dekle, Sr., an assistant state attorney at Lake City, was placed in

---

* The agency's name later became the Florida Department of Law Enforcement.

charge and FDCLE investigator J. O. Jackson was assigned to work with Daugherty and the other detectives.

As a volunteer, I spent a few days in the search, traveling the roads of the remote Osceola National Forest, north and east of Lake City, sometimes slogging into the seemingly endless series of swamps. Then, forty miles to the west, I traveled remote roads, through thick pine forests, along the olive-dark Suwanee River. It was, I concluded, such a vast country, so lonely, so forbidding, they'd never find Kimberly.

On a cold, late February night, Daugherty took me to meet the girl's parents, Tom and Freda Leach, who'd been in seclusion since their daughter disappeared. At their trailer home at the northeast outskirts of Lake City, they welcomed us solemnly.

"We appreciate everythin' that's bein' done—the search 'n' all," said Mrs. Leach. She was a trim, attractive woman, brown-eyed and blonde. She worked as a beautician in Lake City. I had a sense that all her tears had already been shed. She bore only a dry fear and anxiety.

Daugherty and I sat listening in the compact living room of the trailer, as Mrs. Leach recalled the day Kim vanished. "And nobody at the school even noticed she was gone until two-thirty in the afternoon! I jus' don't understand.

"She wouldn't jus' go off with anyone. Only thing I can think is that someone went up to her and told her that somethin' had happened to me or her dad. And he'd told her 'I'm gonna take you to the hospital.' She might go if she thought he was some kind of authority."

Tom Leach, a lean man with dark, curly hair, a truck driver, described the fears they'd had—hoping for, dreading, a telephone call with some news. "We see some of the stuff on TV," he said, nodding toward a television in the corner of the room. "We shore hope that if . . ."

Daugherty interrupted with reassurance. "If anythin' happens," he promised, "we'll sure let y'all know first."

"This Theodore Bundy," said the father, turning toward me, "I understand you know this man."

"Yes, sir, I'm acquainted with him."

The father leaned forward on the chair where he sat,

looked directly at me, wringing his hands. He used soft words to phrase the question in his mind: "You know this man . . . Ah . . . Can you tell . . . Uh . . . How—how . . . These girls . . . What does he *do* to them? How does he kill them?"

I struggled for some reply. How *could* I answer? I settled for evasion. "Mr. Leach," I began, "we . . . uh, the police . . . no one really knows that he had anything to do with this situation here in Lake City . . . with Kimmy's disappearance."

The cases the police investigated out West, I explained, were all young women in their late teens and twenties. "Never a very young girl like Kimmy. So . . . I don't think you should . . ."

Perhaps the father desperately needed a scrap of reasonable doubt to which he could cling. Tom Leach nodded. "I guess any man has to be considered innocent until he's proven guilty," he sighed.

As we departed, Daugherty promised the Leaches again, "We'll sho' let you know of anythin' that comes up." Tom and Freda Leach nodded.

For a moment Daugherty and I stood outside that mobile home, in the darkness that night. I looked upward at some tall pines, the black sky, and the stars.

"Wee-e-e-ell," sighed Daugherty, "ah jus' know we're gonna find that little girl. It may take a while, Dick. But I promise yah—like I promised the Leaches—we gonna fin' her if it takes the rest of my life lookin'."

As we got in his car, the sturdy investigator had one more thought: "Ah'd love just dearly to have 'bout fifteen minutes of conversation in that jail cell with yo' Mister Bundy . . . Jus' him and me."

For a week, Ted Bundy continued his nighttime interviews in the Leon County jail at Tallahassee with Norm Chapman, Don Patchen, and Steve Bodiford. But the detectives knew that he had been collecting his composure and was yielding less and less information to them. His telephone calls to Seattle, to Cas, seemed to settle him.

Fisher and Blakey waited, in rising fury, as Sheriff Katsaris —through his chief of detectives, Poitinger—refused them permission to talk to Bundy. "All we want to ask him about is the escape," explained Fisher. "Where he got the hacksaw blades. And where he got the money."

Poitinger made it clear. Bundy was Sheriff Katsaris' prisoner. And the sheriff was interested in one thing—solving the Chi Omega murders, not solving anyone else's cases.

"If ever Theodore were going to crack, that would have been the time," Blakey, the Colorado prosecutor, would reflect later. "But they just didn't know how to go about it. They didn't understand."

Chapman, Patchen, and Bodiford, all able detectives, agreed—there would have been more success with Ted if just one of them had done the questioning.

"What you really need to have down here is that psychologist from the Utah pen," Fisher advised. "Doctor Carlisle. And he's willing to come. If you'd send him a plane ticket."

In fact, Carlisle had agreed to fly to Tallahassee, either to interview Bundy or to advise his interviewers on the best way to unlock, finally, whatever secrets the man seemed to want to release—if the Leon County sheriff would provide the airplane ticket. "Christ, it'd only be a lousy six-hundred dollar ticket," Fisher argued.

Katsaris and Poitinger ignored the proposal. Carlisle was never called in.

Again the surveillance tape recorder, operated by Poitinger, had failed during an intriguing question-answer session the detectives had one night with Bundy in the Tallahassee jail.

The detectives asked about the FBI reference to thirty-six unsolved cases of murder.

"We asked him . . . if that was an accurate figure, as far as he knew," Poitinger said later. "And he said the figure 'probably would be more correct in three digits.'" That would remain, perhaps forever, an enigmatic, disputable version of what really was said and meant. ("Ted was just playing with them," John Henry Browne, the Seattle lawyer, said later.)

Frustrated and disgusted with Katsaris and Poitinger, Fisher and Blakey flew home to Colorado.

Next it was the turn of the Lake City investigators to be frustrated by Katsaris and Poitinger. Bob Dekle, the Lake City Task Force chief, the Columbia County sheriff, and others involved in the frantic search for the Leach girl asked Katsaris for an opportunity to listen to the tape-recorded interviews which had been conducted with Bundy. "Maybe," explained Dekle, "we could pick up something out of that. Something," he said, "to help us help in the search for Kimberly."

The Leon County sheriff reminded the men from Lake City that the interview tapes belonged to him. But Dekle related later, Katsaris offered a deal. Katsaris said the investigators in the Leach case could hear the tapes—if . . .

If, when the girl's body was found, Ken Katsaris would be notified first so that he could announce the discovery to the news media.

It was an infuriating proposition to the men who were working night and day in the search for the Leach girl. But they agreed.

TWENTY-TWO | Along the Suwanee

"We're jus' willin' to try anythin' now," said Larry Daugherty. There was desperation in the detective's voice. The search for Kimberly Leach had trudged onward persistently, from dawn until after dark, day by day, through the chilly, wet early weeks of March—thousands of man hours spent moving through the woods shrouded with Spanish moss, along rural roads, through the swamplands, in all directions from Lake City, but mostly westward, to and beyond the town of Live Oak and the meandering, brush-lined Suwanee River.

The cool, damp days had been helpful. Then came the warm weather, beginning in late March. Kimberly's body, if it were out there somewhere, would rapidly decompose in the hot Florida spring, and with it evidence could evaporate.

Daugherty, Dekle, and the other men listened patiently to clairvoyants and psychics who described their visions of where Kimberly might be found. By long-distance telephone, the mother of a murdered Utah girl, trying to help the searchers in North Florida, relayed the vision which had come to her.

"I couldn't sleep this morning," said Shirleen Aime, calling from American Fork, Utah. "I was sitting in the living room, looking out the window, thinking about that little girl down there in Florida, and I saw it. The scene. As though it were in broad daylight.

"I could see this road, a dirt road. And, on both sides of it, pine trees . . . And I see the white van . . . and the man, the driver. He gets out and opens the back door and lifts something out. And he carries her into the woods, off to the right." The mother of the murdered Laura Aime had never been to Florida. But she described "a pinkish, reddish road." It sounded like many dirt roads through the pine forests of the search area. "They're searching too far north. Too far north," she said. Dutifully, Daugherty jotted down the information.

Dekle, a tall country lawyer in his early thirties, whose jaw usually bulged with a wad of chewing tobacco, was nervous, impatient. The strain of the exhausting search showed on his unsmiling face. Nothing new or promising was in sight.

"I think we're jus' gonna have to keep workin' along that Suwanee River bank," he told the others in the search task-force office at Lake City. He was counting on those findings in that white van. The suspect vehicle, impounded at the FDCLE lab in Tallahassee, had contained some clues. Lab experts had found traces of blood in it. Perhaps it was Kimberly's blood. But Kimberly's blood type was unknown.

Dirt had been tossed into the rear of the van bed, apparently to blot the blood. That soil, which contained pine needles and oak leaves from particular species (the locally called "spruce pine" and turkey oak, among others) were indicators. Botanists and soil scientists concluded they came from some zone near a North Florida river. "We jus' gotta keep working along the Suwanee," said Dekle.

Through the weeks, scores of items had been picked up by searchers—a big tennis shoe, some towels, underwear, cigarette butts, a five-dollar bill, food wrappings, other things.

Each was tagged, according to its discovery location, then
sped to the crime lab in Tallahassee, a lab which began to
overflow with work. Simultaneously, lab technicians were
microscopically examining the lint, threads, other debris
found in the white van, making comparisons with articles
found in the orange Volkswagen in which Bundy had been
recaptured.

Hot days arrived by early April. On April 6, Dekle
received a telephone message from one of the crime lab men
in Tallahassee. "Those cigarette butts," Doug Barrow had
said. "We just got around to examining them. They looked
pretty good."

The lab man explained that the way those butts had been
smoked, the manner in which they had been twisted, snuffed
out, bore a striking resemblance to the twisted cigarette butts
found in the ashtray of the white van. "Wherever you found
those, I'd go looking back there."

With Suwanee County Sheriff Robert Leonard, Dekle
went immediately to the area—a remote part of Suwanee
State Park. Beside a dirt road, the two men surveyed a
wooded area—mostly hardwood trees: live oak, turkey oak,
and hickory, mixed with some spruce pine. Leonard, a native
of that country, pointed out a large sinkhole. Its dark water
had risen, fed by the spring flood of the Suwanee River.

"Think it'd be a good place to search tomorrow?" asked
Dekle. Leonard nodded.

Next day, April 7, the searchers arrived there early. Scuba
divers from the state fisheries agency dropped into the deep
black waters of the sinkhole, while Daugherty and others
tramped through the forest. At noon, they all paused to lunch
on hamburgers delivered by one of the many restaurants and
drive-ins which had been supplying the searchers.

Florida Highway Patrol trooper Kenneth Robinson, a tall,
quiet man who'd spent weeks searching the woods, the
thickets, the marshes, and swamps, moved into woods on a
low rise above the sinkhole. Brushing away the pesky mos-
quitoes, he noticed a small, abandoned hog shed, with a
weathered metal roof which sagged to within two feet of the
ground. Robinson knelt, peered into the open end of the
abandoned structure and gasped. He could see what looked

like a blue football jersey. Then his eyes rested on the sight of the little girl's twisted body, its skin darkened, almost mummified.

He shouted the news to other searchers.

"Every man out of the woods and up on the road!" That shouted order brought three dozen or more searchers on the dead run, to their cars. "Let's rope off the scene!" shouted Daugherty. He ran to get the divers' nylon line. They used it to cordon off the area around the hog pen. Roadblocks were set up.

Daugherty thought at once of Dekle, who was at Live Oak. They had an agreement. If anything ever were found, Daugherty would send the radio code message: "S.A. One or Two. Ten Forty-Six." Daugherty radioed that message. Within minutes, Dekle was being sped to the scene by Sheriff Leonard.

Dekle had to see for himself. He argued his way past the guards, entering the woods to look into the shed. It was obviously Kimberly, nude, except for a stained turtleneck shirt around her neck. Her clothes were scattered around the partially decomposed body. She'd been found. And there was the possibility of evidence. Crime-scene specialists from the FDCLE were already racing to the scene.

Using his own car, Daugherty drove Dekle back toward his office, where he would begin making the notifications. A chaplain would be sent to the Leach home to inform the parents. As they drove east, toward Lake City, both men were trembling with exhausted excitement. Suddenly Dekle, with a powerful blow, slammed his fist on the dashboard of the car. "Boy, Larry, we DONE IT!" he shouted.

"Yeah, we did," grinned Daugherty.

Dekle smashed another blow against the dashboard. "We're gonna send that Bundy to the electric chair!"

"Right on!" replied Daugherty. "But, Bob, I think you jus' broke loose my dashboard."

A few hours after Kimberly Leach's body was found, the Leon County chief of detectives, Jack Poitinger, sat in a living room in a distant city—Muncie, Indiana. He had traveled there to the home of Nita Neary, to interview, once again, the young woman who'd seen the killer at the front door of the Chi Omega sorority house eleven weeks earlier.

Nita, deeply affected by the traumatic events that night, had left Florida State University to return to her parents' home. Poitinger opened their conversation with preliminary pleasantries. Then he began showing Nita the photo lineup. One after another, Poitinger pulled photographs from a stack—all right profiles of young men—and laid them on a coffee table. The young woman, her face framed by long blonde hair, studied them. She reached out to hold back Number 4. She examined it. Then later, she reached for, and selected, Number 7. Then she returned Number 7 to the stack. And she reexamined Number 4.

It was a right profile photo of Ted Bundy, wearing a dark turtleneck. "Does it resemble him?" asked Poitinger.

"Yes, it does," she replied.

An assortment of circumstances, pointing toward Bundy, had turned up in the Chi Omega murders investigation. There were, for example, identifications by some young women that he was the strange man at Sherrod's, the next door disco, the night of the Chi Omega crimes. But now, with Nita Neary's tentative identification, the prosecution had an important new element in an effort to show "probable cause" for a search warrant—a warrant to take an impression of Bundy's teeth. The Leon County investigators needed a comparison of Bundy's teeth with the marks left on Lisa Levy's body by her killer. The police had an enthusiastic professional adviser. Dr. Richard Souviron, a Coral Gables dentist, was anxious to establish forensic odontology, dental data—especially bite-mark comparisons—as admissible evidence in the courts of law. This dramatic case, the Chi Omega murders, offered a classic opportunity to test the scientific-legal value of bite-mark identification.

During the weeks following Bundy's capture, Dr. Souviron began his comparison work. He studied a news photograph of Bundy, flashing a broad smile, and examined the man's general dental irregularities—the crookedness of individual incisors, canines, laterals in the photo, comparing those with the bite marks in the autopsy photo of the Levy girl's buttock.

At the suggestion of Mike Fisher, Florida authorities

288

secured from the Utah State Penitentiary a full series of X-ray photos of Bundy's teeth, uppers and lowers, plus his dental-work charts. After making his comparisons, Souviron offered the expert opinion that Bundy's teeth "cannot be excluded" from consideration as teeth which caused the marks on the coed.

That conclusion, plus Nita Neary's tentative ID, plus the witnesses who placed Bundy near the Chi Omega house, all added up to probable cause. During the afternoon of April 26, 1978, Poitinger entered the chambers of Judge John Rudd and laid on his desk a warrant, supported by items of probable cause which suggested Bundy's teeth were evidence of the commission of a crime—murder. Judge Rudd signed the search warrant.

In his dimly lighted Leon County jail cell, Bundy, acting as his own counsel on the scores of theft charges, was busy writing motions of his own. He was enjoying the legal sparring with his opponents. For weeks he filed varied motions—seeking access to the press, use of law books, a typewriter for his cell, telephone privileges, outdoor exercise, better illumination in his cell. In Florida, the response of the court was slower, tougher than it had been in Colorado. When Bundy argued for regular outdoor exercise, Sheriff Katsaris replied, "He gets lots of exercise going to and from the court all the time, arguing these motions."

When the guards came to his jail cell that night and snapped the handcuffs on him, Ted asked, "What's up?" Without replying, the officers placed a brace on his leg—one which inhibited his ability to walk—and linked the handcuffs to a waist chain. "Where we going?" Bundy asked.

He was taken down the jail elevator to a waiting car and was driven to a dentist's office which was crowded with police. Dr. Souviron was waiting, too. Bundy was told the dentist would make impressions of his teeth. "You can't do this!" he exclaimed.

Poitinger triumphantly recited the search warrant he held in his hand. It authorized the taking of dental impressions—using force, if necessary. Surrounded by hefty guards, and confronted by a metal jaw-opening device, Bundy decided to submit voluntarily. He settled into the dentist's chair.

When Souviron excused himself to wash his hands before beginning the procedure, he asked Bundy, "You won't bite me now, will you?"

"I'm a very nonviolent person," Ted quipped. Souviron and the cops laughed.

The dentist retracted Bundy's lips, upward and downward, to take color photos of his teeth. Then using a mirror, a reverse-image photograph was taken of the inside surface of the teeth, uppers and lowers. After the soft, mushy Jeltrate was placed in his mouth, Ted was told to bite into it and hold his teeth motionless for a few minutes. Thus a mold was "set" as the material "rubberized." Finally, with the guards watching in fascination, the dentist, by hand, pinched warm wax around the individual teeth, to make a further impression.

Souviron had his molds, into which he could pour sculpting material, to make precise stone casts of Bundy's teeth.

At Lake City, during the steaming days of mid-July, one by one, more than sixty witnesses entered the Columbia County courthouse to give their secret testimony to the grand jury inquiring into the murder of Kimberly Diane Leach.

There was evidence and testimony to connect Ted Bundy to the stolen white van and to place him in Lake City the night before Kimberly vanished. An elderly school crossing guard said he'd seen Bundy driving the white van in the vicinity of the school. But the old man wasn't on duty at the time Kimberly vanished. Specialists from the FDCLE crime lab, through hundreds of hours of work, had made "matches" of fibers from Kimberly's clothing and purse with fibers found in the van.

All that—plus other testimony—remained secret. When the grand jury, on July 21, handed down an indictment, Judge Wallace Jopling ordered it sealed.

That was a Thursday. The following week, 105 miles to the west, a grand jury at Tallahassee began hearing secret testimony in the Chi Omega murders.

Reporters clustered in the corridors outside the grand-jury room of the Leon County courthouse, watching the witnesses enter and leave, many of them Chi Omega sorority sisters.

One was Nita Neary, who had obviously told the grand jury of her glimpse of the killer in the foyer of the Chi O house.

Ben Forbes, the detective from Salt Lake City, had flown in to testify about the pantyhose mask which had been found in Ted Bundy's Volkswagen in Utah, a pantyhose mask almost identical to the pantyhose found at the Dunwoody Street duplex.

On Friday, July 28, the grand-jury foreman, a short, gray-haired man in a tan jacket, informed Judge Rudd, "We have a sealed verdict." Judge Rudd ordered that it remain sealed until the sheriff, as prescribed by law, read it to the defendant. Sitting in the courtroom, wearing a gold polyester suit, Sheriff Ken Katsaris beamed.

News reporters and cameramen were summoned to the Leon County jail that night for a sheriff's press conference. A few early arrivals, including a TV camera crew and two newspaper photographers, were ushered through the outside perimeter of steel doors, into a small interview room near the jail elevators.

"Everybody set?" asked Katsaris. He was now dressed in a photogenic black suit, white shirt, and striped tie.

An elevator delivered Ted Bundy down from his cell into the waiting scene. When the elevator door began to open, a TV light blasted his face with light. Bundy flinched and recoiled in bewilderment. Then he sensed what was happening.

"I'm going to be paraded," Ted said. He was brought into the tiny, brilliantly lighted area, ringed by police and the faces of media people.

He fixed a glare on Katsaris as the sheriff, clutching a lengthy indictment, began to read: "The grand jurors of the State of Florida, empaneled and sworn to inquire . . . do present that Theodore Robert Bundy, on the fifteenth day of January, 1978, in Leon County, Florida, did then and there unlawfully . . ."

Bundy tried to appear blithe as he approached Katsaris to look at the document. "What do we have here, Ken? Let's see. Oh! An indictment!" Now Bundy was delivering lines for the news media. "Why don't you read it to me? You're running for reelection."

Katsaris methodically continued to read. Wearing short-sleeved green jail denims and slippers, Bundy turned away, obviously fuming. Katsaris, eyes on the document, read on: ". . . the said Theodore Robert Bundy did make an assault upon Karen Chandler and/or Kathy Kleiner . . ."

Pacing within the ten-foot-square ring of people, frustrated, Bundy turned to reporters. He gestured toward Katsaris. "He said he was going to get me." Then, turning directly to Katsaris, he added, "Okay. You got your indictment. That's all you're going to get."

Astonished cameramen and reporters recorded it. ". . . unlawfully kill a human being," Katsaris continued, "to wit: Lisa Levy, by strangling and/or beating her and . . ."

Bundy moved toward the standing reporters, exclaiming, "My chance to talk to the press! . . . I'll plead not guilty right now." He grinned toward the cameras, holding up one hand.

"We've displayed the prisoner, now," he snarled at Katsaris, still laboring through his reading of the indictment. "I think it's my turn."

Katsaris interrupted his reading momentarily to tell Bundy he couldn't speak to the press.

"Listen," Bundy protested, "I've been kept in isolation for six months. You've been talking for six months . . . I'm gagged. You're not gagged."

Finally, Katsaris completed the reading of the charge. He handed Bundy the capias, the legal document. At the elevator door, with the cameras and lights still turned on him, his face furious, Bundy held up the paper and tore it. The elevator doors closed.

Most of the reporters were astonished, sickened by the Katsaris show. Joe Nursey, a public-defender attorney, watched it all, seething, his hands trembling with rage. Katsaris, he complained, had exhibited the defendant like a caged animal. "It was disgusting."

Judge Rudd, too, was angry when he learned of the scene.*

---

* Eventually Sheriff Katsaris drew a reprimand from the Tallahassee Bar Association. In a resolution adopted August 7, 1979, that bar association declared that "it condemns the conduct of the Sheriff in reading the indictment of Theodore Bundy on television and further

But Katsaris' circus dominated the television news that night and the following day.

Katsaris and his man Poitinger had, in the view of the Lake City investigators, been systematically uncooperative, impeding their work on the Kimberly Leach case. But with that staged media event, Katsaris unwittingly gave the Lake City detectives and the prosecutor some help.

Next morning, C. L. (Andy) Anderson, a Lake City fireman, sat watching the morning television news when the Katsaris-Bundy scene appeared on the TV set at the Lake City fire hall.

Minutes later, the fireman was talking with Bob Dekle and Larry Daugherty, the detective. "That Theodore Bundy . . ." said Anderson. "He looks like the man I saw walking away from the school with the little girl—that day that Kimberly Leach disappeared."

The prosecutor and the detective struggled to remain calm. Here, belatedly, was an eyewitness in the Leach murder case.

TWENTY-THREE | An Offer of Life

Theodore Bundy and a man with the almost-funny name of John Spenkelink would never know each other. Yet, as though under the force of some dark star, the life and especially the death of John Spenkelink would touch events in the life of Ted Bundy.

In late January 1973, while bright, youthful Ted Bundy was doing law-enforcement research in Seattle, Spenkelink, a lifelong drifter, a robber, an escapee from a California prison camp, was on the run. He'd teamed up with another fugitive.

condemns any such conduct in the future, concerning Bundy or any defendant."

Together they'd driven—seeking the warm climate of Florida —to Tallahassee.

It was a cruel, rather undistinguished murder, committed in a motel not far from the Florida State University campus. Apparently, their argument was over money. Joseph Szymankiewicz, an Ohio parole violator, was found dead in the motel room. There were two gunshot wounds, one through the head. And his skull had been bashed by a hatchet. His companion was gone.

Bill Gunter of the Leon County sheriff's department and Howard Winkler of the Tallahassee Police Department—crime-scene specialists who'd be working other cases together in the future—did the evidence gathering. They found an abundance of clues—fingerprints and some backings from Polaroid films. Those film backings yielded photographs—clear pictures of a dark-haired man with tattoed arms. There were clean fingerprints on a Miller malt-liquor can and an Old Mr. Boston mint-gin bottle.

A few weeks later Spenkelink, the dark-haired man of the Polaroid photos, was arrested in California. The murder weapon was in his possession. His fingerprints matched those at the crime scene. Despite Spenkelink's plea that he'd killed in self-defense, a Tallahassee jury convicted him of first-degree murder on November 28, 1973. The following month, shortly before Christmas, Judge John A. Rudd sentenced him: "It is the judgment of this court and sentence of law that an electric current be caused to be passed through your body until you are dead. . . ." Spenkelink was taken to a cell in Death Row at the Florida State Prison at Raiford.

Gary Gilmore, who'd been a fellow inmate with Ted Bundy at the Utah State Penitentiary, drew national attention when he died before a Utah firing squad January 19, 1977. Gilmore had wished to die. In early 1979, John Spenkelink, who didn't want to die, was gaining national attention as he headed toward his execution in Florida, a state with a constitutionally approved death penalty law.

When Ted was first arrested in Florida, Millard Farmer, his friend and counsel at Atlanta, mourned, "Oh, my Lord—Ted's down here in the Death Belt of America. And Florida —that's the buckle of America's Death Belt." Ted had tried unsuccessfully to have Farmer serve as his lawyer. Judge Rudd had denied the request, a ruling left standing by the Florida State Supreme Court and later by the federal courts.

In May 1979, Farmer was trying to save Spenkelink from execution. Florida Governor Bob Graham, indicating he was willing to go along with executions, had signed the death warrant. Appeals had failed. Spenkelink was scheduled to die May 25.

Other Death Row inmates later told how they had heard Spenkelink resisting, fighting, screaming in his cell, when the guards had come to shave his head and one leg—places on his body where the electrodes would be placed.

Thirty-two witnesses watched through a window while Spenkelink was trussed into the old oak chair which had been manufactured there at the prison decades earlier. His head was strapped. "Do you have any final statement to make?" asked David Brierton, the prison superintendent.

"I can't talk," Spenkelink managed to mutter. "The [chin] strap is too tight." Brierton assumed that meant Spenkelink had nothing to say.

The witnesses saw Spenkelink's eyes—"It was just a wide, wide, wide stare," said one—as the black leather mask dropped over his face. Two black-hooded executioners administered three surges of electricity. The first, 2,500 volts, was administered at 10:12 A.M. Spenkelink's body jerked in the chair. One hand clenched into a fist. After two succeeding shocks and more convulsions, it was over. Spenkelink was dead.

Farmer, a deeply compassionate man, was sickened. An aggressive, articulate lawyer, with a warm-honey Georgia accent and intense blue eyes set in his bony, Lincolnesque face, Farmer was dedicating his life to the battle against, as he saw it, the inhumanity of the state's killing of people.

Farmer worried especially about Ted—a young man he knew and enjoyed as a person. Now Ted was scheduled to go on trial within days—on June 9—in the same courtroom where Spenkelink had been sentenced to die. Some of the people who helped send Spenkelink to the chair were involved in the case against Ted.

The state's evidence against Ted in the Chi Omega and

Kimberly Leach murders was not overwhelming. But the trials, one after another, loomed as ominously billowing black clouds which, added to the storms of dark publicity which constantly raged around Ted, made his outlook bleak. Ted's defense was in disarray. He constantly criticized and debated (often with cause) the public-payroll lawyers who were assisting him—especially Mike Minerva, chief of the Tallahassee public-defender office.

"I think we've got to figure out a way of saving Ted's life," said Farmer in one of his many long-distance telephone calls to Bundy's friends and counselors. Negotiations with prosecutors began, discreetly. The proposal: If Ted would plead guilty to the three counts of murder, he would be guaranteed three consecutive twenty-five year sentences. In a word, life.

Ted contemplated the suggestion with sullen reservations. But eventually he conceded that the odds were overwhelmingly against his winning two consecutive acquittals—especially considering the nature of the crimes and the setting, Florida. With Ted leaning toward the agreement, Farmer flew to Washington State to talk it over with Ted's mother, John Henry Browne, and others. They were supportive. Ted's life, they all agreed, must be saved.

At Tallahassee, Minerva and the other public-defender lawyers were agreeable to a plea bargain. Eventually the state attorneys involved, despite some qualms, began to agree—State Attorney Harry Morrison at Tallahassee, and his assistants, Larry Simpson and Dan McKeever, the men who'd try the Chi Omega case, and State Attorney Jerry Blair and his assistant, Bob Dekle, in the Kimberly Leach case at Lake City.

There were some political risks. Many citizens wanted the highly publicized Ted Bundy to get the chair for the awful murders they believed he had committed. There could be outrage against a state attorney who settled for less.

But for the prosecutors, there were advantages, too. Two consecutive complex trials could be enormously expensive for taxpayers. There also was a possibility Bundy could be acquitted. "You never know what a jury's going to do," said Simpson.

Delicately, the prosecutors in both jurisdictions consulted

with families of the victims. For various reasons, sometimes with great agonizing, they agreed.

The lawyers approached and advised the two judges—Judge Edward Cowart, who now presided over the Chi Omega case, and Judge Wallace Jopling, presiding over the Kimberly Leach case. (Judge Cowart, chief of the criminal division of Dade County, Miami, had succeeded Judge Rudd, who had recused himself after a technical claim of prejudice by the defense was sustained by the Florida State Supreme Court.)

The plea bargain was to be consummated without fanfare, in court the morning of May 31, 1979. There would be no advance word to the news media. John Henry Browne, the Seattle lawyer, Ted's mother, and Ted's newest, closest confidante, Carole Boone, all flew to Tallahassee beforehand to visit Ted and to be with him when his plea was entered and the sentence imposed.

At the Leon County jail, Ted was allowed "contact visits" with Carole that week—private visits without interfering bars or partitions.

The night before it was to happen, Browne and Farmer visited Bundy at the jail. They came away confident. Ted sounded in favor of the plea bargain. Over dinner that evening, Farmer, usually a nondrinker, had three glasses of rosé in celebration of the saving of Ted's life.

Even before nine o'clock the next morning, an expectant crowd began to gather in the courtroom. Word had leaked to many law-enforcement men. Sheriff Ken Katsaris' detectives had been alerted. So, too, had Colonel Eldridge Beach of the Florida Highway Patrol and Ed Blackburn, director of the Florida Department of Law Enforcement, and some of their people. (I was one of a few newspeople who had been advised to be in court that day.)

Before proceedings began, Browne and Farmer left the courtroom to visit Ted in a nearby holding cell. "Everything okay, Ted?" asked Browne. Bundy replied he felt fine. But he added, "I dunno." Both lawyers noticed that Ted held a legal pad, on which he had apparently penciled a lengthy statement or motion of some kind.

While the crowd waited in the courtroom, there was

another brief preliminary conference of the lawyers and both judges in chambers. Minerva was carrying a copy of the plea bargain. "Did he sign it?" asked Dekle. Minerva nodded.

"I don't believe it," replied the Lake City prosecutor. "I gotta see it."

Minerva opened the folder. The document had Bundy's signature.

It was Bundy's confession, devoid of details, that he killed Lisa Levy, Margaret Bowman, and Kimberly Leach. His reciprocal condition: ". . . under the terms of this negotiated plea, I will serve seventy-five (75) calendar years in prison before I become eligible for parole."

When Bundy appeared at the doorway, entering the courtroom under guard, his eyes swept the room. He recognized the faces of law-enforcement men, especially the smug face of Katsaris. As he approached the defense table, Ted glanced at his mother and at Carole, sitting beside her.

There was quiet. Everyone awaited the arrival of the judges. Ted appeared nervous. His left hand rested, palm down, on the plea-bargain agreement which lay before him on the table. With his right hand, he fondled the statement he had written, a statement protesting the quality of his public defender's work.

As though he were weighing the decision, Ted's right hand lowered. His left hand rose. Then his left palm moved downward again, onto the plea bargain. He reached to tug at Browne's jacket. "I'm not going to do it," Ted whispered.

"Oh, Christ," grumbled Browne. The Seattle attorney moved quickly to confer with Minerva. Frowning, Minerva nodded toward the doorway. Together with Farmer, they left the courtroom for a conference with Ted. Sensing something was going wrong, the prosecutors, too, departed.

Ted was adamant. He told the disconsolate defense lawyers the deal was off. Later, back in the courtroom, he began distributing copies of his motion for new legal counsel.

"What the hell's going on?" Dekle asked Blair.

"We've been *had*," replied the state attorney.

At last the judges, Cowart and Jopling, entered the courtroom, a room now filled with an atmosphere of uncertainty. "Are we ready to proceed, gentlemen?" asked Cowart.

"Yes, sir," replied Minerva.

"What is your motion, Mr. Minerva?"

That would have been the moment for the expected plea bargain to be presented. Instead, Minerva told the court that "the defendant has a motion." Judge Cowart scowled.

Ted rose to announce he was moving to seek new counsel. "Recent developments in the case have revealed to me the ineffective state of counsel that I have been receiving in the course of preparing for trial," he began.

The attorneys, glowering, listened as Ted launched a tirade. Mike Minerva, the day before, Ted contended, "was pessimistic because . . . the community feeling is so pervasive and so strong for a belief in guilt in this case that it would be impossible to obtain a fair trial and to find an impartial jury."

In fact, in his written motion, Bundy was alleging that Minerva, his chief public defender, has "revealed his own belief in my alleged guilt."

Bundy closed his angry speech, reciting numerous failures by his lawyers. Then he paused and reached for the plea-bargain document lying on the defense table. Prosecutors watched him warily. Dekle leaned toward Minerva to ask, "He's not going to plead *now,* is he?"

With a shrug, Minerva indicated it looked that way.

"Tell 'im to sit down," growled Dekle. "We ain't takin' no plea now."

Every lawyer in the room knew it was over, even if Ted didn't. He had created a record alleging his counsel was incompetent. So the prosecutors now couldn't touch a plea bargain which had been agreed to by that same counsel.

Minerva tugged at Bundy's sleeve and murmured some advice to him as Ted sat at the defense table. There was a lull, then Bundy spoke falteringly, "Your Honor, there is also before the court . . ."

"Mister Bundy," interjected Judge Cowart, "when you address the Court, stand up please. You are acting as a lawyer now."

Flustered, Bundy stood. He said he was also planning to file a motion to delay the opening of the trial.

"Madam clerk, I want copies of those motions, please," said Judge Cowart. His voice was terse. All the efforts by everyone, all the negotiations, all the agonizing with the victims' families, the willingness of the judges to travel to Tallahassee that day to take a plea bargain—all had been in vain. "This court will be in recess," Cowart concluded.

Farmer and Browne sat stunned. Carole Boone looked at Ted with a round-eyed smile of encouragement. Louise Bundy appeared confused.

It was as though Ted Bundy had been struggling with Ted Bundy. Lawyer Ted probably recognized the legal realities, the probability of conviction, and the wisdom of accepting the bargain. But the impulsive Ted, unwilling to yield control, unwilling to submit to being sentenced (and perhaps miffed at the presence of all the lawmen in the courtroom) had prevailed.

Or was it, as some wondered, a *subconscious act of suicide?* Having created havoc in his defense team, Ted would go on trial first for the Chi Omega murders.

Before heading home to Seattle in disappointment, Browne had some final counsel for Ted: "It was the most stupid decision of your life. But you made the decision. So the only alternative now is to fight like hell."

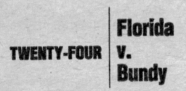

TWENTY-FOUR | Florida V. Bundy

"So there'll be just one camera and one cameraman in the courtroom, and we'll have a rotation schedule on the camera. ABC one day, NBC the next . . ."

A crowd of TV reporters, cameramen, and technicians sprawled on chairs and perched on tables, listened to the plan for courtroom coverage. They were gathered in an expanse of empty space, with some rambling divider walls, on the ninth floor of the Dade County Metropolitan Hall of Justice in Miami.

It was Sunday, June 24, 1979. The trial of Theodore Bundy for the Chi Omega murders would start the following day in a courtroom five floors below.

The media army was getting ready for action. Bundy's trial would be national news. The elements were all there—the savage attacks on the pretty coeds, the debonair, photogenic former law student, the defendant, claiming his innocence. Plus the fact that Florida permitted cameras in the courtroom —one TV camera, one still camera—for graphic coverage.

Cables for audio and video were strung from the courtroom up to the ninth floor where thousands of square feet had been converted into ministudios, crammed with monitors, tape machines, editing consoles, audio mixers, the other gear required for preparation of the daily TV feeds across America.

In early June, Judge Edward Cowart had satisfied himself it would not be possible to empanel an unbiased jury in Tallahassee, where the awful crimes had occurred. When the judge shifted the trial to Miami, Bundy and his public-defender lawyers reacted with grins and sighs of relief.

But now, as the clock ticked toward the beginning of trial, Bundy's cheerfulness evaporated. "Ted's really, really upset," Carole Boone told me as we watched the activity of the TV people setting up on the ninth floor. "The public defenders have been down here in Miami for days now, but Sheriff Ken's been keeping Ted up in Tallahassee until the last minute.

"And Ted really needs to get together with the defenders. They're not anywhere near close to being prepared," Carole added. "Things are really screwed up."

Carole was a tall, auburn-haired woman, in her early thirties, who wore glasses with oversized round frames, giving her a look of perpetual wonder. Her sense of humor was lively, offbeat, often derisive of police and prosecutors. Fondly, almost protectively, she used her own nicknames for Ted, "Bunny" or "Bun."

Carole's relationship with Ted had deepened and intensified, month after month, especially while he was in Colorado. When his Florida trial was about to begin, she had left her job in Washington State to come to Florida, with her fourteen-year-old son, to be near Ted. She was obviously committed to being Ted's most important, constant source of sympathetic support. ("She's always keeping me up," Ted had told me. "She's a very, very gifted person, and she's been important to my morale.").

Shortly before the trial, Carole, who had previously sought anonymity, had decided to "go public." She began to seek media interviews so that she could dispute the mass-murderer image which the news media, she believed, had so casually bestowed on Ted. "I haven't seen anything physical or circumstantial that suggests Ted Bundy belongs in jail," she would say.

At Tallahassee that Sunday, Ted was in an angry mood. When his guards at last came to the Leon County jail, to take him to the airport for the flight to Miami, he was refused the right to carry with him his legal files in the Kimberly Leach murder case, a case which, Ted insisted, required his day-by-day attention, even while the Chi Omega trial would be underway.

One of his guards later recalled that day in the cell. Ted, tossing aside a stack of personal mail, snapped, "And not one letter from my *beloved* mother."

The "beloved," recalled the guard, was uttered with heavy sarcasm.

With Judge Cowart presiding, the case of *Florida* v. *Theodore Robert Bundy,* venue now in the Circuit Court of the Eleventh Judicial District, Dade County, began June 25, 1979.

Seated with Bundy at the defense table were three Tallahassee public defenders—Ed Harvey, Lynn Thompson, and Margaret Good. It was a youthful team. Good was twenty-nine, Thompson and Harvey were in their early thirties. With them was a new face. Robert Haggard, a thirty-four-year-old lawyer in private practice in Miami, had volunteered to help the defense in the trial and his offer had been quickly accepted by the beleaguered defenders.

The prosecution had a capable team of young attorneys: Larry Simpson, calm, reserved, methodical; and Dan McKeever, quick-witted, glib, often smiling. In his own way, each was aggressively effective.

Jury selection, a slow, grueling process, went on for a week. One after another, most prospective jurors said they'd heard about the Chi Omega murders. Many had read or heard something about Ted Bundy.

When one young man was being questioned, he said he couldn't be sequestered with the jury for several weeks because his girlfriend wouldn't like it. "Well," coaxed Judge Cowart, "y'know absence makes the heart grow fonder."

For all his folksiness, his mirth, Cowart was a strong, certain judge. At fifty-four, he was the presiding judge of the criminal courts of the 11th Circuit, a jurist whose decisions almost always held up on appeal. A hefty man with thick shoulders and prominent jowls, Cowart, in his robes, peering down at the courtroom through black-rimmed glasses, accurately resembled a bigger-than-life captain at the bridge of his ship in stern command.

At week's end, Friday evening, June 29, a jury was finally seated. Rudolph Treml, a middle-aged, well-educated petroleum engineer, a stolid man, appeared to everyone as the natural, eventual foreman. The twelfth juror to be chosen was James L. Bennett, a truck driver. He told the questioning lawyers he held some reservations about the death penalty, and he had heard of the case. "You'd have to be in Siberia, not to know about it," he had observed. But the powerfully built black man vowed his consideration of guilt or innocence would be "based on the evidence." (The defense was pleased with Bennett. Perhaps, as a black man in a Southern state, he could sympathize with the problem of police abuse.)

With the jury chosen, Ted leaned back in his chair, apparently satisfied. He smiled and chatted with his lawyers. Ted's jury of his peers included seven blacks, five whites. A clothing designer, a teacher, a bookkeeper, a maid, an engineer. Expectedly, in Miami where the population is heavily Latin, one woman juror, Estela Suarez, was Cuban-born.

The twelve jurors and three alternates, chosen later, were taken by bus to the Sonesta Beach Hotel where they were sequestered through the ensuing days while lawyers battled over defense motions to suppress key elements of the state's case.

Bundy's defense sought to suppress three major elements in the prosecution's case: 1. Nita Neary's "eyewitness testimony" about the man she'd seen at the Chi Omega house that morning; 2. the pantyhose mask found in his Volkswagen when Bundy was arrested in Utah—and which so resembled the pantyhose found at the Tallahassee crime scenes; and, 3. the potentially explosive tape-recorded interviews Bundy had with the detectives after his recapture at Pensacola.

Simpson and McKeever had concerns about Nita, their twenty-two-year-old star witness. She was nervous and apprehensive about her role in the dramatic legal drama, and the defense was ready to attack her rather tentative identification of Bundy on several fronts. She had selected Bundy in a photo lineup, but when police in October 1978 took her to a Tallahassee courtroom to view Bundy in person, she hadn't been positive he was the man.

Before Judge Cowart, Simpson, with supportive, friendly questioning, had Nita recall all the events of that early morning of the murders. She repeated the descriptions she gave to police of the man. She described her collaboration with the artist who drew the sketch of the killer's profile.

Then the prosecutor took her to the final question: The man she had seen in the Chi Omega house that early morning—"is that man in the courtroom today?" "I feel positive . . ." she began.

She paused and continued, "I have never seen the exact profile real—in life—through the whole thing. I've never gotten . . . as good a look as I have gotten this morning. I immediately recognized him to be the man I saw at the door that night."

Simpson urged her onward. "Would you point him out for the court?"

For an instant Nita seemed reluctant to look directly at the defense table, at Bundy. Then her left arm raised rather mechanically. Her index finger—and eyes—pointed directly at Bundy.

With mixed anger and boredom in his voice and on his face,

Ted assisted the court reporter by speaking, for the record, in lawyerlike calm.

"That's Mister Bundy," said Ted.

Judge Cowart ruled that Nita Neary's description of the man she saw leaving the Chi Omega house was "deliberate and careful" and had remained consistent through all her subsequent descriptions.

The prosecution's star witness would be allowed to testify.

Three Utah officers—Bob Hayward, the state trooper who arrested Bundy in August 1975, and Salt Lake County Detectives Jerry Thompson and Daryl Ondrak—had been flown to Miami for the suppression hearing. The defense sought to block the state from using their testimony about the pantyhose mask found in Ted's VW—the pantyhose cut to form a mask—as were the pantyhose found at the Chi Omega and Dunwoody crime scenes.

After listening to the testimony and arguments from both sides, Judge Cowart indicated he would reserve, until later, his ruling on whether the Utah pantyhose evidence would be allowed into trial. Eventually the ruling would be a shocker to the prosecution.

With the jury still sequestered, the defense fought to suppress the tape recordings made while Ted was being questioned following his recapture at Pensacola.

Burly, gentle-mannered Pensacola Detective Norman Chapman sat in the witness chair for nearly three hours, while Judge Cowart and spectators and reporters strained to hear the noisy, barely audible tape recordings of the detectives' questions and Ted's answers during those first predawn interviews.

The "Pensacola tapes" had more than one legal flaw. The tape recorder had been turned off and on, so that some of the questions and answers went unrecorded. That bothered Judge Cowart—the gaps. But the most serious flaw was pointed out by Terry Terrell, a Pensacola public defender. He testified that, on the early morning of February 17, 1978, while Bundy was in the jail undergoing that questioning, Terrell was denied the opportunity to talk with the prisoner.

There was supporting testimony from other Pensacola public defenders. Assistant State Attorney Ron Johnson, they said, had blocked their access, and thus Bundy was denied his right to counsel.

"I just can't understand that," said Judge Cowart. He ruled the tapes out of the trial.

"That really hurt us," mourned McKeever later, in a corridor conversation with reporters. "It was really a disaster. A disaster with a capital D."

Now, suddenly, Ted Bundy's defense had a winnable case.

When Simpson approached the jury that afternoon to deliver the state's opening statement, the youthful-looking prosecutor scooted a blackboard into place, as though he were the teacher, preparing to give the class a complicated lecture. "There are seven charges in this case," he explained to the expectant jurors. "There are two crime scenes." With a piece of chalk, Simpson began covering the blackboard with diagram jottings—the crime scenes, *Chi Omega* and *Dunwoody*, and the crimes, *burglary, burglary, murder, murder, attempted murders.*

Larry Simpson had lived that murder case for months, working long hours with police and lab specialists, on the crimes and evidence, learning everything he could about Bundy and his background. "The toughest part of the case," he once confided privately, "is the complexity of it. How can we present it in a simple way, so that it could be understood, and still cover all the parts of it?"

Simpson described to the jury the apparent chronology of events, beginning with Nita Neary's arrival at the Chi Omega house that early morning and the discovery of the victims at the Chi Omega house, then an hour and a half later, the discovery of the battered Cheryl Thomas at the Dunwoody place. "She had been beaten severely about the head and was laying in a pool of blood on the bed.

"She had suffered five compound fractures of the skull." The jurors listened intently. (Eventually, during the trial, Cheryl would appear as a witness, along with the other survivors. Cheryl, a beautiful, regal girl, who aspired to be a dancer, had to undergo extensive rehabilitation. As she walked across the courtroom, she would falter, as though her equilibrium had been impaired by her severe injuries.)

"An important piece of evidence . . . was a pantyhose

mask," Simpson told the jury. "Remember I told you that Margaret Bowman was strangled [in the Chi Omega house] with a pair of pantyhose. And now we have a pantyhose mask that has been found at the Dunwoody scene." Simpson described how a crime analyst, Patricia Lasko, had found two hairs in that pantyhose and would testify "it is highly likely that the hairs found in that pantyhose mask were those of Theodore Bundy."

Simpson told the jury that bite marks were found on Lisa Levy's body—and the state would show that "within a reasonable degree of dental certainty, the defendant, in this case, Theodore Robert Bundy, was responsible for leaving these bite marks on the buttocks of Lisa Levy."

Haggard, a diminutive man with long blond hair, who was quickly assuming command of the defense legal team, delivered the opening statement for the defense. "Certainly there was a crime committed," he said. "No one disputes that. But there is a true issue in this case—who committed these crimes?"

Haggard continued, "The issue is, did Ted Bundy commit this crime and no other man? Will the state prove that Ted Bundy and no other man committed this crime, beyond and to the exclusion of every reasonable doubt?"

"Object!" Simpson rose to argue that Haggard had strayed into the realm of argument. The judge agreed. Haggard plowed onward with an opening statement interrupted by more than twenty objections from Simpson. At the defense table Bundy scowled at this unfamiliar lawyer who was making such a disjointed presentation of his case to jurors. Among spectators, Carole Boone bit her lip nervously. With Haggard, things were opening badly for Ted.

The parade of state's witnesses began the following Monday, July 9. Jurors first heard testimony of officers who had arrived at the crime scenes and the recollections of the medics who cared for the injured.

To the astonishment of Simpson and others, Ted Bundy, the defendant, arose to act as counsel, to personally cross-examine Ray Crew, the Florida State University officer who was first on the scene at Chi Omega.

"Christ!" exclaimed one of the TV newspeople watching a

monitor on the ninth floor. *"Bundy's* gonna question the witness!" Crowds collected around the TV monitors.

Wearing a sport shirt and tan jacket, Bundy strode to a podium carrying a legal pad in one hand, his other hand casually slanted into his pocket.

In the courtroom, spectators and reporters leaned forward in anticipation and jurors stared, as the defendant softly asked, "Officer, tell me step-by-step what you did when you entered the room."

Crew described finding the bleeding Kathy Kleiner. "Someone was holding a small plastic pail to catch the blood from her chin, to keep it from running all over the place," he said.

Lawyerlike, Ted jotted notes and asked for more details. He wanted to know what the room looked like. He asked about the position of the dead girl's (Margaret Bowman's) arms and legs.

"How was the lady removed from the bed to the floor?"

"Were there any other pantyhose in the room?"

Jurors gazed in fascination as Ted dispassionately asked his questions of the police officer. The jury didn't know it at the time, but Bundy, who was acting as a lawyer in the courtroom at that moment, eventually would never take the stand as a witness in his own case.

Dr. Thomas P. Wood, who conducted the autopsies, testified about his findings. When asked about the cause of death of Lisa Levy, Wood replied, "In my opinion the deceased in all likelihood was rendered unconscious at the time by the blows to the head and shoulder. I think that, following this, the bites to the right breast and the left buttock occurred, along with penetration of the vaginal and anal orifices, and then suffocation by strangulation."

He described the pelvic-area hemorrhaging. Wood theorized that Lisa had been killed first, then the same pantyhose ligature was used to strangle Margaret.

A later witness, Richard L. Stephens, of the Florida Department of Law Enforcement, described the pantyhose which the medical examiner had taken from the neck of Bowman. "Hanes *Alive,* Size D. They are inside out and the right leg is cut off just below the crotch, completely removed.

They are split down the sides on each side of the waistband . . . There's a knot tied in the remaining leg, which would be the left leg. A very, very tight knot tied in the left leg, which leaves a loop with the foot sticking out of the other end of the knot."

Another pantyhose had been discovered belatedly at the Chi O house, several days after the crimes—another crime-scene lapse by police. It had been found, partially covered, on the bed of Bowman's absent roommate. It had been almost identically altered.

Thus the stage was set for the state to introduce the "Utah pantyhose." Again, the Utah officers had been flown to Miami and were waiting, prepared to testify about finding such pantyhose in Ted Bundy's Volkswagen in Utah in August 1975.

Judge Cowart's ruling on the admissibility flabbergasted the prosecution. "I do not think the possession of it, in Utah two years since, in and of itself, would be, in fact, a crime that's creditable for introduction in this particular reference," said the judge. The "Utah pantyhose" evidence was ruled out of the trial.

"I just can't believe it," whispered Simpson. McKeever snapped, "People just don't carry pantyhose masks around with them! With a knot in them!"

Its case weakening, the prosecution pushed ahead with testimony from Patricia Lasko, microanalyst for the FDLE. She told the jury that two hairs found in the pantyhose mask, discovered where Cheryl Thomas had been attacked, came either from Bundy "or someone else whose hair is exactly like his who happened to have been at the Dunwoody apartment."

She conceded that hair is "not like a fingerprint identification." It's not conclusive.

The following morning, July 18, Bundy refused to go to the courtroom. He pulled a sit-down strike in his cell, until Judge Cowart, threatening a contempt citation, ordered his appearance. When the defendant finally appeared, Judge Cowart scolded, "I'm not tolerating any more of this!"

Ted protested his jail conditions and complained his files from Tallahassee still hadn't been delivered. "The sheriff of

Leon County has not complied with this court's order," Ted exclaimed angrily, jabbing his finger in a gesture of emphasis toward the judge.

"Don't shake your finger at me, young man!" snapped the judge. In the ninth-floor media center, newspeople clustered around the TV monitors. "Bundy's blowin' up! Bundy's blowin'!" shouted one of the reporters gleefully. The television crews got dramatic footage of the murder defendant and the judge in a heated confrontation.

Ted had access to a telephone at the Dade County jail, which he used for nightly conversations with Carole. That night he telephoned me, at my hotel room, to discuss his outburst of the day.

"It's so darned frustrating, sitting here, watching myself get put away," Ted said. "This defense team's all messed up." Ted was growing upset with the young Miami lawyer and he was critical of his other defenders.

Ted poured out his frustration with the defense team, which, he said, was making decisions without consulting him. "So here I sit. Isolated. I don't know what to do. Y'know, we can *win* this case! And they keep me isolated from my own case. And they know my life is on the line."

I found myself in sympathy with Ted. Even though he had helped create his own problems, here was the most dramatic, most publicized criminal trial in America in 1979, and the defendant appeared to be without a well-coordinated defense.

The prosecution paraded a series of witnesses before the jury, each adding an element to the pattern of circumstance. Some young women identified Bundy as the man who acted so strangely that night at the disco next door to the Chi Omega house. Henry Polumbo, the young rock musician who lived at The Oak, described seeing Bundy—then known as Chris Hagen—dressed and awake, in front of the apartment at "approximately a quarter to five in the morning." That was soon after the crimes. David Lee, the Pensacola officer, described his arrest of Bundy, an indication to the jury that Bundy was fleeing, evading police.

Simpson knew there could be a lurking question in the minds of jurors: *Why weren't Bundy's fingerprints found in the crime scenes?*

The youthful prosecutor came up with a last-minute inspiration to answer that wonderment. "Call William Gunter," Simpson told the bailiff.

Gunter, the Leon County sheriff's department crime-scene specialist, a fingerprint expert, described going to Bundy's vacant apartment at The Oak, soon after the arrest at Pensacola, and dusting for fingerprints. Gunter told of his exhaustive search for a print—or prints—on closet doors, shelves, bed posts, even an overhead light bulb.

"There was not an area in there that we did not dust for fingerprints," Gunter testified. "The room had been wiped clean."

There was an instant of silence after Gunter's words. . . .

Wiped clean! The jury seemed to absorb the thought that Ted Bundy was fingerprint-conscious.

Simpson and McKeever wound up the state's case with what they hoped would be their strongest elements, Nita Neary's eyewitness identification and the bite-marks evidence.

In the presence of the jury, Nita gave her version of the events that early morning, describing the man she'd seen leaving the sorority house. Simpson asked if Neary saw the man in the courtroom. She nodded.

"Would you point him out for us, please?"

She pointed toward the defendant. The man she saw, Neary added, was the man sitting at the defense table "with the dark pinstripe suit, with the red tie."

"Let the record reflect that she has pointed out the defendant, Theodore Robert Bundy," noted Simpson.

Haggard's prolonged cross-examination raised some doubts about the possibility of police prompting, but did not shake her.

With the jury out of the room, Public Defender Ed Harvey challenged the impending testimony of Dr. Richard Souviron, the Coral Gables dentist, a rather handsome, animated man, the state's enthusiastic key witness on the bite-marks evidence.

Harvey questioned him about the photograph of the bite marks on Miss Levy's body and the yellow plastic ruler which appeared in the photo. The defender drew out the fact that the original ruler had been lost. But there *had* been a ruler in the photograph—and Souviron said he could assume it was an accurate ruler. That preserved the scale of the teeth in the photograph and the validity of comparisons.

Judge Cowart ruled that Souviron could testify in the trial.

For the jury, Souviron presented an elaborate illustrated lecture, with a photograph—enlarged more than six times— of the bite mark on Lisa's skin, and an oversize photograph of Bundy's teeth, with the lips retracted to show the gums and irregular uppers and lowers. Souviron held an acetate overlay, with the pattern of Bundy's front teeth, atop the photograph of the bite marks, to demonstrate the alignment.

"I can tell this is a human bite," Souviron told the jury. Using a pointed on the bite-mark photograph, he went from mark to mark, explaining, "You have some large scrape marks in the upper left hand corner. . . . The overall pattern here would be one of crooked teeth."

The lawyers gathered around Souviron as he stood close to the jury box, explaining, detailing for jurors the points of comparison. "We'll start with Mr. Bundy's right side . . . the first bicuspid . . . tucked down here, but coming to a point . . . his right cuspid. . . . Next, the lateral incisor . . ."

Bundy sat forward, elbows propped on the defense table, watching the juror's attentive faces. "Two large central incisors," Souviron went on, "then the lateral incisor on either side. . . . We have two actual bites there. . . . [He] bit once and turned sideways and bit a second time. . . ." That was fortunate, Souviron told the jurors. It allowed a double check on the accuracy of the comparison.

When the lecture to the jury had ended, Simpson asked, "Doctor, can you tell us, within a reasonable degree of dental certainty, whether or not the teeth represented in that photograph as being those of Theodore Robert Bundy and the teeth represented by the models [of Bundy's teeth] . . . can you tell us within a reasonable degree of certainty if those teeth made the marks on those photographs [of Lisa's body]?"

"Yes, sir."

"And what is that opinion?"

"They made the marks."

Dr. Lowell J. Levine of New York University, chief consultant on forensic dentistry to the New York City medical examiner, a dark, bearded, professional man, delivered his testimony with quiet confidence—without the flair of Souviron, but with obvious effect on the jury. Using an enhanced photograph—given almost three-dimensional quality—of the bite mark on the victim, he compared it with a photo portraying Bundy's teeth. His conclusions solidly supported Souviron's testimony.

Mike Minerva, chief of the public-defender office at Tallahassee, made his only appearance in the trial that day, cross-examining Dr. Levine. Minerva reminded Levine that he had, in 1972, written that flesh "is not a very good medium for retaining dental impressions." "A lot of things have happened in seven years in all the sciences," Levine replied.

On Thursday, July 19, after testimony from forty-nine witnesses, the state rested its case.

Ted's actions—his open-court criticisms of the public defender in Tallahassee—had ruptured the relationship with Minerva. Yet, when Minerva immediately left Miami that day, returning to Tallahassee without saying good-bye, Ted was upset.

That evening, in our telephone conversation, a depressed Ted confided to me, "I just have to pull it together. . . . Here we are with a chance to win this case, and there's no organization, no leadership. We're always making decisions at the last minute.

"I don't like the way the jury is looking at me now. I have to establish some sort of rapport with the jurors, some sort of communication." He confided he was seriously thinking of questioning some of the witnesses for his defense.

Friday night, July 20, Ted had an angry showdown with Haggard in the visiting cell at the Dade County jail. Haggard had aggressively come to dominate the defense strategy. And Ted Bundy was not about to be dominated. Ted announced that Margaret Good—not Haggard—would deliver the important closing statement for the defense. Haggard left in a huff.

Next morning, in the courtroom, Ted announced that decision to the court—that *he* was taking over direction of the defense, that Margaret would handle "the closing. There's no question in my mind, Your Honor, that we can obtain an acquittal with a proper closing statement," he told the judge.

Controlling his fury, Haggard asked permission to quit the case. With a shrug, the judge permitted it. Then a disconsolate Ed Harvey, the "senior" defender in the case, asked to be excused from the case, too. The calm public defender said he and Ted had "irreconcilable differences." Cowart refused that request. Harvey countered with a suggestion that the court conduct a competency hearing for Bundy. In view of the turmoil which the defendant was causing, Ted might be suffering from "a debilitating . . . mental disorder," resulting in his "inadequate ability to consult with lawyers about the case with a reasonable degree of rational understanding."

McKeever objected to a competency hearing at that time. "This man is difficult to work with," said McKeever, with a grin and a good-natured wave toward Ted. "He's almost cunning in his way of working against his attorneys."

But, McKeever concluded, Ted was competent to continue through the end of the trial.

Judge Cowart agreed. As difficult as Ted might be for his co-counsel, he was competent to be on trial.

Sprawled on the bright blue carpet of her room at the Holiday Inn, not far from the jail, Carole Boone, in jeans and T-shirt, was on the telephone with Ted that weekend, discussing his last-minute emergency needs.

"I'm going to call Terry Terrell up in Pensacola," Carole said. "Maybe he can help us get that negative. We can't get anywhere with the *Tallahassee Democrat*. Do you want me to go over and tell the judge that you had straight teeth when you escaped? And that we have photographs to prove that?"

Abruptly in the final hours of the trial, on the eve of closing statements, Carole and Ted were scurrying on a new avenue of defense—Ted's teeth. Ted said he remembered that, while eating a meal in the Leon County jail in mid-March 1978, a chunk of his tooth—his right central incisor—had fallen out. That was after his arrest at Pensacola and before the impressions were made of his teeth. "If that chip did not occur until March of '78, one month or two months after the Chi Omega crimes . . . then there's obviously something wrong with the observations made by the state's odontologist [Souviron]," Ted maintained.

Their last-minute efforts to delay proceedings, to develop some proof about the chipped tooth, ended in limbo. Judge Cowart ordered that closing statements by both sides begin at once.

There was a stern, almost angry look in the blue eyes of Larry Simpson as he began the state's closing statement on Tuesday, July 24. Simpson's argument flowed systematically through a review of Nita Neary's eyewitness identification and the sketch of the assailant. The prosecutor followed a hunch that jurors, in viewing that sketch, could see a resemblance to Bundy. "That sketch," said Simpson, "is an identification of Theodore Robert Bundy as the man going through the Chi Omega house on the morning of January 15, 1978."

Simpson wove together stitches of testimony. There had been Pensacola policeman David Lee's testimony about capturing Bundy during the early morning of February 15, when Bundy had told him, "I wish you had killed me." And why did he wish Lee had killed him? "Here is a man that . . . has committed some of the most horrible, brutal crimes known to the Tallahassee area. . . . He can't live with himself." The powerful circumstances, the eyewitness testimony, and the scientific testimony about the teeth marks—any one of those parts of the case would in and of itself be enough to find Ted Bundy guilty, said Simpson. "There is only one conclusion that you can reach," Simpson told the jurors in a lowered voice. "A verdict of guilty as charged in this case."

Margaret Good, a young woman with long, blond hair, was earnest and businesslike in her appearance. Her specialty in the Tallahassee public defender's office was appellate work. She'd been assigned to the Bundy case at the last moment, just as the trial was being shifted to Miami. But Ted liked her.

And he watched her hopefully as she began, for the first time in her life, nervously delivering the closing statement in a major case, a statement she'd labored over far into the night.

"The defense," Good began, "does not deny there was a great and terrible tragedy that occurred in Tallahassee on January fifteenth. . . . But I ask you not to compound that tragedy by convicting the wrong man. The state's evidence is insufficient to prove beyond reasonable doubt that Mr. Bundy, and no one else, is the person who committed those crimes."

She enumerated all the evidence-collecting failures of police. There were about 260 different fingerprints in the Chi Omega house. But before police finished eliminating all those by comparisons, Ted Bundy showed up as the police's prime suspect. "And they stopped looking."

At length, Good portrayed the police work as a systematic process of induction, shaping, molding, fitting the circumstance to the suspect. Good attacked the state's inference about the lack of Bundy fingerprints at either crime scene. "They want to imply that somehow the assailant was wearing gloves." Yet, she recalled, Nita Neary had testified the man she saw did not appear to be wearing gloves.

She reviewed testimony of Dr. Richard Stephens, the serologist, who had tested a semen stain found on a bedsheet at the Dunwoody duplex. He had explained some men were "secretors"—i.e., their A-B-O blood type antogens are secreted into their saliva, blood, and other body fluids. About 20 percent of the population, he had said, are "nonsecretors." Tests on the stain from the Dunwoody bedsheet, he had testified, were inconclusive as to blood type. Those results, said Good, were "consistent with the semen donor being a nonsecretor" . . . a positive exclusion of Mister Bundy [who was a secretor].

Simpson had a last, hard-hitting summation. The killer, he told the jury, was a smart killer, who took pains to cut holes in a pantyhose mask, who avoided leaving fingerprints, who even wiped fingerprints from his apartment. "He's the kind of man who's smart enough to stand in this courtroom to cross-examine witnesses in this case. . . . He thinks he is smart enough to get away with any crime."

That Tuesday afternoon, July 24, Judge Cowart read his

lengthy instructions to the jury, then told the dozen men and women, "You may now retire to consider your verdict."

Ted, as he was led out of the courtroom to await the verdict, tossed a smile and a wave toward Carole and, sitting beside her, his mother. Louise Bundy had arrived in Miami only hours earlier to watch the finale of the trial.

While we waited for the jury that evening, Ted and I were on the telephone again. "I feel good about the jury right now," he said hopefully. "That's not to say that we have an acquittal. I think there will be several votes."

(I didn't tell him, but the press corps had formed a "pool" on the jury's verdict. Each of us had tossed a dollar into a box and, with it, our predictions of the length of deliberation and verdict. . . . Some local reporters were guessing it would be "guilty" within three to eight hours. A few had predicted acquittal. I had guessed twenty-two hours of deliberation and a hung jury. There was a varied reaction among the media observers to the credibility of some witnesses. Obviously there was "reasonable doubt" in the state's mostly circumstantial case.)

Ted kidded about the credibility of Nita Neary. "If Nita Neary said she saw your spouse in a motel with someone else, would you get a divorce on that basis?" I laughed. It was a good point. "And," Ted added, referring to the suave dental expert, so totally self-assured, "if Dr. Souviron said you had cancer, would you want a second opinion?"

Believability of the state's key witnesses was being decided by the jury.

It was surprisingly quick. About 9:30 that evening the jury filed back into the courtroom, their faces solemn. Sitting at the defense table, wearing a light blue sport coat, matching shirt, and dark blue tie, Ted glanced toward me and flashed a V-for-victory sign with two fingers. It was an unsmiling gesture of irony. It had come so suddenly, I thought it would be an acquittal. But Ted could read it on the jurors' faces—guilty.

"Ladies and gentlemen of the jury, have you reached a verdict?" asked Cowart.

Some heads of the jurors nodded, as they replied in disunison: "Yes, Your Honor."

Treml, the foreman, handed seven verdict slips to the bailiff, who relayed them to the judge. There was deathly silence as Cowart studied each, then handed them to the clerk, Shirley Lewis, and ordered her to read them.

Shirley, a middle-aged black woman, began to read aloud, in a voice with an incongruously cheerful Jamaican lilt:

"We the jury in Miami, Dade County, Florida, this twenty-fourth day of July, A.D., 1979, find the defendant, Theodore Robert Bundy, as to count one of the indictment, burglary of a dwelling and committing an assault upon the persons therein, to wit, Karen Chandler and Kathy Kleiner, guilty as charged. So say we all."

Leaning back in his chair, a steady hand slightly stroking his chin, Bundy watched and listened, eyebrows raised a little.

The ritualistic reading continued. The words "guilty as charged" recurred. Ted Bundy was guilty on all counts.

Near the rear of the courtroom, the face of Louise Bundy contorted with pain. Then the defendant's mother cried in a courtroom once again, as she had in Salt Lake City in 1976. Beside her, Carole looked stunned.

Outside, the horde of reporters and cameras awaited the petite, graying mother. Leaving the courtroom she flinched at the sight. Jamey Boone, Carole's son, a handsome teenager with dark curly hair, put an arm around Louise.

Mrs. Bundy spoke into the lights and microphones: "This is not the final answer. It cannot be. It cannot be. There will be appeal upon appeal."

She was on the verge of tears, yet she maintained her composure.

Very pale, wearing a sleeveless pink cotton dress, she explained to the media horde, it is "absolutely impossible" to think of her son as the killer and attacker of the young women in Tallahassee . . . or anywhere.

Ted managed one last telephone call to me, about forty-five minutes after the verdict. "Dick," he told me, "they didn't take enough time to deliberate." He was controlled, sounding more puzzled than distressed. "They spent six hours deliberating. Good heavens. To read the instructions would take three hours. . . . Well, we don't know what was going on in that jury room. . . . We were bucking a lot of flak and publicity. We don't know what they knew prior to coming in there. We thought we had a reasonably untainted jury. . . . Now there's a potential that they're going to get a head of steam and really try to flatten us in the penalty phase." The prosecution, perhaps the jury, was in a mood for death. Ted sensed it.

He was right. Eventually James Bennett, the black truck driver, about whom the defense felt so confident, would tell *Miami Herald* reporters he considered Bundy a beady-eyed killer "incapable of emotion." Another juror, Alan Smith, would explain he was angered when Bundy, who did not testify, played "lawyer" in the courtroom, questioning a witness. "I was very turned off when he got up. It was a mockery of our system." Smith believed that questioning could and should have been conducted by one of the defense attorneys.

On Monday, July 30, there was only brief testimony before the jury, which was now considering whether or not to recommend the death penalty. The prosecution was prepared to offer testimony about Bundy's conviction of kidnapping in Salt Lake City and his escape from Colorado. Jerry Thompson and Mike Fisher had flown into Miami for that. Carol DaRonch, too, had arrived from Utah and was summoned into the courtroom to testify about how Bundy had kidnapped her. Bundy glanced at her without expression.

The jurors studied the pretty, slim young brunette, but they never heard what she had to say. Hurriedly—to prevent her testimony—the defense stipulated that Ted had been convicted of kidnapping Carol DaRonch.

For the defense, pleading for her son's life, a nervously smiling Louise Bundy testified that, of all her children, Ted had been "my pride and joy." She recalled his growing-up years, his boy-scout days, his hard work in school. She said she felt Ted could lead a constructive life, perhaps working in the law library of the penitentiary, if only he were allowed to live.

She spoke of capital punishment: "I consider it—the death

319

penalty itself—to be the most primitive, barbaric thing that one human can impose on another. . . . My Christian upbringing tells me that to take another person's life under any circumstance is wrong. I don't think the State of Florida is above the law of God."

She left the witness stand, sending a faint, fleeting smile toward her son as she passed the defense table. ("There was so much more I wanted to tell them," she murmured to me later.)

The jury deliberated one hour, forty minutes. Its advisory recommendation: Ted Bundy should die in the electric chair. At the defense table, Bundy, showing no emotion, jotted something on a legal pad. Judge Cowart announced he would make his imposition of sentence the following day.

On the final day of that steamy hot July in Miami, Ted was allowed his chance to address the court. In the hushed crowded courtroom, he blamed the news media for its flood of prejudicial news about him—the press's "vilification," the rush "to make a notorious individual out of me."

His eyes moistened as Bundy looked up at the judge. "I'm not asking for mercy," he said, swallowing. "I find it absurd to ask for mercy for something I did not do. . . . So I will be tortured for, and suffer for, and receive the pain for the act. But I will not share the burden of the guilt."

Then, dispassionately, Judge Cowart, reading, citing the aggravated circumstances in the case, imposed the death penalty. Theodore Bundy, he said, would be taken to the Florida State Penitentiary at Raiford, there to be kept until he shall be administered "a current of electricity sufficient to cause your immediate death."

There were two death sentences—for the killings of Margaret Bowman and Lisa Levy. There were consecutive sentences of ninety years each for the assaults on the other three victims.

Standing before the judge, Ted's face was impassive.

Perhaps Ed Cowart, a father and a grandfather, remembered a day, two months earlier, when he had flown to Tallahassee where, he had been told, Ted Bundy would enter a plea bargain and receive a sentence of life. Life—a sentence for which Ted's mother had pleaded in vain.

But now it was death.

Looking at the handsome Ted Bundy, a surge of words came from the judge: "Take care of yourself, young man."

There was a startled, bewildered silence in the courtroom.

The judge, who had just sentenced Ted to die, said it again: "Take care of yourself. I say that to you sincerely. It's a tragedy to this court to see such a total waste of humanity. You're a bright young man. You'd have made a good lawyer. I'd have loved to have you practice in front of me."

The eyes of Ted Bundy, who'd studied law, whose aspiration was to be an attorney, were turned downward.

"But you went the wrong way, pardnuh," added Cowart. "Take care of yourself."

After a moment of frozen silence, there was an explosion of media activity as the newspaper reporters and the radio and television people, in a noisy, shouting, clattering rush, delivered to the nation that strange final moment of the drama.

In Seattle, where the Miami courtroom action had been daily newsfare, Eleanore Rose wept, saying, "Oh God, I'm so grateful. Maybe now . . ." During the trial in Miami, she had observed, in solitude, the fifth anniversary of that date, July 14, 1974, when her daughter, Denise Naslund, was taken from Lake Sammamish State Park and killed. "Now that there's some resolution of it . . . a conviction," she said, "maybe the police will let me have her remains so I can give Denise a funeral."

At Fort Lauderdale, police officer Bob Campbell had decided not to go to the nearby Miami courtroom to watch Bundy's trial. Instead, Campbell followed the proceedings on television. One evening, as we talked over the guilty verdict, Campbell reflected, "It's very difficult to sit there and look at someone on TV you've been looking for all this time—right there in living color—knowing he's the guy who killed your sister."

Then, thoughtfully, the handsome thirty-one-year-old policeman confided that he had reasonable doubt about the validity of the bite-mark evidence, and he was skeptical of Nita Neary's identification. "I don't know whether to believe her a hundred percent or not. I'm not really sure." But Caryn Campbell's brother added, "I think Bundy did kill my sister."

Ted Bundy was taken quickly from Miami, northward to

the state prison at Raiford, a remote institution in the vast, flat pine forests of North Central Florida, not far from the town of Starke, south of Lake City.

It was seven o'clock in the morning when he arrived. A pleasant senior corrections officer, a man with three silver chevrons on his collar, was one of the first to greet him. The sergeant snapped two Polaroid photos of the celebrated new arrival at Death Row.

Ted's eyes fixed on the silver nameplate on the man's khaki shirt, the name, "D. J. Dekle."

"Are you any relation to Bob?" Ted asked.

"Yes, he's my son," replied Sergeant Jim Dekle.

Small world, thought Bundy. Here was the father of his prosecutor in the upcoming Kimberly Leach case. "Any message for Bob?" asked the sergeant.

"Well," Ted grinned, "tell him I'll see him in court."

That day, Ted Bundy was placed on Q Wing on Death Row, in a cell once occupied by a prisoner named John Spenkelink.

TWENTY-FIVE | The Bride Wore Black

"Bob Dekle's so worked up 'bout that little girl," Larry Daugherty had said, "that I'm worryin' 'bout him maybe gettin' a heart attack."

During those early months of 1978, Dekle, the gangling, tall, rather paunchy, thirty-one-year-old assistant state attorney, a native North Floridian, seemed obsessed by the Kimberly Leach kidnapping. "I 'member the first time I ever saw that picture of Kim," Dekle remembered later. "She looked 'xactly like my li'l daughter. I saw that daggum thing, and it was like a dagger in the heart."

Through those weeks of the search for Kimberly's body, Dekle, Detective Daugherty, J. O. Jackson, investigator for the Florida Department of Law Enforcement, and the other men had slept little. A lode of circumstance had been uncovered—but no hard evidence—to involve Ted Bundy in Kimberly's disappearance from her school the morning of February 9. Step by step, the investigation picked up Bundy's apparent pattern of travel, driving the white van stolen from Florida State University at Tallahassee.

At a Gulf gasoline station north of Lake City, on Interstate 10, a woman attendant identified Bundy as the man who, using a stolen credit card which had been found in Ted's possession, bought gas for a white van. That was February 7. The next day, in Jacksonville, 65 miles to the east, fourteen-year-old Leslie Parmenter was approached by the strange, slightly disheveled man in the K-Mart parking lot. He was posing as a fireman. When Danny, her brother, frightened the stranger away, Danny noted the van's license—13-D-11300, a plate subsequently linked to Bundy in his encounter with the deputy sheriff in Tallahassee.

Then the employees at the Holiday Inn at Lake City positively identified Bundy as the unkempt man, acting peculiarly, who used a stolen credit card for overnight lodging and a meal there the evening of February 8. That was the night before Kimberly vanished from the nearby school.

"His tracks're all over the place," grumbled Dekle. "We got 'im in Lake City f' sure." But it was circumstance only.

While the searchers trudged across the hundreds of square miles of North Florida forests and swamps, there was steady activity in the FDLE's regional laboratory at Tallahassee, 105 miles to the west. Specialists in forensic serology, microanalysts, and latent-fingerprint experts, and others were making an exhaustive search of two impounded vehicles and their contents—the white van and the orange Volkswagen in which Bundy had been recaptured at Pensacola.

On the floor of the white van was found a tiny, red-orange price sticker, a label for a $26 item. Investigator Jackson traced it to the Green Acres sporting-goods shop in Jacksonville, where the owner identified it as a tag from a ten-inch Buck hunting knife he'd sold to a rather ragged-looking man in early February. The physical description fit Bundy.

Carefully, the lab technicians at Tallahassee explored the interior of the van. Dirt had been tossed into the carpeted cargo area, perhaps to blot some blood stains. In the dirt were two faint shoe prints and signs that something had been dragged through the dirt. There was also a shoe tread print on the rear bumper. Lynn Henson, a lab microanalyst, reached a tentative conclusion: the treads from two pairs of Bundy's shoes—an Adidas and a Bass found in the orange VW—could have left the print.

Dirt, lint, hairs, other debris were vacuumed from the van as possible "trace evidence." Dozens of latent fingerprints were within the much-used van. But Doug Barrow, FDLE print expert, reported gloomily, "It looked like the van was wiped down—on the doors and around the inside." No fingerprint of Ted Bundy was found in the van.

"If we can just find the body . . ." Dekle had uttered that prayerfully, repeatedly. "We'll make a case against that goddamn Bundy."

When it was discovered April 7, Kimberly's body, protected from the weather under the cover of the hog-pen roof, had been mostly mummified. The small body, with only a stained, soiled turtleneck shirt tugged up around the neck, was sprawled in a grotesque position—bent, mostly face down, with the left arm beneath the body, under the buttocks, the right arm curled over the head. Around the body, on the ground, lay all her clothing—her shoes, white socks, the blue nylon football jersey, her jeans with panties inside, her bra and coat—plus her denim purse with its multi-colored embroidery.

Within minutes of the discovery, FDLE specialists—Henson, the microanalyst, Jack Duncan, the crime-scene control specialist and photographer, and others—were being sped eastward to the scene from Tallahassee. They performed the photography, made the careful measurements, and helped remove the body. Wrapped in a yellow plastic sheet, it was placed in a gray hearse and taken east, to Jacksonville. Floodlights were set up for the crime-scene workers as darkness fell in the mosquito-infested woods. The specialists picked up each garment and placed it in a sealed bag. They plotted, measured, and scooped up surface soil at the scene. The entire hog-pen structure was dismantled and taken to the crime lab in Tallahassee, a place already overflowing with latent evidence picked up during the Kimberly Leach search and from the Chi Omega murders a few weeks earlier.

When Dr. Peter Lipkovic, medical examiner at Jacksonville, performed the autopsy on Kimberly's body, he noted there had been "a massive loss of tissue in the throat area and in the vaginal-anal area—a continuous loss of tissue, exposing the bones." He reasoned that there had been some wounding there which attracted insects and created larvae activity, causing the eventual tissue loss. Dekle thought about that knife that had been bought earlier at Jacksonville.

Lipkovic's opinion: She died of "homicidal violence to the neck region, type undetermined." Because of the mummification, the deterioration, there was no blood in the body. Serologist Richard Stephens, one of several FDLE specialists who had been flown to the autopsy, later returned westward to the lab at Tallahassee with specimens of Kimberly's bone and muscle tissue—enough for tests to enable him to determine the girl's blood type was Type B. (The trace of blood found on the floor of the van, Stephens had concluded, was human—and Type B.)

On April 14, FDLE microanalyst Pat Lasko, using a spatula, carefully scraped the fabric of Ted Bundy's burgundy shirt—the one found in the VW. (Investigators had noted a tear in the back of the shirt—a tear which, they reasoned, could have been caused by an edge of the low metal roof over the hog pen.)

Those scrapings, plus scrapings from Kimberly's clothing, were placed in sealed bags and turned over to Lynn Henson. Hour after hour, working in the Tallahassee lab, using the microscope, stereoscope, sometimes employing ultraviolet microscopy, Henson examined the minute strands, comparing them all with the mass of vacuumings from the white van.

That June, in a basement meeting room of the FDLE laboratory at Tallahassee, Bob Dekle, lab chief Dale Heideman, and others gathered around a table to hear, one after another, the lab specialists' reports.

There had been blood and cut marks on the girl's coat and blood on her jeans and other garments, reported Stephens. A semen stain on the panties came from a "secretor, with blood type O." Around the room there were nods and shrugs. Ted Bundy was a secretor, blood type O. Millions of other males were in that same category.

Henson began to describe her comparisons of Bundy's shoes with the prints found in the van. "That Bass shoe track was unusual," she said.

"There were very few sold around here. . . ." Dekle took notes, absorbing information. Now and then he spat a stream of tobacco into a large paper cup he held. As a small-town prosecutor, he'd never before had any dealings with the intricacies of the work of these microscope sleuths.

Henson, a studious young woman whose dark hair was pulled back into a bun, continued in a husky, matter-of-fact voice, "Now the carpet in the van is unusual. The threads are twisted polypropylene fibers, of turquoise, blue, and black twisted together. I found a match of that with threads on Kimberly's purse, and her socks and . . ." In excitement, reacting to Henson's words, Dekle began to rise from the chair. She went on, describing how microscopic fibers found on Kimberly's bra and socks were matches for the van carpet. Suddenly, Dekle moved closer to Henson, slumping his big frame on a table where he leaned forward, staring at her. The young woman technician continued systematically, "Now, we also have in the van carpet these fibers of blue, red, white, green, yellow, and orange cotton, which match the cotton embroidery on her purse.

"And the specimens from the burgundy shirt—we have a burgundy polyester thread and a green cotton thread—are a match for the fibers we found from Kimberly's socks. . . ."

"Damn," breathed Dekle. He sputtered, almost choking on his tobacco. "That puts *Kimberly* in the van. And *Bundy* in the van!" Henson nodded.

"And it can put *Bundy* in contact with *Kim!*" Dekle concluded. Henson went on. There were other fiber cross-comparisons.

A few weeks later there would be more. When FDLE obtained, by warrant, a blue jacket Ted Bundy had been wearing in court at Tallahassee, Henson discovered its fibers of blue wool and blue polyester matched fibers on Kimberly's jeans and socks.

* * *

I don't know that it's possible for Ted Bundy to get a fair trial anywhere in Florida," said J. Victor Africano, the private attorney who had been appointed by Judge Wallace Jopling to represent Bundy.

Africano, an able lawyer, an urbane man, had moved his law practice from Miami to Live Oak, the hometown of his wife. He was determined to give Ted Bundy the best defense possible—an attitude which sometimes didn't sit well with some of his neighbors, who loathed Bundy. Africano effectively won some pretrial rounds during suppression hearings.

It was January 1980. The trial was about to begin. Florida and other states had been saturated with publicity about Ted Bundy, the "multiple murder suspect," convicted killer of the Chi Omega girls. At Tallahassee, there were "Burn Bundy" T-shirts, illustrated with the Florida electric chair.

There had been an unsuccessful attempt to seat a jury at Live Oak, in Suwanee County, not far from where Kimberly's body had been found. There, one man wore a T-shirt with the message: FREE BUNDY. The lower line explained: "So We Can Hang the Son of a Bitch."

So the trial was shifted to Orlando, in central Florida. That tourist-crossroads city, home of Disney World, had not escaped the deluge of Bundy publicity. The Orlando *Sentinel Star* had earlier published a lengthy Sunday magazine profile on Ted. Its headline: THE KILLING OF KIMBERLY LEACH.

"I think it's inevitable." Carole Boone muttered the words with a bleak grin. Her man—Ted—had no chance of acquittal, she thought. After his conviction in Miami, Carole had moved with her teenage son from Seattle to Gainesville, where she could be near the prison and have weekend visits with Ted on Death Row. She had found friends among the wives, girlfriends, and other intimates of the men there. "Some really wonderful people around Death Row," she enthused. But because she wasn't a relative, Carole noted, each of her visits with Ted had to be approved, individually, in advance. The two of them had talked about marriage, but prison policy forbade that.

The trial began January 7 in a fourth-floor courtroom of the Orange County Courthouse in Orlando, and as everyone expected, the jury selection process was long and agonizing. One after another, prospective jurors conceded they had read, seen, or heard much about Ted Bundy and the bloody murders at the Chi Omega house. In all, more than 130 men and women were screened.

By January 18, Bundy and his lawyers, Africano and Lynn Thompson, the defender who had worked quietly, effectively on evidence during Ted's Miami trial, sensed they were losing the jury battle. All the defense preemptory challenges had been spent. The prosecutors—State Attorney Jerry Blair and Dekle—had several left. "All they're doing now," murmured Africano gloomily, "is shopping for a foreman."

Patrick Wolski, a production employee of the *Sentinel Star,* a man who remembered reading about the Chi Omega murders ("a pretty gory case," he said) was tentatively seated as the twelfth juror. During a huddle of the attorneys beside the bench, Africano pleaded in vain that Wolski be dismissed for cause. But, noting that Wolski had promised he could weigh the case on the testimony and facts in evidence, Judge Jopling denied the defense motion.

Bundy pressed past the shoulders of his attorneys and, leaning closer to the judge, began a tirade about "the attempt of the state to put people on this jury . . . who have a lot of knowledge about this case—because the state's case is predicated on knowledge outside this courtroom.

"Use your *mind,* Your Honor," Bundy fumed. "Look at what they're doing here. They *want* people to bring that prejudice into the court. . . . And we're playing the game!"

There was continuing outburst of anger by Ted. He railed at the judge and the prosecutors and, at one point, took off his coat jacket, as though to fight an approaching bailiff.

Once again courtroom cameras recorded a Bundy flare-up, but, in contrast to the media mob which had been in Miami, fewer than two dozen news reporters were covering the Orlando trial.

Jerry Blair, Bob Dekle's new boss, the state attorney for the judicial district covering the Lake City-Live Oak area, delivered the opening statement. "It was just another school day for the students at Lake City Junior High School," he began. A trim, handsome, graying man, a devout Christian, Blair told jurors that Kimberly "was looking forward to the Valentine dance which was to be held the following Saturday." But then that morning of February 9, he recounted, after she picked up her blue denim purse from her home room, she began the short walk to the main school building. "Kim was not seen alive by anyone else at the school."

Blair told the jury a key witness, C. L. (Andy) Anderson, would remember seeing a man leading a girl into a white van parked in front of the school that day. "The girl appeared to be upset and crying at the time," Blair told the jurors. "Mr. Anderson will identify the young girl as Kimberly Diane Leach" and would say the man who was taking her looked like Ted Bundy.

Opening for the defense, Africano quietly promised the jurors, "There *is* going to be a defense in this case." He acknowledged directly that "Ted Bundy was in Lake City at the Holiday Inn on February 8, 1978, and while at the Holiday Inn, he did use credit cards that did not belong to him. . . . That is why he is here today.

"The state's whole case," the gentle voice of the defense lawyer went on, "is based on circumstantial evidence" and the testimony of eyewitnesses whose identification of Ted Bundy was influenced by all the publicity of his face and name. The state's case will "rise or fall," he continued, on the testimony of Anderson, the Lake City fireman, who remembered seeing "something" in front of the school one morning —but whose memory was aided by hypnotists working with eager police.

Clarence Lee (Andy) Anderson, the man characterized by the defense as "the state's star witness," a man in his early thirties, testified slowly and in a low voice. He was a fireman for the Lake City Fire Department in early February, he said. On the day of Kimberly's disappearance, while driving to his home sometime after nine o'clock, his car was stopped because traffic was blocked on West Duvall Street, in front of the school.

"First thing I noticed," he said, "there was a white van parked in the westbound lanes. . . . Several cars were going around it. . . . There were two cars sitting behind the van." Anderson told of seeing a man and a girl leaving the school on his left and crossing the street toward the van. "The girl was crying or appeared to have been crying. The man had a scowl on his face." Anderson testified what his own thoughts were:

"Dad's going to take the little girl home and probably give her a spanking or something."

When Blair showed Anderson a photograph of Kimberly Leach, Anderson identified her as "the young girl I saw at that school."

When asked if he could make a certain identification of the man, Anderson replied, "No, sir, I am not absolutely certain."

The prosecutor asked, "Is there anyone in the courtroom who closely resembles that man. . . ?"

"The defendant," replied Anderson.

Blair anticipated Africano's heavy cross-examination of Anderson. Why, asked Blair, didn't Anderson report what he'd seen to police at Lake City at the time? Why had he waited until July 28? (The unmentioned fact was that Anderson's memory had been jogged by seeing a telecast of the sheriff in Tallahassee reading to Bundy the indictment in the Chi Omega murders on July 27.)

"I didn't want to really be involved," said Anderson, his voice faltering. "I wasn't sure I saw anything that was that important. I wasn't sure of the dates. I just knew that I saw a girl who looked like the little girl. . . ."

Anderson testified how, at the behest of police, he underwent hypnosis on July 28, then again on July 31. In between those dates, asked Blair, "were you able to recall the date" of the sighting?

During his first hypnosis session, Anderson couldn't remember what the date was when he'd seen the girl, the man, and the van. He thought it might have been April. He testified that police then told him to "go home and think about it."

"I went home and talked it over with my wife." In that conversation, Anderson said, he recalled that, after arriving home that day, "one of the first things I did was to eat a piece of my daughter's birthday cake." His daughter's birthday was February 8, Anderson testified. Thus he was able to place the date he'd seen the man and girl at the school as the following day—February 9.

During the cross-examination of Anderson, Africano brought out the fact that the fire hall, where Anderson worked, was in the same building as the Lake City Police

Department, the scene of heavy activity during the search for Kimberly. "Why did you wait five months and three weeks?" asked the defense lawyer.

Anderson's voice sounded apologetic, sorrowful. "Because I wasn't sure of what day I saw the girl. I wasn't sure at all. I didn't want to become involved in it."

Prosecution witnesses enumerated the movements of the white van, the identification of Bundy as the driver and user of stolen credit cards. Then came the technical evidence—Lynn Henson's work on the footprints and fabric, the Stephens' testimony about the blood and semen stains, other expert testimony.

Africano and Thompson, with probing, thrusting questions sought to show reasonable doubt. They won some concessions—those fabric comparisons weren't exclusive, Henson said; some of those fabrics were mass-produced. She conceded the tests focused only on Bundy's garments, no one else's.

Repeatedly, Africano suggested that eyewitnesses, like Anderson, had their memory, their identifications enhanced by seeing Ted Bundy on television.

John Farhat, the sporting-goods dealer at Jacksonville, when looking at a photo lineup had initially chosen the face of another man—not Bundy—as the purchaser of that knife at his store. But in the courtroom, he identified Bundy—"That gentleman over there," he said, pointing to the defendant. ("Liar," Bundy whispered loudly.)

Each side produced experts to debate whether or not two hypnosis sessions involving Anderson had been properly conducted. Dr. Milton Kline, a New York psychologist testifying for the defense, said the two hypnosis sessions had been done improperly by undertrained hypnotists—that perhaps enthusiastic police had helped give Anderson "a pseudo memory."

As a final rebuttal witness, the prosecution offered testimony of Dr. Raymond La Scola, a Los Angeles doctor and investigative hypnotist, who testified that "standard and acceptable procedures" were used in the memory-heightening recall hypnosis of Anderson.

Sitting beside me in the front row of the courtroom, Carole Boone peered at my note taking. Then she reached over to scribble a comment on my legal pad, beside my notes on La Scola: "Oink"

And she laughed. La Scola was a man whose hypnosis-training work was with police.

That day, Carole went to another floor of the Orange County Courthouse to take out a wedding license. She and Ted had worked out a sly plan.

Bob Dekle came to that long-planned moment when he began the state's closing argument, asking the jury to convict Ted Bundy for the murder. He produced a chart which portrayed an inverted triangle. At the upper left was the black silhouette of the killer, at the bottom the photo of the white van, at the upper right the enlarged photograph of the smiling, beautiful Kimberly. Systematically, with intensity in his voice, as Dekle reminded jurors of evidence and testimony, he zipped away paper-backed tape, revealing, one by one, thirty-six circumstances printed on the chart, forming the triangle of interrelationships—circumstances which tied Bundy to the van, the van to Kimberly, and Kimberly to Bundy.

"He did a pretty good job of wipin' the van," the tall lawyer told the jury. "Theodore Robert Bundy is pretty smart about coverin' his tracks."

From the defense table, Bundy glared at Dekle as the prosecutor graphically tied all the circumstance and evidence together.

It was an effective presentation, a compelling chart. That pretty face of the dead girl ("like a dagger in the heart," Dekle had said) smiled at the jury from the chart.

In his closing argument for the defense, Africano, in an earnest delivery, struck at each of the circumstances: "There's not one iota of evidence to show that he committed this crime."

An expert had testified that the human body, by natural process, loses scores of head and body hairs each day. In the van "there was hair found," Africano noted, but none of it matched Ted Bundy. . . . "Ted Bundy occupied that van for ten days and didn't leave a *fingerprint?*" Anderson's belated "eyewitness" identification, enhanced by a questionable hypnosis, said Africano, could not be credible.

Africano focused his argument on the microanalyst's testimony about the white van, the shoe, prints, the other trace evidence. "There's eight hundred thousand pairs of shoes in existence that could have caused those footprints," Africano began.

For the jurors, intent on Africano's words, there was a momentary distraction. Bundy, who'd been busily taking notes, rose suddenly from the defense table, walked quickly across the courtroom to the lectern to hand his lawyer a note. Then he returned to the table. Ted couldn't resist a moment of playing lawyer, walking onstage at the critical moment. Africano glanced at the note and resumed.

"Did Andy Anderson see a burgundy shirt? Did Andy Anderson see a blue coat . . .? The constant publicity, the constant exposure of Mr. Bundy's face is all the state has needed to ratify, confirm, and secure the identifications that you've heard in the courtroom the past week and a half."

On February 7, shortly after two o'clock in the afternoon, after less than seven hours of deliberation, the jury returned to the courtroom. An obviously caring Africano, in a gesture of comfort, placed a hand on the shoulder of Ted, as the young man sat awaiting the expected.

Wolski, a stern-looking big man, with a flop of hair swept low across his forehead, was, as the defense had predicted, the foreman. The verdict: guilty as charged.

Dekle and Jerry Blair slapped shoulders and hugged. Larry Daugherty, Dale Parrish, J. O. Jackson, the detectives, and the prosecutors' wives joined in the rejoicing afterward.

The bride-to-be wore black. Sitting beside me, in a front row of the courtroom the morning of February 9, Carole Boone wore black pants and a black, open-knit sweater over a champagne blouse. It was the day the jury would consider its recommendation of sentence—life or death.

When Ted entered the court, Carole laughed. "Oh, no!" she exclaimed. "A bow tie!" Ted grinned at her. On the day of solemn arguments to the jury about the death penalty, Ted wore a jaunty, blue polka-dot bow tie, a light-blue sport coat, and below cotton khaki pants, his bold argyle plaid socks were showing.

It was attire with some cynical symbolism. "He was wearing a bow tie the day he was convicted in Utah," Carole giggled. "I'd thought I'd hidden all his bow ties from him."

Addressing the jury, Jerry Blair solemnly noted the obvious. The jury was considering the death penalty this day, February 9, 1980, on the second anniversary of the date, February 9, 1978, that Kimberly Leach was murdered. The state attorney, a Sunday school teacher, quoted the Bible: "He that shall offend one of these little ones, it would be better for them if a millstone were hanged about his neck and he were cast into the sea and drown."

Death, the electric chair. "Any other penalty," said Blair, "would be a mockery of the system of justice."

Ted's mother had not traveled to Orlando for the trial. Carole Boone took the stand as the lone witness for the defense's penalty-phase presentation to the jury. Her questioner was Ted.

She cheerfully testified how they became acquainted initially while working together at a Washington State government office. Then, she added, "Several years ago our relationship evolved into a more serious, romantic sort of thing . . ."

"Can you tell the jury . . . if you've ever observed any violent or destructive tendencies in my character or personality?" Ted asked.

"I've never seen anything in Ted that indicates any destructiveness toward other people," she told the jury. "I've been associated with Ted in virtually every imaginable circumstance. . . . I've never seen anything in Ted that indicates any kind of destructiveness . . . any kind of hostility toward other people." Ted was, she continued, "a warm, kind, patient man."

She testified about her opposition to the death penalty. "I would hope that you would come back with a recommendation of life rather than the death penalty."

Blair and Dekle—and some law-enforcement men sitting behind them—glowered at the scene with anger.

When it happened, it came so quickly, almost no one sensed what had occurred.

"I want to make this very clear," Ted said solemnly to Carole. "Will you marry me?"

"Yes," she replied. She was smiling, quietly effervescent, her voice barely above a whisper.

"Then I do hereby marry you," added Ted. His voice was lawyerlike. "Thank you." He turned and strode to the defense table.

Carole earlier had arranged for a notary to be in the courtroom at that moment. Thus, with the valid license to wed and the pronouncement, in the presence of a notary— even a judge—the strange wedding was conducted.

Later Ted delivered his own lengthy argument to the jury. He made a reference to the strange wedding which had just taken place. "We didn't do it for your benefit." Ted snuffled and swallowed, as though near tears. "It was the only chance to be in the same room together where the right words could be said. It was something between she and I."

Smiling, gesturing, sometimes choking back tears, he went on with a lengthy review of the trial and a plea for his life. "Was this case sufficient and was your verdict of a kind that . . . ," he faltered for a moment, "that I should be murdered as punishment? Because the bottom line . . . is that the person who murdered Kimberly Leach is not in the courtroom today."

The jury retired to consider its recommended sentence, then returned to the courtroom in less than an hour. The recommendation: death.

I had frequently contemplated the relationship between Carole and Ted, usually with some puzzlement. It had appeared to me that Carole had really a romantic love for Ted—the underdog Ted, the witty, resilient Ted, the Ted who could speak words of compassion. No one, except those two people, perhaps Ted alone, could know if there was a reciprocal romantic feeling for Carole. His occasional glances, waves, and smiles at her across courtrooms had always seemed to me perfunctory, without a convincing glow of romantic affection. But he needed her.

After that strange day in the courtroom had ended, I encountered Carole in the corridor where she stood, waiting for a hoped-for chance to visit Ted before he was taken to his cell.

As I approached, she grinned. "Aren't you going to congratulate me?" she asked. "A kiss for the bride?"

"Oh, hell, yes," I replied. "I'm sorry." I hugged her and

kissed her on the cheek. She hugged back. Hard. A hug of, perhaps, loneliness.

I privately wondered if she ever wondered about a stranger which might lurk within the Ted she knew.

"Ted's been through so much," she sighed. "I just hope his head's going to be okay when we get him free from all this mess." I had no response. I was unable to see whatever ray of hope Carole pretended to see.

"Hey," I asked, "does this now make you Carole *Bundy?*"

"No," she replied. Then, laughing, Carole added: "I'm keeping my name. But he's thinking about taking *mine*. He's sick of his own."

That final day in the Orlando courtroom, as Judge Wallace Jopling was about to impose the death sentence—Ted's third sentence of death—the defendant was permitted to deliver another speech. He went on for twenty-five minutes, attacking the trial procedure—"a sensational and bizarre parody"—especially the jury selection. "While I may bear the awesome consequence of what you're about to do, I bear none of the guilt. I did not kill Kimberly Diane Leach."

Jopling, a careful, restrained country judge, echoed the words of Judge Ed Cowart earlier. "You have every ability that a young man could expect to have to succeed in life," he told Ted. Then he sentenced him to the electric chair. The judge's final words: "May God have mercy on your soul."

Ted Bundy was returned to Death Row. Deliberately, as after every other conviction, he had created a record, tearfully protesting his innocence.

TWENTY-SIX | Death Row

Jubilation prevails in Room 214 of the Harley Hotel, about a block from the Orange County Courthouse at Orlando. Chawin' and grinnin', a barefooted Bob Dekle, lounging in T-shirt and jeans on one corner of his daveno, presides over it all. Detectives, others who worked on the case—J. O. Jackson, Larry Daugherty, Len Register—drop in for a beer and to exchange good-ol'-boy reminiscences of the investigation and, now, the conviction of Theodore Bundy.

Now that the guilty verdict is in and the only things remaining are the death-penalty arguments, I, a reporter, am allowed to sit in.

"Hey, Larry, how y'doin'?" Dekle unwinds his tall frame from the daveno to greet the newest arrival, Larry Simpson. The businesslike Simpson, the brown-haired, boy-faced prosecutor who'd convicted Bundy of the Chi Omega murders, grins and pumps the hand of the man who'd just heard a jury pronounce Bundy "guilty" in the Kimberly Leach murder.

"Good job," says Simpson. "Well, we done it," Dekle exults. "Jerry an' me. An' a hundred others."

Simpson is delivering photocopies of some court documents Dekle needs for his "penalty phase" arguments to the jury. "Here they are," says Simpson, "all true and accurate copies. The judgment and sentence, signed in the courtroom there in Miami. With Bundy's fingerprints 'n' all. I watched 'em being photocopied at the Leon County clerk's office."

We all watch as Simpson leafs through the pages. He pauses at the last sheet and grins. "Hey, you're not gonna believe this, Bob," Simpson exclaims. "Look here."

Dekle peers where Simpson's index finger points to the death-sentence document. The text is legible, but, in the faint photocopy Bundy's fingerprints are mere ghostly rings. Vanished.

"*DAMNATION!*" Dekle hoots in a burst of laughter. "That boy *never* leaves fingerprints, does he? Not even when his fingers is inked and rolled right there in the court!"

"Dave Yocom ought to be here," I tell them. "Then we'd have, all together, the prosecutors who've convicted Ted Bundy. And no one had a fingerprint."

Yocom, in Salt Lake City, had a shy eyewitness, Carol DaRonch, plus circumstance. Larry Simpson, in the Chi Omega case, had an eyewitness of graduating certainty, Nita Neary, some bite marks and circumstance. Jerry Blair and Bob Dekle had an eyewitness, a belated one who was helped by hypnosis, some microscopic wisps of fabric—and circumstance.

Dekle says, though, "Those *crimes* were jus' like fingerprints." He refers to that night when Carol DaRonch escaped her kidnapper in Utah. "And that's at a shoppin' center. Then, right away, that Debbie Kent goes missin' from a school. And we had Leslie Parmenter. He barely misses gettin' her. At a shoppin' center. An' then we have Kimberly go missin'. From a school. Their hair, the way they're dressed, everythin' is like a fingerprint."

In Seattle, detectives ponder some other similarities—the positions of the bodies of the Chi Omega victims on their beds, the nature of the beatings and the fact that the sheets had been drawn up over the heads of the girls. And the investigators recall the sheet which had been pulled up over the head of the girl who was so savagely attacked in her basement apartment in Seattle's University District in January 1974. And the sheet, meticulously drawn up on the bed where Lynda Ann Healy vanished from her basement apartment.

"How many years of appeals do you suppose Ted'll have?" I aim the question at Jerry Blair, Dekle's boss, the restrained, teetotaling Florida state attorney, sitting nearby.

"Spenkelink's the only precedent we have, o' course," replies Blair. "That went five, six years." But Blair notes the obvious: wily, skillful Ted Bundy, who thrives on challenging the system, will stretch the appeals process. "They're still typin' up the transcript from the Chi Omega trial, I hear," Blair explains. "It'll be a while before that appeal ever gets started."

And, Blair has heard, Florida has decided it'll never release Bundy to Colorado to face the Caryn Campbell murder trial there.

Later, outdoors, around the hotel's vacant swimming pool, I'm sitting with Jerry Thompson and Mike Fisher—sharing my six-pack of Budweiser. It's a sweater-wearing, chilly February afternoon, but there's a Florida sun as we stretch in deck chairs. From Salt Lake City and Aspen, the two detectives, adding a few more thousand miles of travel and some more hours and days to their years of Ted Bundy, had flown into Orlando to give brief testimony, to tell the Florida jurors about Bundy's arrest in the West—additional circumstances to prove first-degree murder.

Thompson growls about the "darling little wedding scene" between Ted and Carole in the courtroom on the anniversary of Kimberly Leach's murder. "Those two deserve each other," he grumbles. "Makes me so goddamn mad the way that Carole's goin' around saying that we framed Ted out there."

"Yeah," snorts Fisher. (He held some suspicions about Carole's early December visits with Ted in Glenwood Springs, not long before the escape from Colorado. Carole had emphatically denied any knowledge or involvement in that. Fisher still doesn't know how Bundy got all the money or where the hacksaw blade came from.) "If we were gonna frame Theodore, we'd've come up with more than a straggle of hair." Fisher clears his sinuses again—a rattling sound which echoes around the deserted poolside.

"We coulda gone to the victims' homes—Aime or Kent or Smith—and picked up a piece of their jewelry and put it in that goddamn Volkswagen and then say 'Oh! What have we here?'"

"Yeah," agrees Thompson.

In soul searching, Thompson says he even went back to Carol DaRonch, a year afterward, to ask if she'd been in any way influenced by police questioning. "And she says she knew it was him from the first minute. But she was just terrified all along, 'cause of what had happened to her. So if we framed him, what do *we* get out of it? I'm still just a poor detective. All I ever got out of Theodore Bundy was a pain in the ass."

"And I'm still an investigator workin' my brains out," murmurs Fisher. "Got another Bud?"

I pass him a beer. "Mike," I ask, "how many murders do you give to Ted?"

"Oh, it's hard to say. Y'know, the ones where there's pretty solid circumstances, with the credit cards, where we got him placed, with the right MO and all, it could be, say, twenty-two or so. . . . Maybe more. Who knows where he started?"

I reminisce aloud: "After Kimberly Leach, I thought, 'Oh God! A twelve-year-old. Ted kill a little kid? I don't believe it! So I went home from Florida and went to Tacoma, to look at a case there. A six-year-old girl, Ann Marie Burr, disappears from her house one night, out of the living room, where she was sleeping. That was years ago—1960. No clue, except a tennis-shoe print outside the window on the porch. She apparently was coaxed or lured out. They had the biggest search in the history of the city, but they never found her.

"Ted's house wasn't all that far away from her house. And he's fourteen at the time. When I asked the old chief of detectives on that case if he'd ever thought a fourteen-year-old boy might have done it, he says, 'Yeah, funny you should ask. We did look at a fourteen-year-old suspect.' Only it wasn't Ted Bundy.

"But it's a cold case. No way of ever knowing."

"Well, he'll give his answers before he fries," Thompson predicts. "He's got an ego. There's no way he's going to do it, until he's convinced he's ready to go."

"If we get them, any confessions," Fisher says, "I think we'll get them without a great deal of specificity."

"One cop here," I add, "figures that about the time Ted reaches the chair, he'll suddenly remember details of *one*. Just one. And they'll take him back and listen. Then the next year, when he reaches the chair again, he remembers *another* one."

"At that rate," says Fisher "he'll be around for years." The Aspen cop finishes his beer.

Thompson has another thought: "And yet, you know, he might just say, 'Piss on it.' And go ahead and die. I dunno. . . . Some people truly think that police really framed him in Utah and Colorado and all the way to Florida. So, to them, Ted, he's the greatest goddamn martyr of all times."

"Got another Bud?"

His eyes closed in the sun, the mustached, blondish Fisher, begins a soliloquy:

"I would never, for two seconds, bargain for his life, you know. But goddamn, if he were an individual who would come forth with the total truth . . . IF he could come with total truth, talk about his problem . . . He himself admitted how, when he first escaped in Aspen, that he hadn't had that *urge* of his. He analyzed it as having cured himself of this urge. But, of course, he didn't.

"But maybe somebody can learn something. There are certain things about a personality, maybe in a kid, an indicator, his teachers in school and his mother and dad, if they were trained to recognize any of those traits, you could get a profile. You know, we can get facts about these types, traits. And put 'em in a computer. But then, somebody's already had to lose his life to gain this information. The sorry part is we can't answer the question, where does it start?

"Ted's sane. He's got total control. He's not certifiably crazy. He didn't belong, legally, in an institution. But he doesn't belong in society."

"When Ted got away from Glenwood," I recalled, "one psychiatrist told me, 'If he kills again, it'll probably be a furious kind of thing.' There would be the pent-up urge breaking out, plus his own anger at himself for not being able to control his urge. And it was Chi Omega."

Somewhere around the time Ted was thirteen or fourteen, we've been told, he learned of his illegitimate birth. Dr. A. L. Carlisle, the staff psychologist at the Utah prison, once mentioned to me his inability to penetrate Ted's memories about his boyhood years.

So, in one of our recorded conversations while Ted was in

his cell in Colorado, I made an effort. "Ted," I had asked, "sitting in jail now, isolated away from friends and home and everything, do you ever reflect on some of those boyhood years, like boy-scout hikes in the mountains, things like that—say, when you were fourteen or so?"

"My childhood years?" Ted paused for a long time and drew a deep breath. Then, in a very deliberate reply, he reworked my question, carefully compartmentalizing, moving away from a direct answer.

"Well, you're talking about childhood years as opposed to my mid-twenties, my late twenties? Maybe . . ." He paused. "I . . . I don't think a lot about my childhood now. In fact, I think one of the things I do more and more often is that I try to think less about the past because it is disconcerting, under the circumstances, to be confronted by glimpses of—memories of—freedom, as opposed to the reality of the way I live now."

He described, with rising toughness in his voice, how he had to control himself carefully, adapting to the realities of confinement in steel. "I've come across the guys who've grown up in prison, or who've spent years and years in prison, and one thing you notice about them is they live *here* and *now*. They don't live in the future, and they don't live in the past. In fact they don't have a past. . . . I haven't blocked out the past. I wouldn't trade the person I am, or what I've done—or the people I've known—for anything." Ted paused again. The harshness left his voice. He added almost serenely, "So I do think about it. And at times it's a rather mellow trip to lay back and remember."

I'd gotten no glimpse of those days when he was fourteen, or earlier. And I wondered about the *mellow trip* he was remembering.

A characteristic of the sociopathic personality is the recurring desire to deliver hints of what he has done, to tantalize with suggestions of how very clever he is. Jerry Thompson had experienced it. Ted had told him to keep looking for those straws, to put the broom together. Ted had slyly hinted guilt to me and others. He'd toyed with his Florida interrogators with his line, "The evidence is there. Keep diggin'. You'll find it." Then there was that segment of questions and answers, remembered by the detectives, during one of those late-night sessions, when they asked Ted why he liked Volkswagens:

And he said, "Because they get good gas mileage and it's a common—"

"Well, come on, Ted, what else is there about it?"

He said, "Well, you can take out the front seat."

"Well, why would you want to take out the front seat?"

There was a suggestion that it would be easy to carry someone in the car that way.

He said, "I don't like to use that terminology."

So we fished around for a word that he felt comfortable with.

He said, "Cargo. It's easy to carry cargo in them."

"Why is it easy to carry cargo?"

"You can control it better."

"Is the cargo alive or dead when you put it in the vehicle?"

"I don't like to use that terminology."

Well, we fished around for a word and came up with "damaged." "Is the cargo damaged when it's in the vehicle?"

And "Yes, sometimes it is damaged and sometimes it's not damaged."*

The pathological need of Mr. Bundy to defy authority, to manipulate his associates and adversaries, supplies him with thrills." That was one of the observations of Dr. Emanuel Tanay, a Detroit psychiatrist who had interviewed and examined Ted in May 1979 at Tallahassee.

It was just prior to the Chi Omega trial. Mike Minerva, the chief public defender, had secured a court order for an

---

* From a deposition of Captain Jack Poitinger, Leon County, Florida, sheriff's department.

examination of Ted, to determine if he were competent to go to trial. Dr Tanay recalled their meeting at the cell:

"I believe there were five deputy sheriffs guarding the only exit. Mr. Bundy is a thirty-two-year-old, handsome-looking man, dressed with the casual elegance of a young college professor. . . . He was in total command of the situation. The deputy sheriffs appeared more like part of his entourage than policemen guarding a prisoner. . . .

"Mr. Bundy commented upon the security precautions, saying they were part of the 'Bundy mystique,' which has developed as a result of news media activities. This was presented in the manner of a complaint. It was, however, my impression that Mr. Bundy was taking pride in his celebrity status. . . .

"He was asked about his apparent lack of concern, so out of keeping with the charges facing him. He acknowledged that he is facing a possible death sentence [saying], 'I will cross that bridge when I get to it.' . . .

"The interactions of Mr. Bundy with the police and the whole criminal-justice system have been discussed at length with him and his attorneys. It is my opinion . . . that his dealings with the criminal-justice system are dominated by psychopathology.

"Transcripts of the many hours of his conversations with police officers constitute a variety of 'confessions.' . . . Mr. Bundy confessed the crimes charged against him, while maintaining his innocence. The intellectual denials and emotional admissions are quite apparent from the tapes and transcripts of his conversations with the investigators. . . . This behavior was not, in my opinion, the result of rational reflection and decision-making process, but a manifestation of the psychiatric illness from which Mr. Bundy suffers. . . .

"If one assumes that his sadistic acts, including homicides attributed to Mr. Bundy in Tallahassee, were carried out by him, then psychiatrically, it would be likely that various other similar acts have been perpetrated by him. It could then be argued that he is effective in concealing his criminal activities.

"Such an argument would be only partially true. It would be more accurate to say that he is of two minds on this issue—he attempts to conceal and reveal his involvement."

Tanay's assessment of Bundy was perceptive and, in some ways, prophetic. More than ten days before Ted threw away the plea-bargain offer in the Tallahassee courtroom that day, Dr. Tanay wrote:

"It is my impression that a major factor is his deep-seated need to have a trial, which he views as an opportunity to confront and confound various authority figures . . . not only judges and prosecutors, but also his defense attorneys.

"In a certain sense, Mr. Bundy is a producer of a play which attempts to show that various authority figures can be manipulated, set against each other. . . . Mr. Bundy does not have the capacity to recognize that the price for this 'thriller' might be his own life."

I'd agree with everythin' Tanay had to say in that report," says Bob Dekle. ". . . 'cept the bottom line."

Tanay's bottom line was that, while persons with such personality disorders may not be considered insane for purposes of criminal law, "It is my view that sociopaths, if sufficiently severe, do, in fact, suffer from an illness inasmuch as there is an impairment of a variety of psychic features." That was a recommendation for a plea of insanity—something Ted would never, never consider.

"Regardless of all diagnosis," Dekle concludes, "I see Theodore Bundy as just one of those guys with nothin' more than a damn mean streak plumb through 'im."

Dr. Hervey M. Cleckley, psychiatrist, educator, and author, one of the most respected authorities on the antisocial or sociopathic personality, also disagrees with Dr. Tanay's conclusion. "Most psychiatrists," Cleckley indicates, "view the sociopath, the psychopath, the antisocial person not to be technically psychotic." He alludes to the McNaghten Test, the legal test of whether someone who committed a homicide had the capacity to distinguish between right and wrong. The psychotic personality cannot make that distinction. The sociopath, Cleckley muses, citing an old whimsical definition, "knows the difference but doesn't give a damn."

Cleckley testified for the prosecution during that pretrial competency hearing in Tallahassee. He became interested in Ted Bundy.

345

Now he's asked if there might have been something in Ted's early years, something which might have triggered eruptive behavior.

"Well," says Dr. Cleckley, "you think of how many people have traumatic experiences early in life and yet they seemingly don't act in that way in adulthood. I think there's been an overselling of psychiatric explanations. There is the inference that every time somebody commits a crime, it's because his parents were overprotective or because his parents were oversevere or because it was society's fault in one way or another.

"I think the pendulum has swung too far that way, with too much interpretation being read into the situation."

Perhaps now, he speculates, the pendulum is swinging in the other direction toward a frank conclusion—"the conclusion that we don't know."

Dr. Al Carlisle, the Utah State Prison psychologist, remembers that day outside a Salt Lake City courtroom in 1977, when Ted, who'd just been sentenced to prison for kidnapping Carol DaRonch, asked a pointed, disarming question: "Do you think I'm guilty?"

In an almost counseling tone, Carlisle had replied quietly, "I'm not sure. But if you did do it, I am sure that you will do it again."

"We need to understand more, to learn," reflects Carlisle now. He is still fascinated by Ted and he continues each day to probe, to seek an answer to the behavior of more and more men arriving in prison, convicted of cruel violence against women.

Carlisle questions one of those men at length about his thoughts—a man who, says Carlisle, is like Ted in many ways: "To him the *planning;* the *stalking* of the victim, the carrying out of the attack, the show of power, the ability to outwit and outsmart—all that is very, *very* exciting. And the beating of the victim is so extremely exhilarating. The guy says, 'I just can't put it into words, it's so invigorating. I just come *alive* at that time, with the hurting, the beating.' Afterwards he's relaxed. But then he'll feel the need again, as it builds up. It seems almost akin to the usage of drugs.

"Scientifically we need to understand Ted and these others,

so we can perhaps begin identifying symptoms . . . perhaps catch it early in life."

I drive northward from Orlando, leaving Florida, passing Gainesville where Carole Boone settles into her vigil, within driving distance of the prison and weekend visits with Ted.

And I wonder why Ted came to Florida, a place where he *knew* the death penalty is a way of life now. Its electric chair—"Old Sparky," they call it—is busy again.

Was it a *death wish?* An internal subconscious need to self-impose punishment? Or was it Ted's long-cultivated feeling of omnipotence? To play his thrilling drama on the most ominous of stages?

Ted, driving that orange Volkswagen with all his belongings out of Tallahassee that night in February, was within minutes of the state line. Alabama. Out of Florida. Then further westward, perhaps, to a new place, a new identity. Instead, he turned into Pensacola, the last town in Florida. ("He was trollin'," theorized Mike Fisher. "Lookin' for another victim there in Pensacola. Some girl out walking." Steve Bodiford, Don Patchen, Larry Daugherty, other Florida detectives would agree.) Ted couldn't leave Florida, Buckle of the Death Belt of America.

In northeast Florida your radio picks up WAPE at Jacksonville, where the eccentric, raspy-voiced disk jockey, "The Greaseman," leads the public cheers for capital punishment. Greaseman's morning show once opened with a special message to the inmates on Death Row at the state prison:

"Good mornin', you maggots. Are you up yet? You'd better enjoy the sunrise. There aren't many left for you."

The morning John Spenkelink went to the electric chair, "The Greaseman" turned his microphone to the sound of some bacon in a hot frying pan. As the sizzling sound went over the air, Greaseman cackled, "That's for you, John."

"No," Greaseman tells me, "I haven't done much with Bundy. Oh, after he was convicted in that trial down in Miami, I think I said, 'I'd like to have five minutes in a room alone with him with a baseball bat.'"

Around Jacksonville, around Florida, says Greaseman, the "prevailing mood is 'Let them babies burn.' *God,* it's great! . . . It makes me feel proud to be here. And, lookin' at the opinion polls, it looks like the same feeling is showing up all over the country."

My only visit with Ted at the prison was prior to his Orlando trial. He kidded about his "uniform." Worn over a gray sweatshirt, that bright orange T-shirt was his designation as a Death Row inmate. We were alone together in an eight-foot-square visitors' room, with two barred windows. "I'm not supposed to do this, but . . ." With a grin, glancing to see there were no guards watching, Ted took off the orange T-shirt.

I noticed, as he lifted it over his head, his heavy sweatshirt was drenched with perspiration under the arms. Ted seemed nervous.

Our conversation rambled from the legal work he was doing for fellow inmates, to the inadequate recreation facilities and poor law library at the prison, to literature and politics.

And Ted discussed—satirically—mass murder. The governor of Florida, Ted kidded, was proceeding to sign death warrants for the men on Death Row. "I think there's a hundred and thirty-seven in here now," he guessed. "Graham would have to be some sort of homicidal maniac to sign all those warrants. Now *that* would be a mass murderer!"

Ted's Death Row cell at that time was just three cells removed from the steel door which opens into the corridor leading to the execution room.

I wondered aloud if Ted had anxieties about that waiting door. His answer came with careful deliberateness:

"I don't think about it. It's just a door. Another door.

"A locked door."

When Ted was returned to Death Row after his conviction in Orlando that February, a different reception awaited him. The first time they took him into the institution at Raiford, in late July 1979, it had been early in the morning—a quiet, waking-up time at the pen. This second time, it was midday, so there was bustling activity inside. Scores of prisoners were around the receiving area, sitting on benches, clustered together, talking, when the guards brought Bundy in.

"Haaaaaay, man, there's Bundy!" one of the cons shouted.

"Yeaah, *Bundy,*" some others hooted. Ted, his guards said later, appeared startled by the hostility around him.

His guards took him beyond the steel doors, out of the reception area, but the sounds of jeering followed. Ted, convicted of killing a twelve-year-old girl, was now degraded in the harsh, judgmental prison society, to the lowest of the low—the child molesters, the little-kid killers. His only collateral to deal with the threatening atmosphere would be his ability with the law. As the jailhouse lawyer, he could write writs and give advice on appeals.

Walking along the long corridor toward R Wing, Ted, escorted by the guards, passed other cell blocks of the prison's general population. And the chorus of hoots resumed:

"Hey, man, give us Bundy in *here.*"

"Bundy, you'll get yours!"

"Bundy, we'll get yer ass."

Theodore Robert Bundy, 069063, beads of sweat on his brow, pressed closer to the protective shoulders of the escorting guards in their brown uniforms. "He was scared to death," one prison officer recalled—until Ted reached the safety of his solitary cell on Death Row.

AFTERWORD

During the years following his convictions, Ted Bundy settled into a tedious, strange-world life on Death Row in the prison at Starke, often passing the hours studying legal cases, monitoring the work of attorneys handling his appeals in the Florida courts. His wife, Carole, found a job in nearby Gainseville and was his regular visitor and prime source of psychological support.

Ted, who once enjoyed a generally cordial relationship with the news media, began to disdain reporters' requests for visits and interviews. Vic Africano, the Live Oak attorney who'd represented Ted in the Leach homicide case and who was appointed to represent him in the appeal (a complex one that challenged, among other things, the "hypnosis evidence"), received and passed along several media requests—nearly all of which Ted rejected.

In one thoughtful letter, Ted explained how he felt he had been exploited by many and, he wrote, "I am inclined to be resentful." Through all the years of breathless news coverage of Ted Bundy, the trials and the murders of which he was suspected, no reporter, Ted felt, had undertaken the task of disproving the evidence and circumstance that had been arrayed against him. (On the other hand, when I'd tried, asking him to help me prove he was at some other place at the time a murder was committed, Ted never offered that help.)

The Ted Bundy cases had helped introduce into the vocabulary of law enforcement and American society the phrase "serial killer." It was ironic—and a source of argument and some dark satisfaction for Ted, no doubt—that the Seattle area again became the locale of one of the most baffling serial-killer cases in American history. Through the early 1980s—while Ted was on Death Row in Florida—more than forty young women vanished and most were found slain in what has been dubbed "the Green River Murders." The serial murders took that name from a river in the Seattle vicinity where some of the earliest victims were found. Bob Keppel, the detective of Seattle's "Ted Squad" of the 1970s, worked as a lead detective for Seattle's "Green River Task Force" of the 1980s. Nearly all the Green River victims, he noted, had had some links with prostitution and the killings differed in other ways from those of the 1970s.

As he had in other jails, Ted usually got along well with his guards and came to enjoy some trust within the tight security of his wing of the Florida prison. But that changed abruptly one July day in 1984 when a guard discovered that one bar of Bundy's cell had been sawed through. A search of his cell turned up some hacksaw blades and other contraband hidden in his mattress—affirmation of warnings from Mike Fisher and other Bundy-watchers that Ted thinks constantly of escape.

By late 1985, after the Florida supreme court had rejected all his appeals, Ted's death sentence in the Chi Omega murders was scheduled to be considered by the Florida clemency board. Once again, as he had so often in the past, Ted created an eruption of legal confusion by firing his attorney, Robert Harper of Tallahassee, on the eve of the clemency proceedings. Governor Graham took note of Ted's belligerent behavior in the courts and snapped, "We will not permit our system of justice to be endlessly manipulated and rendered ineffective." He gave Ted thirty days to file his own plea in writing, but there was no doubt about what would happen: Graham signed a death warrant, ordering the execution of Theodore Robert Bundy at 7 A.M. March 4, 1986.

Ted was placed on "death watch" and moved to a cell next to the electric chair.

In late February the legal confusion continued. Ted's hand-written request to the U.S. Supreme Court for a stay of execution was turned down on a technicality. Public and private defense lawyers, foes of the death penalty, scrambled to save him. On February 26, Polly Nelson—a Washington lawyer now representing him—telephoned Ted at the prison to tell him that the high court had granted the stay and would review an appeal.

Ted, said the lawyer, was "speechless." Pale and tense, he was moved off death watch and returned to his cell . . . to await the outcome of his last appeal.

Richard Larsen
Seattle, March 1986

Outstanding Bestsellers!

FREE!!
BOOKS BY MAIL
CATALOGUE

BOOKS BY MAIL will share with you our current bestselling books as well as hard to find specialty titles in areas that will match your interests. You will be updated on what's new from Pocket Books at no cost to you. Just fill in the coupon below and discover the convenience of having books delivered to your home. Please add $1.00 to cover the cost of postage and handling.

BOOKS BY MAIL

320 Steelcase Road E.,
Markham, Ontario L3R 2M1

Please send Books By Mail catalogue to:

Name_____
(please print)

Address_____

City_____

Prov._____ Postal Code _____

(BBM2)